Reader's Digest

How to clean
just about anything

Reader's Digest

How to

just about

Consultant
Gill Chilton

clean
anything

Ingenious secrets for a
fresh and sparkling home

Contents

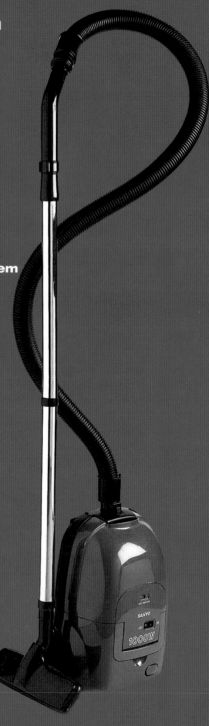

A quick reference guide to 30 cleaning emergencies, from animal accidents and baby sick to water stains and wine spills.

A mini-encyclopedia of cleaning products, compounds, solutions and utensils. Contains all you need to know about buying and using more than 45 cleaning tools ranging from abrasive cleaners and absorbents to steel wool and vacuum cleaners.

Introduction

Cleaning isn't complicated. Anyone (and everyone) can do it. However, the huge variety of materials and possessions that make up our homes these days mean that you do have to know a little about what you're doing. Doing it wrong – and it can be something as simple as using water or too much heat – can be worse than not doing at all.

Armed with this book, that won't be a problem for you. Drawing on the experience of hundreds of cleaning experts, *How to Clean Just About Anything* shows you just how easy it so to clean every single thing that you own and may buy in the future.

After kicking off with the basics – how to get order in your home and a simple regular-clean routine you'll want to use each week – the main focus is on how to clean individual items and surfaces. Just bought a new leather chair or a digital camera? Or perhaps there's mildew in the bathroom that you just haven't been able to shift. Or you've moved into a house with gold taps and an enamel bath? Use this book like an A–Z encyclopedia, and quickly find what you need to know.

We guarantee that you won't need masses of specialist tools and products to get great results: practically everything can be found in major UK supermarkets. If you like 'green' eco-friendly cleaning, we'll show you where to head in the grocery section. If you prefer to get tough with chemicals, then that's covered too. Either way, you can be sure that your home and the things within it will soon be looking a whole lot cleaner. And staying that way.

Gill Chilton

PART

1

the easiest path to a clean home

Clean thinking

You wake early at the weekend with the sun streaming onto the windowsill and wardrobe doors through a gap in the curtains. Immediately you think, 'That sunlight really shows up the dust. Must get up and get to it'. If that's you, you're probably too busy right now with a mop and duster to sit down and read or need this book. But for the rest of us, who know that cleaning is something we have to do to ensure that our homes are as fresh-smelling, pleasant to live in and hygienic as possible, then this book is for you.

This book covers the full spectrum of topics related to cleaning – from smart routines and the right gear to handling unexpected messes and cleaning specific types of items and materials. But underlying it all is one key idea: the more you know about how to clean and the more organised you are about cleaning – the less effort, time and money you will have to spend actually doing it. Too many people see cleaning as an odious chore that can't be avoided, but is all too easy to put off. We're here to convince you of the opposite: that if you have a positive attitude to cleaning and its benefits, then a pristine house becomes something that is much easier to accomplish.

This book has lots of advice on how to clean particular objects in your home. That's not because we think you'll spend ages cleaning a fountain pen or a hair dryer. But if you have these things, learning how to get them clean – and doing so more easily and faster than you have done before – can be very satisfying. With cleaning, it's not mopping the kitchen floor but getting the dirt that collects in the pepper pot holes that will make you feel good.

Too much to do and too little time is something that unites us all these days. So, on page 78, you'll find a fail-safe, tried-and-true system for cleaning your house. ZAP, the Zoned Attack Plan, is a truly time-saving strategy for regular, ideally weekly, housecleaning. It is a super-efficient plan that eliminates going over the same ground twice so that you get your house spick-and-span with minimal effort. It will knock hours off your cleaning time and makes housecleaning almost fun. But first let's take a broader view of cleaning.

The three kinds of cleaning

In a moment, we'll go into the detail of what we call 'clean thinking' – the mindset that you need for easier, faster, more effective cleaning. But to get on top of 'clean thinking,' it's important to understand the categories of cleaning. There are three:

Immediate cleaning prevents small, easy-to-clean-up messes from becoming big, tough messes that take time and energy to shift. Let's say that after cooking dinner, your hob has a few spatters of grease and drops of water on it. You could leave it – it's scarcely noticeable. But if you wipe the stove with a sponge or cloth every time you use it, the job will take only seconds, the stove will be restored to pristine condition and you will be preventing what could eventually become a multilayered build-up requiring hours of serious cleaning attention.

In the immediate cleaning mode, you clean up messes right away. Otherwise, spills accumulate, stains and grime set in, and your family learns that a dirty house is acceptable.

Maintenance cleaning is done regularly, but not necessarily often. This kind of cleaning can be put on a schedule. For example, you could decide to clean the bathroom splashback tiles once a week (perhaps even set the day) and wash the kitchen curtains twice a year. Maintenance cleaning can be organised as a plan – you

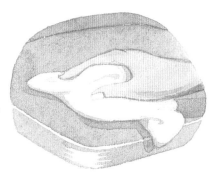

Wipe up spills as soon as they happen to prevent any further damage or staining.

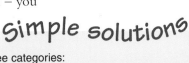

Simple solutions

Contain and maintain Cleaning tasks fall into three categories: immediate, maintenance and remedial.

Immediate
- Towelling off the glass door of the shower after each use.
- Having family members remove their shoes at the door.
- Washing dishes immediately after using them.

Maintenance
- Spraying the shower cubicle with soap scum remover once a week.

- Vacuuming all the dirt that family members track inside.
- Making sure all dishes, glasses, and pots and pans are cleaned up each night before bedtime.

Remedial
- Spending hours by the shower cubicle or with a hand down the toilet scrubbing away a year's worth of scum or limescale.

- Vacuuming only before your mother-in-law comes to stay or neighbours joke about not knowing what colour your carpet is anymore.
- Wasting your Sunday scrubbing hardened food from the week's dishes and pots so you have something to cook with.

might even go so far as to write it down, or block a day off in your diary every now and again. Or, it can be simple habits, like always washing-up and clearing the kitchen worktops directly after dinner.

Remedial cleaning covers cleaning after long periods of neglect, such as tackling the refrigerator after a year's worth of drips and spills have accumulated on the bottom shelf. This kind of remedial cleaning is preventable. You can avoid it by taking preventive steps – for instance, standing a tray on the bottom shelf of the fridge that you can take out and wash, or following maintenance routines. Remedial cleaning also includes what you do after a disaster, major or minor, such as a flood or a pet accident on the carpet.

The big danger is that remedial cleaning can easily become abusive cleaning. That happens when a mild cleaner fails to budge the dirt, so stronger and more abrasive cleaners and tools are called into service. Abusive cleaning may do more damage than the original dirt did – another good reason for keeping on top of things.

Planning for a clean life

The core of the 'clean thinking' philosophy is to clean things at once or on a regular maintenance schedule, so that you almost never have to do any remedial cleaning. Here are some of the easiest ways to achieve this.

Focus on the benefits of cleaning and you'll do it more readily. There are many. You will:

• Be in control instead of out of control.
• Feel renewed pride in your environment.
• Enjoy a healthier, safer home.
• Spend more and better time with your family.
• Have a more active social life – you will have more time and be happy to bring others into your home.
• Experience reduced stress as you will no longer have to wade through clutter and dirt.
• Save money – furniture and clothes that are cleaned with care last longer.

If you hate cleaning and organising, why not try to change your attitude? Look for the value and satisfaction in those activities. Yogis have long taught the value of doing simple chores such as cleaning. They describe the benefits of 'karma yoga' (being in a meditative stage of awareness as you clean or garden) as being calming and focusing. The idea is that you let go of your mental clutter – the bills that need paying, your dispute with your boss – and focus on the job at hand. Even without the yoga philosophy, cleaning can help you to feel more serene. If you're under a lot of stress, doing something mundane and methodical such as cleaning can often be very therepeutic and calming.

Treat cleanliness as a virtue that your whole household shares Dividing up the chores makes sense, especially if there are two adults. But it's particularly important that everyone shares if you are a family. If you get into the habit of being the sole cleaner of the family home, then what are you teaching everyone else? That they can be messy, and someone else will take care of it? Instead, make it the whole family's job to keep your home clean.

Give children cleaning chores from an early age Four or five is not too young to start. When they're this age, they'll enjoy it because they're working with you. Later they may come to see the chores as boring or hard work. But if they've been properly trained, they'll do them anyway. Explaining how to train children to do chores

Simple solutions

Calling in extra help In the USA, you can find people to help with clothes, files, kitchens, basements, garages and even entire houses, offices and businesses. Here, it's yet to catch on, with the exception of the odd wardrobe organiser. But the next best option is your neatest, most practical friend. Having someone else to galvanise you into organising works on several levels.

- Set a definite date and amount of time (three hours is ideal) when you'll take action on a particular area of disorder.
- Two of you working together will get fast results.
- You will be far more ruthless with an audience. It's one thing to keep every birthday card you've ever received, but it's harder to justify why to someone else.
- Your friend may suggest storage ideas you hadn't thought of. For instance, you could add a second rail, half way down, in your wardrobe because you mostly wear tops and skirts which don't need a full length hang. But you'll make nearly twice as much space.
- Finally, your friend comes with a built-in checker system. In a few weeks time, he or she is likely to be back in your home, to see that you've kept up the good work.

is simple – just break everything down into specific steps. The actual training process is less so. When you're pressed for time and they're taking an age to vacuum round a room, or insisting that they can't do it now, because they have to practise penalties in the garden for tomorrow's football match, it's tempting to take over. To avoid this, set only a very reasonable number of tasks that won't eat too much into their free time, then insist that they do what you've asked them to do. No excuses from them, no threats from you. One day, when they're running their own homes, or perhaps at university and living in a bed-sit that isn't a health hazard, they'll thank you.

Build cleaning routines and procedures into your everyday life. This may be the single most important thing for achieving the spick-and-span home of your dreams. It means airing, then straightening up your bed every morning – and teaching your children to do it too. It means always wiping your feet at the door; putting dishes directly into the dishwasher; having a mail-sorting routine that puts bills, catalogues, coupons and correspondence immediately into their right place, and everything that you don't want straight into the bin or paper recycling sack. If you can establish routines like this, you can keep the time spent on housecleaning to a minimum.

Have strategies for keeping your home both clean and neat Neat means worktops are clear, coats are hung up, and clutter is under control. But these things can't happen unless you have enough room in the kitchen cupboards or pegs and hooks in the hall. So you have to set the stage for clean and neat to happen naturally.

Clean also means the floors aren't muddy, the corners aren't cobwebby and the doors aren't smudgy. While the two often go hand in hand, it is possible to have a messy home that's clean, or a neat home that's dirty. Neatening and cleaning need not happen at the same time. But it's certainly easier and faster to clean a room that is already neat. You've heard people who pay someone to clean joke how they clean up before the cleaner comes round. What they actually mean is that they tidy up – put stuff away in drawers, hang up coats – so that their cleaner can spend time doing what he or she is paid to do – cleaning, not tidying and sorting.

Expert advice

Help children see the cleaner picture

Should children do chores simply because they are part of the household? Or is paying 20p for vacuuming fair and motivating?

After the Tsunami disaster in December 2004, a school in Cheltenham used housework as a fund-raiser. Children did chores, ranging from a 4-year-old earning 10p for opening and closing all the curtains, to 25p paid to his sisters for loading up the washing machine.

Because the master list was compiled by a group of people, children did jobs that their parents had not considered. Moral? Children can do and will do housework, but only if they're sufficiently motivated. So if you baulk at paying them personally, why not try the charity option?

Understand the special cleaning requirements of the things you own. What materials are your carpets, furniture, appliances, curtains and clothes made of? The more you know about their material and construction, the better you'll be able to clean them. When you make purchasing decisions, take into consideration how the items should be cleaned. If you resent money spent on dry-cleaning, always buy washable clothes and upholstery covers. If you don't have time for careful hand-washing, only buy clothes with the machine wash symbol.

Don't despair at messes, but rather see the order and cleanliness that can emerge from them. Visualising the result in advance is a powerful tool for clean thinking. Before-and-after pictures are very motivating and energising. But when you're still in the 'before' stage, you have no 'after' picture of your room to inspire you. By visualising, you can make one.

Pick a spot in the house that bothers you because it's dirty or disorganised. It could be a low table in the sitting room, where papers and post get dumped. Conjure up an image of order or cleanliness. You might even draw a picture, or write a description.

Take visualisation a step further and create a small clutter-free area, just to see how it feels. Pick a table that bothers you – or even just one shelf on a display unit or bookcase – and put all the stuff on it that shouldn't be there into a box. For the moment, don't worry about sorting it. After the table or desk is clear, dust it, wash it if necessary, and just savour the feeling of satisfaction that you get from creating order.

Ten golden rules of cleaning

Your primary goal in cleaning is to remove dirt, whether it be in your home or on your garments. But you do need to determine how far you're prepared to go. You don't want to injure yourself or damage the very thing you're trying to clean. And you also want to get it done as quickly and with as little effort as possible. Stick to the following ten golden rules and you will achieve safe, effective cleaning that attacks the problem early and with the minimum amount of effort.

1 Clean up immediately

Spills and stains are generally much easier to clean up when you attack them right away. When you treat the tomato sauce splatter on your shirt at once, for instance, by rinsing it under the cold tap, it will offer little resistance. If you wait until the next day, you'll expend a lot more cleaning solution and time getting rid of it. As a rough rule practically all clothing or carpet stains are easiest to remove when they're fresh. The longer you wait, the more chance the stain has to set.

The rare exception is mud tracked onto your carpet. This is easiest to clean when you've let it dry first. So force yourself to hold back until it's bone dry and crumbly; then just vacuum it up.

2 Clean from the top down

Don't fight gravity when you clean. You'll lose. Working down from high to low almost always works better in cleaning situations.

When you're cleaning the entire house, start on the top floor and work your way down to avoid tramping dirt through rooms you have already cleaned. When you're cleaning a room, first remove any cobwebs from the ceiling and coving. Then dust light fixtures, followed by window frames and wall hangings. Moving downward, sweep over the furniture, skirting boards,

To maximise dust removal, always brush or vacuum your furniture before vacuuming the floor.

and floors. This ensures that any dust shaken loose from on high does not settle on something you've already cleaned below. You don't want to have to dust the room twice.

Similarly, when you clean windows and mirrors, start up high and work your way down, because your cleaning solution obeys gravity and may just drip down. This will save you both elbow grease and time.

3 Think dry, then wet

When you're cleaning a room, start with the cleaning jobs that require dry methods (dusting, sweeping, and vacuuming, for instance). If you still need to clean, then move on to wet methods, using an all-purpose cleaner and glass cleaner, mopping and similar jobs. This way, there will be less dirt floating around in the room to cling to wet surfaces.

4 Start with the least harmful approach

Use your gentlest cleaning methods first and move up to more aggressive techniques only if necessary. If you've tried everything you know to be safe, make a rational decision about whether it's worth carrying on. Generally, you may feel it is better to suffer a small spot on your hob, than to ruin the surface by scrubbing it with steel wool.

5 Let time do the work for you

Here's a little time management trick to make your cleaning easier and faster. When you start to clean a room, spray on your cleaning chemicals first and then find another little job to do while the cleaner does its dirty work. In the kitchen, spray your cleaner on the worktops and appliances, then occupy yourself with removing old food from the fridge while the cleaner soaks in. When you come back to wipe clean, there should be little or no scrubbing to do.

6 Carry your supplies with you

Keep your core cleaning products with you. This will save you from making multiple trips around the house looking for the right tools and cleaners. Use one of the following to carry your tools:

• A **simple plastic tool caddy** from a DIY store – the sort painters use – with two deep pockets each side of a handle, is perfect.

• A **sturdy, large plastic bucket** with a good handle.

• An **apron with roomy pockets**.

As well as cleaning solutions and cloths, put in clean rags, paper towels, and a stack of bin liners for emptying all of the wastebaskets around the house. If your home has more than one floor, consider setting up a caddy for each level. However, only do this if you have somewhere safe, away from children, to store cleaning products safely.

If you have room and secure space in the toilet and bathroom, you might prefer to leave speciality products here, rather than carry them with you.

7 When in doubt, test it out

Before you use a new cleaning technique or product, test the method on an inconspicuous area of the object you're cleaning. This rule also applies when you first clean an object that is delicate and might be damaged by a cleaning compound. Testing will show you whether the object is colourfast and whether the cleaning method is likely to cause damage.

8 Don't soak, go easy on the spray

When you clean an item that could be harmed by a liquid cleaning product – electronics, computer screens, framed artwork, or framed photographs, for example – first spray the cleaner on your cleaning cloth and then wipe. Don't spray cleaner directly on the object you're cleaning. Liquid slopping into your electronics could cause serious damage, and solution dripping through a frame and soaking the matting could harm your artwork.

9 Read the directions

You've probably heard this before. But the makers of all of the furnishings in your home do know best how to clean them. And the manufacturers of your cleaning products know the best way to use them. So where possible, follow the manufacturer's directions when cleaning anything. This goes for everything from toasters to silk blouses. File the directions and cleaning tips that come with any new appliance, rug or other household item and keep them. Unlike guarantees, cleaning instructions are valid for as long as you have the item. Don't remove care labels on clothes, linens and other washable objects – they are there to help you.

10 Get some protection

Last but not least, take care of yourself. Many cleaning products contain acid, bleach, abrasives and other ingredients that can damage eyes, skin, nose, and even lungs. Don't let your cleaning products get mixed together. Some combinations – chlorine bleach and ammonia, for instance – will produce poisonous gases. When you're using cleaning chemicals, make sure the room you're in is properly ventilated. Even with these precautions, you still need to take care.

Your cleaning kit needs to include **a pair of rubber gloves** and **protective safety glasses**. If it's not too hot, wear clothes that cover your legs and arms in case of spatters from cleaning products. Tie long hair back and, when you're working overhead, consider wearing a light garden hat, cap or headscarf.

If you don't get on with gloves, then at least protect your nails. Dab a line of petroleum jelly underneath your nails to keep out dirt. Dot more on your cuticles to keep them from drying out, roughening and splitting from exposure to cleaning chemicals.

Stopping dirt at the door

What's the best kind of dirt? The sort that you never allow into your house in the first place. That's dirt in its proper place – dirt that you don't have to clean up. It's much easier to head off a problem before it takes root, than to fix it after the damage is done. So here's lots of advice on how to stop dirt in its tracks.

Keep dirt on the mat

Actually, what you want to do is stop the dirt in your tracks – specifically, on the soles of your shoes. There are other ways that dirt gets in – and in particular, you may be thinking of dirt that comes through the air and open windows – but what you bring in on your feet is of far greater significance.

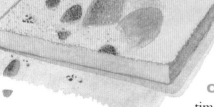

Put a doormat outside all your exterior doors to cut down on mud entering your house.

So use doormats at every entrance to your home, inside and out. Most of the grime in your home comes from the outside, the bulk of it coming in unnoticed on shoes that don't appear to be either muddy or dirty.

Choosing the right doormat will reduce the time you spend cleaning and chasing down dirt. The key here is the size of your mat. For a mat to work thoroughly, it has to be longer than a typical stride. A mat should be long enough so that you can walk across with both feet before entering the house, with the width no wider than the door itself. So people coming into the house literally walk along it, shifting off dirt onto the mat as they do so.

Acrylic with either a vinyl or rubber backing is the best choice for an indoor mat as you'll be able to vacuum or shake it outside to get rid of the dirt. Buy one that will co-ordinate with your décor, but several shades darker. That way, it will hide the worst of the dirt. Mats for outside your door are usually made of rubber. If you live in the country, or have a driveway that gets very muddy, keep a wire rack underneath the mat. This will be handy if your family or guests need to scrape mud from their boots or shoes before they enter the house.

Floor mats also are a good idea near high-traffic or spill-prone spots such as the fridge, the bath and the toilet. However, you should always weigh up whether you might slip or trip on a rug, plus how you view its appearance. So most people choose not to have a mat in front of the kitchen sink. It doesn't look good and there's a risk you could trip, possibly when carrying hot liquids.

Doormats need minimal maintenance Just take them outside occasionally and give them a good shake to remove the dust as well as a once-over with the vacuum cleaner now and then.

When mats are really grimy, hose them down and scrub them with a squirt of **washing-up liquid** in **warm water**. Rinse and allow to thoroughly air-dry. If you prefer, **upholstery shampoo** is also fine. Make sure the mats are completely dry before you put them back on the floor. Moisture trapped underneath could damage your floors. Replace mats when they get threadbare, as worn ones are less effective at trapping dirt.

To reduce the dirt entering your house, limit the number of entrances that are used. This way, you'll cut down on the places where people and pets can walk dirt in. And if most people enter your house through a room that has an easy-wipe floor, most of the grime will never make it past first base and into the rest of your home.

Make your house a shoeless zone for everyone. Politely ask family members, guests and friends to shed their shoes just inside the entrance. Provide a decorative basket or some other receptacle where people can stash their shoes.

Design to reduce grime

It's not every day that you buy new furniture or redecorate the kitchen or bathroom. But when you do, choose the fabrics and surfaces wisely. Always think as you buy, 'will this increase the work I have to do around the home?'

Easy-care decorating choices abound Laminate and solid wood floors almost look the same, but only one needs waxing and re-finishing. The laminate mostly just needs a vacuum. For kitchen worktops, you'll find that solid surfaces – rather than tiles, and in particular, small tiles –

don't have grooves and indentations where dirt can gather. Over time, curtains and blinds can become magnets for dust and cobwebs. Instead of dust-catching materials, choose fabrics treated with a stain-and-dust-resistant finish, or treat the fabric yourself with a product such as *Scotchguard* fabric protector, following package instructions.

To childproof a child's bedroom, a playroom, or the kitchen, use *Dulux Real Life Paint* (available at DIY stores) on the walls. It is up to ten times more durable than standard paint. So when you go to scrub off everyday stains made by children, such as crayon and poster paint, you won't also scrub off the top layer of your painted wall.

Have you made a mess of a family room wall by taping and tacking children's artwork to it? You can have a full-wall gallery in your home without the damage. Just cover the wall in two coats of *Kidicraft Magnetic Paint* (look on *www.kidicraft.co.uk* or call 01200 447192 for stockists) and use magnets to post the work of budding Michelangelos.

Patterns camouflage dirt and grime but solid colours are much less forgiving. And don't forget your pets when you redecorate. If you have a black Labrador retriever or another dark-haired breed, light-coloured surfaces may not be the wisest choice, while a dark carpet or sofa will show every white or ginger hair from a lighter coloured pet.

Stop grime in the kitchen

The kitchen can be one of the dirtiest rooms in a house, which is alarming considering it is where you cook and eat. As you heat food, it's inevitable that grease particles will rise into the air, ready to land on all surfaces, especially walls, ceilings and cupboards. But you can minimise this.

Suck up some of the airborne grease by turning on the exhaust fan every time you cook on the hob. The noise of the fan can be irritating, but the time spent washing down grimy kitchen walls will be greatly reduced.

Cut down on soup and tomato-based sauces jumping out of their saucepans, by using larger pots and pans, with their lids. If you frequently deep-fry, sauté, or otherwise cook foods that spit, you could consider fitting an

Expert advice

STAIN LAB

Clean, then protect

Thoroughly clean surfaces before applying products that prevent them getting grimy, advises Anita Kelly, who works at a Merry Maids cleaning franchise. For instance, lemon oil works wonders in preventing residue build-up on shower doors and curtains, but you have to rid them of mildew, soap scum, and other gunk before applying it. The same goes for fabrics: the spray-on fabric protectors that repel stains and spills also require that the fabric be clean before you apply the protectant. So while using one of them will become a short-cut, actually kick-starting the process does mean a bit of extra work for you. Fail to take off the dirt first, and all you will do is seal it in, underneath the fabric protector.

extra line of tiles behind the oven, so that you have a deep splashback.

For oven splatters from a pie or casserole bubbling over, sprinkle the stains with **salt** to keep the smoke down and make the eventual clean-up job much easier.

To protect the fabric on kitchen chairs, which is always under assault, especially from food spills, choose ones with laminated fabric (or oilcloth). You can also buy the material and make new covers yourself, out of fabric squares that tie with ribbon around each corner. When guests come, remove the laminated ones and enjoy the clean, non-greasy originals. Or choose chairs with a wipe-clean surface.

As a quick, temporary measure, sprinkle salt on oven splatters.

Keep your tools clean

Worn-out cleaning tools – such as sponges, mops and squeegees – are a waste of time. They make it much harder to get the job done. Dirty cleaning tools are worse, because they're downright counterproductive, smearing grime and germs all over the things you're trying to clean.

• Throw away cleaning tools when they look chewed-up and tired. They won't work as well, are difficult to clean and can actually spread dirt and germs around.
• Regularly wash cleaning rags in your washing machine, using **detergent**, **hot water** and **100ml of white vinegar** or a **scoop of oxygen-boosting additive**, such as *Oxi Clean*, to cut through grease.
• Wash cellulose sponges very frequently in the **washing machine** or in the top rack of your **dishwasher**. Get into the habit of putting them in each evening. After four weeks of use, throw them away.
• Replace the **bag** in your **vacuum cleaner** at least once a month – more often if you have pets that shed lots of fur. Vacuum bags need air inside to suck properly, so be sure to change them when they are two-thirds full. Keep vacuum brushes clean, too. Take vacuums without bags outside the house to empty them. Even if you are careful, holding them upside down and then tipping directly into a plastic sack,

very tiny particles of dust will still escape and settle right back down onto the surfaces that you have just sucked them up from.

Close your doors

Dirt just likes to travel. It's happiest when it can roam freely all over your home, hiding in nooks and crannies where it's most labour-intensive to find and remove.

So stop dirt at the borders. That is, habitually keep your doors, drawers, cabinets, wardrobes and other barriers closed. This will keep dirt out in the open, where vacuum cleaners and cleaning cloths will be able to deal with it more readily.

If you're working on a messy, dust-producing project in the house, keep the doors to the room you're working in closed. Better yet, hang **plastic sheeting** across the door and any air vents to confine the dust to one room.

Periodically wash venetian blinds and other dirt-trapping window coverings such as net curtains. Remember that dirt loves company and acts as a magnet for more.

Smart tricks for pets

Any pet with easy access to the garden will bring plenty of the great outdoors in on its coat and paws. Keeping your dogs and cats clean, and taking preventative measures when you know they have got especially dirty, will reduce the amount of dirt they can bring into your house.

Brush your dog outside to stop it shedding hair in the house.

• Keep a **clean rag** by the door that your pet uses so that you'll be more likely to remember to wipe off muddy, wet paws and claws before your beloved animal makes unsightly tracks through the whole house.

• Once a week, take your dog outside and give its fur a good going-over with the type of **brush** recommended for its coat. Do this well away from the house, so that the tufts won't tumble back inside.

• The miracle way to lift pet hair from furniture and other surfaces is to wipe with a **damp sponge** or **cloth**. The hair will gather in clumps, and onto your cloth. An excellent alternative is a lightly-dampened **rubber glove**, rubbed quickly back and forth. It will pick up bundles of hair. Or you could use one of those special **rubber brushes** with nubs on it that is intended for grooming cats and finer-haired dogs (available at pet shops).

• Nothing beats your **vacuum cleaner** for pulling pet hair out of your rugs and carpets. If you have a number of pets or an animal that sheds a great deal, it could be worth considering a vacuum cleaner which has been specially designed to deal with fur. Typically they have greater suction power for sucking up fur and special filters for trapping potential allergens.

Clearing out clutter

Thousands of years ago, our ancestors had to save and store whatever they could because they had so little. And what they had was subject to attack by the elements, predators and marauders. In the 21st century, this hoarding tendency is far less useful. Here's how to deal with the stuff you've hoarded, how to store and display what you want and discard what's no longer needed. Finally and most importantly, how to stop clutter from building up in the first place.

What is clutter?

There is no single definition, because one person's clutter is another's delight. But people who help others declutter their surroundings agree on a few principles.

Some basic ideas about clutter:
• It is anything that bothers you and interferes with your enjoyment of each day because it is disorganised or chaotic.
• It is things you don't love or don't use, unfinished projects or too many objects in too small a space.
• It makes you feel overwhelmed, smothered, not in control of your space, victimised or unfulfilled.
• It may be a symptom of a lack of clarity about who you are and what your life is about.
• It is like the static on a radio. It's a distraction and an interference that stops you from focusing on what is important in your home and your life.
• It is stressful.

The first step in getting rid of clutter is to make the decision either to accept it and stop complaining about it – or to do something about it. And start at once. The benefits of removing clutter include these:

• You will find that cleaning up is easier.
• Your desk, table, room or house will look tidy. At a quick glance, neat spaces appear to be cleaner too.
• You'll have more time for things that are important to you.
• You'll feel better.
• You'll be able to buy things that you truly do want for your home, because there is now the space for them.

Organising wardrobes and cupboards effectively makes life much easier.

Confront your clutter

Looking at clutter typically makes people feel paralysed and overwhelmed, but luckily the process of getting rid of it is actually very simple.

Organising your home, office, files, desk, or anything else boils down to three steps.

1 Eliminate the things you don't need, want, use, or love. These are things you can throw out right now. Without another thought.
2 Categorise what remains by grouping similar things together. If everything you need to handle paper is together – hole punch, paperclips, staplers – it will be so much quicker to do so.
3 Organise the categories by having a place for everything and everything in its place – such as allocating a drawer just for items you use to file and collate paper.

Whatever system of organisation you come up with should fulfil three requirements. The system should be:

• **Beautiful**, in the sense that it makes you happy to look at it and work in it.
• **Functional**, because you want it to be efficient as well.
• **Easy for the user to maintain**. If it takes too much time, you'll just use the 'leave it where it is' option.

Spot the clutter crisis points

Some people know where their clutter problem lies – perhaps they can never throw out a magazine, or have to hang onto every piece of paper their child's pencil has ever touched. Make a list of your worst clutter blackspots and try to understand why they start to build up.

Paper Usually, there are two patterns here. Either you build up unread newspapers and magazines, old mail, unorganised clippings that, one day, you faintly assume you'll get around to. Or, you hoard paper items because you believe them to have either a sentimental or a practical purpose. This includes children's school papers, old love letters, notes, lists, bank statements from the 1990s and car service records dating back to the car before last.

Expert advice

Do you need de-clutter therapy?

A lack of organising skills is why many people continue to live amid piles of clutter. If that's you, it might take time, but one day, when a friend or family member shows you the brilliance, say, of storing Christmas decorations in one place instead of scattered all over the house, a light bulb will go off in your head. You'll learn the skill and easily become organised.

But there's a second group who may have deep-seated reasons for cluttering, going back to childhood – such as a feeling of deprivation or insecurity. Having lots of things may give these people a feeling of false prosperity. Getting to the root of that insecurity and recognising why you feel the need to surround yourself with things is probably necessary before you can start to address the clutter itself.

Clothing Is your problem that clothes aren't organised, or is it that you're chronically unable to get rid of things that no longer fit, are out of style, worn out or never worn?

After those two categories, clutter patterns look like the many tributaries of a mighty river – they're all over the map. Some common kinds are clutter related to home office space, pets, books, videos and CDs, electronics, hobbies, children's toys and kitchen utensils.

Before you begin your clutter attack, recognise that the feeling of being overwhelmed goes with the territory, and don't let it stop you. Break the job into small parts – each tiny part that you conquer will lift your spirits.

To pick a starting point, find the area that bothers you most. If it's a large area, like a home office or a spare bedroom, pick one tiny part – a bureau you've stored there. Now pick one tiny part of that – a single drawer.

Or maybe your most irritating area is the kitchen table, where you can hardly find space to eat because of all of the papers and other stuff. Pick a pile from a corner of the table.

Three steps to success

Imagine you've now got one small area of clutter to tackle. To do a thorough job, you're going to have to look at each item individually, yet swiftly. Tell yourself there are only three things that you can decide to do with this item:

1 Discard.
2 Keep.
3 Take action.

In practice, your discard pile may include items to be put into the bin, donated to the charity shop, sold on *eBay* or recycled. Items to keep may be papers to file, clothing to hang up, or sports equipment to put away. Things to take action on might include bills to pay, school papers to sign, library books or videos to return or unworn, recently bought clothes to take back to the shops for a refund.

Make your judgments quickly To linger is fatal as your natural instinct will be to keep everything. Be ruthless. Depending on how old your pile is, you've managed without some items for weeks, months, or years. You can probably do without them.

If you have things you are going to keep and store away – for instance, children's clothing that will be handed down to younger siblings in a few years – sort and label them clearly. For example, have separate boxes for '1–2 years,' '3–4 years,' and so on. Don't mix everything together or you are simply creating a future nightmare when you want to find something.

If you have a lot of sentimental memorabilia, ask yourself whether there is some other way to keep it. Instead of saving your daughter's science project, for example, take a photo of her with the project, plus a close-up photo of the project and throw the project away. Keep photo albums and scrapbooks up to date, well labelled and easily accessible.

Stem the tide

Clutter is continual. However well you do today at reducing what's in your home now, you'll need to change future behaviour and storage patterns if you want to stem the problem long-time. Think of your clutter as an overflowing bath. Before you mop up the water on the floor and bail out the bath, you turn off the tap. So for total victory over clutter, you have to reduce the items that are going to come into your home next week and next year.

For less clutter in your life:
• Focus more on doing and being in your life, not having.
• Whenever you're tempted to buy something, decide whether your buying impulse falls into the 'worthwhile' or 'future clutter' category. Like the right marriage partner, the worthwhile items will be just as worthwhile if you wait.
• Buy cloth or string shopping bags and use them to cut down on bags you bring home.
• Stop subscriptions to magazines that you somehow never get around to reading.
• Instead of buying things you'll use just once or very rarely, rent them – DVDs and videos are prime candidates.
• Start buying family members birthday and Christmas presents that are immediately consumable – or experiences. Does your child really need another cuddly toy or wouldn't a day trip to the zoo or an activity park be more fun?

Expert advice

Blending two households

Remarriage creates special clutter challenges. People bring far more stuff – including children and their clothes, toys and books – to second marriages.

One approach is to make a written inventory of both sets of household goods. It's easier to decide on paper what to weed out and what to keep, rather than bring everything along. Doing it this way can also open up communication about hidden assumptions.

Of course, people who remarry are not the only ones who need help with merging possessions. University students, those who live with a landlord or other sharers and even household guests who try to take over the shelf in the bathroom, need to know something about organising and respecting another person's space.

Laundry loads of advice

Doing the laundry used to be a muscle job – the dirtier the clothes, the harder you scrubbed. But as machines and laundry products have evolved over the years, so have fibres and fabrics, with many becoming, if not delicate, then certainly not suited to hard scrubbing. The result is that today laundering is mostly a mental exercise, a matter of deciphering care label symbols, keeping up with new improved laundry products, recognising the differences between fabric types and understanding the chemistry behind stain-removal techniques.

Everyone has clothes to clean. Not everyone cleans them as well as they could. They wing it or get by on the bare minimum. This chapter will help you to do a better, more thorough job on your laundry. You will be more knowledgeable, more confident and more efficient. More importantly, your clothes will be cleaner, brighter, fresher and last for longer.

Sorting your clothes

Most of us put dark clothes in one pile, and whites in another. But if you really want to keep your clothes looking their best, it is well worth sorting them by similar fabrics and dirt level.

Sorting by colour Separate whites from colours and light colours from dark colours. This is most important if you want to choose different detergents, for instance a 'colour' product such as *Ariel Colour*, which doesn't contain optical brighteners and so won't dull coloured clothes. Read care labels to be on the look-out for garments that need to be washed separately. This is because the dye colours may run. You won't just find this with red or black tops. Even tiny amounts of a beige dye can transfer to other fabrics, making lighter clothes look discoloured and dingy.

Sorting by dirtiness Separate heavily soiled or greasy items from lightly soiled ones. Lightly soiled clothes can pick up some of this dirt and grease, making whites look grey or yellow and colours look dull. If you have a load of particularly dirty clothes, you should also put fewer of them in the machine and use the maximum dose of detergent.

Sorting by fabrics Separate out clothes that are loosely knit or woven and items that have delicate trimmings or unfinished seams that could fray. Wash those on a shorter cycle that features more gentle agitation. Also separate lint producers – such as fleece sweat suits, chenille items, new towels and flannel pyjamas – from lint attractors, such as corduroys, synthetic blends and dark things. In the long run, it is quicker to do more loads of washing than spend time getting pale lint out of a pair of corduroy trousers.

Getting ready to wash

Just a little careful preparation before you put your clothes in the washing machine is essential to get the cleanest clothes. Resist the temptation simply to chuck everything in and shut the door. A few routine steps – like checking pockets and so removing crayons from your child's trousers – can prevent a laundry disaster.

Empty pockets Be especially alert for tissues, which can also be wedged up sleeves or stuck in pockets. Keep a small brush handy to brush dirt and lint out of cuffs.

Close zips and Velcro This prevents snags and keeps Velcro from getting matted with lint and thread and so losing its effectiveness.

Bag tights Put tights, stockings and items with long ties, such as bikini tops, into a mesh bag to keep them from snagging and tearing. You can get these from *www.lakelandlimited.co.uk*

Getting tough with stains

It's always best to try to remove stains when they are fresh. From page 46 there are detailed techniques for removing stains at this stage. But here, we look at what to do when you first spot a mark as you go to load the clothes into the washing machine. Modern, premium brand detergents are actually rather good at shifting most stains these days. The trick is to wash your clothes at the

For best results, always pre-treat stains before washing.

maximum temperature allowed on the care label and not to put too many clothes into the machine. Also, choose the correct dose of detergent. If the staining is particularly bad and you don't feel confident that your detergent will shift it, try the following first.

Soak protein stains in cold water These include egg, milk, faeces, urine and blood. Soak for half an hour in cold water, then run under a cold tap, gently rubbing the fabric together with your hands to loosen the stain. Avoid warm or hot water, which can 'cook' proteins, setting the stain permanently.

Pretreat oil and grease stains with liquid laundry detergent or pre-treatment spray. Apply the detergent or a spray, such as *Vanish Pre-wash Stain Remover Spray*, directly on to the stain.

Soak tannin stains such as coffee, tea, soft drinks, fruit and jam for half an hour in a solution of 1 teaspoon of liquid detergent (a biological one containing enzymes) per 2 litres of warm water. Do not use soap or a soap-based product. Soap can make the tannin stain harder to remove.

After washing in the machine check to see whether the stain has gone. If it hasn't, do not dry and especially do not tumble dry. Try again to remove the stain and then repeat washing.

All about washing machines

Most of us pick up our laundering skills in bits and pieces. We start in our teens, desperate to wash a favourite top to be ready for a special occasion, then perhaps alternate with launderettes and home washing during student years. Chances are, you may have missed out on some of the following essential tips.

Evenly distribute clothes in the washer The spin cycle relies on a balanced load. The best mix is large items such as sheets with smaller hand towels and socks.

Don't overload the washer The wash cycle depends on clothes rubbing together to remove dirt. If the washer is too full, the clothes will not have enough space to rub together. Powdered detergent may not have room to adequately dissolve, and you may end up with clumps of white powder stuck on your clothes. Moreover, there must be enough free-flowing water to carry away the dirt removed from the clothes. Check your washing machine manual for the recommended maximum load. Most are between 5–6kg. Considering a woollen jumper can weigh 1kg and a duvet cover 1.5kg, a full load soon mounts up.

Pick the right setting Most clothes use the normal or regular setting. In fact, even if your machine has 22 programmes, you may have previously just used this one for everything. But do try to switch to the gentle or delicate setting – sometimes marked as quick wash. Typically, it has a shorter, slower spin cycle and is ideal for lingerie, loose knits, washable woollens and synthetic fabrics that can get damaged and stretched by over-spinning.

For optimum results, check out all the fabric care options on your washing machine.

Choose the right water temperature On many machines, the hot cycle draws directly from your household hot water supply, then heats it to the required temperature. This is usually a choice of 60°C or 80°C, although pricier machines have an override, that lets you choose exactly the temperature that you want for every wash programme. The warm 40°C wash on most machines takes water from the cold water supply, then heats it to the desired temperature. Check care labels to set the temperature.

• **Hot (95–60°C)** Only use the 95°C option for 'boil wash' safe items, such as white cotton sheets. The 60°C hot wash is easily hot enough for whites and colourfast fabrics and heavily soiled clothes that say on the care label that they can withstand this temperature. Water this hot can kill most bacteria (not true at 40°C). When starting a hot-water load, make sure no one is about to take a shower or bath otherwise they'll be disappointed to get no hot water.

• **Warm (40°C)** Use for noncolourfast fabrics, moderately soiled loads, synthetics, wrinkle-free fabrics, knits, silks and woollens. Detergents including *Ariel*, *Persil* and *Surf* are specifically designed to be as effective at this temperature. So it can make sense to choose this most of the time: your clothes will look just as good and you'll save energy and money on fuel bills by not over-heating the water.

• **Cold (30°C)** Use for dark or bright colours that you know will bleed. Powdered detergent will not dissolve well in cold temperatures, so use liquid detergent instead.

Add the right amount of detergent Especially if you use both powders and liquids, it's easy to lose sight of just how much detergent to use with each wash. So take the extra minute to read the packet and use the measure scoop. Or switch to tablets (powder) or liquid capsules. The main cause of clothes coming out yellow, grey and dingy is not using enough detergent.

Although detergents and powder both work well, liquid detergents have the edge with cold water washes and on oily stains. Powders are great for removing ground-in dirt and mud. Biological is always best for cleaning, but if you have sensitive skin that is irritated by the enzymes in biological powder (these actively improve the detergent's stain shifting ability) then you'll have to use non-bio instead.

Soften your water More than 50 per cent of the UK has hard water. This means there is excess magnesium, calcium and other minerals present in the water and detergent has to work harder to combat them. In a soft water area, soap and detergents will lather up more easily.

If your clothes come out of the wash looking grey and dingy and feeling rough, you may have a hard-water problem. Other symptoms of hard water are rings around the water line in your bath, white residue around taps and drains, and soaps and shampoos that don't lather well. The easiest solution is just to add a little more detergent. You may also want to protect your washing machine's pipes from becoming coated with mineral deposits that may lead to long term damage. A water softening product, such as *Calgon*, which can be added as a tablet with each wash, solves the problem.

Laundry extras

These days, detergent and fabric conditioner are not the only laundry options. There are many other products you can use in the wash to enhance the look and feel of your laundered items. All-fabric bleaches, softeners and wash-boosters are among the most popular.

Bleaches come in two varieties
• **Chlorine bleach** (sometimes labelled as sodium hypochlorite)
• **All-fabric bleach** sometimes called oxygen bleach, contains hydrogen peroxide, or another chlorine substitute.

Chlorine bleach is the most effective whitener and sanitiser – it can be used to turn ordinary water into safe drinking water, with the correct dilution. But the downside is that we all know – mostly from personal wash-day disasters – just how strong chlorine bleach really is. It can fade or alter the colour of fabrics and can weaken fibres.

However, it does have a place as a pre-soak for whites that are very soiled or greying. But use it with care. Never pour full-strength liquid chlorine bleach directly into the washing machine. Always dilute it, then dispense it through a machine's bleach dispenser, following the instructions found on the bleach container – one part bleach to 10 parts water is typical. Don't soak cottons in a bleach solution for more than 15 minutes. If the stain remains after 15 minutes, that means it's not going to go away using this solvent. Don't use chlorine bleach on silk, wool, Lycra, polyurethane foam, rubber or anything with rubber or Lycra elastic.

Specialised laundry products can make your washdays a breeze.

All-fabric, oxygen bleaches are less harsh and are safe for some coloured fabrics. At the same time, they are not as powerful or fast-acting as chlorine bleach. You'll find oxygen bleach in many commercial wash boosters. *Ace Wash Booster* goes directly into the wash cycle in a dispenser ball. It whitens whites and brightens colours, rather than fading them, as a cholorine bleach would.

Enzyme pre-soaks are good for loosening and removing stains, especially hard-to-shift protein stains like milk, egg, urine and faeces before the wash cycle. When added to the wash cycle, they act like boosters to improve the washing. Many, like *Biotex*, are quite safe for delicate fabrics and contain no bleach.

Prewash stain removers are often spray products containing some combination of concentrated detergents, alcohol, mineral spirits or enzymes. These are especially good for removing oily or greasy stains from synthetic fibres. Their great advantage is that you can directly target the stain. A product like *Shout Stain Removing Spray* is effective on even low temperature washes.

Detergent boosters help detergents do their job by increasing stain and soil-removal action, altering the pH of water and brightening clothes. *Glo-White Ultra Wash Booster* works for colours as well as whites. However, with a quality detergent and not too many clothes in the wash, boosters aren't generally needed.

Water softeners are quick fixes for hard water. Added directly to the wash or rinse cycle of your machine, products such as *Calgon* soften the water, making the detergent work more effectively.

Fabric softeners in liquid form are added to the final rinse cycle of your wash load or come in sheets that you add to the dryer. These products make fabrics softer and fluffier, reduce static cling and wrinkling, and make ironing easier. Don't go overboard: if overused, fabric softeners can reduce the absorbency of towels. Dryer sheets which are placed with the wet washing into the drum of the tumble drier may, if used too often, leave oily looking splotches on medium-coloured items. The latest softening products – fabric conditioners sealed in one dose capsules – are handy if you tend to slosh in too much fabric conditioner.

Starches and fabric finishes are rarely used these days. However, used either in the final rinse or after drying, they temporarily stiffen fabrics, so they look crisp and fresh.

Drying your washing

Having a tumble drier doesn't just mean you can turn round clothes and laundry within a couple of hours, rather than the best part of a day. In winter and on wet days, it also gives you back a home without wet clothes on the radiators or dripping into the bath. But before you get tumbling, spend a moment on the following.

Check clothes for stains before drying If you overlook a stain you could set it permanently by drying it at a hot temperature. If you find a stain, treat it and rewash.

Shake damp pieces before drying This loosens them and helps them dry faster and more completely. Pull out anything that needs to be line or flat dried and has a 'no tumble drying' symbol on it. Woollens may shink and delicates such as bras may 'melt' in the hot dryer.

Don't overload the dryer A dryer needs some airflow to do its work. Clothes that are bunched up in a dryer will take longer to dry and will wrinkle more easily.

Don't underload the dryer A nearly empty dryer does not work as well as one that is fuller, but not too full. The tumbling effect is reduced in dryers with small loads, prolonging the drying period. If you must dry only one item, find a few towels that are already clean and dry and of a colour similar to the wet garment and put them into the dryer to improve the process.

Throw in a dryer sheet with damp synthetics to reduce static cling.

Use the right setting Most dryers have the following automatic settings.
• **Regular** for loads made up mostly of all-cotton fabrics.
• **Permanent press** for synthetics.
• **Cool** or **low** for lingerie, hand-washables, washable woollens, and heat-sensitive items marked 'tumble dry-low'.

The permanent press cycle typically features a cool-down period after the drying is completed to reduce creasing.

Avoid overdrying This causes shrinkage, static build-up, and creasing. Overdrying can actually set creases, making them harder to remove.

To reduce creasing remove items from the dryer as soon as they are dry. And don't let them sit in a heap in the basket. Hang up or fold them as soon as possible. Remove permanent press items while they are damp and hang on a rustproof hanger. Close buttons and snaps, straighten creases, and brush out any wrinkles.

Clean the lint filter after each use. Not doing so is a serious fire hazard. A filter without lint also means a better airflow and improved drying performance.

Use a mesh bag for drying tights It will protect them from snagging.

For items that call for flat drying such as sweaters, squeeze out excess water, but don't wring, or you may cause creasing. Roll the garment in a clean, dry towel to absorb water (see page 44). Then shape and lay out flat on a dry towel or drying rack. Over the bath is ideal.

Outdoor drying

Even if you've got a tumble drier, your clothes and bedding will appreciate the full, fresh dry off you can only get from the wind blowing them dry.

Turn clothes inside out if it's sunny – it will stop coloured garments fading in strong sunlight.

Peg with care Avoid making ridges that will need extra ironing by pegging trousers at the waistband and shirts at the underarm seam, rather than on the shoulders.

Check on your washing regularly to avoid over-drying. You will need to bring in synthetics and nylons well before cotton items are dry.

Remember to wipe down the washing line if you haven't used it in a while, otherwise you will get a line of dirt across your freshly-washed clothes.

Pressing on with the ironing

Ironing can be a real bind – whose heart hasn't sunk at a seemingly endless pile of crumpled clothes? But you can cut down the time you spend at the board with these tips.

Wash and dry your clothes correctly Follow the previous advice for reducing creasing during the washing process. The most important rule for easy ironing is: don't overload your dryer and don't over-dry your clothes. Sometimes all you need to do is smooth a garment (such as t-shirts, sweaters, casual jeans) with your hands and fold it or hang it and put it away. Dry things well, and you will cut your ironing time down considerably.

Try touch-up ironing Instead of ironing the whole garment, could you run your iron over collars and cuffs?

Read care labels Look out for advice on any parts of the garment that should not be ironed – for instance, a specially-finished embroidered section.

Keep your equipment handy Don't pile boxes in front of the board or leave your iron's cable in a tangle. The hassle of setting up will discourage you from ironing – leading to a much bigger job when you do get round to it.

Keep your ironing board and iron clean Launder the ironing board cover regularly; wash the iron soleplate – once it is completely cold – if necessary using very fine steel wool to remove dirt. Otherwise, you may stain clothes the next time you iron them.

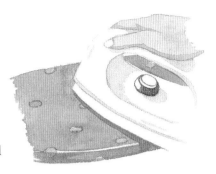

Keep your iron and board clean and have an allotted space for them so they are always handy.

Sort items by ironing temperature Start with low-temperature fabrics, such as silks and synthetics and move on to items, such as cottons and linens that need a hot iron. Iron clothes while they are still damp. This makes the job easier, since creases are not as set in the fabric. When you've finished ironing, hang your garments immediately to help them stay fresh and pressed.

To keep wrinkling to a minimum, start ironing with small areas, such as cuffs, collars and sleeves, and then work your way to the larger areas. Iron lengthwise on fabric to prevent the fabric from stretching.

Never iron stains Check very carefully for stains before ironing. The heat will set the stains permanently.

No stain, no pain: the miracle of nanotechnology

Picture the scene: you're at a dinner party having a great time when wine splashes into your lap. You don't panic. You don't cry. You simply wipe the spill off your clothes with a paper towel and ask for a refill. You're wearing stain-resistant clothing made possible through nanotechnology.

Scientists are using nanotechnology – the manipulation of materials on an atomic or molecular scale – to treat certain natural and synthetic textiles so they are stain, crease and waterproof. One way is by coating a fabric's fibres with microscopic liquid-repelling molecules.

The application of nanotechnology to textiles works better than the more familiar method of stain proofing fabrics – coating them with a special layer of fabric protector such as *Scotchgard*. Such treatments wear off and make fabric stiff, even shiny. Fibres that have been altered molecularly don't change so you can't even tell there's a stain-resistant treatment on it. That is, until a spill hits it. Then the spill simply beads up and rolls off or waits patiently to be removed.

Developed by a company called *Nano-Tex,* which licenses its techniques to manufacturers, nanotech textile products are already on the market, under brand names such as *Lee, Gap,* and *Land's End*. The next breakthrough from *Nano-Tex?* Clothes that don't absorb odours. Smells like a good idea.

Know your fabric

There's no substitute for checking the care label in everything that you clean, but items you already own may still not have their labels attached. So consider these tips for specific materials.

Acetate Often used in linings because it does not pill or suffer from static cling, acetate is also made into dresses, suits and sportswear. Most acetates are dry-clean only. For those that are washable you can hand-wash in warm water with mild suds, but don't soak items with collars. Do not wring and lay flat to dry. While still damp, press inside out with a cool iron. For a 'finishing' iron, if it is needed, on the right side of the fabric, place a cloth – a fresh linen tea towel is perfect – between your garment and the iron. When removing stains never use acetone, or a nail polish remover that contains acetone, as it will dissolve the fibres.

Acrylic Known for its ability to wick moisture away from the body, acrylic is a popular material for socks and sportswear. Acrylic can be washed or dry-cleaned. Generally, you should machine-wash, using a warm-water setting and and fabric softener. Acrylics are heat-sensitive, so tumble dry at a low temperature. To avoid creasing, remove from the dryer as soon as they are dry. When hand-washing is required for delicate items, use warm water and a mild detergent. Rinse and gently squeeze out the water, smooth out the garment, and dry on a rustproof hanger. Lay sweaters and knits flat to dry. When ironing, use a moderately warm iron.

Alpaca Made from the fine, soft hair of the alpaca, a cousin to the llama, alpaca is gaining in popularity as a substitute for wool. Nearly all alpaca can be dry-cleaned, and some can be gently washed. Woven items should be dry-cleaned, but knitted garments, such as sweaters, should be washed by hand in cool water with a mild, undyed soap or shampoo. Don't twist or wring and lay out flat to dry, pressing with a dry towel to remove excess water. Touch up with a cool iron as needed.

Cashmere A fine wool made from the undercoat of the cashmere goat, cashmere is exquisitely soft and luxurious. Most cashmere can be dry-cleaned and some can be gently washed. Most woven cashmere requires dry-cleaning to retain its shape. But knitted cashmeres, such as sweaters, can be hand-washed. Use a natural, undyed soap and cool water. Move the sweater around in the cool water for a few minutes. Rinse repeatedly until the rinse water is clear. Lay out the sweater to dry, pressing it with a dry towel to remove excess water. If you need to touch it up with an iron, do so carefully, using a pressing cloth.

Cotton Not even boiling hurts cotton fibres, although cheap, loosely woven cotton is prone to shrinkage and cloth that has been poorly dyed will bleed. But unless the care label says otherwise, feel free to machine-wash items that are 100 per cent cotton in high temperatures using any good detergent. Watch out for cotton-mixes: you'll need to follow the wash instructions for the less robust nylon or polyester. You can use chlorine bleach safely on cotton whites but only in short bursts: never soak for more than 15 minutes, since the bleach will break down the fibres. Use all-fabric bleach on dyed cottons. Cotton is an absorbent fibre and requires lots of drying time. Because it creases easily, it often requires pressing. Use a hot steam iron.

Linen Linen is made from flax, one of the oldest textile fibres, dating back to at least 5000 BC. Today, you can wash some varieties of linen, but others should be dry-cleaned. Linen has a natural pectin that keeps it stiff and crisp. Washing removes the pectin, making it softer. So if you prefer crisp linen, have your linen dry-cleaned. Otherwise, machine-wash it in warm water and tumble dry, and consider adding starch. Linen tends to crease and needs a steam iron on medium or high heat.

Lycra Developed in the late 1950s, Lycra (a brand name for spandex) is lightweight, durable and known for being extremely flexible. That's why it is used in swimwear, tights and to add a flattering shape to t-shirts, leggings and shorts. You can machine or hand-wash most items containing Lycra. Don't use chlorine bleach under any circumstances. Either let drip dry or put in a dryer on a low setting. When ironing, use a low temperature setting and iron in swift strokes, never letting the iron linger in one spot.

Nylon Relatively easy to care for, nylon can be machine-washed in warm water. To reduce static cling, add a tumble dryer conditioning sheet such as *Bounce* to the dryer and remove clothes from the dryer as soon as they have finished drying. If you need to iron nylon, use a warm iron – it can scorch easily and quickly at hotter temperatures.

Polyester Strong, durable, shrink and crease-resistant, polyester is a modern miracle fibre. However, it does tend to take on oily stains easily. Most polyester can be washed or dry-cleaned. Wash in warm water and tumble dry at a low temperature setting. To prevent pilling (bobbling) and snagging, turn knits inside out. To reduce static cling, use a dryer sheet and remove garments as soon as they have dried. When ironing polyester, use a moderately warm iron.

Ramie A vegetable fibre similar to flax, ramie comes from the stem of a shrub that originated in Asia. The fibres are strong, but have low twisting and bending strength, do not shrink, and have a lustrous appearance. Much like linen, ramie can be machine-washed in warm water and tumbled dry or dry-cleaned. It does tend to crease and so often requires pressing. Use a steam iron on medium or high heat.

Rayon (Also known as viscose.) Developed in 1910, rayon was the first synthetic fibre. Originally, most rayon was dry-clean only, but there are more and more washable rayons on the market. Check the care label for any rayon garment you're unsure of. Dry-clean-only rayon that gets wet – even in the rain – can bleed dyes, shrink and grow stiff. Washable rayon is typically hand-wash only. Since it loses up to 50 per cent of its strength when wet, rayon can be destroyed easily by the agitating action of most washers. Wash in lukewarm or cool suds, squeezing the suds through the fabric, and rinse. Never wring or twist rayon. Shake out or smooth the garment and hang it on a rustproof hanger to dry. Lay sweaters flat to dry. While the garment is still damp, iron inside out on a low heat. For finishing on the right side, use a pressing cloth.

Silk Made from protein fibre produced by the silkworm – the finest silk fibre is produced by worms that eat mulberry leaves – this ancient material connotes fabulous wealth and exotic locales. It is expensive and delicate and must be treated accordingly. Most silk is dry-clean only, since laundry detergents can harm silk. If the care label says that hand-

The lowdown on labels Sewn-in care labels are a legal requirement in all clothing sold in the UK and EC states. Most, but not all, countries have similar laws. In theory, even that ethnic shirt you pick up on holiday should have a care label. The labels give instructions for the best way to care for a garment, including how to properly clean, dry and iron and what techniques and products to avoid. Here's a handy explanation of the symbols:

WASHING	DRYING	IRONING

MACHINE WASH

Normal
The number shows the maximum temperature for safe washing. Can cope with a full spin.

Use a programme suitable for synthetics. Reduced spin.

Gentle/delicate/wool programme.

Hand wash. Look for maximum temperature in the wash bowl.

Warning signs

Do not wash.

BLEACH

Any bleach (when needed)

Chlorine bleach may be used

Warning signs

Do not bleach

TUMBLE DRY

May be tumble dried.

Tumble dry on high setting.

Tumble dry on low setting.

Warning signs

Do not tumble dry.

AIR DRY

Line dry/hang to dry.

Drip dry.

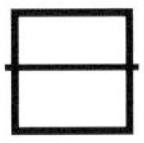

Dry flat.

IRONING

Hot iron – maximum setting.

Medium iron.

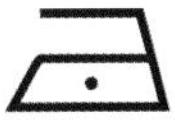

Cool iron – Use minimum setting.

Warning signs

Do not iron.

DRY CLEANING

Normal cycle Dry-clean.

Warning signs

Do not dry-clean.

washing is safe, use a mild soap and lukewarm water. Never use bleach with silk. When ironing, iron inside out on a low heat and use the iron lightly.

Wool Known for its warmth and ability to shed creases, this natural fibre made from the fleeces of sheep, can be cared for in different ways. If there is no care label guidance, dry-cleaning is safest: hot water on wool can lead to serious permanent shrinkage. However, most of the knitwear you can buy today is washable, some if it even by machine. If it's a hand-wash item, use warm water and a mild detergent that contains no bleach. Don't soak. Rinse thoroughly.

Drying a woollen jumper
1 Trace your jumper's shape before washing.

2 To remove excess water, roll the jumper in a towel and then pull back into shape using the template above to dry.

To dry, roll the sweater in a clean towel and squeeze out excess water. If you think that the item will shrink – and you will have to stretch it back into shape after washing – a tip is to trace round the item onto a piece of wrapping paper before you wash. Put a piece of clear plastic over this (to stop dye transfer) and you'll then have a template to lay the washed item onto afterwards – so you can pull it back to its original shape, but no more. So there should be no risk of making sleeves that stretch to your fingertips.

Problems and solutions

Ordinary dirt and difficult stains are one thing. But sometimes even when there is no definable stain, clothes just don't turn out right. Here are some common problems and the likely solutions to the problems.

Clothes come out grey or yellow You may need to increase the amount of detergent in the next load, use a **detergent booster** or increase the temperature of the wash water. However, the grey could be from dye that has bled from darks to lights, suggesting you need to sort better.

Detergent residue on clothes Powdered detergent isn't dissolving properly. Put fewer items into the washing machine. Use **liquid detergent** with 30°C cycles. If the problem is caused by hard water, remove hard-water residue from clothes by soaking them in a solution of **1 cup white vinegar** per **1 gallon warm water**. Rinse and rewash.

There's lint on your clothes You probably need to sort better. Separate lint producers, such as fleece-backed sweat suits, chenille items, new towels and flannel pyjamas, from lint attractors, such as corduroys, synthetic blends and dark fabric. To remove the lint, use a **lint roller** or pat with the sticky side of **masking** or **packing tape**. Check to make sure pockets are empty of tissues and other paper before you wash. Make sure the washer and dryer lint filters are clean and free of lint.

Use a lint roller to remove lint on garments before you wash them to stop it building up in the washing machine or dryer.

You have a problem with pilling This is most common with synthetic fabrics and makes even new items look old and shabby. Try turning synthetic clothing inside out before washing. You can also wash synthetics together in a gentler, shorter cycle. Using a liquid detergent will help. It is possible to remove pills but be aware that it is also very easy indeed to create holes in the fabric beneath. So going at your own risk, and with care, pull fabric tight over a curved surface and carefully shave the pills off with a **safety razor** or a battery-powered **pill remover** available from haberdashers.

Everyday stains & seasonal pests

No matter how careful and houseproud you are, accidents do happen. In particular, you will always need to know how to treat stains and prevent and deal with the insect and rodent pests that get into your house. In the main A–Z of cleaning, we give advice on how to clean just about any object or surface in your home. This chapter looks at how to deal with everyday spills and soiling that can happen anywhere but usually occur on the furnishings and clothes that you love most.

Take immediate action

Taking swift action can often stop a spill or sudden accident from turning into a stain. That doesn't mean that you should panic. Things usually get more difficult when the spill has dried up, and become 'locked' into the fibres of the material that it landed on. Even on a hot day, most things will not dry out immediately.

Stains aren't really very mysterious. Most fall into one of four main categories: protein, oil-based, tannin and dye. The rest are usually a combination of those categories. By understanding what is in a stain, you can determine the best and safest way to remove it.

Before moving on to stain-removal specifics, read the general guidelines box opposite. Always consider the material on which the spill has occurred. Some treatments may remove the stain, but if the fabric is delicate, it may be ruined in the process. So you must always make a judgment about whether the stained item can be safely treated, or if the lesser of two evils is actually to live with the stain but keep a favourite item in one piece.

There are three main categories of textiles that can be stained: washable fabrics (clothing, linens and towels), carpets and upholstered furniture. Below are general steps to follow when trying to remove stains from all three.

Washable fabrics One of the main advantages with washable items is that you have access to both sides of the stain. That simply isn't possible with a fitted carpet or fixed upholstery on sofas. Pre-treatment often consists of pushing the stain out from the back side of the fabric. Attempt stain treatment on washable fabrics using the steps below.

1 Remove as much of the stain-causing material as possible by blotting with **paper towels** or scraping with a **dull knife**.

2 Pre-treat the stain by soaking or applying a **cleaning solution**. It helps to lightly agitate the fabric being soaked or to gently rub together the stained fabric with your hands.

3 Launder in your **washing machine** according to the instructions on the fabric's care label.

4 If necessary, repeat the preceding steps, possibly using a stronger cleaning solution.

General guidelines for successful stain removal Follow the instructions on care labels. Most fabric items, including clothes, rugs, linens and upholstery, have care labels. Because fabrics differ in so many ways – type of material, type of weave, colour, style – don't assume that items that look similar can all be treated the same.

● **Remove spills and drop-ons before they become stains.** Blot up spilled liquids, scrape away solids, and begin your step-by-step stain removal as soon as possible. Factors such as heat and evaporation make stains that are older than about 24 hours much harder to remove.

● **To remove stains from dry-clean-only fabrics**, first remove as much of the stain residue as possible and then have the item dry-cleaned as soon as you can (within a day or two).

● **Be patient**. As effective as stain-removal know-how can be, it is often a multi step approach, from mildest to harshest treatment. Try one tactic and if that doesn't work, move on to a stronger cleaning solution. If you lose patience and try to jump ahead, you may make things worse.

● **Test cleaning solutions on an inconspicuous part of an item**, such as an inside seam or hidden corner. That way, if the fabric or fabric colours react poorly to the cleaning solution, you haven't ruined the whole thing. To test a chlorine bleach solution, mix 1 tablespoon of bleach with 100ml water. Use a cotton bud to apply a drop of the solution to the fabric. Let the garment stand for two minutes and then blot dry with a clean cloth. If there is no colour from your garment on the cotton bud, it's safe to continue with that cleaner.

● **If a stain persists**, don't put the item in the dryer, because the heat could set the stain permanently. Because your first approach may not remove the stain, always check for persistent stains on items after they've gone through the wash. If the washing machine didn't remove a stain, pull that item out from the tumble-dryer pile and let it air-dry. Likewise, don't iron or press something if a stain remains on it.

Carpeting Typically you have access to the top side only for stain removal. But you should never soak carpet stains, because most carpets and rugs have rubber or synthetic-based lining under them. Getting cleaning solutions into those pads can actually attract dirt and lead to other problems, such as mildew and glue deterioration. Try these methods instead.

1 Remove as much of the stain-causing material as you can by blotting with **paper towels** or scraping with a **dull knife**. When blotting up a large stain, always blot from the edge of the stain to the centre to contain it. Standing on the blotting paper will increase its ability to blot up more. Jump up and down if you like.

2 Avoid rubbing, which can push the stain deeper into the pile. Avoid using a circular motion, which can destroy a carpet's texture.

3 Because you should never soak a carpet, **spray bottles** are good for applying a small amount of water-based cleaning solution and rinse water. You can buy them very cheaply from garden centres.

4 To dry patches of carpet that have been rinsed with water, lay a **pad of paper towels** on the spot and place a **weight**, such as a brick, on the pad. To prevent transferring colour from the brick to the carpet, put the brick in a **plastic bag** or wrap it in **foil**. When the carpet is dry, remove the paper towels. **Brush** the carpet pile to restore a consistent texture.

Spray bottles are good for squirting liquid onto carpet stains *(right)*.

Always put the brick or other heavy object into a plastic bag to prevent colour transfer to the carpet *(far right)*.

Upholstery You rarely have a chance to get at both sides of the stain with upholstered furniture. Even if you can remove the covering material, most manufacturers warn against washing cushion covers separately from the cushions because of possible shrinkage and fading. So one small mark can quickly escalate to a big washing job. The trick, as with carpeting, is to remove the stain from the top side without soaking the cushion beneath. So follow the steps for removing carpet stains, listed above, to deal with similar upholstery stains.

Protein-based stains

Baby food and formula milk, cream or cheese-based foods, eggs, faeces and urine are all protein stains.

Fresh protein stains **Cold water** may be all you'll need to remove them. Don't use hot water, because it can 'cook' the proteins, causing the stain to coagulate between the fibres in the fabric and become locked there for ever. For washable fabrics, soak in **cold water** for half an hour, put the stain under **running cold water** and gently rub the fabric against itself to loosen the stain. Launder in the **washing machine** in **warm water**.

Old or dried-on protein stains With this kind of stain, you may have to take your stain-removal tactics to the next level. Soak washable fabrics for half an hour in a solution of **1 teaspoon of liquid detergent** (choose a biological one containing enzymes – the label will say whether it has them) per **2 litres of cold water**. Follow this soaking by laundering the fabric in your **washing machine** in **warm water**. Inspect the item before drying. If the stain is still there, soak the fabric for an additional half hour and then wash again. If the stain remains after that, your only option may be to add the recommended amount of **oxygen bleach** to the next wash cycle, especially if the stain was caused by a coloured ice cream or baby food.

Mayonnaise, a mixture of eggs and oil, will make a classic protein-based stain.

Fresh protein stain in carpeting or upholstery Spray with **cold water** and blot, repeating until the stained area comes clean.

Dried protein stain in carpeting or upholstery Lightly apply a solution of ¼ **teaspoon mild washing-up liquid** (one that doesn't contain lanolin) in **1 litre cold water**. Apply the solution to a **cloth** and use a blotting motion to work the solution into the affected area.

Blot with a **clean paper towel** to remove the solution. Rinse by lightly spraying the stain with **water** and then blotting. Do this until all the suds are gone. Then spray again lightly with **water**. Don't blot this time. Instead, lay a **pad of paper towels** over the spot, put a **weight** on it, and let it dry. (Refer to step 4 of removing stains from carpeting, on page 48.)

If the stain persists, repeat the procedure with a stronger solution: ½ **teaspoon of liquid detergent** (a biological one containing enzymes) per **litre of cold water**.

If that still doesn't completely remove the stain, moisten the stained tufts with a solution of **3 per cent hydrogen peroxide** – you can buy this from the chemist where it is sold as a mouthwash. Let it stand for an hour. Blot and repeat until the carpet or upholstery is stain free. No rinsing is necessary following this procedure, because light will cause the peroxide to change to water. To dry, use the method mentioned above involving a **pad of paper towels** and a weight. But be careful: hydrogen peroxide is bleach and can drastically fade colours.

Oil-based stains

Oil-based stains aren't as difficult to get rid of as most people think. They include auto grease or motor oil, hair oil and mousse, hand lotion, kitchen grease, lard, butter, bacon, oils, ointments, salad dressing and suntan lotion. Many pre-wash stain-removal products, such as *Vanish* and *Shout*, are formulated with special solvents for removing oil and grease.

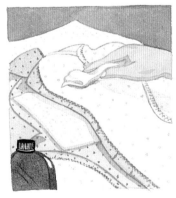

Use paper towels to blot up any excess cleaning fluid as you work on a stain.

Oil-based stains in washable fabrics Pre-treat new and old stains with a **commercial pre-wash stain remover**. Alternatively, apply **liquid detergent**, or a paste made from **powder detergent** mixed with **water**, directly to the stain. Work the detergent into the stain. Immediately after pre-treatment, launder the item in the **washing machine** in **hot water** (if that is safe for the fabric). Before drying the fabric, inspect it. If the stain is still evident, repeat the process until it is gone. For heavy stains, lay the stain face down on a **clean white towel** or **stack of paper towels** and press a **dry-cleaning solvent** – sold in supermarkets as dry clean stain remover – onto the stain, forcing it out and into the towels. Repeat and launder.

Oil-based stains in carpets and upholstery

Apply **methylated spirit** to a **clean white cloth** or **white paper towel** and blot the stain. Discard the dirty towels and repeat using **fresh paper towels** and alcohol until the stain is gone. Don't let the alcohol penetrate the carpet backing, as it can destroy the rubber lining. If that doesn't remove the stain, try the method recommended on page 49 for removing dried protein stains from carpeting and upholstery.

Tannin stains

Alcoholic drinks, coffee or tea without milk, fruits and fruit juices, soft drinks and wine all have tannin as the base of their stains. Most jams also contain tannins, but cherry and blueberry jellies should be treated as dye stains.

Tannin stains in washable fabric Soak for half an hour in a solution of **1 teaspoon liquid detergent** (choose a biological one containing enzymes) per **2 litres of warm water**. Then launder in the **washing machine** in the **hottest water** that is safe for the fabric, using laundry detergent. Don't be tempted to give it a quick go with soap first: natural soaps – including soap flakes, bar soap, and hand wash detergent containing soap – make tannin stains harder to remove. To remove stubborn tannin stains, you may need to wash with **bleach**. If all the sugars from one of these stains aren't removed, they may turn brown when put into the dryer, as the sugar will caramelise. So check first before you attempt to dry.

Tannin stains in carpeting or upholstery Lightly apply a solution of ¼ **teaspoon mild dishwashing liquid** and **1 litre water**. Use a blotting motion to work the solution into the affected area. Blot with a **clean paper towel** to remove the solution. Rinse by lightly spraying with **water** and blotting to remove excess water. Do this until all the suds are gone. Then spray lightly with water again, but don't blot. Instead, lay a **pad of paper towels** down, **weight** it, and let it dry. If the blemish persists, repeat the procedure using a solution of ½ **teaspoon liquid detergent** (a biological one containing enzymes) per **litre of water**. If that doesn't completely remove the stain, moisten the tufts in the stained area with **3 per cent hydrogen peroxide**.

Oops!

A bottle of red, a bottle of white

A butler who wishes to remain anonymous was horrified to find a large red stain in a cream-coloured carpet. He called a carpet-cleaning company, which agreed to come immediately.

Before the cleaners arrived, he surprised two of the family's children sneaking across the hall with a half-empty bottle of expensive white wine. They had been told that they could remove a red wine stain with white wine and they were testing the theory. 'All I will say', adds the butler, 'is that the red wine/white wine stain theory cost them a very large amount of their pocket money.' Moral: while it is indeed true that white wine will shift a red wine stain so will fizzy mineral water. Now which would you rather pour away?

Let stand for one hour. Blot and repeat until the stain has disappeared. No rinsing is necessary following this procedure. To dry, lay down the weighted pad of paper towels mentioned above.

Dye stains

Blackcurrant, cherry, grass and mustard are all dye-based stains and can be real nightmares to shift. After all, dyes are meant to stick. But all is not necessarily lost.

The juice of dark fruits such as cherries is a powerful dye and one of the most difficult stains to get rid of.

Dye stains in washable fabrics Pre-treat with a commercial **pre-wash stain remover**. Or apply **liquid laundry detergent** directly to the stain, work the detergent into the stain, and rinse well. Next, soak the fabric in a diluted solution of **oxygen bleach** (identified as 'all-fabric' on the label), following the directions on the packaging. Launder. Check to see whether the stain is still there. If so, try soaking the garment in a solution of **chlorine bleach and water**, following dilution instructions on the label but be aware that you may be putting your item at risk.

Dye stains in carpet or upholstery You may have to call a professional cleaner or, in the case of a solid-coloured carpet, cut the stained part out and patch it with clean carpet. But before you go that far, try the procedure described on page 51 for tannin stains on carpet or upholstery. It helps to go very carefully: when you are using **hydrogen peroxide**, dab a little onto a **cotton bud** and try to absorb the stain from the carpet into the bud.

Combination stains

Many common stains are a mixture of both oils or waxes and dyes – stains from makeup are always a type of combination stain. They are commonly divided into two categories for the purposes of treatment.

Group A combination stains include those from lipstick, eye makeup including mascara, pencil, liner and most kinds of eye shadows, various types of furniture polish and, perhaps worst of all, shoe polish.

Group B combination stains include chocolate, gravy, hair spray, face makeup (foundation, powder, blusher), peanut butter and tomato-based foods.

To remove these stains, you must first remove the oily or waxy portion, and then you can try to remove the dye. As with any tough stain, your success is not guaranteed. But, by following the steps below, you do stand a chance, especially if you get to the stain while it's fresh.

Washable fabrics with stains in Group A Start by applying a **dry-cleaning stain remover**. Next, rub with a **liquid detergent** and scrub in **hot water** to remove the oily or waxy part. Then launder, using a **laundry detergent** and an **oxygen** or **all-fabric bleach**. Inspect before drying. If the stain persists, wash with **chlorine bleach**.

Washable fabrics with stains in Group B Skip the dry-cleaning solvent. Rub the stain with a **liquid laundry detergent** and launder in the **washing machine** in the **hottest water** possible for the fabric. If that doesn't work, try **oxygen bleach** and then, if that fails, **chlorine bleach** (but only on white fabrics).

Combination stains in carpets and upholstery Begin by removing the oily or waxy part first. Apply **methylated spirit** to a **clean white cloth** or **white paper towel** and blot the stain. Discard the dirty towels and repeat using **fresh paper towels** and more **methylated spirit** until the stain is gone. Don't let the alcohol penetrate the carpet backing, as it could destroy the rubber lining.

If the alcohol treatment doesn't remove the stain, lightly apply a solution of ¼ **teaspoon of mild washing-up liquid** (one that doesn't contain lanolin) and **1 litre of water**. Use a blotting motion to work the solution into the affected area. Blot with a **clean paper towel** to remove the solution. Rinse by lightly spraying with **water** and blotting. Do this until all the suds are gone. Then spray again lightly with **water**. Instead of blotting this time, lay a **pad of paper towels** down, put a **weight** on it, and let it dry.

Finally, if that doesn't completely remove the stain, moisten the stained tufts with **3 per cent hydrogen peroxide** and let stand for one hour. Blot and repeat until the stain is gone. No rinsing is necessary following this procedure. To dry, use a pad of paper towels and weight.

Simple solutions

Collar treatment
To remove lipstick stains from fabric, rub some toothpaste into the stain as a pre-treatment and then wash as usual.

Other stains

Stains produced by perspiration, glue, paint, mud and nail polish are all fairly hard to remove and need to be dealt with differently from the previous categories.

Deodorant and perspiration stains Treat these as you would dye stains. The aluminium or zinc salt build-up from deodorants can make them particularly stubborn.

Removing glue Begin by scraping off whatever you can with a **dull knife** (rubbing **ice** on the glue first to harden it). If the glue is white school glue, treat it as you would a protein-based stain, so don't use hot water – the hot water could cook the proteins. If it is model-aeroplane glue, treat it as an oil-based stain. If the glue won't come out, place the stain face-down on **absorbent paper towels**. To force the stain out, blot the back of the fabric with a **cloth** moistened with **dry-cleaning solvent**.

Removing emulsion paint Treat while it is wet – immediately is best. Soak the fabric in **cold water** and then wash it in **cold water** with **laundry detergent**. If the paint has dried,

Simple solutions

Tracking down mystery stains You don't always have the luxury of knowing what caused a stain. In many cases, especially if you have a family, it probably isn't on your clothes anyhow. So how do you handle a mystery stain? Like a detective, of course.

Start by using your senses to pick up clues: how the stain smells, what colour it is, and where it is on a garment. For example:

• You typically find food stains on the front of clothes.

• Black grease, the kind you find on cars and other heavy machinery, often turns up on trousers and skirts at the level of your car door latch.

• Colours can be misleading.

For instance, old dried blood can be black, not red.

If you can't figure a stain out, use trial and error to remove the stain. First off, avoid washing unknown stains in hot water, which will set protein-based stains, such as egg or blood. Try the mildest method first, then escalate:

• Soak in cold water, which might remove a protein-based stain.

• If that doesn't work, pre-treat by rubbing with liquid laundry detergent and then wash with warm or hot water.

• If that doesn't work, try spraying with a pre-treatment product or blotting with dry-cleaning solvent.

• Still no luck? Time for the bleaches, beginning with oxygen bleach. Use a diluted chlorine bleach soak as a last resort.

even for as little as six hours, treat it as you would one of the Group A combination stains.

Removing gloss paint Spot treat while it is still wet using **paint thinner** or **white spirit** and a **sponge** or **cloth** until the paint is loosened and as much is removed as possible. Before it dries, wash in **hot water** and **detergent**.

Removing mud Handle mud as you would a protein-based stain, with one exception: it's best to wait until mud has dried before cleaning it. Once it has dried, scrape off the excess solids. Then follow the protein-stain procedures.

Removing rust stains If a rust stain remains after removing the mud, treat it with a **commercial fabric stain rust remover**. Since rust removers can be toxic, follow the directions on the container carefully. A solution of **lemon juice** and **salt** sometimes removes rust. Sprinkle salt on the stain, squeeze lemon juice on it, and put the item in the **sun** to dry. Be sure to test the lemon juice first, since it can bleach some fabrics. Don't use chlorine bleach: it will make rust stains permanent.

Removing nail polish Blot with a **clean cloth** moistened with **acetone** or **nail polish remover** until the stain is gone. If possible, lay the stain face down on **white paper towels** and blot from the back side to force the stain out the way it came in.

Removing yellowing from white fabrics Fabrics can take on a yellowish tinge for several reasons: not enough detergent in a wash cycle, too much detergent, insufficiently hot wash temperatures, colour transfer from other items while washing, or the loss of a fabric's artificial whiteners. Your best bet for restoring brightness and whiteness is to launder with the correct amount of **detergent** – read the labels to find one that has both **bleach** and **optical brighteners** in it. Most **biological powders** have the greatest whitening power. If that doesn't work, try **oxygen bleach**. As a final resort, try a cycle with **chlorine bleach**.

Stain specifics

Almost any surface can become permanently stained if you don't know how to deal with the substances that you have dropped on it. From hard surfaces like porous marble worktops and concrete, to soft carpets and textiles, most will respond if dealt with swiftly and correctly. Protein stains such as egg, blood, grease and pet accidents are frequent offenders and can stain for good if left. Here's how to blitz just about anything that you drop unsuspectingly in your home.

Bloodstains

These are much more difficult to remove once they have dried and set – so act promptly. Keep in mind the following three points when treating a bloodstain on any surface.

• **Always use cold water** Any heat from water or tumble drying, could set the stain.
• **Be gentle** Scrub too vigorously and you'll dilute and spread the stain into the clean fabric that surrounds it.
• **Work from the outside in** to avoid spreading the stain.

Bloodstains on clothing Blot with a **clean rag** you've wetted with **cold water**. If staining persists, mix a few drops of **washing-up liquid** with a **cup of cold water** into a bowl and dab the stained item into it, leaving it submerged for 10 minutes. Then blot with a **dry rag**.

Hydrogen peroxide is the next step, but only use it with white or colourfast clothes. (Test on a hidden area first.) Spread the stained area out over the **sink**, and then pour **full-strength hydrogen peroxide** through the stain. Scrub with a **scrubbing brush** or **toothbrush**. Rinse thoroughly in **cold water**.

Commercial stain shifters can be highly effective. Choose an oxygen based one like *OxiClean*, mix **1 scoop of the paste** into a **cup of water**, scrub into the stain and let it sit for two hours. Rinse in **cold water**.

Bloodstains on washable upholstery and carpeting Cover a fresh spot with a **mix of flour and cold water**. Rub gently and dry, either by turning up the

Treat fresh bloodstains on washable upholstery immediately to avoid permanent staining.

radiators or exposing the item to the sun if possible. Brush off the paste once it has dried. You can also try this with **talcum powder**.

Bloodstains on bedding **Shampoo** is an unlikely success story here. Make sure the shampoo covers all of the stain, rubbing it in until fully absorbed. Wet with **cold water** then, once it has lathered up, scrub with a **stiff nylon scrubbing brush**. Rinse in **cold water**. If a ring remains, repeat.

Burns

If your clothing has a burn mark, most professional cleaners will tell you that reweaving by a professional is your only option. That may be true. But you can certainly significantly improve the appearance by cutting out the burn and making a patch underneath from the fabric. Here's how.

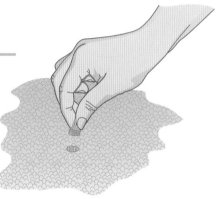

Remedy a small carpet burn by snipping off a few fibres from elsewhere and gluing them into the burn hole.

1 Lay the garment on a **table** with the lining, if there is one, facing towards you. With **scissors**, snip a couple of inches of lining loose at the seam. Then cut a small piece of the garment fabric, about the size of the burn, from the inside seam.

2 Locate the burn on the inside of the garment. Take a piece of **gaffer tape**, large enough to cover the burn fully, and apply the tape to the burn on the inside of the clothing. With a **needle and thread**, sew the lining back into place temporarily with long, loose stitches. Turn the garment over to see the burn from the outside.

3 Using your **scissors**, snip the small piece of garment seam fabric into the smallest pieces you can. You want the cut-up fabric to look as much like fibres as possible. Then press the 'fibres' into the burn so that they adhere to the **gaffer tape** underneath. It won't be as seamless as reweaving, but you will be the only one who knows.

Burns on upholstery The trick here is to try to disguise the scorch mark. Wet a **paper towel** with **plain water** and dab it on the burn. Blot with a **dry paper towel**. If that doesn't take most of the charred spot out, put a drop of **mild liquid laundry detergent** on a **wet paper**

towel and blot the spot. Follow up by blotting with first a **wet paper towel** to remove the detergent and then with a **dry paper towel** to absorb the char stain.

Burns on fake leather upholstery You may be able to fix burns on this type of material with a **hole-patching kit** which you can buy from car supply stores. This repair will involve spreading a coloured paste over the hole and letting it dry. Follow the package directions to the letter for the best results.

Burns on wood floors and furniture You may be able to remove enough of the burn to make it unnoticeable.

An alternative solution for burns on floors

If there's not too much damage, lightly sand the burn, then wipe away the reside with a damp cloth and polish the floor. For deeper burns: scrape out the burn with a sharp knife, then apply putty, which you'll have to disguise by using a crayon the same colour as your floor, or by sticking in a very fine slither of wood. Sand this level with the floor, then use wood stain to match the colour.

• **If the burn is small**, use a **cotton bud** to apply a little **turpentine** to it. If the char remains, rub lightly with some **superfine steel wool (0000)**. If this takes out the burn, but leaves a small indentation in the surface, fill it in with clear **nail polish**. Be prepared to apply several layers.
• **If the burn is mostly just a scorch**, try **methylated spirits**. Put a little on a **soft cloth** and dab it on the scorch. It will dry quickly, but take a little of the scorch out each time. Repeat until you are satisfied. Or try **bicarbonate of soda** on a **wet sponge** – rub in small circular motions.
• **If it's burned beyond a scorch** but not too deeply into the surface, try a **thin paste of cigarette ashes** mixed with **vegetable oil**. With a **soft cloth**, gently rub in the direction of the grain. Follow with coats of **clear nail polish** to restore a flat surface

Chewing gum

Freezing chewing gum with ice makes it easier to scrape off.

When chewed-up chewing gum ends up in your carpet, clothes, or hair, you've got a sticky situation that will only get worse. Gum hardens over time, making it increasingly difficult to remove. So act promptly.

Use ice cubes to freeze gum and make it easier to remove from carpets, upholstery and washable clothing. Scrape off as much of the gum as possible with a **dull non-serrated knife.** Then put **one or two ice cubes** in a **self-sealing sandwich bag** and rub the bag over the spot until the gum freezes. Using the knife, scrape away more gum. Repeat as needed to remove all the gum.

If that doesn't work, try heat The next trick is to try melting the gum. Start by heating it with a **hair dryer** for a minute or two. Now, with a **plastic sandwich bag** on your hand, lift off as much of the heated gum as possible.

Next, try massaging ½ **teaspoon of deep-heating rub** evenly into the spot. Turn the hair dryer on high and heat the area for 30 seconds. Then use another **plastic bag** to lift off the remaining residue. Finally, add **1 teaspoon of mild detergent** to **1 cup of water** and blot the spot with **paper towels** or a **cloth rag** to lift any stain. **Spot remover** or **dry-cleaning solvent** are also worth trying.

Removing gum from clothing Follow the procedure described above for carpets, but apply the deep-heating rub to the opposite side of the cloth. After 30 seconds of blow-drying, the gum should peel off. Then wash the garment as usual, whether by hand or in a washing machine.

You can also try this variant of the ice-cube treatment. Seal the garment in a **plastic bag** and place it in the **freezer**. After it is completely frozen, just scrape the spot with a **dull knife** to remove the gum and launder as usual.

Removing gum from hair Work **peanut butter** or **oil** into the gummy spot for a minute to soften the gum. Then gently pull out the gum with a **paper towel**, then **shampoo** and rinse the area.

Crayon marks

Lavish on them all the pads of paper in the world, and still crayon-wielding youngsters will be mysteriously attracted to the walls of your home. Pint-sized artists are also known to leave their mark on clothing, furniture, carpet and other flooring. And crayons forgotten in a pocket often get into the wash where they can melt and stain clothing.

Removing crayon from smooth surfaces If the marks are on painted walls, glass, metal, tile, marble or porcelain, spray them with a **penetrating lubricant** (specifically, *WD-40*), then wipe with a **soft cloth**. The lubricant *WD-40* lifts off the stain by getting between the mark and the surface. Spray a little *WD-40* in an obscure spot first to make sure it won't harm what you're cleaning. If it doesn't do the trick, dip a **sponge** into a solution of

Simple solutions

Chew on this

Removing chewing gum from pavements is a huge and costly burden especially as councils have to keep doing it all the time.

In the UK, more money is now spent clearing up gum than cigarette butts. For removing gum on a massive scale, chemical solvents are the main cleaning method.

But if gum on your drive drives you mad, try some non-toxic, high-velocity water. Attach a jet nozzle to your garden hose, the kind used for power spraying, put it on its most powerful setting, and fire away at the spot. The quicker you attack the chewing gum, the more easily it will come up.

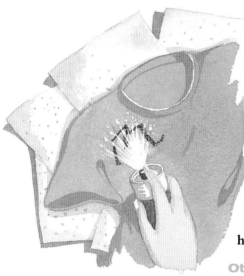

WD-40 spray is the magic ingredient for removing crayon marks from clothing.

dishwashing liquid and **warm water** and wet the crayon mark, rubbing with a circular motion. Rinse with **warm water**, then air-dry.

Removing crayon from clothing Place the item on **paper towels**, then spray with a **penetrating lubricant** (again, *WD-40*). Spray more on a **clean rag** and apply it to both sides of the stain. Allow it to sit for two minutes. Then, using your fingers, rub **1 or 2 drops of washing-up liquid** into the stain on each side. Replace the **paper towels** as they absorb the crayon. Launder the clothing in the washer using the **hottest water** possible and the **heavy soil setting**.

Other approaches that you might try
• Use a light touch on the stain with a **dry soap-filled steel wool pad**.
• Or rub the stain gently with **baking soda** sprinkled on a **damp sponge**.
• At a pinch, pre-treat with **hair spray** before washing.

Removing crayon on upholstery and carpeting
Scrape up as much crayon as you can with a **metal spoon** or **dull knife**. Then wet the mark with *WD-40* and let it stand for 5 minutes. Scrub with a **stiff-bristled brush**, then wipe with **paper towels**. Spray again with *WD-40*. Dab **1 or 2 drops of washing-up liquid** onto the stain and work it in with the **brush**. Wipe with a **damp sponge**.

Removing crayon from floors
• **On vinyl no-wax flooring**, use **silver polish**. Rinse well with **water** and dry with a **paper towel**.
• **On a wood floor**, place an **ice-filled plastic bag** on the mark to make it brittle, and then scrape with a **spoon** or **dull knife**. Or place a **clean rag** on the mark and heat it with an **iron** (no steam). It will soak up the melted wax.

Drying up greasy floors

To remove grease from a concrete floor, sprinkle dry cement over the grease. Once it has absorbed the grease, sweep it up with a broom and a dustpan.

If you have no dry cement handy, try **cat litter**. If that fails, wet the stained area of concrete with **water** and sprinkle it with **powdered dishwasher detergent**. Wait a few minutes and then pour **boiling water** on the area. Wearing **rubber gloves** to protect your hands, scrub with a **stiff-bristled brush** and rinse with **water**.

Hard-water deposits

If you live in a hard-water area, you should know it. Surfaces that get wet frequently will have colourful stains, whitish spots or crusty deposits. Limescale may build up enough to interfere with the function of fixtures like showerheads and taps and washing machines. Soaps will seem to leave a residue and it will take more detergent to get things clean than it has in other places you've lived.

The effects of hard water include dull, sticky hair, dingy, scratchy clothes; and spotted dishes. The culprits? Minerals in your water, especially calcium and magnesium.

Preventing mineral deposits Keep hard water from pooling on the surfaces it typically damages.
• Wipe taps dry.
• Keep lawn sprinklers away from windows.
• Fix leaks and dripping taps.
• Rinse sinks, baths and the shower base after use and then wipe dry with a towel.

Removing mineral deposits The chemical approach involves choosing a **toilet or bathroom cleaner** specially formulated to remove limescale. For small spot areas, such as around the tap and plug hole, **vinegar** or **lemon** also work well. Fix a **half lemon** onto a tap overnight (hold with sticky tape). In the morning, scrub away at loose mineral deposits with an **old toothbrush**. Other ideas that work:

• **Ceramic tile/acrylic baths** Acid-based kitchen-bathroom cleaners formulated for mineral deposits and soap scum, such as *Kitchen Power*. Or rinse repeatedly in **1 part white vinegar** to **4 parts water**.
• **Formica and other plastics** Rub a **wet cloth** dipped in **baking soda**. Wipe off with a **dry cloth**.
• **Glassware** Soak in **undiluted white vinegar** for 15 minutes. Rinse and dry. Sadly, this won't work if limestone cloudiness and progressed to deep etching of the glass.

How hard is your water?
Visit **www.calgon.co.uk**, type in your postcode and find out if you're in a hard, medium or soft water area.

Simple solutions

Limescale on enamel baths

Limescale can be very difficult to remove from enamel baths, because the acid-based cleaners you need to shift it can damage the enamel. One answer is to use a solution of half water, half white vinegar. Using a soft cloth, rub only the limescaled area and rinse frequently. Sometimes you can shift the top layer of a heavy deposit by sheer elbow grease and persistence. Try the blunt end of a disposable razor handle and rub at the mark – this will take a good deal of time, maybe 30 minutes plus – and some of the scale will rub off.

Ink

A good deal of the ink used in fountain pens is washable. Simply flush the stain out at once, holding the item inside out, so that you push the ink back out the way it came.

Simple solutions

Out, damned spot

1 Always treat an ink stain immediately.

2 If you're dealing with washable ink, use cool water.

3 Permanent pen and biro needs methylated spirit. But give it time to work – generally 30 minutes.

4 Apply alcohol to the stain with a clean white terry cloth towel. Later, blot the stain with a fresh white towel.

Biro is trickier: here **methylated spirit** is the best bet. Take care as it can be just too strong for many fabrics. Use a **cotton bud** dipped in **methylated spirit**, then lift up the ink, with a **fresh, dry bud**. If you think the fabric can take it (test for colourfastness on a hidden area first), let the solvent sit on it for 30 minutes to give it time to dissolve the ink, before blotting it up. For large areas, use a **cloth** rather than a cotton bud. Rinse with a **solution of one part white vinegar per 10 parts water** and again with **plain water**.

If the ink resists removal try **foam shaving cream** (gel shaving cream does not work) or **hairspray**. Different biros and pens react to different solvents and you have to take a try-everything approach in the hope you'll find the right one. On larger stains, remember to blot but not to rub – it will break down the fibres of the material – and work from the outside of the stain, towards the centre, to stop the stain from spreading. Also, protect your work surface from the ink as you don't want to remove one stain to start another. Lay an **old white towel** underneath.

Removing ink from fabric Remember that polyester reacts differently to ink from cotton and other fabrics. If **methylated spirit** doesn't completely remove the ink, rinse the fabric with **cool water**, apply **3 per cent hydrogen peroxide**, then rinse again. The hydrogen peroxide will bleach what is left of the ink so that it won't be noticeable. Test for colourfastness and don't use on a wool, silk or a Persian carpet.

Removing ink from carpeting Moisten a section of a **clean white towel** with **methylated spirit** and gently blot the spot. Wait 30 minutes for the alcohol to dissolve the ink, and then press the knuckle of your index finger into the barely damp rag. Work your knuckle forward and backward over the stain. Change to a clean spot on the towel and repeat, this time working your knuckle left to right. To finish, again press your knuckle into the damp towel, but this time twist your wrist clockwise. Carpet fibres are twisted clockwise. This motion will help remove stains from between the fibres without causing the carpet to go fuzzy. Rinse with a solution of **1 part white vinegar** to **10 parts water** and then rinse again with **plain water**, applied using a **fresh towel** and the same knuckle technique described previously.

Mildew

Don't let mildew get a grip in your home. It can destroy fabric and upholstery, eat through plasterboard, disintegrate wallpaper and trigger allergies. Yet it starts with just a few black dots. However, with simple tools and a little know-how, you can defend your home against this musty-smelling micro menace.

Foaming shaving cream may remove a biro mark if methylated spirit doesn't work.

Mildew occurs when moisture combines with mould, which is always present in the air. Mildew flourishes in damp, warm, dark places. The moisture that it needs can come from dripping pipes, a leaky roof or simply high humidity, which is why bathrooms are prime sites. When conditions are right, mildew begins to grow within 24 to 48 hours and will continue until you address the problem.

Preventing mildew Dry out water-damaged areas thoroughly as soon as you notice them. Keeping your house clean, dry and well-ventilated will prevent most mildew problems. Cleaning with **soap** and **water** will often take care of mildew stains, but actually killing mildew requires the power of **bleach**. Don't use straight bleach as it's too powerful and can create toxic fumes.

Removing mildew from the bathroom Mix **1 part bleach** with **11 parts water**. Wear **rubber gloves** and use a **sponge**, **cloth**, or **soft-bristled brush** to apply the solution. Rinse with a **damp sponge** and then wipe down the area with a **squeegee mop**, to get out every last bit of moisture. Turning on a **vent fan** before a shower or opening the window afterwards cuts down on moisture.

Removing musty odours in an unused room Sprinkle **cat litter granules** over the floor. Let it soak for a day and then sweep or vacuum it up. If you use a **vacuum**, dispose of the bag. If you sweep with a **broom**, collect the residue in a **dustpan** and dispose of it outdoors.

Removing mildew stains from fabric or upholstery Take the item outside and knock off the surface mildew with a **stiff brush**. Then air out the piece in the sun. If spots remain, wash the item according to the manufacturer's instructions. Use **hot water** and **laundry bleach** if the fabric can tolerate it.

Removing mildew from leather Use a **cloth** dipped in a solution of equal parts of **methylated spirit** and **water**. Wring out the cloth and wipe the affected area. Follow with a **cloth** dampened only with **water** and then dry the item in an airy place.

Odours

Did you know that certain odours – ammonia for instance – can cause physical pain? Most smells: pet urine, the stench of cooked fish, refrigerator odours, are merely unpleasant. Odours are tricky to shift because you are trying to clean something you can't see. Masking the smell with perfumes and air fresheners is a temporary solution. To truly quell a smell, you must remove its source.

An open box of bicarbonate of soda will absorb fridge odours.

Removing the smell of smoke If you have a culinary disaster and the kitchen fills with smoke, exchange the sooty, smelly air for fresh air. Turn off the oven. If the stove has an exhaust fan, turn it on high. Open windows to create cross-ventilation – windows on opposite sides of the room are ideal. If possible, close doors leading to other parts of the house to confine the smoke.

Removing lingering cooking smells Use a **clean sponge** or **cloth** to wipe down kitchen surfaces (other than those that come into contact with your food) with a **kitchen cleaner**. You are trying to remove tiny particles and grease, carried by smoke, steam, and splatter, in the same way that you would spots you can see. Wipe walls and other surfaces close to the stove. If the smell is still there, as heat rises and is drawn to cool areas, you'll need to wipe down windows, light fixtures, and high kitchen cabinets. If it's still smelly, wash kitchen curtains and exposed dish cloths.

Reducing rubbish bin smells Clean the bin regularly – once a week is ideal. Take it outside and hose it out. Then scrub thoroughly inside with a **nylon-bristled brush** and a solution of **50ml bleach** to **5 litres of warm water** plus a couple of squirts of **dishwashing liquid**. Air-dry until is is completely bone-dry.

Deodorising your waste disposal unit Grind **lemon** or **orange peels** into the unit every so often.

Cut down on fridge odours Don't let old food creep to the back of shelves. Wipe inside the fridge with a **sponge** and **plain water**. Be sure to clean the rubber door seal as it can attract mould. Keep an open box of **bicarbonate of soda** on a shelf and another in the freezer to absorb odours. Replace both boxes several times a year. **Cat litter** and **ground coffee** work just as well.

Removing musty smells in a basement First ventilate your cellar, basement or other rarely-used room. The musty smell comes from mould and mildew, which thrive in dank, dark environments where the air is stale. Open windows and doors, use fans to circulate the air. If it is a persistent problem, consider buying a **dehumidifier** – from DIY and electrical stores. See also **Mildew** on page 63 for additional advice on how to tackle the problem.

Pencil marks

It sounds too obvious, but most pencil rubs out with a rubber. So try it, taking care not to rub too hard, on painted walls and fabric. Remember to choose a white rubber. If that doesn't work: on walls, press a slice of fresh bread into the stain. On clothes, a quality biological detergent should do the trick.

Pests

To prevent pest invasions, tighten up entry points into your home, especially for crawling insects. Fill gaps between the wall and floor with plaster and inspect boxes and gardening equipment for ants, woodlice and spiders.

Next, cut off the pests' food and water supplies. Make sure the tiles behind the sink aren't coming away. Repair leaky taps. Keep food in tightly sealed containers. Wipe down

Simple solutions

Dealing with nasty smells

Removing kitchen odours
Boil up 100ml of white vinegar and a litre of water. The rising heat will carry the vinegar particles to the same surfaces on which the smoke and grease landed and it will neutralise the effect.

For sweet smelling hands
To reduce an onion smell on your hands, rub them before and after you cut onions with the sliced end of a celery stalk. A little vinegar rubbed on your hands before or after cutting onions has the same neutralising effect. If that's too late, use a stainless steel hand washer, from hardware and kitchen equipment stores. The onion residue simply clings to the stainless steel as you wash your hands with this soap-shaped piece of steel. Result, no smell.

Desperate measures
Get a smelly basement to stay fresh for a few hours by placing half an onion on a plate and leaving it out.

worktops. Remove food spills on the sides of and behind the stove. Also attack pest breeding and living areas by filling holes in walls and floors, removing piles of cardboard and paper bags inside or around the house and eliminating general clutter.

To kill ants, avoid sprays and instead use a long-life insecticide that ants take back to their nest. As a prevention, use an insecticide 'pen' (sold in supermarkets and DIY stores) to draw a line through the point that ants usually enter your home. They won't cross the line.

Preventing a flea invasion If you have pets, you'll need to take steps to prevent fleas. Fitting a **flea collar** on your cat is just one element. Even though your pet probably attracted the fleas, it's keeping your home clean that counts just as much, because 90 per cent of a flea's life cycle is spent off the pet and in its bedding or your rugs in its egg, larva and pupa stages.

Designate a pet sleeping area, such as a tiled utility room, that is easy to clean and clean it regularly – more often than the rest of the house if necessary. Cover your pet's bed with a **machine washable blanket**. Then all you have to wash is the blanket, not the bed. When you pick the blanket up, carefully lift all four corners, so flea eggs don't roll off. If you have fleas, vacuum rugs and upholstered furniture, then empty the cylinder or dispose of the bag outside the house. **Steam cleaning carpets** is even more effective.

Killing fleas on your pet Bathe your animal with a **specialist flea shampoo** from your vet and use a product such as *Frontline* (also available from your vet) that can be put onto the back of the neck with a dropper.

Eliminate clothing moths Thoroughly clean clothes before storing them out of season. Moths are attracted to the food, perspiration and urine on soiled fabrics rather than to the wool or cotton itself. So if clothes are totally clean, there is no problem. For long-term storage, put clothes (except leather, which needs to breathe) in **airtight bags** or **plastic containers**. Those with a vacuum seal will take up significantly less space. Steer clear of commercial moth repellents which may contain naphthalene, which is harmful if swallowed. Instead, dab **essential oils – cedar, eucalyptus and lavender –** on a **handkerchief** or **piece of cotton** that you can store with your clothes.

Make mice vanish for good Did you know that in six months, two mice can eat four pounds of food and leave behind some 18,000 faecal pellets? It's an alarming thought. While plenty of people have tried, it's hard to invent a better mousetrap than the **standard snap-back trap**. Poisons can be dangerous to your pets and can leave dead mice out of reach, where they can become a food source for other household pests. Buy traps at hardware stores.

Bait traps with **peanut butter**, **oatmeal**, **cheese** or, if you'd rather not leave out food, **cotton wool balls** (mice will use them for nests) and spread them strategically around the house. Put them perpendicular to walls that mice run along. Mice are renowned for their powerful noses, so wear **gloves** when baiting the traps to avoid leaving your scent.

The classic baited mousetrap is still one of the best ways to catch mice.

Pet clean-up

Furry pets and a sparkling house are not an easy combination. They spread hair on carpets and furniture, walk muddy paws on clean floors, are messy eaters. And then there are the accidents, which need swift attention if they are not to stain and leave a lasting odour.

Removing pet hair from furniture Start with the **vacuum cleaner**. Buy a **lint-brush attachment** for your vacuum if you don't already have one. This gadget first prises up and then sucks up short, wiry hairs that have imbedded themselves in your upholstery. As an alternative, wear a **damp rubber glove** and rub your hand across the sofa cushion. The hair will clump together for easy removal.

Stopping your pet from shedding Use the **brush attachment** on your vacuum to literally hoover your pet. As long as you are careful and your pet does not mind the sucking action and noise, this is a good way to make a preemptive strike against hair that is bound to fall out. You might find that your dog, or even your cat, loves the attention. It feels like a pet massage. If your pet is afraid of the vacuum, regular combing or brushing will do.

Cleaning up pet vomit Start with the chunks of solid stuff. Remove them with a **paper towel** or **spatula**. If the vomit is on a hard surface, such as a vinyl or wood floor, simply wipe up the liquid with **moist paper towels** and then thoroughly **mop** the spot with clean water.

Cleaning pet vomit from fabric, carpet or rugs
If your pet has thrown up on a carpet or upholstered furniture, blot up as much of the liquid as possible using **paper towels**. Next, apply a **cleaner with active enzymes, designed especially for pet mess**. Available at pet stores, these cleaners actually digest the proteins found in the vomit. They usually take a while. So let the cleaner stand for as long as the product's directions suggest. Then, for clothing, wash and rinse or dry-clean according to label instructions. For carpeting or furniture, blot with **clean, cool water** to rinse (but avoid using too much water, especially if there is a pad under the carpet or stuffing in the upholstered furniture). Remove excess liquids by either repeatedly blotting with **fresh, dry paper towels** or using a **wet vac**. As with any pet accident, the key to success is to clean the mess up immediately.

Cleaning up pet faeces Begin by removing any solids with **tissue paper**. Flush down the **toilet**. If there is little or no residue (as with firm faeces on a hard floor), clean with **soapy water** and **paper towels**. Then rinse with **clean water** and **paper towels**. If there is residue (as with loose faeces on a carpet), follow the steps listed for cleaning up vomit: blot up as much of the liquid as possible using **paper towels** and apply a **specialist pet cleaner**. Wash and rinse according to the type of material.

Cleaning up a fresh puddle Wipe up the urine using **paper towels**. The sooner you clean up your pet's indiscretion, the more likely it will be that you'll stop the odour and keep your furry friend from revisiting the spot for a reprise. Urine is by far the worst pet odour in a home. Once it has soaked in and dried, it can be tough to remove.

Removing urine from a carpet Soak up as much of the liquid as possible with **paper towels**. Then cover the spot with a thick layer of **dry paper towels**, with **newspaper** on top of that. (Make sure the newsprint doesn't rub off on the carpet.) Stand on the padding for a minute or so. Then remove the soaked padding and take it to your pet's bathroom area – the cat's litter box or the dog's designated outdoor area – to lure your pet there the next time. Repeat the process. Apply a **specialist pet cleaner**, designed to digest proteins, to help remove the urine smell.

Then rinse the accident zone by blotting with a **cloth** soaked in **clean water**. Remove excess water by blotting with paper towels (as above). Don't use fragrant chemical cleaners, vinegar or ammonia. As with the urine smell, these odours could draw the pet back to the scene of the crime.

Rust

Rust is unsightly and destructive. The natural reaction of metal to water and air, it affects iron, steel, chrome, baths, toilets, sinks, concrete, garden tools, metal outdoor furniture, carpeting and fabric, among other things. But if you step in and deal with it before it gets too bad, rust is relatively easy to shift.

Iron and steel Remove the rust by rubbing it with **fine glasspaper** or **steel wool**.

Metal baking dishes and other cookware Sprinkle **powdered detergent** onto the spot and scour with the **cut edge of half a raw potato**. Or pour **cola** on the rust and let it work overnight. Wash off in the morning.

Baths, toilets and sinks Use **rust-remover** designed for cars. On stainless steel sinks, **lighter fuel** will get rid of the rust but this is a job to be done with extreme care as lighter fuel is highly flammable. Wash thoroughly afterwards.

Concrete Sprinkle **dry cement powder** on the rust and use a **small piece from a broken patio slab** to rub out the stain. The combination of powder and stone acts like pumice to rub away the rust.

Metal garden furniture Try wrapping the rusty spots with a **cloth** soaked in *WD-40* for a few days. Wipe off, then sand with **medium glasspaper**. Wash, rinse and dry thoroughly and then paint with a **rustproof paint**.

Carpets and rugs Mix **water** and **bicarbonate of soda** into a paste. Apply the paste to the stain, allow it to sit for three or four hours and then follow with a **commercial carpet shampoo**. Use this according to the directions on the package.

Simple solutions

Stop garden tools from getting rusty

Garden tools are among the most rust-prone pieces in any home. To stop them from rusting, mix some fine sand with just enough old motor oil to make a clumpy constituency in an old bucket. Push the head of each tool down into the sand for storage. Wipe before using.

Clothing Apply a paste of **lemon juice** and **bicarbonate of soda** to a hidden spot on the garment to make sure the colour holds. If all is well, apply the paste to the rust stains. Let it sit an hour before hanging the garment outside to dry, then wash as usual.

Removing rust from white clothes Mix **cream of tartar** with **lemon juice** and apply it to the stain. Allow the garment to dry and then rinse thoroughly before washing.

Smoke

'Smoke Gets in Your Eyes' sounds almost benign, even romantic, in the famous song. But, in reality, there's nothing appealing about the stale smell of smoke in your house or on your clothes. Whether the smoke comes from cigarettes or cigars which have left their own special odour in your home and clothes or you've had a more serious cooking accident or fire, it is possible to get rid of smoke smells and staining.

Fabric deodorisers will neutralise any residual smoke odour.

To remove smoke odour from clothing, whether it's from a fire or cigarettes, hang the clothes outside in the sun. Sunlight breaks down smoke molecules and fresh air is great for the fabric. You may want to attach a fan to an extension cord and allow the fan to force air across the clothes. Check the clothing every two hours and leave them outside until the smell dissipates. You'll have more effective results in the wash – your next step.

To wash smoky clothes, first pre-soak the garment in a sink filled with **100ml of bicarbonate of soda** and **10 litres of water**. Then place the garment directly into the **washing machine**, using a **detergent** with **oxygen bleach**, such as *Ace*. These detergents remove the odour, not merely mask it with a perfume. Wash smoke-contaminated clothing separately from your general family laundry.

After washing, hang the clothes to dry Using a dryer is not recommended, because the heat can set the smoke odour into any fabric from which it hasn't been completely removed. Neutralise any residual smoke odour with a **deodoriser** such as *Febreze*.

If the clothing label says 'Dry clean only', that's what you should do – and be sure the dry cleaner specialises in smoke removal. Don't forget to air the clothing first. Your dry cleaner will appreciate the gesture.

Removing protein-generated smoke – from cooking ham or chicken, for instance – can be more difficult because these items produce heavy, greasy smoke that fabric readily absorbs. (Wood smoke tends to be flaky and easier to clean.) Air clothing affected by protein smoke on a hanger near a source of fresh air.

To remove just a little smoke from a small area in your home, such as a chest of drawers, use **bicarbonate of soda**. Or try placing a **dish of sliced apples** nearby – it really does work. If smoke has penetrated a large part of your home, understand that you have an extensive clean-up job on your hands involving a variety of materials that require different cleaning techniques. Your safest bet is to contact your insurance company and professional cleaners.

To clean smoke from walls and ceilings, first **vacuum** up any visible residue. Wipe down the walls with a **chemical sponge** (available at chemists and online). Then dilute a **special smoke-removal cleaner** (available at cleaning supply stores and conservation suppliers) according to the package directions. Fill a **spray bottle** with the cleaner. Spray and wipe one section of the wall or ceiling at a time, using a clean cloth. For walls, start from the bottom and work your way up to avoid streaking. You may have to repeat the process several times. Oil-based paint will hold up well to washing. Be careful as emulsion paint can wear off if you scrub aggressively or wash it too many times.

See also Soot.

Soot

The oily black film that is soot can be very difficult to clean. A by-product of smoke, this combination of oil, carbon and tar can settle into microscopic cracks in myriad objects in your home. Run your finger across a wall with soot on it and the oils in your finger, combined with the soot, will permanently mark the surface. Even after you clean the wall, the soot mark will remain.

So what should you do? Before you start, assess how widespread the soot contamination is to see whether you need to call a professional. Test in two or three rooms in an inconspicuous, high area. Take a **paper towel** folded into a pad, dampen it with **water**, and wipe across the surface. If the paper towel turns grey, you've got dust. If it turns black, you've got soot. If there's a lot of the black stuff, it's worth calling a specialist cleaner.

You can treat light surface soot if it isn't widespread. But you'll need to systematically plan your cleaning. The general rule is to work from the top to the bottom of an area – except when using the wet method described below. Then you'll need to work from the bottom up.

First remove as much soot as you can using a dry method. Wear **old clothes**, **rubber gloves**, a **scarf** or **cap**, **disposable paper dust mask** and **safety goggles**, especially when removing loose particles.

The dry method for cleaning soot

• **Vacuum, sweep or feather dust** using a quick, flicking motion with a **broom** or **duster** or keep the **vacuum head** about 1cm from the surface to avoid scratching. Don't rub, unless you want a huge smear to clean. Place **newspapers** under affected surfaces to catch soot for easy removal.

• **Vacuum upholstery.** If this doesn't work, call a professional fire and smoke restorer or dry-cleaner who specialises in soot removal.

• **Take small but sturdy objects** such as lampshades outside to blow off the soot.

• **Use a special soot sponge or chemical sponge** (available at hardware stores, industrial cleaning supply stores, conservation suppliers, and online at *www.conservation-by-design.co.uk*) on walls and ceilings or on unfinished wood (but not on vinyl wallpaper). Apply to the surface in methodical lines so you can keep track of where you have cleaned. To apply to ceilings or walls, attach the sponge to a **pole**. When the sponge is filthy on all sides, wash it alone in the washing machine. Don't wring it, or you will ruin the chemical treatment.

The wet method for cleaning soot is the last resort after you've removed as much of the soot as possible by vacuuming (or dusting or brushing) and using the soot sponge. Put down a **plastic dust sheet** and wash the

For light soot, a quick flick with a duster should solve the problem.

surfaces with a solution of **warm water** and a couple of drops of **all-purpose cleaner**. Apply liberally to the surface with a **sponge**, **rag** or **hard-bristled scrubbing brush**. Rinse with water and wipe dry. If necessary, repeat this procedure.

If a small stain remains after repeated washing, apply **turpentine** carefully with **cotton swabs** made by tightly rolling **cotton balls** around the end of a **wooden skewer**. These are preferable to commercially available cotton swabs, because solvents can dissolve the plastic stalks. Lightly moisten the swab with the turps and gently roll it across the object. Don't rub or wipe, since this might ingrain the soot and carbon in the surface of the object. Never fully immerse an object in solvent. Work slowly and methodically. Test this method on an inconspicuous part of the object first.

Use a degreaser and scrubbing brush for bad soot stains.

Tips for specific soot-removal jobs

• **On objects with a glossy finish,** such as coffee tables and vinyl surfaces including wallpaper, vacuum first. Use a damp cloth to wipe up carefully.

• **To clean ceilings, vacuum** and use the **soot sponge** for a flat painted ceiling. Then use the wet method.

• **To use the wet method on walls,** clean from the bottom up. Start in small sections, wipe the **wet sponge** onto the wall in circular motions, then wipe dry with an **old towel** or **rag**. Wipe up any soot drips immediately.

• **Clean floors first and last.** Before attacking any other part of the room, **vacuum** thoroughly to get up any loose material so it won't be ground into the flooring. Then protect the floor with **dustsheets** while you clean the rest of the room. Return to the floors again for a thorough cleaning at the end. Try **water** first on wood (but don't overwet) and tiles. For carpeting use a regular **carpet shampoo** applied either with a **carpet-cleaning machine** or a **wet vac**. If a wood floor won't come clean, you will have to refinish it. If small soot stains remain on the carpet, apply **turps with a cotton bud**, scrub, rinse and then shampoo the carpet again.

• **If sooty marks remain on walls, ceilings or cabinets** despite your best efforts, re-painting is the final option. First, seal the mark using a **stain-resistant primer-sealer**, available at DIY stores.

Stickers

Gummy, hard-to-remove stickers and price tags are plastered on just about everything we buy. Even when they're designed to be easy-peel, if left too long all stickers can be very frustrating to remove.

Removing stickers with water-soluble glue
Soak the sticker in a basin of **warm water** until the glue dissolves and the sticker comes off. If you can't soak it in water, soak a **towel** in water and apply that to the sticker.

Removing pressure-sensitive adhesive labels
These are the ones that are peeled from a backing and then pressed into place. Peel off as much of the label as possible. Rub the remaining adhesive off with your fingers. Coax up difficult bits with your **fingernail** or a **dull knife.**

Removing old or dried out sticker adhesive
Try removing it with **warm, soapy water** or a **50–50 solution of vinegar** and **warm water.** You might also try **salad oil,** *WD-40,* **acetone** (or an **acetone-based nail polish remover**). If these tactics don't work, move up to solvents, such as **paint thinner,** but bear in mind that you may damage the surface of your object. It may be easier and less harmful to just leave the sticker where it is.

Removing peelable stickers from wood
Heat with a hair dryer to remove.

Vomit

Parents and pet owners, sadly, this one is for you, whether it's a baby regurgitating milk or soft food onto your shoulder or a more significant accident on the floor from a pet or older child.

Removing vomit from a floor or other hard surface
Pour **clean cat litter** onto the fresh vomit. It will absorb most of it and can then be swept up. Follow by wiping with a **damp sponge** or **cloth**. If you don't have any litter, use **bicarbonate of soda**.

Removing old vomit from a hard surface
Scrape off as much as possible with a **putty knife**, **kitchen knife**, or **spatula**. Wash the surface with a little **undiluted**

washing-up liquid applied to a **sponge** or **cloth**. Then rinse and dry. If the acid in the vomit has eaten away wax or an underlying finish, renew it with a spot application.

Cleaning vomit from a carpet or upholstery
Lift off any solids with **paper towels** and then sponge with **cool water**. Follow by covering the spot with plenty of **bicarbonate of soda**, which will absorb the liquid, neutralise the acid and wipe out the odour. Allow to dry. Then **vacuum**. Later, sponge the stain with a sudsy solution of **washing-up liquid**. Rinse and blot dry.

Cleaning vomit from clothing, bedding or table linens Shake the item over the **toilet bowl** and flush. Next, flush fresh messes with **cold water**. Hold the item under the tap with the soiled side down. Don't use hot water – it will cook the protein and make it harder to remove. For dried vomit, scrape off any solids and then soak in **cold water**, using a **biological presoak**, for several hours. For both new and old stains, follow by rubbing a little **undiluted liquid detergent** into the stain and washing in **warm water** with **detergent**. If any stain remains, repeat or use **chlorine bleach** on white fabrics or **oxygen bleach** on coloured ones. If possible, dry on a clothes line rather than in a dryer. Dry cleaning isn't effective at shifting vomit so always try home washing as your first line of assault.

See also **Pet clean-up** on pages 67–68.

Water stains

It seems a little ironic that the most abundant cleaner, water, is itself capable of leaving one of the toughest stains to remove. Choose from the following methods.

White water stains on wood Unless advised otherwise, rub with a **cloth** dipped in a **wood cleaner**, going with the grain of the wood. Follow by buffing with a **clean cloth** and applying **furniture polish**.

The following methods all work – some of the time.
• A 50-50 mix of **baking soda** and **white toothpaste** (not coloured or gel).
• **Mayonnaise** – let sit for an hour.

• **Petroleum jelly** – let sit for a day.
  • A solution of equal parts of **vinegar, boiled linseed oil** and **turpentine**.
• **Olive oil**, applied with **superfine (0000) steel wool**. If none of the above solutions works, refinishing may be the only cure.

Black water stains on furniture Strip off the finish and bleach the wood. The finish is likely to be damaged already, so removing it shouldn't be too difficult. Use a **paint and varnish remover**. Let the piece dry; then treat it with **oxalic acid bleach**. This is highly toxic. Follow the directions on the labels.

Water stains on painted walls or ceilings Dab with a mixture of **1 part chlorine bleach** to **10 parts warm water**. If several applications don't work, you'll need to repaint. But first apply a sealant so the stain won't bleed through. *Zinsser BIN Primer Sealer*, available at hardware stores and *www.decoratingdirect.co.uk* is a good one.

Water stains on carpets or upholstery Try a **50-50 solution** of **water** and **white vinegar**. Wet a **cloth** with the solution and gently blot the surface.

Wax

If you burn candles, some wax is bound to spill. Minimise damage in advance by burning only white candles. The dye in coloured candles is much harder to remove.

White wax on carpets or upholstery
Use the fire-and-ice approach:
1 Put some **ice cubes** into a **plastic bag** and place it on the wax for a few minutes to make the wax more brittle.
2 Scrape off the wax with the dull side of a **table knife**.
3 Use a **hair dryer** on high to soften the remaining wax.
4 Scrape again.
5 Put a layer of **paper towels** or **white rags** over the wax and pass a **warm iron** over the area. Keep moving a clean area of the towels or rags onto the spot.
6 Test some **dry-cleaning solvent** on an inconspicuous area, and if it does no damage, blot a little into the remaining wax stain. The solvent is available at DIY stores.

Ice cubes will harden wax for easier removal.

Place a wax-stained tablecloth in the freezer to harden the wax

White wax on table linens or clothing

Use the above methods, with these changes:
• Put the item in a **plastic bag** and then into the **freezer** for half an hour before scraping.
• On washable items, saturate the final stain with a solution of **1 part methylated spirits** to **2 parts water** and let it sit for half an hour. Rinse and then launder in the **washing machine**. Send non-washable items to the dry-cleaner.

Removing coloured wax

1 After freezing and scraping, use **turpentine** on the rest of the wax. Test first and work on only tiny areas at a time, blotting with a **rag**. Only you can judge whether the treatment is worse than the disease, because it may damage some materials. Some dyes may not be removable.
2 Treat washable colourfast fabrics with **bleach**, following directions on the package. Then launder.
3 For fine rugs or upholstery, consult a professional.

Removing wax from dishes and glass

Heat with a **hair dryer** and then wipe with a **cloth**. Then keep wiping and polishing with **used fabric softener sheets**.

Simple solutions

No-wax mahogany

The birthday party ended with your aged aunt blowing out the candles – and wax spots all over your beautiful mahogany table. But don't worry, wax comes off fairly easily from wood surfaces.
1 If you get at the wax while it is still warm, wipe up all you can with a clean cloth.
2 If the wax has hardened, soften it first with a hair dryer set on medium and then wipe.

The ZAP top-to-bottom cleaning system

Here's a foolproof way to get your weekly housecleaning done, top to bottom, as swiftly and efficiently as possible. Just imagine how good you'll feel whipping through regular chores, spending less time yet getting better results. Read on and discover how simple it is. Professional housekeepers say you need just two things to do a speedy but thorough job of cleaning your home: focus and organisation. Here's how to start.

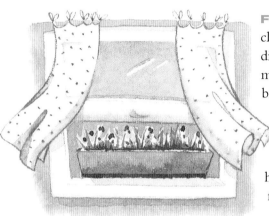

A clean and tidy house is like a breath of fresh air. Enjoy the benefits of being focused and organised in your cleaning.

Focus For the three hours or so that you will spend cleaning your home from top to bottom, strip the distractions out of your life. Don't dawdle over magazines you should be stuffing into the recycling bin. Don't pick up the phone if it rings.

Organisation You need a clear plan. This establishes a pattern, and because you work in the same order week in, week out, leads to speed. And here's the good news: there's no need to go searching for a plan. We have one right here. The Zoned Attack Plan (ZAP) is so named because you concentrate on one portion of your house at a time. It's the ultimate time-saving strategy for weekly housecleaning.

Ground rules for cleaning

Before we get down to the specifics of how to use the ZAP plan in your home, it's worth setting out some time-saving ground rules.

Clean from left to right and top to bottom in each room. A systematic, clockwise approach to a room eliminates any retracing of steps. And a top-to-bottom system lets gravity work for you and avoids duplication of effort. You don't want the dust from window ledges falling on a freshly cleaned table, for instance.

Keep cleaning supplies together and close at hand to make every movement count. Interrupting the bathroom cleaning to track down window cleaner slows your momentum.

Deal with the clutter in your home separately
The ZAP approach assumes you will have laid down the
law with other family members: no clothes strewn about the
bedroom and no dishes left in the sink.

Move furniture toward the centre of the room
when it is time to dust. The dust from the skirting board,
carpets and windowsills will settle to the floor, where it's
easy to vacuum up. Once you've vacuumed the outside of
the room, push furniture into place and vacuum the rest.

Set a deadline for completing your cleaning
Knowing up-front how much time you'll spend cleaning
can make the list of chores less daunting.

Learn to multitask If you must answer the phone
while you're cleaning, do some low-concentration tasks,
such as cleaning windows, polishing a table or loading the
dishwasher at the same time.

Don't turn on the television Instead, entertain
yourself with upbeat music to keep energised.

Use both hands while cleaning Dust or wipe
surfaces with one hand while lifting objects with the other.
Scrub counters with a cloth in each hand. Squirt spray
cleaner with one hand and wipe the surface with the other.

Pull an old, clean cotton tube sock over your
dusting hand and lift objects with the other hand as you
clean. If you have problems with hand dexterity, try a
rubber glove on the hand you use for lifting objects.

Spray a lint-free towel with window cleaner
and keep it handy for cabinets or tables with glass inlays.

If you have pets use rubber gloves and a circular
motion to collect pet hair from chairs and couches.
Throw the rolled-up hair on the floor and suction it up
when you vacuum the floor later.

A sock on one hand makes
dusting easy while lifting objects
with your other hand.

If you live in a multistorey house and come across
items that belong elsewhere, place them in a plastic bin near
the stairs and take them up next time you make the trip.

Get a 6-metre extension cord for your vacuum
cleaner so you won't have to plug it in in every room.

If it's truly not dirty, don't clean it Don't waste
time on a rarely-used room. Dust lightly and forget it.

Assemble your arsenal

An effective cleaning system starts with good tools and products. Use a plastic or rubber cleaning caddy with dividers, stocked with everything you'll need as you make your rounds.

Check your tools regularly to make sure they are up to the task. A crumbling sponge mop or worn-out broom will make extra work. A vacuum cleaner with a broken guard will damage baseboards and furniture.

For a house with several floors, it's worth keeping a completely stocked cleaning caddy on each floor, providing that you have somewhere safe to store chemicals out of children's reach. Also keep basic tools, including a broom, dustpan, and mop, on every level.

Alternatives to the caddy, especially if you have a smaller house or flat, are a **large plastic bucket**, or an **apron with large pockets**. Arrange items in the caddy so that it is well balanced. Avoid specialised items that accomplish only one job, such as soap scum cleaner or special counter spray. If you must have such cleaners, store them near the place that you're most likely to need them.

Cleaning schedules At top hotels, silverware is polished each week. But in the real world, with no army of cleaners and table staff, plenty of jobs can be done far less often, without anyone being any the wiser. Here's a schedule that makes practical sense to follow alongside the weekly ZAP routine.

Every day
- Put things away when you finish using them.
- Wash dishes, wipe kitchen worktops, clean up cooker spills and empty trash as needed.
- Sponge down showers after use to prevent mineral deposits and mildew.
- Wipe sinks.
- Make beds and straighten rooms.

Twice a week
- Dust-mop hardwood floors to prevent scratching from dirt.
- Put away clutter.
- Vacuum if you have children

and pets who walk in lots of dirt. Otherwise, vacuum weekly.

Once a month
- Wipe or vacuum skirting boards and blinds.
- Sweep the garage, patio and paths.
- Vacuum upholstered furniture with the brush attachment.
- Clean ceiling fixtures in one room per month (rotate).
- Wash throw rugs.
- Clean the oven.

Every three months
- Polish wood furniture.
- Wash windows inside and out.

Every six months
- Declutter storage areas in the loft and garage.
- Vacuum, flip and rotate mattresses.
- Polish silver.
- Air out pillows.

Once a year
- Move heavy furniture to clean behind and underneath.
- Vacuum rug pads and the backs of large rugs.
- Clean curtains and carpets.
- Turn large rugs 180 degrees to even out wear patterns.
- Wash walls.
- Clean chandeliers.

Fill your caddy (16) with these items:

1 **Glass cleaner**
2 **General-purpose cleaner** Choose one in a spray bottle – supermarket own-labels are good.
3 **Heavy-duty degreasing cleaner** Or a mousse product, like *Cif*, which is fast to use.
4 **Wood polish**
   Powdered scouring cleanser such as *Astonish* or *Bar Keeper's Friend* (not shown).

You'll also need a few extra tools Some of these items may not be mentioned in the weekly ZAP routine described below, but you will need them for some of the cleaning jobs you'll be doing:

5 **Lambswool duster**
6 **Nylon scrub pad**
7 **Stiff-bristled toothbrush** for scrubbing around taps.
8 **1cm soft-bristled paintbrush** for dusting lampshades and removing cobwebs.
9 **Toilet bowl brush**
10 **Rubber gloves**
11 **Clean cotton rags**
12 **Micro fibre cloth (E-cloth)**
13 **Large rubbish bag**
14 **Plastic squeegee** for bathrooms.
15 **Safety glasses** to protect your eyes from splattering cleaner or airborne dirt.
   Plastic bin for collecting items that belong elsewhere (not shown).

Divide and conquer

ZAP is a systematic cleaning plan for getting your home spotless, top to bottom, every week. It divides your home into four zones and you completely clean each zone before moving on to the next. ZAP is designed to eliminate going over the same ground, or cleaning surface, twice, extra trips around the house and counterproductive moves like wiping dust onto a just vacuumed floor.

Here are the four zones

Zone 1 Bedrooms, bathrooms and halls.
Zone 2 Kitchen, informal dining area and family room.
Zone 3 Formal living room and formal dining room.
Zone 4 Laundry room, home office and other miscellaneous spaces.

A lot of people have no idea how to clean and may typically start with the room nearest to where they store the vacuum cleaner. But professional cleaners work in a specific way. And now you can too. With the ZAP system, you've an efficient step-by-step process that couldn't be easier to follow.

ZONE 1 Bedrooms, bathroom & hall

Vacuum after dusing each room to maximise dust pick-up.

1 Go into each bedroom, strip the sheets off the beds, and throw them into the hall. Go into the bathroom and throw the towels, washcloths and bath mats into the hall, too. Gather all of these washable items in a laundry basket and put them near the washing machine. Start a wash load with the bath mats and a couple of towels.

2 Get the cleaning caddy you keep upstairs and go into the upstairs bathroom and start spreading around the cleaning chemicals. Spray bowl cleaner inside the toilet bowl. Spray all-purpose cleaner or bathroom mousse, if you prefer, on the basin and basin surround and bath.

3 Empty the rubbish bin into the plastic bag that's in your cleaning caddy.

4 Now for some cleaning. Spray a clean rag with window cleaner and clean the mirror. Scrub the inside of your toilet bowl with the toilet bowl brush, then flush. Wipe down the basin, bath and surrounds. Rinse basins and baths. Spray all-purpose cleaner on the toilet seat and exterior and on the shower walls. Wipe everything down. (Note: this prevents mixing two cleaners in the toilet, which you must avoid.)

5 Mop the floor, backing out of the room.

6 Go into a bedroom and empty the rubbish basket into your plastic bag.

7 Move any light furniture or other obstructions toward the centre of the room, away from the walls.

8 Dust the entire room, starting at the entrance and moving from left to right (clockwise). Using your lambswool duster, take one wall at a time, working from top to bottom, including pelmets, window frames, pictures and furniture. Because your duster is on a pole, this isn't the hard bending and stretching work it might sound.

9 Now vacuum around the entire outside of the bedroom. (That's why you moved the furniture.) Return the furniture to its original position. Starting at the far corner of the room, vacuum the rest of the room, backing out the door.

10 Go into the other upstairs bedrooms and repeat steps 6 to 9.

11 Give the upstairs hall a quick dusting, moving left to right, top to bottom, one wall at a time. Dust the tops of pictures and any skirtings.

12 Put away the upstairs cleaning caddy. Vacuum the upstairs hall, moving backwards toward the stairs. Take the rubbish bag with you and back down the stairs, vacuuming as you go.

13 Dust and vacuum the downstairs hallway.

14 Unload the washing machine – it should be finished by now. Put everything but the rubber bath mats into the tumble-dryer (if you have one – otherwise hang it up to dry with the bath mats). Load the machine with dirty sheets and towels. Hang the bath mats on a clothes rack or peg on the line to drip dry.

Simple solutions

Faster, faster!

When you really need to speed clean, try these work-faster tips.

- **Time yourself**. One week, set the stop-watch, and you'll discover that you spend 8 minutes in a bedroom. Next week, challenge yourself to do it in 7.
- **Wear trainers**. You'll whizz up and down stairs with ease.
- **Listen to favourite, upbeat music** on a Walkman, an iPod or other carry-round-the neck system. Having it with you means there is no need to stop and change CDs and you won't linger longer in the only room where the music is.
- **Share the work**: the four zones of ZAP divide neatly into two. One week, your partner does the harder first sections, next time you swap.
- **Plan a treat** for immediately after your cleaning is finished. You'll want to hurry along to get to a favourite foodie snack, TV show, swim/gym class or hairdresser/beauty salon appointment.

ZONE 2 Kitchen, dining area & family room

You already have some of the biggest cleaning jobs behind you. Now it's time to tackle the real high-traffic spots: kitchen, casual dining area and the family room.

1 Get your downstairs cleaning caddy. Go into the kitchen and pull out a microwave-safe bowl. Pour in 2 cups of water, put the bowl of water in the microwave, and heat on high for 3 to 5 minutes.

2 While the microwave is running, go around the kitchen and wipe all surfaces, left to right, top to bottom. Spray on a cleaner that's safe for your hob (make sure it's cool first), then also spray an appropriate kitchen cleaner onto the oven and refrigerator doors, and the worktops. If in doubt, the safest solution is sudsy water, made with warm water and washing-up liquid. Pour it into an empty plastic spray bottle (sold at garden centres for misting plants, cost around £1). Then you're ready to go.

3 Take a cleaning cloth and move from left to right around the kitchen, wiping down the work surfaces and appliances. While you're at the stove, wipe any food spills from the cooking rings. Move worktop appliances such as the toaster and kettle and wipe under them as you go. When you get to the microwave, make sure the water has cooled for at least a minute. Pour the water out and wipe down the steamed interior of the microwave.

4 Pick one section of cabinets to clean each time you clean the kitchen. Spray that section with all-purpose spray and wipe. Each month or so, you'll have worked right round the room with no need to ever make cleaning cupboard doors a separate major cleaning job.

5 Throw out old food in the refrigerator and pick one shelf or drawer to clean. At the sink, carefully wash it with sudsy water. Then rinse very thoroughly. Dry glass shelving using a fresh, lint free linen tea-towel.

6 Clean the sink. Stainless steel can scratch, so you should avoid using anything abrasive. A light scouring cream like *Cif*, is generally suitable. But if in doubt, simply use a cloth and washing-up liquid. Shiny taps are the trademark that a

Simple solutions

Do your sums

If you have a big family and a small house, you'll need to increase the frequency of your cleaning, since key items will get a lot more use.

Conversely, if you live alone in a big house, you can get away with less frequent cleaning.

In particular, you may be able to cut down on vacuuming: even more so if you keep the doors of rooms that you rarely use shut. However, this rule doesn't apply to areas where time – as much as usage – is the main factor. So whether the kitchen and loo are used by one person or six, bacteria left on worktops and handles will multiply just as fast.

professional cleaner's been in – use a microfibre cloth to dry them, and you'll get a polished look in no time.

7 Mop the floor.

8 Go to your casual dining area. (If you have an eat-in kitchen, take care of the table and chairs in step 3.) Dust your way around the room, left to right, top to bottom. Dust the light fixture. Pull the chairs away from the table. Wipe up any spills or crumbs from the table and chairs. Mop or vacuum under the table and move the chairs back. Clean the rest of the floor.

9 Go to your family room. Move any light furniture into the centre of the room. Move around the room dusting – from left to right, top to bottom, one section of wall at a time. Dust the pelmets, window frames, pictures, furniture and electronic devices.

10 Vacuum the outside of the family room. Put furniture back in its original position. Vacuum the rest of the room.

11 Take the towels, washcloths and bath mats out of the dryer or off the line and set them on a worktop. (Don't bother folding.) Take the sheets and towels out of the washing machine and put them in the dryer. Load any remaining sheets and towels in the washing machine.

ZONE 3 Formal living & dining rooms

Take a deep breath, a swig of water and pat yourself on the back. You're almost done – and by using the ZAP system, you've left the easiest for last.

1 Go into your formal living room. Move any light furniture, including lamps, into the centre of the room.

2 You know the drill by now. Dust the room, moving from left to right, one wall at a time. Dust from top to bottom, including pelmets, window frames, pictures and furniture.

3 Vacuum the outside of the living room. Return the furniture to its original position.

4 Lift the seat cushions out of the sofa and armchairs and vacuum underneath with the brush attachment. Vacuum the centre of the floor.

5 Go to the dining room and repeat steps 1 to 3.

6 Dust the dining room table and chairs.

7 Pull the chairs away from the table and vacuum under the table. Return the chairs to their original positions and vacuum the rest of the room.

ZONE 4 Laundry room & other spaces

This is the home stretch – it's time to polish off the last couple of rooms and wrap up any loose ends.

1 Remove the sheets and towels from the dryer or washing line and add them to the unfolded pile on the counter. Move the last of the laundry from the washer to the dryer or the washing line.

2 Empty the rubbish bin into your plastic bag.

3 Since this is not a high-traffic area, a quick dusting will do. Move around the room left to right, top to bottom, dusting the shelves, worktops and sink. Wipe up any detergent spills with a damp rag.

4 Mop the floor.

A regular light mop prevents serious dirt build-up and tougher cleaning jobs.

5 Continue the pattern of dusting and then vacuuming or mopping in the other miscellaneous spaces of your home – conservatory, enclosed porch and office.

6 Empy the vacuum cleaner cylinder (or check on the bag level) then put it and your cleaning caddy away.

7 Take your plastic bag full of rubbish out to the dustbin.

8 While you're outside, take your doormats and shake them out thoroughly, into an unobtrusive spot.

9 Take all your dirty cleaning cloths to the laundry room and put them in the washing machine.

10 Once all of the sheets, towels and other household laundry items are dry, spread out one of the sheets from an upstairs bedroom and put all of the other laundry on top of it, along with the bathroom mats that were drip-drying. Pull the corners of the sheet together to make a sack. Take it all to the first-floor bedrooms and put the sheets back on the beds. (This is why you didn't bother folding.) Return the towels, washcloths and bath mat to their usual places. Then carry the remaining laundry upstairs and repeat. Of course, if you have several sets of bedding and you like to rotate, you'll need to fold the sheets up, then take fresh supplies from the airing cupboard.

11 Take a bow. Or take a nap – it's your choice and you're bound to have plenty of time, because the beauty of ZAP is how fast everything gets done.

Maid to order We all need a break from housecleaning once in a while. And, while you may not be able to budget for this every week, most domestic cleaning firms are happy to do one-off cleans. Having a cleaner come once a fortnight is another option: in between, it's you and the ZAP system. Particularly if you're not physically up to the bending and stretching of cleaning, this can be an acceptable solution. On your cleaning weeks, the skirting board and ceilings can wait.

Before you look for someone to clean your home:
● Decide whether you want to hire a cleaning service or a single housekeeper. Cleaning services typically dispatch teams of two to four, who complete the work more quickly. But solo cleaners will often take on tasks that the services avoid, such as washing laundry, doing the dishes and picking up and tidying clutter.
● Ask for references from current and former clients. Call those people and find out what they liked and disliked about the arrangement.

● Ask the company whether they conduct background checks on their employees and what type of insurance they carry to cover damage or theft.
● Before you hire anyone, nail down precisely what they'll clean, how long they'll be in your home, and whether they'll bring their own cleaning tools or use yours. (They typically clean when you're not around, so you won't be there to supervise.)
● If there are items you don't want cleaners to touch, such as the frame of an original oil painting or your child's delicate clay models, point these out to

the cleaner in advance to avoid any grief later.
● Rates vary widely according to where you live. An individual may clean from around £5.50 per hour (from £8 in London) while a cleaning service is more likely to charge around £20–£40 basing their charges on completing the job, rather than precise timing.
● If your house needs a thorough spring clean, expect to pay more for the first visit, because workers may need to spend significantly more time on heavy-duty cleaning than they will on subsequent visits.

PART 2

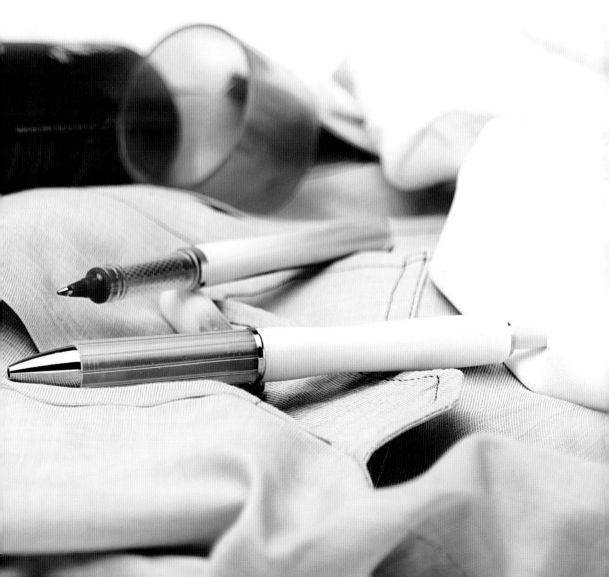

A-Z of everyday cleaning

A-Z of everyday cleaning

Here's a complete A–Z guide to cleaning just about any object or surface inside or outside your home. From aquariums to attics, to bicycles and binoculars, from CD players to chandeliers, from silver to shower cubicles: if you own it, we can probably tell you how to clean it. Whether it's everyday maintenance or a complete scrub down and overhaul, you'll find detailed instructions on how to start, what to use and how to maintain your object in pristine condition.

Air & allergens

We use air every minute of every day. The problem is, hot and cold air don't come free, so we spend much of the year with our homes hermetically sealed to save money, but with fans or heaters on. But trapped in there, in our centrally-heated, double-glazed homes, are dust mites, airborne chemicals, cooking fumes and, for some of us, cigarette smoke, carbon monoxide from fireplaces, pet allergens (fur, skin and saliva) and many other irritants.

Some simple air-cleaning solutions cost nothing.
• **Good ventilation** will do more than anything else to freshen the air in your home. When you get up in the morning, open a window in each room of the house for five minutes no matter what the temperature is outside. If you absolutely can't bear to do this at least do the bedrooms.
• **Smooth surfaces** – tile or hardwood floors, for instance – will keep the air cleaner, too, because allergens collect in upholstery, curtains and carpets. So if you have a particular condition, such as asthma, that means you really do need clean air, consider swapping to these.
• **Don't rely on smells** to tell you that the air is fresh. Using **bicarbonate of soda** or **vinegar** to absorb odours may reduce smells, but they do little to clean the air. The same is true of aerosol spray air fresheners, which pump more chemicals into your environment.
• **Clean any fan vents** in the bathroom regularly.

For super sneeze control

For more serious allergen control, consider buying an air filter unit – especially if allergens are a medical problem and less expensive approaches haven't solved it.

There are several technologies to choose from, but for general removal of particles from the air, you'll probably have the most success with a HEPA filter (high efficiency particulate air). Most are small units, costing from around £30, that sit in the room and trap microscopic particles by drawing air through fine disposable filters and returning the purified air to the room. Remember that you will need one in every room. The filters are so efficient that they're often used in hospitals and industrial 'clean rooms'. If you have a cyclone-style vacuum cleaner you can also get a HEPA filter for it, which ensures that the cleaner picks up and retains microscopic particles as it breezes around your home.

Control the humidity in your home Heating systems can create extremely dry air, which can be corrected with a **humidifier** or much more simply and cheaply by placing **bowls of water** near your heat source, for example on windowsills above radiators. You might think houseplants would do great things to clean up the air in your home, since they gobble up carbon dioxide and expel oxygen. But very moist pots of soil can be splendid breeding grounds for mould. So it's a question of balance.

To control allergens in the air around you, you have to go to the source.
• **To control pet allergens and mites,** wash dogs frequently – every two weeks if someone in your home has allergies. Few cats are likely to tolerate this, but some may allow damp combing which cuts down on shedding.
• **To keep smoke to a minimum,** limit the number of fires you have in the fireplace and, if you or another member of your household simply must have a cigarette, always smoke it outside.
• **To keep dust mites under wraps,** put an **anti-allergen mattress cover** over the mattress on your bed. You spend a third of your life here so it's worth keeping it clean.

See also **Fireplaces** and **Humidifiers.**

Air conditioners

Portable air conditioners are a boon if you have a small room that overheats unbearably in the summer. A child's attic bedroom is a good example. The unit will be cheaper to run if kept clean.

Dirt and debris can restrict airflow through the filter and around the cooling elements, forcing the unit to work harder and use more electricity than necessary to do its job. Most portable units have a pull-out tray, which enables you to clean the filter regularly. Shake out any dirt into a **plastic sack,** then use the **crevice tool** on your **vacuum cleaner** to suck dirt out of the grills.

Alabaster

As early as the 5th century BC, thin slices of translucent alabaster were used as windowpanes in the Middle East. Today, you're more likely to find this delicate, porous stone used for vases, urns, bowls and figurines. Translucent varieties are used to diffuse light in light fixtures.

The safest way to clean alabaster is just to wipe the object clean with a dry, **pure cotton cloth,** because the stone is easy to damage. Don't soak an alabaster object in water, don't use any other cleaning chemicals and don't use any abrasive materials.

If a piece needs more cleaning, squirt some **mild washing-up liquid** into **water,** dip a **sponge** into the soapy water and squeeze. (You don't want the sponge dripping.) Sponge the water on and rub gently. Rinse the sponge with **fresh water** and gently wipe the object again. Dry with a **cotton cloth.** If the alabaster is from a light fixture, let it dry at room temperature for two hours before returning it to use. Otherwise, the heat could cause the damp alabaster to expand and crack. After cleaning, give alabaster a soft glow and remove the appearance of surface scratches by rubbing over **petroleum jelly.** Dip a **soft cloth** into the jelly, then rub this onto the alabaster, with a circular motion.

Aluminium

Much of the aluminium that enters your life these days is extremely easy to care for.

Cleaning aluminium window and door frames is straightforward. They are sold with a tough coating – white, primarily, but sometimes bronze or brown. Aluminium can scratch, so it's important to use only a **smooth cloth** and avoid any cleaners with abrasives. A **sudsy bowl of washing-up liquid** is the best bet. Afterwards, be sure to dry thoroughly.

Cleaning older bare aluminium presents more of a challenge. It may have started out shiny, but it tends to oxidise from years of exposure to the air, turning it a darker grey and giving it a rough feel. To clean the aluminium apply some *WD-40*. Spray it on or apply it with a **cleaning rag**. Then go over the aluminium with **fine steel wool (00)**. Move the steel wool back and forth (not in circles) and don't rub so hard that it scratches. When you're finished, wipe the *WD-40* off with a **clean rag**. Test this method on an inconspicuous area first. This technique will make your aluminium lighter and brighter, but the effects of oxidation can't be totally erased. If you're still not happy with the appearance of your aluminium, consider giving it new life with a coating of **outdoor emulsion paint**. (Oil-based gloss paint that you'd usually choose for wood window frames might crack due to the expansion and contraction that aluminium goes through as the temperature outdoors changes during the seasons.)

Pollution-stained aluminium

If aluminium frames on an outside extension, shed or conservatory have dark streaks, they were probably caused by pollution and there's a good chance that they will not simply respond to washing with detergent. In that case, you have nothing to lose by using a mildly abrasive cleaning cream, such as *Cif*. Dampen a cleaning cloth with a little water, dab on some of the cream and rub it into the cloth. Then rub the cloth just on the streaks, very lightly. Rinse immediately with a garden hose.

Animal bedding & cages

The fabric used for bedding for cats and small dogs is likely to be machine washable – so check the labels. Ideally, wash at 60°C to kill fleas and other insects and their eggs and then dry on a washing line.

Washing pet bedding in the bath is an option if it's too big for the machine (but remember to thoroughly clean the bath afterwards, with **very hot water** and **bathroom cleaner**). Or use either wicker or plastic – then place a cushion pad or quilt inside that can be easily washed.

Or – our top cleaning and hygiene choice – use a cardboard box, that you can throw away every month. Wicker beds should be vacuumed each week. Every few months **hose** them down outside, on a sunny or blowy day, to ensure that the basket dries relatively quickly.

All cages need to be cleaned regularly Make life simple for yourself and have a second, spare cage for your bird or rodent to stay in. Knowing your pet is secure will mean you won't rush the cleaning. With gerbils, hamsters and other rodents, scoop out soiled wood shavings and replace with fresh daily. Each month, thoroughly disinfect the cage, using a **specialist cleaner** from the pet shop. Do not use kitchen spray cleaners on toys or bars as these can be too intense for your pet. Apply to the cloth and wipe each rung of the cage. Wipe again with a **just damp cloth**.

Antique clothing

When cleaning antique clothing it's worth avoiding most modern conveniences, which are generally too harsh for fragile fabrics. So for clothing with a history, you should use cleaning techniques from yesteryear.

The safest way to clean fragile garments is with a sponge bath. Before you start, fix any tears in the fabric – as the stress of cleaning may make matters worse. Then mix a squirt of **mild non-biological detergent** in a **washing-up bowl** full of **water** and dab the solution on gently with a **sponge**. Rinse by sponging on **clean water**, taking care not to get the garment sopping wet.

Hands off hand-me-downs

Always wear gloves when you touch delicate antique clothing, says the UK Institute of Conservation. Acid from your hands can get onto the fabric then, over time, cause it to rot. Remember also to take off rings and jewellery which could scratch.

To remove browning or stubborn stains that don't respond to a sponge bath, treat them to a long soak in room temperature water to which a few drops of **3 per cent hydrogen peroxide** (sold in chemists, as a mouthwash) have been added. Place the garment and the solution in a **plastic tub** and let it sit – don't agitate – for one to three days. Then rinse with **fresh water** until it rinses clear. If your tap water is hard, use **distilled water** (or boil tap water first, then allow to cool) for rinsing instead so that minerals won't discolour the fabric.

Drying an antique garment is a delicate operation. Never wring antique fabric. Lay it flat to dry and be careful when moving whilst wet. Just the weight of the water can tear the fibres. To move the garment, lay it on a **bed sheet** and carry the sheet.

Storing a fragile garment also requires special care. Don't starch an antique garment before storing it. Starch attracts insects and will stress the fabric along folds. If possible, store the garment spread out flat. If space doesn't permit flat storage, roll it up. Rolling the garment around an object isn't necessary, but if you feel you must – don't use wood or a cardboard tube as they could brown the fabric. Protect the cloth from any such material (wood drawers and cardboard boxes, for example) with sheets of **acid-free tissue** (available at sewing shops). Don't store your garment in a plastic bag – it needs to breathe.

Rules of the game

Easy does it

When cleaning antique clothing, here are the basic guidelines to follow:

1 Avoid regular dry-cleaners – find one who specialises in antique textiles.
2 Mend any rips before you clean.
3 Don't use your washing machine or tumble dryer.
4 Sponge clean.
5 Never wring. Dry flat – don't hang.
6 Don't starch before storing.

Antique furniture

When cleaning antiques, less is always better. Some of the cleaning methods you'd readily use on everyday furniture can ruin the look and reduce the value of an antique.

The safest approach to cleaning antiques is to limit it to simple dusting once every week or two. Wipe your antiques down with a **soft, dry, non-abrasive cloth** or **chamois**. Avoid furniture polishes – they will just leave a film that will attract more dirt and polishing can damage the finish, the patina of your piece, and diminish its value.

A more aggressive cleaning method can be considered if you're willing to risk it. But first make sure that the finish isn't too fragile (breaking down, separating or,

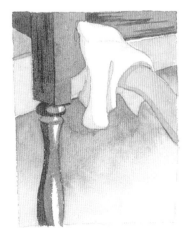

Keep antique furniture protected by applying a thin coating of paste wax with a soft cloth. Rub the wax off with a clean cloth.

Simple solutions

THE GREAT STAINGO

Protect your antiques

- Don't store antiques in a dry room. A humidity level that's comfortable for your skin will be fine for the furniture as well.
- Don't store antiques in a room with fluctuating humidity or temperatures. Both can cause cracking.
- Keep out of direct sunlight.
- Don't place drinks on antique furniture. Wipe up any water immediately with a dry cloth.
- If a piece has gilding (gold leaf) anywhere, be extremely careful. A damp cleaning rag can wipe water-based gilding right off. Use a dry rag and a delicate touch to clean gilding.

in the case of veneer, lifting). If the finish is in good condition, wipe it down with a **slightly damp cloth** and follow up immediately with a **dry cloth**. (Never saturate an antique with water – that would ruin even a stable finish.) If you need stronger cleaning power, mix **1 teaspoon of mild washing-up liquid in a litre of water**. Dip your cloth in the solution, wring it out and wipe the furniture down quickly. Follow up right away with a dry cloth. Test this method on a hidden spot to ensure the finish holds.

Waxing antique furniture is something you should do no more often than every three years – and again only if the finish is stable. A **dark paste wax** (available at hardware stores) is a good idea, because it won't leave a whitish residue in crevices, which lighter waxes do. Apply a thin coating of the paste wax with a **soft cloth**. Follow up right away with a **clean cloth**, rubbing the wax off until it's dry. (Normally, you would let the wax dry before buffing, but this technique allows you to apply a thinner coat and is friendlier to the finish, because it does not require you to rub as hard.)

If an antique has a water stain – and the item is not very valuable – you can try waxing the mark. Start by using a **soft cloth** to apply a **paste furniture wax** to the stain itself to see how much the surface darkens. Work your way outward from the stain, attempting to create a match with the surrounding surface. If your antique is valuable, however, don't attempt to fix the stain yourself. Get help from a professional restorer.

Appliances

To find out how to clean a specific item – a washing machine for example – look under the name of the appliance itself.

To clean a small electrical appliance first unplug it – and let it cool if it's been in use recently. Wipe down with a **damp cloth**. If it has food splatters on the outside, mix a solution of **warm water** and **washing-up liquid** to dip your cleaning cloth in. Keep the water and suds away from the electronics of the appliance. Never put an appliance in water unless instructions say it's safe to clean it that way. Some appliances have washable parts that should be removed from the electronic base to make cleaning easier and safer (can openers and slow cookers, for example).

See also **Coffee grinders, Coffee makers, Fridges & freezers, Food processors, Irons, Microwave ovens, Ovens, Sandwich makers, Toasters, Tumble driers, Washing machines** and **Waste disposal units.**

Aquariums

Proper cleaning is a life-or-death issue for fish and should begin on the day you buy a new aquarium. Clean all of your new gear – tank and accessories. Soap and detergent are not suitable as the residue will hurt the fish. For new equipment, just use plain warm or cold water.

Check your aquarium's water once a week for its pH, nitrate, nitrite and ammonia levels, using **water testing equipment** sold at the pet shop. Read up on the chemical tolerances of your particular fish species, so you will know when it's time for a change of water. How many fish you have, how big they are, the species, the size of the tank, your lighting and the kind of filtration you're using, all affect how often you must change the water. So get expert advice, right from the start. You should never change *all* the water at once. Just change 10 to 25 per cent of the water in your aquarium and expect to do it about every two weeks.

To change the water round up enough **buckets** to handle 10 to 25 per cent of the water in your tank. Use a **siphon hose** to draw the water out. A **clear hose** is best, so you can see what you're sucking up.

Don't refill the aquarium with water straight from the tap. Nearly all tap water has chlorine added and that will hurt your fish. Many pet shops will test a sample for you or you can use a home water chemical test kit. To remove the chlorine, either use a **dechlorinating product**, or let the water sit in a fresh bucket for 24 hours before pouring it in to the tank – this will have given the chlorine time to dissipate naturally. In any case, make sure the new water is about the same temperature – within one or two degrees – as the water left in the aquarium.

Simple solutions

Nature's vacuum cleaners

Why not hire some live-in workers for your tank? The following species are happy to gobble up algae so you won't have to. Just make sure they're compatible with the other creatures in your tank. You're inviting them to have dinner, not be dinner.

Freshwater
Siamese Algae eater
Bristlenose
Whiptail catfish
Mollies

Saltwater
Turbo snails
Certain hermit crabs

Simple solutions

THE GREAT STAINGO

An underwater dirt devil

The gravel at the bottom of your aquarium isn't just decorative. It's also a biological filter that traps gunk in the water. Give it a gentle vacuuming each time you change your aquarium's water with a vacuum you can easily make yourself.

Attach a clear plastic siphon hose to the top of a small plastic soft drink bottle. (The hose needs to be large enough to fit tightly over the bottle and to run out into a bucket at the other end.) Cut the bottom off the bottle. Then place the bottle on the bottom of the tank. When the siphon starts drawing water, it will suck up the dirt, waste and old food without disturbing the gravel. Move from one patch of gravel to the next, working your way across the aquarium floor.

Since you'll be using this technique at water-changing time, you'll have to stop when you've removed your target amount of water. It may take you two sessions to cover the entire aquarium floor.

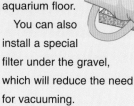

You can also install a special filter under the gravel, which will reduce the need for vacuuming.

To remove algae use **algae scrub pads** (available at your aquarium store or pet shop) and clean the inside walls of your aquarium whenever the fuzzy green stuff becomes visible. If you don't like sloshing around in the water with your hands, try a **magnetic cleaning system**. One magnet, attached to a scrubbing pad, goes on the inside of the glass and another magnet goes on the outside for dragging the scrubbing pad around. Remember, algae thrive on light, so the more light your aquarium gets the more algae you will to have to clean up.

Clean the filter in your tank once a week – or more often, depending on the feeding habits of your fish and how many fish you have. Most tanks have a **mechanical filter** and models vary; follow the instructions that come with yours for removing, cleaning and replacing the filter. A clean filter means better water, which means healthier fish.

Another filtering tool is **carbon**. It gives your water a sparkling-clear look by removing the yellowish cast caused by food and waste. Carbon may already be a part of your mechanical filter. If not, you can buy a carbon holder or even make your own. Put the carbon (available at the aquarium store or pet shop) into an old pair of **tights**, tie a tight knot to secure and cut away excess fabric. Place the carbon filter where it will get good water flow in the tank.

To thoroughly clean an old tank – especially if fish have died in the tank – remove any fish to another water-filled container and empty everything out. Refill, with fresh water and add **2 teaspoons of bleach** for every **4 litres of water**. Let it sit for at least 30 minutes. Empty the tank, rinse it well and then refill. Now neutralise any bleach residue by adding a **chlorine neutraliser** (available from pet shops). Empty the water once again and rinse. Then fill your aquarium with the water that you have let sit for a day and pop the fish back in.

Because tank cleaning is such a chore here are ways to cut down how often it needs to be done:

• **Keep it out of direct sunlight** and you'll grow less algae. You will also have the same problem if you leave your aquarium lights on for too long.

• **Start with freshwater fish**. They're less sensitive to variations in the chemical levels in the water so even if you get it slightly wrong, they should still be safe. Besides, tracking the salt levels of a saltwater tank is yet another thing to do that could push a beginner over the edge.

• **Don't give your fish too much food**. Fish don't have fridges, so the leftovers float around, driving up the levels of harmful chemicals. Watch your fish at feeding time. When they begin to slow down their rate of eating, dinner's over so don't add more food.

• **Inspect your fish every day** to see whether they have any injuries, infections or parasites. When you buy new fish, let them stay in a 'guest room' for a month – a separate quarantine tank – so you can monitor them for any diseases that could kill the rest of your fish.

Artwork

With unframed paper-based artwork, such as prints, etchings and drawings, it's best to approach cleaning with a healthy dose of forethought and prevention. Paper is easily damaged and any medium applied to it is likely to remove the art as much as the dirt and dust. Prints, etchings, drawings, watercolours and pastels just can't be cleaned, except professionally (which may involve another artist re-filling in colour that's been cleaned off). So do the wise thing and preserve artworks that you love under glass and framing. That way, you are cleaning the exterior casing, not the artwork itself. And the value and longevity of your artwork will increase.

To clean a framed work take it off the wall and lay it flat. Remove dust by wiping all surfaces – front and back – with a **soft, dry cloth**. Don't use a feather duster or a paper towel, which could scratch the glass or frame. To clean the glass, lightly moisten a soft **cleaning cloth** with **glass cleaner** and wipe the surface. Don't spray cleaner directly onto the glass. The cleaner may get behind the glass and damage your artwork.

When cleaning oil paintings there are more don'ts than do's. The good news is that dust doesn't tend to settle on paintings themselves, because they hang vertically. Don't attempt to dust a painting. Feathers from a feather duster or fibres from a cloth can snag on the paint surface and damage it. And leave the vacuum cleaner with its brush attachment in the cupboard, too. If you simply can't resist dusting a painting, wave a **feather duster** at it, making sure it doesn't actually touch the surface and the resulting wind will do the job. Don't blow on your painting – there's inevitably some damaging saliva in human breath.

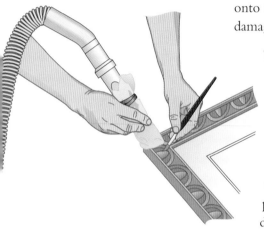

The only safe way to clean in between delicate mouldings on frames is with a watercolour brush. Use a vacuum cleaner with a soft flannel over its nozzle to suck up other bits of dust.

Dust will settle, of course, across the top of your painting's frame. But you still have limited options. The frames around valuable paintings often have delicate gilding – feather dusters and cloths are a no-no. If you have modern frames, they are safe to use. But all is not lost. Remove any attachment from your **vacuum hose** and put a **soft flannel cloth** over the end, secured with a rubber band, to reduce the suction. Dislodge dust from the nooks and crannies of your delicate frame with a **soft watercolour brush** and use the covered hose to catch the airborne particles.

If you have a smoker in your family, you have no alternative but to shield your paintings by covering them with glass, to prevent nicotine stains. You can wipe the glass, with a **cloth** sprayed with **glass cleaner**.

Cleaning sculptures is an exercise in the art of light-touch simplicity. Avoid the kind of harsh chemicals you get with commercial cleaners. And avoid soaps of any kind, since it's hard to know how they will affect various sculpting materials and finishes. Also resist the temptation to use feather dusters, as the feathers can get caught in crevices and break off a piece of the sculpture, or damage delicate veneer finishes. Clean plaster of Paris objects with a **cloth** lightly dampened in **distilled water**. For harder, more durable sculptures you can use **plain tap water**, but make sure you dry it carefully to avoid any watermarks

To dust a wood sculpture spray a few drops of **eucalyptus oil** onto a **soft cloth** (old T-shirts are ideal) and gently wipe the entire surface once a week, pulling dust out of crevices. You can use a **very slightly damp cloth** on your wood sculpture, too, but take care that no moisture is left behind to damage the wood. This is not speed work. Proceed very carefully, because some areas can be more delicate than others. Don't use silicone-based products which will soak into the wood and build up. If your sculpture is stained from long-time exposure to impurities from a fireplace or a heating system, get expert advice and don't attempt to deep clean yourself.

You can also use the dusting method described for paintings to clean sculptures. Cover your **vacuum cleaner hose** with **flannel**, secured with a **rubber band**. Then use a **soft brush** to get up the dust and suck it up with the vacuum cleaner.

To wax a wood sculpture first remove any build-up from furniture polish or furniture cleaning soap. As a test, dip a **cotton bud** in **white spirit** and dab it on a hidden spot to see whether it damages the finish. If not, apply this to a **soft cloth**, such as an old T-shirt and gently stroke the cloth over the sculpture. (Don't breath in: inhaling dust could cause lung damage.) Be careful not to snag the cloth on any end grain of the wood, which could pull off chips and splinters. Then apply the wax to another **soft, clean cloth** (again, a T-shirt) and gently rub it into the surface. **Carnauba wax** works well (from specialist suppliers, such as *www.thepolishingcompany.com*) and comes in a variety of colours or clear for a white sculpture. Or try **brown shoe polish**, which will match the colour of the wood and help cover any scratches. Talk to a conservator before waxing stone, marble, plaster of Paris or a painted surface.

See also **Photographs.**

Expert advice

Pass on the potatoes and bread

There's a folktale floating about that claims you can clean a painting by rubbing it with a cut potato or a slice of bread. The theory is that mild enzymes or acid in the potato will clean the artwork and that the bread will absorb dirt particles. But don't be fooled: while both tricks can work with robust wallpaper, they are not suitable for delicate artwork. In fact, painting restorers spend more time fixing the cleaning mistakes of well-intentioned amateurs than cleaning up age-old dirt. So keep your food in the kitchen, where it belongs.

Asphalt

Without a doubt, asphalt is tough and hardwearing, but there are a surprising number of cleaning considerations where the rubber meets the road.

To clean your driveway or other asphalt surface, give it a good wash once a year. Remove leaves and dirt with a **broom** or **leaf blower**. Mix **1 scoop (60ml)** of **detergent** in a **bucket** with **4 litres of water**. Splash some onto the driveway as needed for spot cleaning and scrub with a **stiff broom**. Then give it a good rinse with a **garden hose**. Avoid high-pressure hoses or steam washing, which could damage the asphalt.

Blot up petrol and oil spills on an asphalt drive with paper towels then wash clean with a hose.

Clean petrol and oil spills as quickly as possible. Asphalt is a petroleum-based material. This means a puddle of petrol or oil could eat a hole in your driveway. Soak up a spill with **paper towels** and spray away any of the remainder with a **garden hose**. For a little more cleaning power, mix **detergent** in **water** as described above and work at the spot with a **stiff-bristled scrubbing brush**. And next time, take preventive measures. Lay down some **cardboard**, **newspaper** or **plastic** when you add oil or petrol to your lawn mower or oil a bike chain on the drive.

To remove asphalt stains on clothing pretreat the stain with a **biological stain removing product**, then machine wash. If you get asphalt on your shoes, spray them with *WD-40* and scrape the asphalt off with a **paint scraper** or **putty knife**. Make sure to rinse your shoes well before you wear them in the house.

To remove asphalt from your tools again the *WD-40* trick works. Spray it on, wait a few minutes and wipe it off. Turpentine, paint thinner and white spirit also work but we don't recommend them here, because they're highly flammable.

To remove asphalt from your car go to a garage or car supplies store and buy an **asphalt** – or **tar-removal product** designed for that purpose and follow the package directions carefully.

Even if you don't have any marks to tackle there are still things you can do to make your asphalt driveway look better for longer.

• **Reseal with a commercial sealant** every two or three years to protect it from the weather and to maintain its looks. If you reseal more often, you will get a thick build-up of the material, which can start to crack.

• **Fill cracks in asphalt without delay**. Eventually, your driveway will crack – heat and cold alone will cause this. But asphalt-patching products (available at hardware and home improvement stores) can cover cracking and doing so prevents weeds from growing in the cracks. Weeds accelerate the problem because – as plants grow and take root – your driveway will become even more cracked.

Attics & lofts

Neglect your attic and you could have a dust and mould factory hanging over your head. Give it a thorough clean once a year and you'll not only remove a source of these irritants from your home, but you'll also have a valuable storage space that you won't dread going into. So you'll use it more often and the rooms in the rest of the house will be less cluttered.

Before you start – especially if it's been several years since you even went into your attic – you should gear up to protect yourself. Wear a **full mouth-nose dust mask** (from DIY stores) to protect your lungs from dust, allergens and other nuisances. You may need an **apron** to protect your clothes, **goggles** to protect your eyes and **heavyweight rubber gloves**. If your attic is already used for storage, make sure everything's organised before you attempt cleaning. This means storing small items in labelled boxes, grouping together boxes that contain like items and opening up walkways so that you can get to any box in any part of the loft space.

To actually clean the attic use an extension lead, so that you can **vacuum** and start sucking up dust from the

Conquering attic mould

Mould in the attic is a sign that you have a moisture problem – maybe a leaky roof, maybe poor ventilation. To get rid of the mould, you need to cut off the source of moisture that's allowing it to flourish so freely. Get the leak fixed or improve the airflow so that the attic stays dry.

When you're sure all is fine, vacuum up what you can from the affected areas. Then, wearing a respirator mask, use a stiff brush to loosen any mould that remains and vacuum again. Finally, paint over the affected areas with a mould-inhibiting paint.

top down – ceiling, beams, walls and floor. If your attic already has things stored in it, don't just clean around the boxes – clean under them, too. Once the major grime has been vanquished, you're ready to give the area a light once-over with a **damp cleaning cloth** dipped in a solution of **water** and **mild washing-up liquid**.

Awnings & canopies

A dirty awning or canopy can mar the look of your whole house. After all having one is meant to make your house look as if it is often bathed in bright sunshine, not drowning in dirt. Keeping your awning clean will also help it last a lot longer.

Cleaning acrylic awnings is usually very simple because most have a soil and stain-resistant finish. Where necessary, use a **stepladder** to reach the awnings. Spot-wash by applying a solution of **warm water** and **mild washing-up liquid** with a **sponge**. Rinse thoroughly with **clean water** and air-dry. For stubborn stains, use a **fabric stain remover**, following the directions on the container. Again, rinse well and air-dry.

Mildew on an acrylic awning is usually found not on the fabric itself but growing on dirt, leaves and other materials that are not removed from the fabric. Acrylic awnings themselves do not promote the growth of mildew. To remove mildew, mix **50ml of bleach** with a squirt of **mild dishwashing liquid** in **5 litres of water**. Apply to the entire area and allow it to soak in (but not to dry).

Scrub with a **sponge**. Rinse thoroughly and air-dry. Don't use **bleach** on any logos or prints that decorate the awning.

Cleaning vinyl or fabric awnings is usually done with spray cleaners that work best if you don't wet the awning before cleaning it – a **garden furniture upholstery cleaner** (from DIY stores) is fine. Stand on a **stepladder** so that you can evenly mist on your vinyl cleaner. Start from the bottom and work up. Before the cleaner dries, scrub the awning with a **sponge** or **soft to medium-bristled brush**. (Brushes work best on fabric awnings.) Never use abrasive cleaners or scrubbers. Rinse by spraying with a **garden hose** until the water runs off clear. You must remove all the cleaner, because leftover cleaner will leave a chalky film once it dries. Don't use a pressure washer to clean your awning. It's ineffective and can cause permanent damage.

Mildew on a vinyl or fabric awning can be removed using a solution of **50ml bleach** per **5 litres of warm water**. Before using the solution, however, test it by rubbing a solution-soaked **cotton bud** on a hidden section of awning to make sure it does not cause the colours to fade or run. Don't let the bleach solution dry on the awning. Rinse thoroughly with water.

Immediately after applying a spray vinyl and fabric cleaner, give the awning a good scrub with a sponge or brush, then rinse thoroughly and allow to dry.

Baby equipment

Babies require a lot of equipment and you will spend more time than you might imagine meticulously cleaning every item that your newborn baby comes into contact with. Your baby's new immune system is just developing and needs to be carefully protected from 'everyday' germs that you'd shrug off without noticing.

It's important to find the right balance between cleanliness and germ phobia. With a healthy baby, it isn't necessary to scrub down and sterilise everything in sight, but you should be careful with anything that may end up in your baby's mouth: bottles, teats, dummies and utensils used for feeding.

Sterilising baby bottles is a first year essential. Some bottles may be dishwasher safe but in reality you'll only get a thorough clean by hand washing. You will need to rinse out again anyway, to ensure there are no traces of detergent. Wash the bottle and teat in **hot water** with **sudsy washing-up water**. Use a **bottle brush** and a **teat brush** to get right inside and so remove any caked-on milk in the interior corners. Force soapy water through the hole in the teat. Rinse thoroughly with **running water**. Now sterilise, according to what kind of steriliser you have. A microwave one, which fits inside the microwave, holds up to eight bottles and takes only around five minutes, is easily the top choice. If you don't have a microwave, a bulkier, plug-in steam steriliser works just as well. Follow the instructions. Do not touch the teats when you go to make up the formula: use teat tongs instead, to manoeuvre them back onto the bottle.

To keep a changing table clean, use an **antibacterial cleaning spray** after each change. These don't need rinsing off. So give it a simple spray and wipe and you're done. Antibacterial wipes are faster still: but at 2p–5p per go and up to 10 clean ups a day (yes, really) in those first, frantic weeks, using them can work out very expensive.

To clean prams and buggies sprinkle **bicarbonate of soda** on a **damp paper towel** or **clean cloth** and wipe down the item, then rinse with **warm water**. (Bicarbonate

A quick spray and wipe with an antibacterial will keep your baby's highchair hygienic.

b

The hands that rock the cradle

When it comes to baby hygiene, the paediatrician's clarion call is simple and straightforward: 'Wash your hands'.

'That is a very important factor in how disease spreads', says Dr Marianne Neifert, a paediatrician and mother of five, 'I always wash my hands before I handle a baby'.

A newborn's immune system starts working on its own at about six weeks. Before that, the sum of a baby's immunity consists of whatever the mother supplied during pregnancy and continues to provide through breast-feeding. To fend off bacteria, train the entire family to wash their hands before holding the baby and don't be afraid to ask guests to do the same. Frequent hand washing with soap and water will stop the spread of most common germs. No special antibacterial products are required.

of soda is a mild alkali that can make dirt dissolve in water. It acts as a mild abrasive when not totally dissolved.) If that isn't strong enough, use the **suds** only from a solution of **washing-up liquid** to dab away at the dirt.

Cleaning highchairs The trick is to keep on top of the enormous amount of food that your toddler will push into every crevice of the chair. So after each meal, give a thorough wipe down. A **blunt knife** is useful for getting up dried in deposits. Use **cleaning wipes** and then follow with an **antibacterial cleaning spray**. On the wooden surrounds: use **soapy water** and then dry promptly.

Cleaning a cot Use **bicarbonate of soda** (as described above) to wipe cot rails. Wash baby bed linen in a **washing machine**, using hot water, ideally at 60°C to kill bacteria.

Cleaning baby toys Remember that many plastic and rubber toys will stand up to the rigours of the **dishwasher**. Put them in regularly to keep microbes or organic material on the toys to a minimum. Wash stuffed animals in a **washing machine**, using **hot water** (60°C) to kill dust mites. If you feel this is too tough a treatment — many soft toys say surface wash with a sudsy cloth only — then use the **freezer** as a dust mite killer. Pop a toy in a **sealed plastic bag** for 48 hours: no creature can survive that.

Most plastic toys will withstand a short cycle in the dishwasher once in a while.

Backpacks

Clean a school nylon book bag in the washing machine on the gentle cycle with your regular detergent.

Cleaning a hiking backpack is simple. But with its stiff frame, a hiking backpack won't fit into a washing machine. Instead, use a **vacuum cleaner** to remove dirt from the zips and seams. Applying **water** will work too, but it's messier. The important thing is not to let the grit build up, because it will damage the zips and weaken the seams.

Always tend to the backpack soon after a hike. Remove the items inside. If there is a food spill or crusted mud, wipe it off with a **damp sponge** dipped in a **bowl of warm water** with a little **washing-up liquid**. Remove stubborn stains with **spot remover** made for clothing. But there's no need to get carried away: most hikers view a well-worn backpack as a badge of honour, proving they've walked the walk.

Banisters

A beautiful staircase and banister can be the centrepiece of a home's entrance, so don't let everyday grime diminish its wow factor.

Dust a painted banister with a **soft, water-dampened cloth**. If it's especially dirty, add a couple of drops of **mild washing-up liquid** to **warm water**. Then wash and rinse a small section at a time, keeping the cloth well wrung out and wipe with a **dry cloth**. Oil polish is best avoided on painted wood, since it can cause discolouration. Wax is rarely needed, but if you use it, choose a light-coloured wax for light-coloured paint.

Dust a wooden banister with a **soft cloth** and **furniture polish**. That will restore moisture to the wood and keep the dust collected on the cloth from floating back onto the balusters (the posts or spindles that support the banister). When dust collects in the intricacies of the balusters, use a **cotton bud** to get into crevices and clean out the really tight spaces.

Barbecues

Outdoor cooking is delicious and fun, but before you start the barbecue, make sure it's ready to cook with. A clean machine makes for tastier, healthier meals.

Cleaning a barbecue Remove the grill grates and clean it inside and out with **2 parts hot water** to **1 part washing-up liquid**. (With gas barbecues, you'll need to cover the gas receptacles with **aluminium foil** to stop water leaking inside.) Scrub with a **nylon brush** to prevent scratching (or just a cloth, if you're concerned that even that might be too much), follow with a **hot water** rinse and towel dry. Finally, apply **vegetable oil**, using a **clean cloth**, to the barbecue's outside surface. This will keep the body of the barbecue shining and lubricated against the elements.

If your barbecue instructions say the racks are dishwasher safe you're lucky. If not, several methods work well. First scrub them with a **wire brush** and the **hot water** and **washing-up liquid mix** described above. If they're too encrusted, spray them with **oven cleaner**. Place the treated grates in a **rubbish bag** lined with **paper towels**, tie the top closed and stash the bag in the garden shed, out of reach of pets and children for a couple of hours or even overnight – powerful chemicals are at work. When you re-open the bag to remove the grates, point the opening away from your face to avoid inhaling potent fumes. Thoroughly hose off the grates, wipe them down with **hot water** and **washing-up liquid** and rinse.

If you have a self-cleaning oven, your clean-up couldn't be easier. Just put the grill grates in the oven and let the intense heat do the work for you.

Cleaning a gas grill You need to take these additional cleaning and maintenance steps, ideally when you get the barbecue out after the winter.

1 First make sure the gas bottle is disconnected.
2 Inspect the burners for cracks and corrosion and if they are damaged, replace them.
3 Using a **pipe cleaner** or **non-metallic bottle brush,** clean the tubes, which carry gas to the burners. These tubes make an excellent hiding spot for spiders, whose nests can block the flow of gas and cause an explosion.

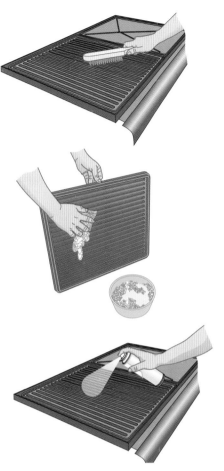

Cleaning a barbecue
1 Use a stiff wire brush to remove most of the burnt-on food and grease.

2 Sponge both sides of the grate, as fat droplets often congeal underneath.

3 Re-season and protect the cleaned grate by spraying it with vegetable oil.

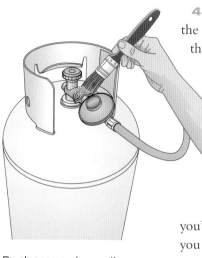

Brush soap suds over the connections between the gas bottle and hose, turn on the gas and watch for bubbles.

4 Check for leaks in the connector hose. Brush around the connections between the gas bottle, the regulator and the hose with **soapy water** (see left) and turn on the gas. If you smell gas or see bubbles, turn off the gas, tighten the connections and repeat the test. If the gas is still leaking – a potentially dangerous problem – you'll need a new hose.

Cleaning lava rocks Use a **stiff-bristled brush** or remove the rocks and clean them with a **degreasing cleaner**. One batch of lava rocks should see you through the whole summer, even if you're an enthusiast. Simply turn them over every third time you cook, to burn off the dripped grease.

To cut down on mess try to eliminate some of the grease. When you've finished cooking, leave the burners turned on for 10 to 15 minutes with the cover closed. Let the grill cool and then scrape away the residue with a **wire brush**. This job will be even easier if you coat the grates with a **non-stick cooking spray** each time you cook.

Basements & cellars

Dealing with a dirty or recently flooded basement can be one of the most daunting tasks on a home owner's cleaning list. Short of calling in the professionals, there aren't many shortcuts.

So roll up your sleeves and make sure you're well protected with a **dust mask** and a strong pair of **rubber gloves**. Begin by knocking down cobwebs with a **long-handled broom**, then thoroughly sweep the floor and brush away debris from the walls. In a **bucket**, mix **hot water** and an **all-purpose cleaner**, according to the label directions. If the walls need cleaning, wash them first, using a **strong-bristled floor brush with a long handle**. Always start at the bottom and work up to prevent streaking. While standing in one spot, wash as much as you can reach, then rinse with **warm water, from a second bucket**. Continue until the walls are finished.

Next, scrub concrete floors, using **hot water** and **household detergent**. Because concrete is porous, strong odours, such as animal waste, can be hard to eradicate. If a strong scrubbing doesn't do the trick, you can seal the floor with a **concrete sealer**, which is stronger than wax. Follow the label directions and spread it on with a **mop**. Repeat the application for really tough odours. After cleaning, open any doors or windows to air out the room and help the drying process.

If mould or mildew is a problem, take an extra step after cleaning. Mop the walls and floors with a solution of ½ **cup of chlorine bleach** to **2 gallons of water**, then rinse well. Keep in mind that the bleach will kill existing mildew, but the mildew will return unless the source of the moisture problem is addressed.

Baskets

To clean an unfinished wicker basket, a gentle vacuum is all that's required, since too much moisture will damage the basket. Don't use the vacuum cleaner on fragile baskets though – its suction may be too powerful. Instead, dust a delicate basket with a damp cloth.

Cleaning a varnished or painted basket Start with a gentle **vacuum**. Then use a **spray bottle** filled with **water** and a **tablespoon of vinegar**. The spray allows you to penetrate the small areas between the wickerwork. Wipe the basket dry with a **very soft cloth** such as an **old T-shirt**, which is less likely to get caught on rough edges. Use a **cotton bud** to get to the tight places. Air out the basket in the sun, but keep it away from direct heat sources like radiators, which can warp the basket.

Cleaning most other baskets Use a **vacuum cleaner**, followed by a **mild solution of water** and a **drop of washing–up liquid** on a **soft cloth**. Apply with a **soft brush** if needed for problem spots. Avoid any cleaner with phosphates, which can eventually cause the basket to disintegrate.

Simple solutions

New life for an old basket

To rescue a worn-looking basket, give it a coat of spray paint. First, check whether small pieces of broken wicker are sticking out. If so, use wire cutters to trim them. Then hang the basket on a metal clothes hanger, attach it to a tree and spray-paint it. Let it hang there for several hours to dry out thoroughly.

Watch out

When using any new cleaning product that you're unsure about, always test it first on an inconspicuous area to see that it doesn't cause damage to the material you are cleaning. And don't mix bathroom cleaners, in case you create a toxic stew with noxious gases. Mixing chlorine bleach with ammonia is particularly dangerous.

It's safe to use more than one type of cleaner as long as you rinse well between applications.

Baths & sinks

For everyday care, wipe down the bath after each use with water and a cloth or sponge to keep soap scum under control. Staying on top of the problem like this goes a long way, especially considering that most acrylic baths come with dire warnings about the danger of abrasive cleaners because their layer of acrylic is now so thin. And it's certainly true that if you scrub your way through the tub's protective finish, you'll soon have stains that are embedded in the glassfibre, porcelain or enamel.

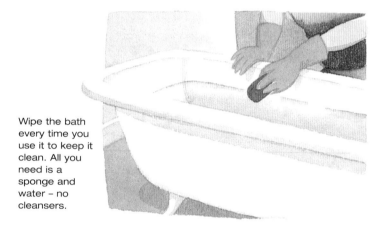

Wipe the bath every time you use it to keep it clean. All you need is a sponge and water – no cleansers.

Cleaning porcelain Most bathroom cleaners are safe. To polish stainless steel on fixtures, rub with **bicarbonate of soda** on a **damp sponge**. Rinse well with water.

Removing rust stains Squeeze **lemon juice** over the spot and use circular motion with an **old toothbrush** to gently rub the rust away. Be aware, however, that there may be permanent damage to your bath surface underneath, especially if the rust has been there for some time. Rinse with **water** and repeat if necessary.

Removing blue-green stains These are caused by water with a high copper content. Combine equal amounts of **cream of tartar** and **bicarbonate of soda** (usually a tablespoon of each is enough) and add some **lemon juice** drop by drop until you have a paste. Rub it into the stain with your fingers or a soft cloth. Leave it for half an hour and rinse well with **water**. Repeat if necessary.

Cleaning an enamel bath Always check that your cleaning product specifically says it is 'safe for enamel'. If it doesn't don't use it. The problem isn't so much with new,

super shiny enamel, but with enamel that has started to wear. Cleaning products hit on the weak spots, taking off the sheen from the surface. Stay with **enamel-safe cleaners** and you won't have a problem. **Mousses** work most quickly. So spray on, wait a while as instructed, then rinse off. For a good shiny finish, towel dry.

Cleaning acrylic tubs can be difficult because mild cleaners have little impact on a seriously soiled unit but abrasive cleaners applied with too much scrubbing pressure will quickly dull the finish. For everyday cleaning, spray on a **bathroom cleaner** that's designed for acrylic and wipe with a **soft sponge**. If the dirt and grime has reached the point where you have to be more aggressive, use a mildly abrasive cleaner, like *Cif* and a **light-duty scrubbing sponge**. Be sure to rinse well with **water** so that the chemicals won't stay on the surface.

Beadwork

The ancient craft of beading has taken on a new life in recent years and baubles are showing up on everything from vases to denim jeans to picture frames. Some beads are remarkably durable and can withstand a spin in the washing machine, but others are quite fragile.

Beadwork on casual clothing can be cleaned at home more readily than the fine beading on formalwear, which is best left to professionals. Beads used on jeans and casual wear are typically made of plastic and can usually be put in the **washing machine** with **mild detergent** on the gentle cycle. Always double-check the manufacturer's cleaning instructions on the label.

Loose glass beads are the easiest to deal with. Wash them in a bowl of **warm water** and **mild washing-up liquid**. If the beads are textured, use a **soft toothbrush** to loosen grime in the crevices. Then rinse thoroughly with **water** and **towel** dry.

Use a soft old toothbrush dipped in a solution of washing-up liquid to clean grime from your beads.

Strung beads are more vulnerable than loose beads, because the thread that holds them all together needs special consideration. Wash a beaded necklace or bracelet in the same solution of **warm water** and **washing-up liquid** in a bowl, but don't let the beads soak. Rinse them with **water** immediately after cleaning, pat dry with a **towel** and leave them lying flat – not hanging, which can stretch the thread – until the thread has had time to dry completely. Or use a **soft toothbrush** that has been dipped into a bowl of **dry bicarbonate of soda** and brush the beads gently. Then rub them with a **soft cloth**.

Vintage beads require even more caution. Instead of submerging them in soapy water, wipe them gently with a **damp cloth** dipped in a solution of **1 part vinegar** to **4 parts water** and air-dry.

Beams

To dust beams, get out your vacuum cleaner and its extension wand, snap on the brush attachment and get ready for some Michelangelo-like neck stretches. Or you can attach a lint roller replacement tube to a paint roller and run it across the exposed surfaces.

If the beams are really dusty and dirty, you'll need to wash them, so you may need to use an **extension ladder**. For wood that has been varnished, mix a **mild detergent** with **water**, then wipe down and rinse a small section at a time using **flannels** or, for harder-to-reach areas, a sponge mop. Go easy with the water solution – you are just wiping the beams, not drowning them. If beams are unfinished, don't use water. Or if you absolutely feel you must, restrict it to a **damp cloth**, but with no detergent.

Beds

Sometimes the biggest cleaning challenge is getting under the bed, rather than actually cleaning the divan or wood slats. It's worth doing both regularly, to increase the working life of your bed. Mattresses are covered in a separate section, as are stains that land on beds: hot drinks, alcohol, bodily fluids, blood, ink and jam.

Wooden slats Clean these several times a year. Use the **crevice tool** on the **vacuum cleaner** to lift up dirt and dust from each slat. While doing this, take the opportunity to check the holding screws. They may need tightening to keep the base of the bed sufficiently supportive.

Wood headboards and support posts Use a **cloth** wrung out from a **solution of sudsy washing-up liquid** to remove grease and dirt. Rinse, dry and polish with a **dry cloth** (a **microfibre** one will give the best shine). Avoid using polishes as you'll smell the residue at night.

Fabric headboards You'll need to clean these grease and dust traps often. Get into the habit of giving the headboard a quick **vacuum** as you do the floor and you'll ward off the worst. But it's unlikely to be enough to keep the bright, fresh colour that attracted you to the headboard when new. So, in the morning, use **upholstery cleaner** and open the windows to air the room. Protect the mattress with a towel before you spray on the cleaner. It's important not to get chemicals into the mattress, which could inhibit the action of the springs.

Divans Stick with **vacuuming**, unless it is particularly greasy. Try using a **wrung out cloth**, as above – but take care not to over-wet. If the divan is still dulled with grease, try to absorb particularly bad patches by rubbing in **baby talcum powder**, then brushing off with a **stiff brush**. Using a mattress protector and a valance will shield your divan from dirt. The highest risk time is the day that you change the bedding. If you remove the sheets, and want to put them back on later that day, take care not to use your uncovered bed as a dumping ground. And close the door if you have cats, unless you want a snagged base: an uncovered, undisturbed divan makes the world's most wonderful scratching post.

See **Duvets, Mattresses, Pillows & sheets.**

Bedspreads

Laundering a bedspread, particularly if it's large or padded, can be difficult to do at home. Most washing machines and dryers just aren't big enough. So you may want to take your bedspread out for a little trip – to a local launderette, where the washers and dryers are bigger than most home varieties.

Single men need waking up in bed

A survey by *Guardsman*, the UK's largest provider of mattress protectors, found that single men typically change their bed linen every two months. Practically everyone else nips the bedding off to the washing machine weekly including single guys once they get partners.

Before washing Check the care label to make sure that your bedspread is in fact washable and weigh it to check that your washing machine will be able to deal with the load – if not, you may need a trip to the launderette. Pre-treat any heavily soiled areas with a **pre-wash product**, such as *Shout*. Set the washing machine to a delicates programme with a normal spin cycle. Add the bedspread and some **detergent**.

Drying a bedspread Transfer it to the **dryer** and select the setting appropriate for its fabric type. Add a couple of **clean, dry towels** and then toss in several **clean tennis balls** that will knock against the spread to keep its filling from clumping. Stop the dryer twice to make sure it isn't getting too hot. Shake the bedspread out once, too, to make sure padding doesn't jam in one corner.

To fluff up a candlewick bedspread – the durable, still-popular knotted or tufted kind your grandmother probably had – try this clever approach. Wash as described above, then hang it on an **outside clothes line** in a stiff wind, with the knotted sides facing. The knots will perk up as they rub against one another. Or, once your candlewick spread is dry, spread it on a clean floor and sweep the surface with a **pristine broom**.

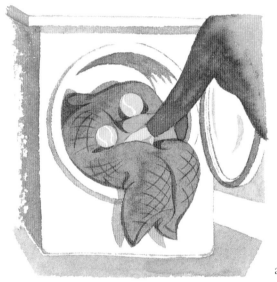

Tennis balls thrown into the dryer with your bedspread will stop the filling becoming lumpy.

Belts

Dry-cleaning or machine-washing a fabric belt is almost always a bad idea. This is because fabric belts are usually backed with vinyl, cardboard or plastic, which can stiffen, crack or bleed when cleaning solvents are used. An all-fabric belt – one without these backings – can usually be dry-cleaned as long as the buckle isn't metal and the belt is sewn and not glued together. Check the edges to see how it was made. Grimy or perspiration-stained fabric belts can be spruced up at home, as can leather ones.

Cleaning a fabric or woven belt Cover your work area with a **towel** and spread out your belt. In a bucket, mix **50ml of gentle fabric cleaner**, such as *Woolite*, with a

litre of cool water. Dampen a **cleaning cloth** with this solution and apply to a small part of the belt's edge to see whether it is colourfast. If the colours don't bleed, carefully dab at the belt, without rubbing, one section at a time. As the cleaning cloth gets dirty, rinse and moisten again with solution. Use another **cloth**, wrung out in water, to rinse and to blot. To dry, blot with a **dry towel** or use a **hair dryer** on the lowest setting. Another tactic is to spread the belt on a **towel** to air-dry. If the buckle is metal and got wet in the cleaning process, buff with a **cloth**.

To protect a new leather belt and prolong its life, apply a **leather protector** – one that contains no wax or silicone – according to the package directions. You'll find them on sale at heel bars. Should your belt get dirty or stained, clean it with a **damp sponge** or **cloth** dabbed in saddle soap. Wipe off the excess and buff it to a shine with a **dry cloth**.

Bicycles

A clean bicycle is also a safe one, because each wash provides an ideal opportunity to inspect the tyres for wear and tear. Bent rims can create small pinches that grow over time if the tyres aren't properly inflated. So be sure to inflate your tyres to the recommended levels.

To make cleaning easier, consider buying a **bicycle work stand**. It will stabilise the bike as you wash it and let you take off the wheels if you want. They cost from around £15 for a budget, folding stand to more than £70 for a solid, professional support. Another alternative is to suspend your bike with **ropes** from a **strong, low-lying tree branch**. If you're concerned about the mess that caked-on mud might make beneath you, spread a **groundsheet** underneath. Leaning the bike against a wall is another option, but makes your work more cumbersome and your bike more likely to topple over.

Start cleaning your bike by gently knocking off any visible dirt with a **brush**. Then use a **garden hose** on low pressure to rinse it. You want the water to trickle out, rather than spray with force, because water under pressure can force grime into the chain and other moving parts. For the

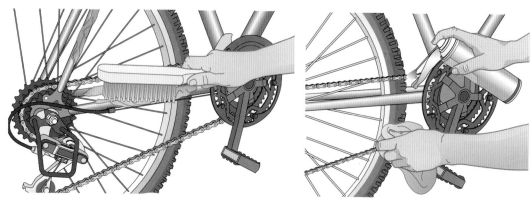

A brush is all you need to knock obvious dirt such as caked mud, off your bike frame *(left)*.

Lubricant attracts dirt, so use it sparingly and wipe off the excess with a soft cloth *(right)*.

same reason, never use a power washer or put your bike through a car wash.

Next, degrease the drive train The hardest bike parts to keep clean are always the chain and linked, moving parts – the pedals, derailleur, rear hub and such – so tackle them first. It's a good idea to protect your hands with **work gloves**. Then apply a **degreaser**, such as *WD-40*, to a **soft cloth** and clean the chain, a few links at a time. Move the pedals forwards to work on a new section of chain. Once you've cleaned the chain, carefully remove it from the chain ring (also called the chain wheel) – the metal wheel whose pointed teeth keep the chain in place. Using a **small screwdriver**, carefully remove any caked-on dirt caught between the teeth. Then slip a **cloth** between them, rubbing it back and forth as if you were flossing your teeth.

Now wash the entire bike Use a **big sponge** and a bowl of **strong, sudsy washing-up water**. Don't forget the seat and its underpinnings, handlebars and handgrips and be sure not to miss the brake levers and under the fork that connects the handlebars to the frame. Wash the wheel rims and tyres. Gently soap the drive train to remove any residue from the degreaser. Rinse the bike completely with a **garden hose** and then ride it in the work stand to slough off excess water. Towel off the bike and ride it around to shake off more water. Then towel it off again completely.

Lubricate the chain with more *WD-40* or a **specialist bike lubricant**. Turn the crank backwards as you spray. As lubricant attracts dirt, wipe off any excess with a **soft cloth**.

Wax a clean bicycle for the same reason that you polish new shoes. The wax protects the bike and deflects dirt, keeping your bike looking new for longer. **Bike waxes**

are sold at any cycle shop. Following the instructions, apply **wax** with a **soft cloth**, being careful to hit the bike's various tubes, joints and other hard-to-reach spots. Or simply spray your bike frame with an ordinary **furniture polish** that contains wax, such as *Pledge*.

Binoculars & telescopes

Don't let a tuft of dust or a screen of grime spoil your birdwatching, stargazing or special safari. Keep your binoculars and telescopes in good working order with these simple procedures.

Cleaning binocular lenses First blow gently on each lens, without spitting, to remove loose debris and dust. Or use a **lens cleaning pen**, which has a soft natural brush at one end and a cleaning tip on the other, to get right into the crevices.

Brush off the lens lightly with a **sheet of lens tissue**. With a **clean sheet of lens tissue**, sprayed lightly with **lens cleaning fluid**, wipe the lens with a circular motion. Gentleness is the key here, since rubbing too hard can remove the protective coating. With a **third sheet of lens tissue**, remove the remaining fluid. Repeat with the other lens. When you're outdoors, never be tempted to use an edge of your T-shirt or a facial tissue for this job because their fibres could scratch the delicate lens coating. Also resist the temptation to use a commercial glass cleaner on your lenses. The ammonia in most glass cleaners will eat away the coating.

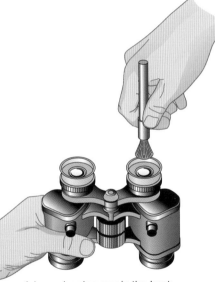

A lens-cleaning pen is the best tool for removing dust particles from binocular lenses.

Cleaning the exterior of binoculars
Dampen a **soft cloth** with water and wipe the outer casing of your binoculars. Keep rubber eyecups and focus knobs lubricated with a **vinyl** or **rubber preservative**, such as *Armor All Protectant*, from car spares shops.

Cleaning a telescope Remember that less is always more. Telescope optics should be cleaned no more than two times a year because their reflective coatings are easily damaged. In fact, if you use **canned air** (sold at camera shops) instead, to blow away the dirt, you should never have to move onto contact cleaning at all. If you feel you must, carefully remove the mirror from the tube, use a **camel-hair brush** – sold at most camera stores – to remove surface dust and dirt. Dampen a **sheet of lens tissue** with **lens cleaning fluid**. Wipe the mirror, eyepiece and lenses from the centre to the outer edge, using minimal pressure. (Telescope optics are even more delicate than binocular lenses and don't take kindly to being rubbed in circles.)

Should the optics collect dew outside, don't wipe them dry. Instead, let them air-dry, then clean with **distilled water** and a **lens tissue**: distilled water leaves no spots.

Protecting your telescope Always use the dust caps and keep your telescope inside when not in use to prevent rusting. Most telescopes have an aluminium coating that should last 10 years if it's kept clean. Before you store a telescope, wipe the outside dry with a **soft cleaning cloth**.

Birdbaths, feeders & birdhouses

Just as our baths, kitchens and sleeping areas need constant attention to keep them clean, so do the identical spots we set up for our feathered friends. Keep birdbaths, feeders and houses free of fungi, algae and bacteria and the birds will happily return for more. To get to work, simply use an old scrubbing brush and a tired toothbrush.

Clean a birdbath once a week during warm weather. Birdbaths with stale standing water can turn into fertile breeding grounds for mosquito larvae, so dumping out old water and cleaning inside is essential.

First, use a **scrubbing brush with stiff bristles** and **warm water** to scrub out the birdbath. If the bath has a telltale ring from algae or other deposits or feels slimy to the touch, mix a solution of **1 part bleach** to **10 parts water** in a **clean bucket** and use that to scrub the bath. Wear **rubber gloves** to protect your hands. If you don't like the notion of using bleach, mix equal parts of **white vinegar** and **water** and scrub. Rinse with **fresh water** and air-dry.

Clean bird feeders every two weeks all through the year. This is because birdseed and other bird food gets damp and mouldy in humid conditions and the birds feeding at

Ring around the birdbath

Soap residue left behind in a birdbath, feeder or house is not good for birds. It's much better to use bleach instead. Bleach will not harm the birds, as long as you use it in a weak concentration. Because it breaks down quickly in the environment, there will be no chemical residue either. The only risk is that bleach can sometimes whiten a wooden bird feeder or house. So don't let either soak in a bleach solution. Instead, rinse thoroughly and swiftly and then dry.

However, do shy away from treating wooden birdhouses and feeders with any wood preservative containing petroleum compounds. The fumes they emit could harm birds.

your trough may get sick. If you can, take your wooden feeder apart. Dust off the pieces with a **wire brush** and then scrub with **warm water** and a **stiff–bristled scrubbing brush**. If the feeder is really dirty, wear **rubber gloves** and mix **1 part bleach** to **10 parts water** in a **clean bucket**. Vigorously scrub it, both inside and out. Rinse thoroughly and then dry. For plastic or metal feeders, brush them out, then rinse with **warm water** and dry with a **soft cloth**, or simply leave to air-dry.

Clean a birdhouse during cold weather when birds aren't feathering their nests inside. If the birdhouse has a removable side or top panel, take it off and dip the pieces into a solution of **1 part bleach** to **10 parts water**. With an **old toothbrush**, dig into the cracks and crevices – this is where feather mites, which feed on bird feathers, often lurk. You don't want these bugs infesting the next generation to take up residence in your birdhouse. To guard against mites, as well as fleas, flies, larvae and lice use an **aviary dusting powder**, from pet shops.

An old toothbrush will get into tight spaces on a bird house to brush up dirt and scrub away germs.

Blankets

It's a myth that you can't wash blankets, because they'll shrink and distort. These days, most blankets, including some made of wool, can be washed at home. Check the care labels and make certain that your washing machine and tumble dryer will hold the blanket comfortably. Weigh the blanket first, if you're unsure and check it against your machine's maximum weights. Don't just cram it in and go – the blanket won't rinse or dry properly if there isn't really enough room. In that instance, take your blanket to a self-service launderette with a commercial-size washing machine and tumble dryer.

Use the bathtub if your large blanket won't fit into the washing machine.

Before washing a wool blanket, check the label to make sure it is washable. If it isn't, have it dry-cleaned. If you are going to wash it, measure the blanket and save the measurements for later – you may want these as a guide as to how far you want to stretch the fibres out to afterwards. Pretreat any spots or stains with **stain remover**, following label directions. If the binding (the narrow fabric along the edges) is really filthy, use a **nylon-bristled scrubbing brush** to gently scrub it with **washing-up liquid** or make a paste of equal parts **non-biological detergent** and **water** and apply it carefully. Gentleness is critical here because the binding may shred if it's old and worn.

To machine-wash a wool blanket use a **non-biological powder** that's safe for wools and choose the **gentle cycle**, with a minimal spin. Most machines have a specific wool programme that you should choose.

To hand-wash a wool blanket – if your blanket won't fit into the machine, or you're worried that it will be too much – fill the bath with **cold water** and add 1 measure of a **hand wash detergent** that is suitable for wools, such as *Woolite*. Put the blanket in the tub and press down to wash.

To rinse, fill the tub several times with **fresh, cool water**. Squeeze out, but don't wring, excess water by rolling up your blanket in **two or three large white towels**.

To dry a wool blanket you have several drying options:
• The first is to use your **tumble dryer**, but only if you have a *No heat* setting.

• Alternatively, spread out **dry towels** on a **clean garden table**, flatten the blanket out on top and stretch it to its original shape, using the measurements you took previously.
• Hang the blanket over **two tightly strung clothes lines** that won't droop under its weight.

If you chose the second or third approaches, plump up the blanket afterward in the **dryer** on the *No heat* setting.

To clean a cotton or acrylic blanket Simply wash as you would other cotton or acrylic items – in the washing machine, following the maximum temperature on the care label. Dry a knitted cotton blanket in a **dryer** on **low heat** so it won't pill. For other cotton blankets, the regular setting is suitable. Or hang a cotton blanket from a taut **clothesline** to dry. Tumble-dry an acrylic blanket on low heat.

Blinds

Blinds – and especially the slatted versions such as venetian blinds – are like miniature dust-collecting shelves. Ignore them and you'll have a full-scale dust library in no time. So make giving them a really thorough clean and dust a regular part of your routine.

Dusting blinds Use the **brush attachment** on your **vacuum cleaner** and adjust the blinds to expose the flat surface. Then, from top to bottom and left to right, vacuum the entire surface. Reverse the slats and repeat.
Other options:
• Use a **lamb's wool duster** to clean the slats.
• Rub an **old paintbrush** along each slat.
• Wear an old pair of **thick absorbent cloth gloves** and wipe the slats by hand. *Lakeland*, (*www.lakelandlimited.com*) sells a Venetian blind duster, that is specially angled so you can move up and through the slats with speed.

Blinds made of natural materials can be damaged by water.
• Parchment, paper or rice paper should not get wet at all. Clean them as you would non-washable wallpaper – with **commercial cleaning putty** or an **art gum eraser**. Or find a **spot remover** that claims to work on the material at hand and test it on an inconspicuous area first.

Simple solutions

Taking it outside
If your blinds are washable, why not take the job outside? Spread an old shower curtain or piece of plastic on a level part of your patio, open the blinds and spray them with a garden hose. Then use sudsy water to clean the slats with gloved fingers. Rinse thoroughly and air-dry.

An old pair of thick, absorbent old gloves are great for dusting between the slats of your blinds.

• Wood and bamboo blinds should not be immersed in water. Wipe them down with a **damp rag** soaked in a solution of **washing-up liquid** and **water**. Then dry them quickly with a **fresh rag**.

Washing aluminium and vinyl blinds is fine, but don't use harsh cleaners or abrasives on them. And don't use any cleaner with ammonia on aluminium, because it will damage the finish. To clean aluminium or plastic blinds, you have a couple of choices. You can wash them where they hang, using **water** and a squirt of **washing-up liquid**, then rinsing off afterwards, or you can take them down and wash them in the shower or tub.

To give blinds a bath raise them, unlock the brackets at the top and remove them from the holder. Run enough **warm water** in the tub to cover the blinds and add around **100ml of washing-up liquid**. Protecting your hands with **rubber gloves**, place the blinds in the water and extend them. Dip the blinds several times to loosen grime. Then let them soak for five minutes. Use your gloved fingers to clean both sides of each slat. Drain the dirty water and either rinse the blinds in a **fresh tub of water** or give them a spray under the **shower**, if you have a showerhead over the bath. Spread out the blinds on a **clean towel** and blot with another **towel**. When the blinds are completely dry, wipe **fabric softener sheets**, such as *Bounce*, on each slat. This keeps them from attracting dust, hair, insects and other grimy stuff.

Boats

Sitting at anchor in the harbour or exposed to the elements on dry land, boats get covered in all manner of grime. Buoy your spirits by washing that dirty boat.

When washing a wooden boat your cleaning has to take into account the quality of the paint finish. If it's getting old, you should not use chemicals or abrasives that could eat through the paint. When your boat is out of the water, fill up a **bucket** with **warm water** and a scoop of **mild, non-biological detergent** and use a **large sponge**

(a car cleaning one is ideal) to clean your boat from stem to stern. If dirt is particularly stubborn, use a **cleaning pad** with a slightly abrasive surface to it, but work with care, so as not to take off any paint. To keep a bare wood boat sparkling, mix **1 part ammonia** to **10 parts water** in a **bucket**. Scrub with a **soft–bristled nylon brush**.

To wash a glassfibre boat imagine you're washing your car or a caravan. You simply add the pressure of water and perhaps a **little car shampoo** to remove dirt that's sitting on the surface. A **washing-up liquid solution** is also suitable: if your boat is big, you're going to get through quite a lot. Thoroughly rinse the boat with **water**. *Star Brite One Step Cleaning Wax* will bring your boat back up to a shine. If you hit any particularly scratched spots – again, take a leaf from car cleaning and use a **specialist surface restorer**. Boat supply shops sell a good range of liquid rubbing products that will do this nicely. Or, if it's easier – and you can get a better colour match – try out a **car restorer product**.

To wash a polyethylene vessel – canoes, kayaks and other small boats today are sometimes made of this durable yet pliable plastic – give it the standard mild-detergent–and-water treatment described above. If you have obstinate stains, apply a touch of **turpentine** or **acetone** on a **soft cloth**. But be aware – prolonged contact can weaken plastic. Work fast and with minimal product. Test on an inconspicuous area first.

Wash your painted aluminium boat as you would a painted wooden one. (See instructions above.) If your vessel is unpainted, consider it almost indestructible. That means that you can use solvents, such as **white spirit**, to remove hardened grit.

Boilers

Having your boiler cleaned is an annual job for a professional. So never open it up. Your should only ever clean the cover. Wipe it with a just damp cloth, then dry. To remove any scratching on the painted metal, rub petroleum jelly, in a circular motion over the mark. Wipe off, then buff to a shine.

Books

Lined up on a bookshelf or stacked on a table, books can be real dust magnets – and they're also often victims of spills and greasy hands. It's usually best to just dust them, using a vacuum cleaner armed with its soft brush attachment or a feather duster. Assuming that you're dusting in situ because time is tight, just go over the exposed spine and top of each book.

Simple solutions

A book fan

A simple technique for ridding a book of its musty smell is to open up the book and set it out near an oscillating fan. Mustiness tends to be caused by dampness. So doing this will get your book totally dry. Then, if you feel some smell remains, sprinkle the pages liberally with unperfumed talcum powder. Give the book a shake, then use a soft brush to remove any excess.

If you do pull out a few volumes and notice that the cover of a book is smudged with fingerprints or smeared with food, use a **damp rag** to remove spots. If you need more cleaning power, mix ½ **cup of mild detergent**, such as *Dreft*, in a **bucket of cool water** and test it on an inconspicuous spot. Covers can break up if you use too much soap and water, so it's best to test first. For a cover that appears durable, wipe with a **rag** slightly dampened with the **detergent solution**, then dry with a **soft cloth**.

Use a **soft eraser** to clean up a grimy paperback. Be careful, too much pressure can rub off some coloured inks.

When cleaning leatherbound books use restraint. Try wiping with a **clean cloth** first, or use the **vacuum cleaner** to remove visible dust. Some antiques booksellers sell **leather cover cleaners**, but some conservationists no longer favour using products that contain neat's-foot oil, lanolin, or other oils that can permanently darken or stain the cover and give it a greasy feel. Another consideration is that leather-bound volumes treated with oil tend to go mouldy when they're crammed in a bookcase. So doing nothing may well turn out to be the best thing.

Boots

Many boots come with a protective coating that keeps them shiny and bright until they take their first step outdoors. But in most cases the coating will wear off, so dirt and grime can work their way in, clogging the pores that allow the boot to breathe and dry and breaking down seams as well as the leather or fabric itself.

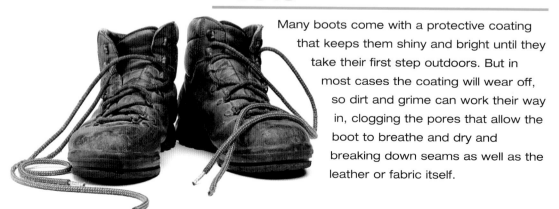

To dislodge dirt first bang your boots together. Then wipe off surface grime and dust with a **damp cloth**, paying special attention to creases and wrinkles. Go into the stubborn stitched areas with a **dry, stiff nylon brush** or an **old toothbrush**.

To clean a boot close the zip (if it has one). Wet the **nylon brush** and rub it on one side of a **bar of soap**. Then scrub down the zip channel. Wipe it dry with a **soft cloth**. Then undo the zip and, using a dry corner of the **soap bar**, rub down each side of the zip to lubricate it for an easy slide. Wipe off the excess with a **soft, dry cloth**.

If your boots become very stained you may want to get rid of the waxed layer, so that you can add more polish more easily. Using either **saddle soap** or a **fabric cleaner**, such as *Woolite*, and a **dry cloth**, rub the whole of the outside in small circles until the stains disappear. Then stuff the boots with **crumpled newspaper** and let them dry at room temperature. Now they are ready to be polished. If you have salt stains on your boots, get rid of them immediately – salt can break down leather and fibres. One option is to use a **specialist shoe stain remover**. An alternative is to dampen the salt stains again, so that they dissolve in the water, then brush your boots firmly to remove them. Rubbing leather with **milk** can also help to restore an even colour.

> ### Scuffs aren't so tough
> Use a pencil eraser to get scuff marks off boots – it works more often than you might imagine. If they're bad, but still won't shift, use a wax crayon in a matching colour to restore the appearance of unblemished leather.

Bottles

Cleaning the outside of an ordinary bottle is as simple as any other glass-cleaning task. The real challenge, of course, is removing dirt from the inside.

To clean the outside of a bottle use **warm water** and **washing-up liquid**. Mildly abrasive **washing-up pads** are fine for use on modern glass. For antique glass, stick to a **smooth cloth**.

To remove hardened residue inside let the bottle stand full of **soapy water** (**warm water** and **washing-up liquid**) for several hours, until the residue softens and can be loosened by shaking or by use of a **bottle brush**. If dirt still remains inside the bottle, here are two ways to provide a little extra help:

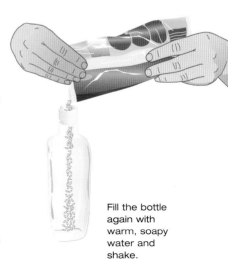

Fill the bottle again with warm, soapy water and shake.

• Pour **1 tablespoon of dry rice** or **sand** into the bottle.
• Fill the bottle with **water** and dissolve a **denture-cleaning tablet.**

A tough white crust can build up inside a bottle that has held water for a long time. You may be able to remove this by filling the bottle with **white vinegar** and letting it stand for a day. The vinegar will then work as an excellent odour absorber in the dishwasher until your next wash.

See also **Baby equipment** and **Decanters.**

Brass

There are two kinds of brass to consider when cleaning: brass with a protective lacquer coating – this is most common today – and raw brass. Raw brass is the bigger challenge to care for, since this copper-and-zinc alloy oxidises when it is exposed to air, resulting in tarnish. Removing tarnish requires some elbow grease.

Removing dirt from lacquered brass Mix **mild washing-up liquid** with **warm water** and apply it with a **soft, cellulose sponge** or **cloth.** Rinse with **fresh water** and dry thoroughly with a soft cloth. Buff with an extremely **soft cloth** such as an **old T-shirt** made into a

Natural ways to clean brass

Like many natural methods, it's a bit messy, but think how satisfied you'll feel that just half a cut lemon and a dash of salt has restored your brass to its former glory. Sprinkle the cut lemon with salt, then squeeze it over dirty, unlacquered brass. Wipe off with a cloth, then buff up with a second, clean cloth.

Alternatively, make a paste of bicarbonate of soda and water (or just use non-gel toothpaste, also a mild abrasive). Apply the paste to a soft cloth and then rub the brass. Wipe clean with a fresh cloth.

Once it's clean, rub the brass with a light coating of mineral oil, olive oil, or lemon oil to protect it from further tarnish. Lacquered brass doesn't need this protection.

pad or **chamois**. Avoid paper towels, because they will scratch the surface of the brass.

Removing tarnish from raw brass Take a tip from antiques dealers and the armed forces and use a **metal polish** like *Brasso*, which contains cleaners to eliminate the tarnish, abrasives for polishing and oil to protect the brass from the air. Follow the instructions on the package and use only a thin layer of metal polish – more is not better. Repeat every few months.

To brighten up soot-grimed brass fireplace equipment the cleaning techniques above may not be sufficient. Rub the brass with **extra-fine steel wool (0000)** or a **very fine emery cloth**. Be careful, you're in abrasive territory now. Rub the metal in one direction only – not with a circular motion. Once the brass is clean, follow up with a **commercial brass polish**.

Brick

Exposed interior brick can be cleaned by simply putting the brush attachment on your vacuum cleaner and running it over the wall. The brush will loosen the dust and dirt and the vacuum will suck it up.

On exterior brick, particularly in a damp and shady spot, mould, mildew and algae are often a problem. To kill and remove the growth, mix **50ml of bleach** with **5 litres of water** in a **bucket**. If you find you need more strength, increase the bleach or try *Thompsons Moss and Mould Killer*. Wearing **rubber gloves**, dip a **stiff-bristled brush** (not metal) in the solution and scrub the brick. To rinse, hose the brick down with **fresh water**.

For cleaning dingy brick some masonry specialists swear by **caustic soda**, an ingredient in powerful cold oven cleaners. Follow the instructions precisely, as you would when you clean the oven and only apply if you can be sure that children or pets won't have access to the wall, while it is sitting in this extremely strong solvent.

Oven cleaner will be a very expensive option if you have a large section of brickwork to wash. So instead, just use the caustic soda – *Starpax* do one, on sale at DIY stores.

Rules of the game

Cleaning under pressure

A high-pressure hose can work magic in cleaning brick, but be careful – the pressure can damage both mortar and bricks, especially bricks with a sand finish. Use a low setting and keep the nozzle 60cm from the wall. Keep moving as you spray: it's the concentration of water on one spot that will lift off loose brick particles. Aim for the brick, not the mortar.

Because it is so powerful (it will cause burns instantly) always get the water bucket filled first, then add the caustic soda to the water. This minimises the risk of getting splashed with the concentrated product. Wear **rubber gloves**, **long sleeves** and **protective goggles**. Apply the solution with an **old rag**. Let the cleaner sit for 15 minutes and follow up with a **scrubbing brush**. Apply the cleaner again if necessary and scrub once more. Rinse with **water**.

To brighten soot-stained brick try this old masonry trick. Mix a can of a **cola soft drink** (its acid adds cleaning power), **100ml of an economy all-purpose household cleaner**, such as *Tesco All Purpose Value Cleaner* and **4 litres of water** in a **bucket**. Sponge the solution onto the sooty brick and let it sit for 15 minutes. Scrub with a **stiff-bristled brush** to loosen the soot. Rinse with a **clean sponge** and **fresh water**. If you are working outside, use a **hose**. To make the solution more powerful, add more cola. As an alternative, buy a **commercial soot remover** from a shop that sells fireplace equipment and use following the product's directions.

Bridal gowns

Unless your gown specifically says that it can be machine washed, never try to clean it yourself. If you've bought a second-hand gown, take it to a professional dry-cleaners. If yours is new and you're just panicking about on-the-day disasters, this emergency know-how will keep you calm.

To fix a last-minute stain do not use spot cleaner on your gown. Instead, use **talcum powder** as a disguise. Just sprinkle some talc onto the spot and let it absorb the moisture. Brush off lightly. If your dress is slightly too long and a rehearsal has left scuff marks along the bottom of the gown, mark over them with a piece of **white chalk**.

For liquid spills try **fizzy mineral water**. Depending on the location of the stain, you might have to undress and dress all over again. Working from the inside out, use a **clean, white handkerchief** to blot up as much of the stain as possible. Be sure to dab, not rub. Then wet the handkerchief with the **mineral water** and dab again, working again from the inside.

If the gown needs a final touch-up press only on the inside of the gown. And don't use steam. If the fabric hasn't been pre-washed, steam can create spotting or a colour change. Place a **dry handkerchief** between the iron and the gown. Then press in a downward direction. Don't move the iron back and forth – this will destroy delicate fibres. Press one area and then move the cloth to another.

When the honeymoon is over don't put off taking your gown to the **dry-cleaner**. You might want to hand it down to someone or sell it and, without the proper care, it will become yellow and useless to anyone else.

First, take off any easily removable trimmings or shoulder pads. Then search out any spots you may have ignored while you were partying at the reception. Dry cleaning usually removes the obvious – makeup, grass stains, food spills – but you may also have acquired some invisible spills – champagne is a classic – that show up later. If you can remember where they are, you will give the dry-cleaner a head start. Otherwise, when your gown is preserved and stored, the champagne stains will be, too.

When you store your gown, don't put it in plastic or expose it to sunlight. Instead, ask the dry-cleaner to wrap your gown in **acid-free tissue** and store it in an **acid-free box** to slow the ageing process.

Simple solutions

Weddings and 1999 other uses for WD-40

It's inevitable. Your husband's Aunt Sally, who wears too much makeup, will make her way to your wedding gown. And she'll most likely smudge you with a lipstick kiss or a hug just before the pictures are taken.

Luckily, there is something you can do. A light mist of *WD-40*, the all-purpose lubricant, will lift up the stain. Of course you won't be carrying one with you, But, chances are, your photographer might: it's also used to clean up tripods and grubby metal. So he may have one in his kit bag. Removing lipstick is just one of 2000 uses for this mini miracle in a can. Visit *www.twbc.org/wd40.htm* and you'll have the fun of viewing 2000 ideas suggested to the company by people who clearly just can't get enough of the stuff. The ideas aren't verified – just people telling what works for them. But if you fancy some inspiration on cleaning everything from printer toner off clothes to sticky residue off floor tiles – and shifting lipstick of course – you won't be disappointed.

Briefcases

To clean the inside, empty the briefcase and shake it over a rubbish bin to get rid of broken pencil leads, paperclips, scraps of paper, old crumbs and the general grit and grime that accumulates in offices, airports and car boots.

Vacuum out everything else, using a **hand vacuum cleaner** or the **crevice attachment** of a regular **vacuum cleaner**. Use a **spray bottle of water** (the sort you use to mist over plants) to lightly spray the lining. Pour a little **washing-up liquid** on a **small cloth** and rub lightly on any persistent stains. Immediately wipe down the lining with a **dry cloth**. Don't close the case – let it air-dry.

To clean the outside use a **liquid saddle soap** or put a couple of drops of **detergent** in a small bowl of **warm water**. Swirl to create some bubbles. Dip a **face flannel** in the water and quickly wipe down the briefcase. If your briefcase has a zip, take a **dry bar of soap** and rub it down the zip. It will clean and loosen the zip at the same time. Remove excess soap with a **dry flannel**.

Brocade

Brocade is a combination of fabrics woven into a raised design. When cleaning brocade, you must consider the fabric contents of the weave. It can be made of wool, cotton, silk, synthetic fibre or a combination of these. If there is no care label, then clean according to the most delicate element. So with cotton and silk, clean as silk.

To remove a stain from brocade First, remove as much of the stain as possible by lifting it off with a **dull-edged knife**. Then start to force the stain out from the wrong side of the fabric (you may have to remove the fabric from furniture to do this). Then place the fabric, stain-side down, onto an **absorbent tea towel. Fizzy mineral water** will help lift the stain. But if you don't have any, use **lukewarm tap water**. Pour a little on a **paper towel** and dab it on the stain, forcing it onto the tea towel. Dab a spot, then move to another spot and dab again. Keep dabbing until the stain disappears.

Bronze

Artists using special paints can re-create the look of weathered bronze in a faux finish called *verdigris*. But if you're patient, real bronze will do the job all by itself. With time, bronze creates its own protective patina – a pretty, earthy green colour. But even with the no-cost natural process, you still have to clean it and you must be careful to remove water residue. Lingering moisture and even grit can degrade bronze. If you lose a little of the patina while cleaning, don't worry – it will come back again.

When cleaning bronze you're essentially cleaning two different metals at once. An alloy, bronze is a combination of copper and any other metal except zinc. Like any decorative surface that is exposed to the environment, bronze can accumulate a layer of film or dust (or dusty film) that needs removing. First, wipe away any loose or surface dirt with a **soft cloth**, then work at it again with a **soft toothbrush** to get into crevices and ornamental work.

For a more thorough cleaning carefully wash the bronze with a solution of **1 tablespoon salt** dissolved into **3 litres of water**. For the toughest grime, dissolve **1 teaspoon of salt** in **150ml of white vinegar**, then add enough **flour** to make a paste. Let it sit on the bronze for 15 minutes to an hour. Rinse with **clean, warm water**. Be sure to towel-dry the piece thoroughly, because moisture and salt by themselves can degrade the bronze.

E is for excellent

You can buy bronze with a factory-finish lacquer which will protect it from changes in colour as well as corrosion. Never apply a chemical cleanser to lacquered bronze. A weekly swipe with a damp cloth will keep it in good shape. Linda Cobb, author of *Talking Dirty with the Queen of Clean*, recommends using a damp microfibre. 'It's like thousands of scrubbing fingers that remove dirt', she says. Best of all, you might not have to polish, because microfibre cloths polish as they clean.

Although you can buy cheaper imitations, *E-Cloths*, from around £5, remain just about the best. Buy them direct from *www.enviroproducts.co.uk* or haberdashery sections of department stores, including John Lewis.

Butcher's blocks

Ask a professional chef how to clean a butcher's block with a protective coating and he or she will probably tell you to take it to the dump. Varnish or polyurethane should never be an ingredient in food preparation. Professional butcher's blocks never have a varnished finish.

To clean a butcher's block don't ever use any household chemical cleaners. They could be harmful and, at the least, the residue will be distasteful on food. All you need to keep preparation surfaces hygienic is **10ml of chlorine household bleach** mixed with **2 litres of water** in a **bucket**. Dip a **small scrubbing brush** in the chlorine water and scrub in hand-sized circles, taking care not to saturate the wood. When wood absorbs water, it swells. Then, when it dries out, the wood will crack, making a convenient trap for food, grime and germs. So brush the butcher's block clean and quickly wipe away excess water with a hand towel.

As an alternative Mix just enough **salt** into **a few drops of lemon juice** to make a paste. Rub it, with a **cleaning cloth** or **sponge**, hard enough onto the wood to free stuck-on or wedged-in food particles. Then rinse out the cloth or sponge and wipe the butcher's block clean. The result won't be as germ-free as cleaning with bleach, but it's a good, fresh-smelling alternative.

If the surface is oily or sticky even after a brisk scrub, you might need to get out the toolbox. Scrape up any build-up with a **putty knife**. Then gently attack the block with **very fine glasspaper**, graduating to finer grades, until you're satisfied. Then wipe clean with a **damp cloth** or **sponge** and season the block, as described in the panel left.

Simple solutions

Season liberally

The first step in keeping an unvarnished butcher's block like new is to season it when you first bring it home. Warm a little vegetable oil in a small saucepan on the stove. Don't let it get hot – warm oil will penetrate the wood nicely. Using a soft cloth dabbed into the oil, rub in the direction of the grain. Let the oil soak in for four or five hours, then wipe off any excess using a soft, dry cloth. Repeat the process. Seasoning your butcher's block once a month sets the stage for a clean, hygienic work surface.

Buttons

Before beginning, make sure you know what your buttons are made of. You should never put strong metal polish on buttons with a gold or silver finish or wash leather buttons in a washing machine. If your buttons are covered with the same fabric as the garment or if they're plastic, care for the buttons the way you would for the garment.

To clean leather buttons

remove them from the garment. While a wool sweater might make it through a machine wash, leather and some other natural button materials won't. Never use shoe polish: when you next wear the item, your body heat could transfer polish to the garment. Instead, choose **saddle soap** or a **leather cleaning and conditioning solution with lanolin**.

You'll find them most easily at heel bars. A handy idea if you're cleaning just the odd button is to choose a **saddle soap wipe**, such as *Carr & Day Martin Glycerine Saddle Soap Wipe*s. One quick wipe and your buttons are done.

Let this or traditional saddle soap dry, then buff it to a shine with a **soft cloth**.

To clean wooden buttons remove them from the garment and use a **wood oil cleanser**, such as *Orange Glo Wood Cleaner & Polish*. Follow the directions on the bottle. The buttons will absorb most of the wood oil soap. Remove any residue with a **soft cloth**.

To clean bone or ivory buttons remove them from the garment. Mix a small amount of **lemon juice** with enough **salt** to make a paste. Lightly brush it on with a **soft toothbrush** and wipe them clean with a **damp cloth**.

To clean buttons made of horn dampen a **soft cloth** with a small amount of **vegetable oil** or **baby oil**. Rub to remove stains, then wipe with a **dry cloth**. Do not immerse horn in water.

To clean metal buttons you can try the age-old remedy of **non-gel toothpaste**. Avoid anything that boasts 'tartar contro' or 'whitening'. As an alternative, dissolve **1 teaspoon of rock salt** in **1 litre of water**. (Don't use table salt, as this can cause discoloration.) Dampen a **soft cloth** in the salt solution and polish the surface. Rinse well with water. Then polish with a **soft, dry cloth**.

Simple solutions

How they button up at sea

Because boats have lots of rubber, sailors know how to keep the stuff clean. Try this traditional nautical tip for rubber buttons. Buy a small bottle of glycerine from the cake ingredients aisle at the supermarket. Rub the glycerine into the buttons with a towel. They'll come clean and repel water and dirt for a long time to come.

Calculators

To clean a calculator thoroughly, dust both sides with an eye shadow brush, being careful to brush away lint and accumulated dust or dirt. If there is a great deal of lint, brush it off with a soft, dry toothbrush.

Keeping the keys clean can be difficult. Because fingers transfer all kinds of dirt – such as newspaper ink and sticky sugar – the keys are like magnets for lint and grime. To get rid of anything that doesn't belong, dip a **cotton bud** into a small amount of **methylated spirit**. Press the bud onto a **paper towel** to eliminate excess alcohol. Dab each key lightly. For the bigger surfaces, such as the back of the calculator, you can use a **cotton ball**, dipped in methylated spirit, to get rid of unsightly dirt.

Clean the keypad on a calculator with a cotton bud dipped in methylated spirits.

Camcorders

Most camera experts will tell you not to clean your own camcorder. There are too many integral small parts that can be easily damaged. If you cause problems while cleaning your camcorder, most camera repair shops won't be prepared to take responsibility for any subsequent problems. But there are times when it just makes good sense to have a go – when a child splashes juice on it, for instance, or when you've brought home a little of the beach in your camera case.

Deal with outdoor exposure to salt, moisture or dirt as soon as you can. Reporters who cover extreme weather, such as hurricanes, know how quickly exposure to the elements – especially salt – erodes and rusts a camera and its workings. Although you should not get inside the camera to clean it, you can do what reporters do. Dampen a **clean, soft cloth** or **towel** with a tiny amount of **methylated spirits** – as little as possible in fact – and wipe the surfaces thoroughly. Make sure that the dock where you load the cassette tape stays closed.

When cleaning a lens, it's best not to touch it or a viewfinder with anything other than **lens tissue**, available cheaply from anywhere that sells camera equipment.

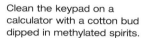

Simple solutions

Clean tapes equal a clean machine

Get into the simple habit of always putting your tapes back into their boxes. Dust from the tape is the easiest route for dust to get into your machine. So putting your tapes in boxes will ensure the minimum transfer of dust.

Ordinary facial tissues frequently contain additives, such as lanolin, that will cause damage to the lens. The only other acceptable alternative is a **soft, natural-bristled brush** (an artist's brush or a makeup brush). If you use the brush, make sure it's new. Even brushes that have been washed can contain residue that you don't want to transfer to your lens and viewfinder. Alternatively, **canned air** (sold in camera shops) is an easy, non-contact way to blow off dust.

To clean the heads in a camcorder go to the shop where you bought your camcorder and buy a **dry cleaning tape** that is compatible with your camera. Simply load the tape, press Play, and let it run for the recommended amount of time.

Cameos

The intricate carvings and grooves that make cameos so charming provide excellent hiding places for grime that can dull their beauty. Cameos are made of coral, resin, stones and, most commonly, seashells. Different coloured layers provide the characteristic contrast between the relief carving and its background. These delicate materials need protection from dirt and becoming too dry.

Cleaning a cameo is simple, no matter how complex the design. A periodic dusting with a **soft-bristled brush** will help keep particles from settling into crevices. The brushing may be followed by rinsing with **warm water** and drying with a **soft, lint-free cloth**.

Give a cameo a soapy bath about twice a year. Never use a harsh cleaner. Put a few drops of **mild washing-up liquid** or a **gentle hand wash solution**, such as *Woolite*, into a bowl with about **300ml of warm water**. Swish the cameo around, wet a **soft toothbrush**, and scrub gently. Never let cameos soak, because soaking may damage the shell. After the soapy bath, rinse the cameo in **warm water** and dry it with a **soft cloth**.

Moisturise a cameo after its bath A cameo that is too dry may become cracked or chipped. Use a fine oil, such as **olive oil**, **vegetable oil** or **baby oil** – or follow the old-fashioned practice of using **oil of wintergreen** (teaberry – sold as an essential oil at health shops), to give your cameo a fresh and surprising scent. Use a **cotton bud** to apply a little oil to the surface. Let it sit overnight, then wipe off any oil you can still see with a **soft cloth**.

Always store cameos in a **soft cloth** or **lined box** well away from heat and light.

Cameras

Cameras are compact bundles of extremely delicate parts. Cleaning them without causing damage in the process is a daunting task. What you use to clean them is also somewhat controversial. At one end of the spectrum, it's just air (canned) and minimal contact; the other uses contact cleaning and solvents. But the real trick is in preventing dirt and damage in the first place.

To clean the lens first examine it with a **magnifying glass**. Any kind of foreign material, including dirt you can't see with the naked eye, will mar your pictures and may damage your lens.

To get rid of dust or dirt on the lens start with air. Camera shops sell a blower brush, which combines a brush with a blower. The blower on most of them is actually ineffective. A better alternative is a **bulb syringe**, which you can get at any chemist, which will shoot a puff of air. Still more effective is a **can of compressed air**. Also known as 'canned air', it's an aerosol can containing air under pressure and a nozzle extension. Some say canned air gives too big a blast, but it is widely used. *Jessops*, the photographic chain, sell a selection from around £6.50.

If your lens is removable, check the back end occasionally and clean it in exactly the same way as the front.

A magnifying glass helps spot dust and dirt on your delicate camera lens.

To remove persistent specks that don't respond to the air treatment, brush them away with a **blower brush** or **soft watercolour paintbrush**. You can also use a **cleaning cloth**. But you don't want to move specks around – that will only damage the lens or its coatings. So take care in choosing a cloth. The best is a **microfibre lens cleaning cloth**, which can also be used on the body of the camera and can be washed and reused. These cloths trap particles among their fibres rather than on the surface. You can get them from around £5 from *www.enviroproducts.co.uk*

To remove fingerprints or really persistent specks, you may need to use **lens cleaning fluid**. There are many types on the market. Check your owner's manual for recommendations. If your camera has a plastic lens, make sure the lens cleaner is suitable for plastic as well as glass. Use a few drops of **lens cleaning fluid** on a **microfibre cloth** – never put it directly on to the lens – and clean with a light, circular motion. Fingerprints should be cleaned immediately in this way. If left for a long time, fingerprints can actually etch themselves into the glass.

Fingerprints are also a great source of food for glass mould, a type that doesn't need as much moisture as most other moulds. The mould will also feed on dust, and it can destroy the surface of a lens. Using your camera in the sunshine every so often will usually be enough to prevent glass mould. If you aren't going to be using your camera for a long time, take it out of the case. Camera cases can build up moisture and grow mould quite easily.

To clean inside a traditional film camera use **compressed air** and a **soft watercolour brush** to banish dirt from the film chamber, followed by a gentle wiping with a **microfibre cloth**. Don't forget the inside of the lens cap and the inside of your camera bag.

Keep it simple and everything will click

Ed Romney has made a career of restoring really filthy cameras. He has sometimes been obliged to use substances like diesel starting fluid as cleaning agents. Ed has helped foster a growing interest in antique cameras and their restoration. But his advice to the average amateur photographer is always the same, 'Don't clean it – keep it clean.'

For maintenance, Romney subscribes to the basics of cleaning a camera, but that's about it. 'It's a pity to do unnecessary things to a camera', Romney says. 'More lenses are destroyed by cleaning than anything else. Over-polishing a lens is an awful thing to do.'

Romney is also worried about the mould that can attack lenses and literally eat them. To kill it, he wipes the lens with a rag dipped in a 50–50 mixture of ammonia and hydrogen peroxide.

More cameras are thrown away because they are dirty than because they are broken, he maintains.

So keep yours clean and it will repay you with a long and effective working life.

When cleaning a digital camera slip the battery pack out to make sure it is powerless before you start. A new product for use with a digital camera is a **lens pen**, which combines a retractable brush on one end with a cleaning tip on the other. They cost around £9 from *Jessops*.

Some simple precautions will help keep your camera clean and well functioning:

• Protect the lens with an **ultraviolet filter** (even if you remove it for picture taking) and lens cap. With many new cameras, you can't lose the lens cap because it just slides aside. But you still must remember to close it after use.
• Don't store a camera where it will be exposed to direct sunlight, high humidity, rapid changes in temperature (which may cause condensation) or temperature extremes.
• Wipe off the batteries and the contact points in the battery chambers before inserting new batteries. This will help to prevent corrosion.
• Consult the owner's manual for hints about preventive maintenance and specific information about your camera.

Can openers

It's a wonder that we are not poisoned by our can openers. When you consider the mixture of substances – chicken soup, tuna fish, dog food and other debris – that congeal on the blades, a can opener's potential toxicity isn't surprising. The juices left on the blades have been shown to harbour the bacteria that cause food poisoning, skin infections, pneumonia and other ailments. To avoid trouble, always wash the blades carefully after each use.

Cleaning a handheld can opener is simple. Just wash it with the dishes, either by hand or in a **dishwasher**.

Cleaning an electric can opener is also easy, because most have blades or cutting assemblies designed to be removed and washed with the dishes. Older models may not have detachable blades. In that case, clean the cutting parts, being careful not to cut yourself, with a **cloth**

dampened with **water** and a little **washing–up liquid**. If you're dealing with accumulated dirt, scrub with an **old toothbrush**. Regular cleaning thereafter will keep the machine clean. To clean the machine's body, wipe it with a **clean damp cloth** with the unit unplugged. Never immerse an electric can opener in water.

Candlesticks & candelabra

The easiest way to clean wax from candlesticks is to wipe the wax off while the drips are still warm and soft. But this may seem overly fastidious in the midst of a dinner party.

To remove hardened wax try this general–purpose method. First, remove all you can with your fingers or with assistance from a soft wooden stick – one from an ice lolly is ideal. You could also use warm water to soften the wax. Never use a knife or other metal object.

If there is still some left after this, try to get the wax harder still. Wrap **ice cubes** in a **plastic bag**, then push them onto the old wax to freeze it solid. When you've got it all off, polish the candlesticks with nylon material – an **old pair of tights** is ideal – and finish according to the sections on copper, brass or silver as relevant.

Watch out

- Don't be tempted to put the entire candlestick into the freezer. Some candlesticks are actually made from two or more kinds of metal, which could expand and contract at different rates.
- The candles themselves are a different story. If you place candles in cold storage for a couple of hours before using them, they'll burn more slowly and with less dripping. That'll mean less mess to clean up

Caning

Used on antique and contemporary chairs, footstools and other small pieces of furniture, caning is made of woven bamboo or reeds. Historically, it was often intended to support cushions, which also helped protect it. Using cushions with caning is still a good idea.

To clean caning use the **brush attachment** of a **vacuum cleaner** regularly to suck out loose dirt, or dust it with a brush, such as a **paintbrush**. To wash dirtier caning, use a little **mild detergent** in **water** applied with a **sponge**, **cloth** or **medium–stiff brush**. Rinse with **clear water** and dry with a **towel** or **soft cloth**. Don't use harsh detergents or cleaners.

To prevent stains on caning clean up any spills promptly with a **wet cloth** or **soap and water**. A stain may be impossible to remove. If you do get a serious stain, your best bet may be to paint or stain the cane.

To fix a sagging cane seat provided the material isn't broken, wet the seat thoroughly from underneath. The underside is more porous than the top and will absorb better. Then let the caning dry in the sun.

Carpeting

For routine carpet cleaning, a vacuum cleaner is the best tool. Vacuuming removes about 85 per cent of carpet dirt. But to get down to the deep dirt, you will need to give your carpeting a more thorough cleaning than a vacuum cleaner can provide. How often depends on your lifestyle, but the recommended range is every 6 to 18 months.

Vacuuming your carpeting every day would be ideal. Many people settle on once a week, even if it doesn't appear dirty. If you can, vacuum heavily trafficked areas a little more often. And be sure to vacuum up any obvious soiling before it gets ground in.

For vacuuming your carpet, the more powerful your machine is the better. You can use either an **upright vacuum**, which has the advantage of having a brush bar to beat more dirt up out of the carpet, or a **cylinder with a power nozzle**, which relies on suction alone, but can come in handy if you lack the strength to push an upright, or find it awkward on stairs.

• Persistence is essential for effective vacuuming. You may need to have to go over a piece of carpet up to seven times to remove all the dust and dirt you'd like to. So whilst whipping around quickly with the vacuum will do a fair job, spend longer and you'll do a better job.
• Set your vacuum for the pile level of the carpet – unless it has an automatic adjustment.
• When you vacuum an area, use slow, even

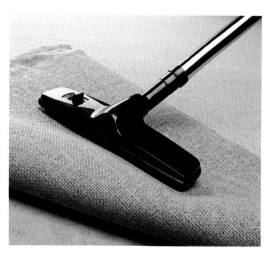

Vacuum the underside of rugs occasionally to prevent a build-up of dust and other allergens.

strokes and go back and forth several times, so that you
work both with and against the grain of the carpet pile.
Finish with strokes that all go in the same direction. In
plush carpets with pile, this will give a smooth finish, rather
than just-cut lawn stripes.

• Move light furniture into the centre of the room before
you start. See the **ZAP** cleaning method, on pages 78–87,
for a full explanation of this.

• If you have a rug, occasionally turn it over and vacuum
the underside.

• If your vacuum cleaner won't suck up cat hairs, threads or
other fine items, use a lint roller or a piece of doubled-over
tape to pick them up.

• New carpeting produces a lot of extra fluff. It's normal –
there is nothing to worry about.

Steam-cleaning units can be hired
from a rental shop. Check listings
in your local directory.

Professional steam cleaning is the ideal way to
remove ground in dirt from your carpet. There are
several types of professional carpet-cleaning
methods, but the Rolls-Royce of them all is **hot
water extraction**, or **steam cleaning**, done by
professionals using a **truck-mounted unit**.
However, a good compromise is to shampoo the
carpet, using a **water-extraction machine**. You
can hire these from DIY stores and supermarkets
for around £20 per day, with cleaning solutions
for a typical home doubling your final cost. Or,
you can buy your own machine: *Bissell* do a
range, from around £250. So the cost soon gets
paid back. Plus, there's the huge advantage that you can
just shampoo after a stain accident in one room.

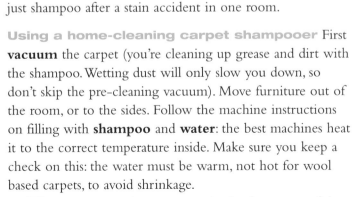

Using a home-cleaning carpet shampooer First
vacuum the carpet (you're cleaning up grease and dirt with
the shampoo. Wetting dust will only slow you down, so
don't skip the pre-cleaning vacuum). Move furniture out of
the room, or to the sides. Follow the machine instructions
on filling with **shampoo** and **water**: the best machines heat
it to the correct temperature inside. Make sure you keep a
check on this: the water must be warm, not hot for wool
based carpets, to avoid shrinkage.

When you are ready to go, start in the far corner of the
room, and move very slowly up and down. Move too
quickly, and your machine will still lay down the wet
shampoo solution, but won't have the time to suck it up.

Rules of the game

Carpet clean-ups made simple

Many people's first reaction to a carpet spill is to make it worse by rubbing. Yet rubbing will only grind the spill more deeply into the carpet's fibres.

While the treatment of spills will vary with the materials of the carpet and of the substance spilled, here are a few principles that apply to all:

1 Scoop up any solids and use something absorbent to soak up any liquid that hasn't sunk in yet.

2 After you've absorbed everything you can, blot the spot with white towels or rags. Work from the outside in so you won't spread the stain.

3 When you've blotted up all you can, use water to dilute what remains, and continue to blot.

4 If that doesn't complete the job, proceed to a low-tech cleaner. If that doesn't work, call in the professionals. Many amateurs do harm by overdosing on harsh, but ineffective cleaners.

Which means your carpet will stay wet for far longer than needed. Accept that you'll have to keep stopping to empty out the dirty water, and refill with shampoo and fresh water.

A very dirty house that is fully carpeted could mean you emptying 20 to 30 buckets of filthy water. If it's very bad, take it straight out and pour it down the drain. You don't want the extra job of clearing a sink blocked with grease. When you've finished, open the windows to air the room. Wait until the carpet is quite dry until putting back heavy furniture or walking on it in shoes. Wet carpet is most vulnerable to damage. Finally, use the machine to whizz over any washable, fixed upholstery before you take it back to the hire shop.

Removing spots on carpeting is something you have to expect to do yourself, because onto every carpet a little wine must fall – or tomato ketchup – or pet mess. The techniques for attacking stains are as varied as the stains themselves, so if you want advice on how to clear up a particular problem, look up what you've spilled in the index. You'll find a plenty of suitable suggestions in **Everyday stains and seasonal pests** (pages 46–77) and in **Cleaning crises** (pages 400–409). The approach you use depends in part on how much you value your carpet. If your carpet is old and beaten up, you can afford to be daring. If it's brand-new, of high quality and you want it to last for many years to come, be more cautious.

Choosing a spot-removing strategy is a bit like picking foods from the Food Guide Pyramid that divides meats from vegetables, from cereals. On the food pyramid, you're supposed to eat a lot of the foods depicted at the bottom (fruits, vegetables and grains) and eat the foods at the top (fats, sweets and oils) sparingly. On the Stain Removal Pyramid the broad bottom section includes that most gentle and universal of cleaning substances – water. The higher you go on this pyramid, the more extreme the treatment and the less of it you should use.

Before we examine each step in the pyramid, you need to remember a few basics: stain removal usually requires tenacious blotting. Be sure to blot, not rub. Before moving on from one step in the pyramid to the next, test the next solution on an inconspicuous area of carpet. Put a little of the treatment on the carpet, let it sit for about 10 minutes, and blot with a **clean white rag**. Inspect the rag for any dye from the carpet, and inspect the carpet for any damage from the cleaner. If either occurs, the solution isn't really a solution; it's another problem. In the case of wool, if it doesn't respond to water and the mild soap solution, you should call a professional.

Here are the techniques to try, in order, as you ascend the **Stain Removal Pyramid**. Use these techniques only one at a time, and rinse well between steps.

1 Blot up liquid spills promptly then dilute what remains with **water** and blot some more. You can also dilute spills with **plain mineral water**. The fizziness and salts it contains will sometimes help it work better than tap water, and it's just about as safe.

2 Next, try a **general-purpose spot cleaner**. Mix **1 teaspoon of mild washing-up liquid** with **100ml of warm water**. Blot it on the spot. Be sure to rinse thoroughly with clean water.

3 Try a solution of **15ml of ammonia** and **50ml of water** on old spots, blood and chocolate.

4 Try a solution of **1 part white vinegar** and **2 parts water** on mildew stains and spills with a strong residual odour, such as urine.

5 Try full-strength **3 per cent hydrogen peroxide** (from chemists, where it is sold as mouthwash) on tomato-based stains, red drinks, alcoholic drinks, fruit juice, grass stains, coffee and chocolate. Dab the solvent onto a **cotton bud** and press into the stain. Get a **fresh cotton bud**, and use to lift off the solvent and, you hope, the dissolved stain.

6 Use **methylated spirit** full strength, on oily stains, ballpoint pen ink, candle wax residue and grass stains. Use the **cotton bud** treatment, as above.

Special situations may call for special techniques:
• **For oily spills**, such as mayonnaise, salad dressing and butter, try saturating the spot with **cornflour**, a good absorbent. Allow it to dry, then **vacuum**.
• **For candle wax** dripped onto your carpet, use a **warm iron** over a sheet of **greaseproof paper** to take up as much wax as possible. Then dab on **methylated spirits**.

The Stain Removal Pyramid

6 Alcohol

5 Hydrogen peroxide

4 Ammonia and water

3 Vinegar and water

2 Mild washing-up liquid and water

1 Tap water or plain mineral water

Simple solutions

Don't try some salt with your wine

Say you're celebrating your home renovation, which included new beige carpeting. And someone – possibly even you – has spilled wine on the new carpeting. And it's red wine. Now you may have heard the tip about adding salt to minimise the spread of spills. And yes, it's true. For spills on worktops, machine washable tablecloths. But not carpets. Whilst it will stop the spread, it can also leave a residue in the carpet that you will never be able to shift. So reach for the paper towels instead and get blotting.

If there is still a stain, move on to the general-purpose spot cleaner described above. (See step 2.)

• **Pet accidents** produce odours as well as stains and the problem is compounded when urine is not detected immediately. The longer it stays, the worse it gets. First, flush the spot with **water** and blot with an **old towel** or **rag**. Then use the general-purpose spot treatment. (See step 2.) Rinse that with the **vinegar mixture**. (See step 4.) Rinse again with **water** and blot. Finally, apply a 1cm thick layer of **dry, clean white rags**, **towels**, or **paper towels**, weight them with a **heavy object**, and allow them to sit for several hours. If they're still damp when you remove them, repeat with a fresh layer of absorbent materials until they come up dry. (This is also a good formula for treating spilled beer.) The odour will not come out as long as any urine remains. So you just have to keep repeating this, until you're sure

What's your carpet made of?

How your carpeting responds to dirt and your efforts to eradicate it depends on the material – of the carpet and of the dirt. Unfortunately, most people have little idea about the materials their carpets are made of, unless the carpet is wool. The majority of UK carpet sold is now synthetic, with polypropylene and acrylic as top choices.

• **Polypropylene** Inexpensive and fairly stain resistant. If you move into a house, and have no clue as to what the carpet is made of – chances are that it is this. It is the only carpet material that can sometimes accept bleach. Its chief disadvantage is fibres that crush easily.

• **Acrylic** Also relatively inexpensive, it resembles nylon in some ways, but has a softer look and touch. It is not as strong and is unsuitable for high-traffic areas, so bedroom carpets are often acrylic but stair and sitting room ones rarely are. And it is susceptible to pilling and fuzzing.

• **Nylon** Tough and resistant to soil and stains, but has a tendency to conduct static. So it is not a good choice for bedrooms or places where you want to walk barefoot. If the fibres get compressed by a heavy object sitting on them, they can be revived with steam.

• **Blends** These will have characteristics of their components, but since those components react differently to stains, removing stains may be more difficult.

• **Natural fibres** Include wool, sisal, hemp, jute, and sea grass. Wool is durable and naturally resistant to stains and dirt. It also washes beautifully. The downside is the cost – you may spend up to four times as much on a wool carpet, even the more usual 80 per cent wool, 20 per cent synthetic mix.

• **Sisal, hemp, jute and sea grass** are all made from plants and they come in a wide variety of weaves and prices. Plant-based materials are more likely to be found in area rugs than in wall-to-wall carpeting. These carpets will not stand up to shampooing or steam cleaning. Use as little liquid as possible when treating stains.

you've hit success. Most commercial products sold to eliminate odour just mask the smell temporarily.

• **If a carpet has a musty smell, bicarbonate of soda will help.** If you've been removing spots from the carpet, let the carpet dry out completely first. Then sprinkle bicarbonate of soda over the entire carpet, let it sit for three to five hours, and vacuum it up.

• Not all substances can be removed from carpeting. Chlorine bleach, iodine, mustard, insecticides and plant fertilisers, to name a few, are likely to create permanent stains. Many foods, drinks, medicines and cosmetics contain dye, and their spots also may be permanent.

Sometimes a professional restorer can fix a permanently damaged area by spot-dyeing, reweaving or retufting. Or a professional installer can replace a section of carpet using a scrap or a piece taken from an inconspicuous spot. As a last resort, get a pair of nail scissors and snip off the very worst of the stained pile. Then, leave a small ice cube to melt on the spot. The remaining fibres should swell a little to help plug the gap.

A liberal sprinkling of bicarbonate of soda followed by thorough vacuuming will rid your carpet of musty spells.

Cars

For most of us, cars are our second most expensive possession. We choose them to reflect our personalities and our dreams – yet, when it comes to cleaning, the rules are nearly all the same.

Over the metal frame exterior of your car, is a layer of primer, then a single layer of waterborne acrylic paint with pigment and then several layers of paint with no pigment, called clearcoat. While the clearcoat adds depth and brightness to the colour, it gives no additional protection, so total coverage is often no more than 5mm thick. That's not a lot between the metal and any corrosive elements. Or between a surface scratch taking out the entire colour.

So the idea is to boost your car's ability to cope with the elements and brush contact with other surfaces (prickly hedges spring to mind) by regularly adding a solid protective layer of wax.

Interior surfaces take a beating from the elements as well – just think how often you open the car doors when you

drive on wet days – so they need regular care as well. The International Car Wash Association recommends washing your car every 10 days and waxing every six months. Beyond aesthetics, it's a way of protecting your investment and avoiding damage.

Choosing a car washing site is the first step. Don't wash your car under a tree, as debris, pollen, leaves or bird droppings will undo your good work. Direct sunshine is also an enemy. When intense heat dries the car very fast, you're more likely to be left with irritating water spots, as the heated metal of your car's bodywork dries soap into a film before you can rinse it off and your wax crusts into hard-to-wipe streaks.

Better choices are a carport, a garage with good ventilation and drainage or a shady area not directly under a tree. Another alternative is a coin-operated car wash bay.

You need a good four hours to devote to the process if you want to do a totally thorough job (although in practice even a quarter of that is time well spent if it means you wash your car regularly). Remove your watch and any belt buckle or jewellery that might bang against the car and leave scratches where you just want shine.

Now get together your tools and supplies.

Selecting the right cleaner is important. Remember that washing-up liquid is strictly for dishes. Used on a car, it can do more harm than good. The detergent can thin the vehicle's protective layer of wax or, if the finish is worn, it can actually scratch or further break down the paint.

You'll find **detergent-free car cleaners** at car supplies shops, such as *Halfords*. Avoid those that promise a shine, because they are likely to contain silicone, which can streak your paint and result in glare from shiny interior surfaces.

Mix the cleaner according to the label instructions for the exterior and in a more dilute mix for interior surfaces (1 drop per litre). Look for established brand names like *Autoglym, TurtleWax, Mer, Zymol* or a recognised own label, such as *Halfords*.

Selecting cleaning rags is a matter of personal choice, but a near-universal favourite is a piece of **100 per cent cotton towelling**. Towelling is very absorbent and grows softer with use and age. It is especially good for drying. Be sure to use a really old towel. New towels contain unstable dyes and silicone for sizing, which could leave unwanted silicone streaks on your car.

All-cotton T-shirts and **rags** are fine for interiors, but their weaves can be abrasive on your car's tender outside. And be careful when using sponges on the paint. Some, such as natural sea sponges, are notorious for hiding grit in their holes. Other options are **disposable wash mitts** filled with **car soap**, **microfibre towels** and **chamois cloths**. Chamois tends to cling, so use it only to push water across the car, not to dry. Never drag it flat across the finish – it will drag away wax.

When you machine wash your cleaning rags don't use fabric softener and dryer sheets. These products contain silicone, which causes streaking.

Using a garden hose for rinsing makes life a lot easier. If you don't have a hose at home, you can use the **wand** in a **coin-operated car wash**. Spray in a steady, medium flow, not a high-pressure blast, which can grind dirt granules into the paint. With a continuous, moderate stream, the water flows across the car's outer surface in sheets, gently washing away sand, salt, pollen, dirt and other debris as well as soap. The wheels are the exception – there, a strong blast works well.

When rinsing, spray in directions that water normally travels across or down the car, because that's the way the car is designed to slough off water. Otherwise, you may shoot water into body vents and other design features where water isn't meant to go.

Selecting a polish should be done with care. Made with fine abrasives, polishes are designed to lift light oxidation so you can see the true colour of the paint better. As their name implies, they brighten the finish. Read labels

carefully. Find a polish that indicates that it is 'safe for modern car finishes'. And always apply polish onto a clean car with a cool surface.

Selecting a wax is easy because a number of good brands are widely available. **Liquid waxes** are easiest to use. With a **paste wax**, it's easy to transfer grit into the original container – putting your finish at risk. Not only does wax give the paint its glossy sheen and sharpen the colour, but it also preserves the paint by helping it retain oils that reduce oxidation, the process that leads to rusting. It's also a layer between your paint and the world, a barrier to ultraviolet rays, pollutants, bird droppings, grime, bugs, tar and tree sap. If you live near the coast, rust can be a particular enemy. So you may want to wax more often, possibly every three months. And if your car is red, black or white, consider waxing more often, since these colours are more susceptible to acid rain and UV rays.

Be very careful with spray-on, wipe-off products that promise to help maintain that freshly waxed look between wax jobs. Many are alcohol-based, so they actually strip wax.

Clear the drain holes early in the car-washing process. Many people are astonished to learn that cars have drain holes that need occasional attention, but the life of your car is at stake. The drain holes are located under each bumper and at the bottom of each door panel. The rubber eyelets let out rainwater and melting snow that would otherwise leak down the outside of the bumpers, panels, and windows. If the holes are plugged with debris, the moisture gets trapped inside the body and can cause the vehicle to rust from the inside. Clear the holes by running a **cotton bud** into and across the opening. When you rinse the car, any build-up will drain out.

Clean the drain holes to prevent water from being trapped inside the car body which can cause the car to rust.

Start cleaning the car interior by **vacuuming** the seats and seat crevices (use the crevice attachment), then the floor mats and floor carpeting. If you don't have a driveway and are washing your car on the street or away from your house, you will need a **cordless hand-held vacuum**.

Cleaning floor mats is the next step after vacuuming. Take out the mats and, if they have carpet tops, simply vacuum. Hose down rubber mats. Fill a **bucket** with **water** and add two or three drops of **all-purpose cleaner**. Dip in a **stiff-bristled brush** and scrub. After scrubbing, rinse the mats until the runoff is clear. Let them air-dry.

Cleaning doorjambs By starting with the parts of the door you don't see when the doors are closed, you won't risk getting cleaner and wax on already-clean surfaces, such as your seats and carpet. Open the door wide and thoroughly clean around the door opening and the edges with a **soapy rag**. Afterward, take a **dry exterior-use rag** and wipe the inner door and sills dry. Dry all the painted surfaces, then polish and wax. (See Waxing on page 154.)

Cleaning carpets Scrub the carpets with a **stiff-bristled brush** and **carpet/upholstery cleaner**. (A household brand will do.) If you're using a **wet/dry vacuum**, don't be afraid to wet the carpet with a little water to loosen tough deposits of dirt before you scrub it. Then sweep up the water, loosened salt, soil and debris.

Cleaning seats Unless you often have children in your car, these will need only a quick once-over. With child passengers, you may want to turn to pages 58–59 and see how to remove chewing gum and food and drinks stains.

You can choose between using **upholstery cleaner** and a **soft-bristled brush**, **vinyl cleaner** and a **rag**, or **saddle soap** (for leather interiors) and a **dampened sponge**.

To remove pet hair from upholstery, wrap **wide masking** or **packing tape** around your hand and wipe with the tape.

For leather seats, make sure your rag or sponge is barely damp, because too much water will damage them. After cleaning the leather, apply a thin, even coat of **protective leather conditioner**, such as *Zymol Leather Cleaner*. Don't over-condition. Leather needs to be able to absorb moisture from the air.

Cleaning door panels is tricky because their surfaces have lots of crevices and, usually, electrical switches. After first wiping the panel with a **soapy rag**, dampen (don't get it sopping wet) an **old toothbrush** and a **thin cloth** and use the toothbrush to clean out crevices. Wrap the cloth around a **plastic picnic knife** to clean the electrical switches, repositioning the cloth as needed to keep soft fabric over the knife edge. Remember that a just-damp cloth won't drip into switches and cause them to fail or

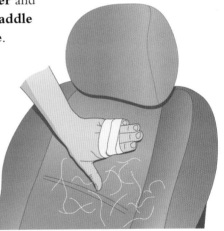

Thick tape wrapped around your hand makes short work of removing pet hairs from car upholstery.

To wax or not to wax?

Use a bead test to find out whether you're still getting good protection from your wax, regardless of your timetable for waxing. Rinse the entire car with the hose and notice how the water droplets bead up around the car. Tight, rounded beads mean things are looking good. If they are more than 10mm across or if the water stays on the surface in sheets, it's time to wax.

short-circuit. You can also use the same method for dials and switches on the dashboard. Wipe dry.

Cleaning window interiors Use a solution of **1 part white vinegar** to **8 parts water**, mixed in a **spray bottle**. Or use a **non-ammonia glass cleaner**. (Ammonia-based household glass cleaners and foam glass cleaners can dry out neighbouring plastic, rubber and vinyl.) You may hear hot water recommended for cleaning glass, but when the air temperature is low, the hot liquid may cause cracking.

Newspaper is an old favourite as a glass-cleaning wipe and is reputed to have a polishing effect. It may not be as effective as it used to be, as formulations used in printing newspapers have changed. Also, it's ridiculously messy, when a clean cloth does just as well. If you do use newspapers, be careful to not leave smudges on non-glass parts of the car. For no-streak drying, use a **low-lint cloth**, such as an old pillowcase. Finally, roll door windows down and clean the tops, where dirt and film tend to be thickest.

Cleaning the dashboard, steering column, centre console and other vinyl and plastic surfaces is the finishing touch for the interior. If they are dusty, first wipe them down with a **household dusting cloth**. A convenient new alternative are **non-woven disposable dusting cloths**, such as those made by *Spontex*. Use a small, **dry natural-bristle pastry brush** to dust hard-to-reach areas such as vents and dashboard corners.

Mix **1 part all-purpose household cleaner** – a supermarket own-brand is fine – with **8 parts water** in a **spray bottle**. Spray and wipe with a **clean cloth**. Use a damp, cloth-covered plastic knife on dashboard dials and switches. (See Cleaning door panels, above.) If there are any scratches on the clear plastic lenses on your dash, mask them by rubbing on **baby oil** or *WD-40*.

Add a finishing shine to the dashboard and other non-upholstered, nonglass surfaces. It will also help to prevent cracking and fading. *Williams F1* make a suitable **silicone-free protectant**.

Start cleaning the car's exterior by checking the finish and trim for insects, bird droppings and asphalt and tar. Deal with these first. Use a **soft dampened cloth** and even a **flattened finger** to prise off what you can. Then check individual stain shifter methods on pages 46–77.

Washing wheels and tyres is one activity where it's all right to blast the car with **water**, since it takes force to dislodge stubborn road grime. Use a **pressure nozzle** to hose out inside the wheel wells and give the tyres a cleaning blast. Mix **detergent-free car cleaner** with **water** in a **bucket** according to the package directions. Then scrub the wheels with the solution, using a **stiff-bristled brush** or a **rag**. A **soft-bristled toothbrush** will let you get at places where the scrubbing brush won't fit.

Remember that once you've used rags, brushes and car-wash solution on the wheels and tyres, you should not reuse these same dirty materials anywhere else on the car. They are ready for a hot machine wash – or just put them straight in the dustbin.

Washing the car body Start by using a **hose** to spray the car – working from the roof downward. With the first rinse, water will flow through the newly unplugged drain holes and wash away any residue from inside the doors and body. Mix **non-detergent car cleaner** with **water** in a bucket. Apply the solution with a **car-wash mitt** or a **soft rag**. Go for a mitt that's all wool or a wool-polyester blend – 100 per cent polyester is too rough for your paint.

When hosing dirt from wheels and tyres, do it on the grass if possible so the water soaks into the soil.

Never shampoo the entire car and then rinse, because that will give the cleaner time to air-dry and leave a film. Work your way around, soaping, rinsing and drying the metal and trim in sections no larger than you can reach without moving your feet (about 1m by 60cm). Work from the roof down, making sure your rag stays free of stones, tar and debris. Don't use a mitt that has fallen on the ground.

Keep **two buckets of car cleaner solution** on the go at one time. Either designate one for 'rough' or especially dirt-prone surfaces and the other for smooth, less debris-laden ones or use one bucket for your first soaping (the 'dirty' bucket) and the other for a second soaping (the 'clean' bucket). Segregate your rags accordingly.

Wash and dry painted metal gently. There's no sense in thinning its protective wax layer or making it uneven by rubbing too hard. For gentle drying, hold a **towel** at both ends and drape it over the wet surface. Drag it across the surface toward you. That way, you don't apply any potentially wax-stripping pressure, as you might when

Simple solutions

Setting up a clean getaway

Make it shady During cleaning, the sun is not your car's friend. Park in shade – but not directly under a tree.

Round up your supplies You don't want to have to drive a soapy car to the motor supply store because you forgot something.

Know your suds Dishwashing soap is for dishes. Buy a non-detergent car cleaner.

Bag a good rag With cotton rags, use soft, 100 per cent cotton, clean and free of any fabric softener or sizing. Old bath towels are perfect.

Rinse right Resist the impulse to blast away dirt and grime. Hosing with a moderate stream and constant flow of water creates a sheeting action that gently washes away debris and cleanser without scratching.

Don't be a drip Letting your car drip dry leads to water spotting and soap film. Work in sections, washing, rinsing, and drying as you go.

rubbing with the rag in your hand. Do two rounds of drying as well, to make sure you've done a thorough job.

Cleaning the trim is the next step. Spray vinyl and plastic parts with an **all-purpose household cleaner solution** (see Cleaning the dashboard, above) or use a **non-silicone vinyl cleaner** with a matt finish according to the label directions. Clean chrome with **chrome cleaner** according to label instructions. Use **fresh water** to rinse completely under any mouldings – debris and dirt can collect there, creating a layer that can trap condensation. Trapped moisture will eventually lead to rust.

Cleaning window exteriors is no different from cleaning their interiors. Just spray and wipe the glass with a **vinegar solution** or **non-ammonia cleaner**. (See Cleaning window interiors, above.) Use **low-lint cloths** for drying.

Once the car is clean, unless it's brand-new or you're sure the wax layer is holding up (see box on page 152), you may need to polish, wax and buff it.

Polishing removes surface paint that has oxidised. Use a **car polish** if your paint finish appears bright, not hazy, and follow label instructions. A visible haze on the paint indicates more oxidation damage than a polish can fix and means your car could benefit from a professional re-wax.

Waxing can be done with either a **liquid** or **paste wax**. Follow the label instructions to the letter. As noted earlier, it's easy to pick up grit with paste wax, so be careful how you handle the applicator. A favoured method for applying and removing wax is to use long, straight strokes that follow the same pattern that air takes as it moves around the car. This is because straight strokes don't leave behind the swirls in the finish that circular motions can. And if, by chance, you scratch the car, straight scratches are easier to remove. However, always read and follow label instructions for applying the product you're using. Again, work in sections. When your applicator or rag starts to drag as you pull it, flip it over or use a clean section. If the product instructions say to wait until the wax dries to a haze, do it – this gives the wax time to work and makes it easier to remove.

Keep wax away from plastic mouldings and rubber seals and trim, from which it will be next to impossible to remove once it dries.

There is no need to scrub as you apply or buff wax. The idea is to leave a good coat of wax behind. Even pressure, just using the weight of your arm is all that's needed.

For buffing use your **softest rags**. Do it in the same straight motions you used to wax. When your rag moves smoothly across the surface and the residue is gone, your hard work is complete.

Cassette players

If you have a cassette player – be it at home or in the car – chances are that it may now be losing its highs and lows. The audio problem may very well be caused by dust and grime combined with the oxide build-up that occurs when a tape moves through the player. You can improve the sound by cleaning the tape path.

To clean the tape path, you need to wipe over everything that the tape touches as it's played – the heads, tape guides, chrome pin and black rubber roller. Saturate three to four **cotton buds** with **methylated spirits** and thoroughly swab each area. The chrome heads should be wiped both vertically and horizontally. Keep cleaning until the final cotton swab comes away with no brown residue. Don't worry about black residue from the roller – that is from the rubber.

You can also buy **cassette cleaning tapes**, which generally don't clean as thoroughly as the cotton swab method but are a good alternative if you lack the careful finger work to get right into the tape deck.

Wipe the inside of the cassette player with cotton buds soaked in surgical spirit or methylated spirit.

To extend the life of cassettes, store them properly. Keep them out of extreme heat (that includes the back seat of your car or the dashboard in summer) and away from direct sunlight. Store them in their cases in the car's central console. Clean the player after every 75 hours or so of use and at least twice that often if some of your tapes are of poor quality.

See also **CD players & CDs** and **DVD players.**

CD players & CDs

When your CDs start skipping or the disc won't spin, there's a good chance the player's laser lens needs a quick shine. A clean machine will give a better sound, and regular maintenance will mean you won't miss a beat.

Cleaning the laser lens is inexpensive and simple on top-loading players and portable units. Front-loading players and carousel units require removing the player's cover and finding the lens. Often there are too many mechanisms in the way, and extensive disassembling should be left to the professionals. In those cases, you can attempt to clean the lens with a **cleaning disc**, available for under £5 at CD shops and on the internet.

The disc looks like a CD, but its shiny side has tiny brushes on it and as the disc spins it brushes the lens. However, the lens has to be able to 'see' before the disc can spin, so a really dusty laser lens often won't respond when a cleaning disc is inserted.

But if your player's laser is in plain view in a top-loading model, even the most inexperienced home mechanic can clean it. Before you begin, unplug the CD player. If it's battery-powered, make sure the unit is off. Then do the following:

1 Locate the laser lens, which is a round glass bubble about a quarter-inch in diameter. The slightest bit of dust can prevent the laser from 'reading' the CD.

2 Dip a **cotton swab** in **methylated spirits** and, wearing **plastic gloves**, squeeze out the excess into a **paper towel** so it doesn't drip.

3 Using a circular motion, gently rub the lens for 5 to 10 seconds. The lens will move a little, but that's not a problem.

4 Let it dry. Depending on how much alcohol was left on the lens, it will take 10 to 20 minutes to dry. The CD player won't turn until it has sufficiently dried out.

Cleaning your CDs from time to time is also important, not only so that they play without distortion but also to prevent dust on the CDs from clogging up the player's works. The quickest way is simply to use **CD wipes** – at around £3 for 12. But if you prefer, you can use a **CD**

cleaning cloth or just about any **lint free soft cloth** moistened with a little **methylated spirits**. Hold the CD by its outer edge in one hand while cleaning with the other. Wipe it from the centre to the outer edge, as though you were wiping the spokes of a wheel from hub to rim.

Proper storage of your CDs will go a long way toward extending their playing time. Store them in their cases, and inspect them periodically for dust and fingerprints, which can cause a tracking error. Keep your player and CDs out of direct sunlight.

One last tip If the player is brought directly from a cold location to a warm one, moisture may condense on the lens, which will prevent the unit from playing. If this happens, remove the CD and wait about an hour for the moisture to evaporate.

See also **Cassette players** and **DVD players.**

Ceilings

If you want to brighten the view overhead, take aim at your grubby ceiling. Ceilings attract airborne dirt, cigarette smoke and grease. Cleaning them is a project that's tempting to put off, since ceilings are hard to reach and awkward to clean. Whenever possible, use long-handled tools instead of balancing on a ladder or step stool.

Dusting the ceiling is sometimes all that's needed and, to do that, all you need is a **long-handled duster**. If you'd rather not take up storage space for an item you won't use that often, simply tie a **duster** onto the end of a **broom**. Or you can suck, rather than sweep up dust, using your **vacuum cleaner** with a **brush attachment**.

To clean a truly dirty ceiling you'll have to use water. First, do a little preparation work. Lay down **dust sheets** or **newspapers** to protect furniture, electronic equipment and floors. Wear **safety goggles** or other eye protection, because you're likely to dislodge small particles you can't really see coming at you. You should also wear **rubber gloves** and wearing **sweat bands** designed for sport on your wrists will stop dirty water dripping up your arms as you work.

Simple solutions

Face up to a drippy situation

If you use liquid cleaners to clean your ceiling, there's a good chance that some of that liquid will come dribbling down your arm onto your clothes or into your face.

Wear rubber gloves and fold the ends up into cuffs, so anything that drips from your hands stays in the glove. Or if you really, really hate drips, wrap a child's thick nylon headband (the stretchy sort they wear for ballet and school) round your wrists twice, to catch all drips.

To wash the ceiling, use a **sponge mop with an extender handle** (the one you use for the kitchen floor). Working upside down from your usual floor cleaning isn't that natural a thing to do, so you'll have to be careful to apply even pressure and get an even distribution of the cleaning product so it won't streak. Or you can use a **dry foam sponge**, and stand on a **stepladder**. Take care to follow basic safety rules, such as placing the ladder securely on a level surface to prevent tipping and never standing on the top step. Don't lean over too far. Break the ceiling into imaginary small squares and get off and move the stepladder each time you go to start a new 'square'.

For painted ceilings, whether they're covered with emulsion or gloss paint, a **general-purpose cleaner**, such as *Flash*, works well. Or use a concentrated one, like *Zoflora*, mixing both to packet instructions. Dip your **sponge** in the solution, wring out the excess and wipe the dirty area. Rinsing is necessary only if the ceiling is heavily soiled, but whether or not you rinse, you'll need to wipe away the excess moisture with a dry towel to prevent bead marks.

Artex ceilings and those that have a rough surface are best kept dry. So keep running over it with the **vacuum cleaner** and the **soft brush attachment**.

Ceiling tiles

An easy remedy for dirty acoustical ceiling tiles is hydrogen peroxide, an environmentally friendly product that contains powerful oxidising agents.

To clean vinyl-coated ceiling tiles use **3 per cent hydrogen peroxide solution**. Wear **goggles** to keep debris and the peroxide mist out of your eyes. Mix about **15ml of hydrogen peroxide** in **500ml water** and pour it into a **spray bottle**. Peroxide, a mild bleach, will whiten the tiles. Best of all, no rubbing is required – simply spray the mixture on the tiles, applying it evenly and let it air-dry.

To clean non-coated ceiling tiles – which generally aren't washable – wipe with a **just damp sponge**, then dry thoroughly by re-wiping with a **fresh sponge** in an even, sweeping motion.

Ceramics

Handmade ceramics used only for display run the greatest risk of being damaged during handling. So use both hands when lifting and support the item from its base. Wearing a clean pair of cotton gloves makes this easier: also, the hand that is holding your object won't make it any greasier with natural dirt that is always present on hands.

You should only have to dust a decorative ceramic item very occasionally.

Cleaning a ceramic item

• **Machine-made, functional ceramic bowls** and other pieces that do regular kitchen duty can be cleaned in the **dishwasher**.
• **Handmade ceramics** that are soiled should be cleaned by hand, using a **soft cloth**, **mild washing-up liquid** and **water**. Don't soak the item in water, which can lead to staining, especially if there are small cracks. Instead, dampen a **cloth** with **soapy water**, wipe away the dirt, rinse with a **clean, damp cloth**, and let the piece air-dry in a **drainer** to avoid the risk of it slipping through your fingers as you dry.

To protect decorative ceramics

on display in your home, use a dab of *Blu Tack* under your item to hold it firmly, yet invisibly in place. If someone bumps into the table where it's displayed – or your pet brushes up against it – it won't go tumbling. The *Blu Tack* can be easily removed, yet will hold firmly enough that you have to twist the object to remove it.

Dusting mitts are idea for gently dusting and cleaning the surface of smooth ceramic items.

Ceramic tiles

The beauty of ceramic tiles, besides their attractive appearance, is their durability and low maintenance. An alcohol-and-water solution is usually all that's needed to keep ceramic tiles shining, assuming that they were properly sealed during installation.

If you're are not sure of this – perhaps with ageing, hand-fired tiles, play safe and use just a **dampened sponge**. Water and chemicals will easily penetrate unsealed areas. You could then repaint the tiles, using a primer, then a top coat.

On all kinds of tiles, overly harsh cleaners will do more damage than anything else, because the wrong cleaners can strip away the sealant that protects them.

Cleaning ceramic tile floors regularly is important so that tracked-in dirt isn't able to build up and scratch through the protective sealant. Begin by removing loose dirt using a **vacuum cleaner**, a **broom**, or an **oil-free dust mop**. Then add an **all-purpose floor cleaner** – a supermarket own label brand is fine. Avoid products that contain natural waxes – you don't want to slip up later. The waxes can penetrate into the grout (the substance in the seams between the tiles) and cause it to discolour.

Two rinses with **clean water** are recommended, because you need to remove any chemicals that could break down the sealant. When the water rinses clean, dry the floor with a **clean, soft cloth**.

Cleaning ceramic wall tiles doesn't need to be done as frequently as cleaning a tile floor, but it's a good idea to wipe them down once or twice a month using **all-purpose cleaner**, or, if you're in the bathroom, the same **bathroom cleaning mousse** that you use on the sinks and bath. Areas such as the shower surround and the sink backsplash which collect soap scum and spatters, may need more frequent attention, especially in a large household.

Gunning for the grimiest grout

For really grimy grout that stubbornly resists standard cleaning methods, try a solution of chlorine bleach and water. Make sure the area you're working in is well ventilated and wear rubber gloves. Then mix together 40ml of bleach and 2 litres of water in a bucket. Using a toothbrush or nylon scrubbing brush, scrub the dirty areas, then let the solution soak for 10 to 20 minutes before rinsing with clean water. Rinse a second time – again with clean water, not the water you used in the first rinse – and wipe the area dry with a clean cloth.

After the grout has dried thoroughly, apply a silicone sealer (available at DIY stores) to reduce future maintenance. Grout manufacturers generally recommend resealing grout joints twice a year to prevent staining, but of course it is in their interests to do so. Good care means your grout should look good for years, without constant renewal.

Cleaning the grout between tiles especially floor tiles, is occasionally necessary. Mix together **30ml of vinegar** with **3 litres of water** and scrub the grout with a **toothbrush** or **nylon scrubbing pad**. Don't use steel wool, because it can scratch the finish. If the grout is really dirty, see the box on page 160.

See also **Baths & sinks.**

Chandeliers

It's only when they are sparkling clean that expensive, elegant chandeliers can be told apart from cheap imitations. You can buy the finest crystal in the world, but if it gets dirty, it's indistinguishable from cheap crystal. So if you are fortunate enough to have a fine example, clean it up and show it off.

A chandelier should be cleaned whenever it looks dusty, milky or cloudy. There are several methods to restore a chandelier's dazzle, depending on how dingy it has become. But if you maintain it regularly – say, a couple of times a year – you probably won't have to remove all the crystals and wash them by hand.

If a chandelier is not too dirty set up a **stepladder** in one or two spots where you can easily reach the chandelier without stretching and use one of these two methods to clean the crystals:

1 Make sure the switch is off, then lightly dampen a **chamois cloth** with a little **water** and wipe down each crystal while it is still attached to the chandelier frame. To clean the chandelier frame itself, wipe it with a **dry cloth**.
2 The two-glove method is also popular. Buy a pair of **white cotton gloves**, available in supermarkets and DIY stores, and dampen one glove with a **glass cleaner**, such as *Windolene*. Spray the cleaner onto the glove – never directly onto the chandelier – massage each crystal with the damp glove and then wipe it immediately with the dry glove.

If a chandelier is really dirty, you'll have to take down the crystals and wash them by hand – there are no dishwasher shortcuts. Start by climbing your **stepladder**

Expert advice

Completing the crystal maze
Before you start removing dusty chandelier crystals for hand washing, make absolutely sure you know how to put the chandelier back together again.

Either clean a small section at a time or use the diagram that came with the chandelier. If the diagram is long lost, whip out a digital camera and take a photo of the intact chandelier or do a drawing before taking it apart.

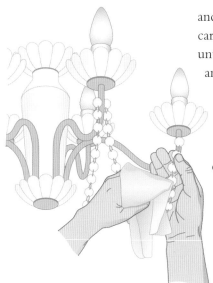

To remove surface dirt, wipe each crystal gently with a chamois dampened with water.

and removing the bulbs and setting them aside. Then carefully remove the crystals. Run **warm water** in a **bowl** until it's about a quarter full. Add **30ml of white vinegar** and **1 drop of washing-up liquid**. The combination will remove any grease or residue on the glass but will minimise the amount of suds created, which are hard to rinse off.

Place a **folded towel** in the bottom of the sink – you don't want to break a crystal if it slips through your grasp. Wipe each crystal with your hands, then individually rinse each one under **running water** and dry with a **soft cloth**. If you don't dry them properly you'll end up with unsightly water spots.

Finally, wipe the light bulbs with a **damp sponge**, dry them with a **cloth**, return them to their sockets – and enjoy the light show.

Chimneys

Where there's fire, there's smoke – and when it's in your fireplace, you'll eventually have a chimney that needs a clean sweep. Sooty chimneys can lead to chimney fires, which occur when creosote, a highly combustible residue created by burning wood, ignites. The resulting flames burn many times hotter than the wood in your fireplace and could set your home on fire.

To prevent such disasters, you should have your chimney cleaned regularly by a professional chimney sweep (find one using *Yellow Pages* or *www.yell.co.uk*). Cleaning chimneys is difficult, dangerous work that requires special brushes and equipment tailored to fit the precise measurements of your fireplace flue. However, you can and should clean out the ashes in your fireplace when they start piling up.

Shovel the ashes into a **metal container with a tight lid** – never use a paper bag – and store it away from any combustible materials (including a wooden deck) before final disposal. There's no need to shovel up every last ash, except when you're doing a clear up after the last fire of winter. Get the very last ashes up by just damping your shovel, so that they stick onto it.

We would not recommend that you ever try to inspect a chimney yourself. Being on the roof is best left to experts.

To cut down on creosote build-up, burn wood that's been dried for six months to a year. Freshly-cut wood has a higher moisture content than seasoned wood, which results in a smokier fire. Hardwoods such as oak, maple, elm and ash burn more slowly and with a steadier flame than softwoods such as spruce and pine, which cause faster creosote build-up.

See also **Fireplaces** and **Fireplace screens & tools.**

China

The term 'fine china' evokes images of fragile delicacy, but most china manufactured today is made to be functional as well as elegant. So most china made in the past 25 years is dishwasher safe and says so explicitly on the bottom of the piece.

A notable exception is fine china with a band made of a precious metal such as platinum or gold. Although you'll probably have few problems, one day the high heat of the dishwasher's drying cycle may cause the metal to soften and small pieces become dislodged. Hand washing is also necessary for antique or hand-painted china. The force and heat of the dishwasher is too much for fragile pieces.

Line the sink with a tea towel or rubber mat and use a soft cloth when washing delicate china.

Washing china in the dishwasher does require a little extra care. Load the pieces carefully so they won't bump into each other and chip. Make sure aluminium utensils and lightweight foil containers don't rub against dishes during the wash cycle, because that can create black or grey marks.

To hand-wash antique or hand-painted china, start by lining the bottom of the sink with a **rubber mat** or **towel**. Half-fill the sink with **warm water** and a **mild washing-up liquid**. To prevent chipping, take care not to

Give your china a face-lift Don't put up with stained or finely cracked china. Try these tips instead.

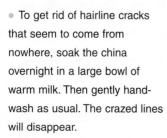

- To get rid of hairline cracks that seem to come from nowhere, soak the china overnight in a large bowl of warm milk. Then gently hand-wash as usual. The crazed lines will disappear.
- To get rid of black specks, sprinkle a little baking soda on a damp cloth and rub the spot. Or try some non-gel toothpaste on a plastic scouring pad.

- To lift tea stains from cups, mix 2 tablespoons of chlorine bleach in a litre of water. Soak the cup in the solution for no more than two minutes and rinse immediately.
- Hard water sometimes causes a film to develop on china. To remove it, fill a bowl with 150ml of chlorine bleach and place it in the lower rack of the dishwasher. Load your china into the washer and run it up to the dry cycle (don't add any dishwasher powder – you already have the bleach), then turn it off.

Empty the bowl, rinse it out, pour in 300ml of white vinegar, and return it to the dishwasher. Turn the dishwasher back on and let it run through the rest of the cycle.

overload the sink with dishes. Remove any rings and jewellery to prevent scratching the china and, for the same reason, wash cutlery separately. Use a **soft cloth** or **sponge** for cleaning.

Here are some more tips:

• Wash or soak the items as soon after dining as possible, to prevent the problem of dried-on food and staining. Acidic foods such as mayonnaise and eggs can damage the glaze if left on for long periods.
• To remove dried food, soak the china in a **bowl of sudsy water** and then scrub gently with a **nylon scouring pad**. Never use a metal pad, and avoid steel wool and gritty cleansers as well.

• Be careful when placing the dishes to dry to prevent scratches and chips. A **drying rack** means two dishes won't have to touch.

Wash china figurines and sculptures by hand using **water** with just a few drops of **washing–up liquid**. Hand-dry with a **soft cloth**. If the piece has a wooden base, don't let the wood get wet.

Christmas decorations

Good storage is the key here – 11 months is a long time for paper, plastics, metal and glass to sit in a box. If your storage room is damp, many won't survive. So when you box up on January 5 each year, give careful thought to where everything is going to go. The attic is fine, if it's dry. Ideally, you should not put anything away dirty. But if you're pressed for time, concentrate on providing secure, safe storage. Removing the odd piece of *Blu Tack* or mending a fallen angel can wait until next December.

To clean painted ornaments, separate them so you can pick them up one at a time by their hangers. Lightly dust each ornament with a **feather duster**. Try not to handle the ornaments, since the oils in your hands can damage the paint. If you need to touch the ornament, wear **rubber gloves** (a must if your ornament is old and fragile).

To clean glass ornaments, spray **ordinary glass cleaner** onto a **soft cloth** and wipe gently.

To clean porcelain or crystal ornaments, use a **feather duster**, brushing across the surface in a downward motion. Don't handle crystal decorations unless you wear gloves. A **buffing jewellery cloth** is also fine for use on crystal. Simply wipe over the surface with the cloth.

To clean resin and wood ornaments, a **soft cotton cloth** works well. Again, just wipe across the surface of each piece.

Sterling silver and gold-plated ornaments will come clean when wiped with a **jewellery polishing cloth**. Apply the cloth in circular motions to remove dust, grime and fingerprints.

Cleaning glittery ornaments is a tricky business. Try using a **feather duster** on one area. If a lot of glitter comes off, it may be best to leave the decoration alone.

Cleaning leaf garlands Use a **hairdryer** on a low setting to get dust out of wicker rings. They may fall apart if you try the more usual method of giving them a shake.

Storing your clean ornaments properly will ensure they will be sparkling, dust free and ready to hang the next year. Here are some tips:

• Store ornaments in a **box** that is large enough to be useful, but not so big that it becomes too heavy to carry safely. Aim for around 60 by 90cm.

• Place a thick layer of **crunched-up tissue paper** (use only acid-free paper) in the bottom of the container.

• Put the more sturdy ornaments on the bottom and the delicate ones on top. Don't use more than two layers. Try to offset the top layer so that they don't sit directly on top of ornaments below. Don't pack the ornaments tightly, because they may break.

• Wrap each ornament individually with **one layer of tissue paper**.

• Lay a full layer of ornaments on top of the crunched-up tissue paper.

• Lay one or two layers of **flat tissue paper** on top of the first layer of ornaments.

• Place a new layer of wrapped ornaments on top of the tissue paper over the previous layer of ornaments.

• Store your container of ornaments in a cool, dry, out-of-the-way place.

Chrome

Chrome is all around us: old car bumpers are plated with it, as are toasters, electric frying pans, appliance handles, showerheads, metal shower frames and taps. Since chrome is usually plated onto another metal, be gentle when you clean it or you can scrub it right off. And don't get abrasive with chrome. Cleaners with 'scratch' in them can indelibly mar the surface.

When cleaning chrome, remember never to wash removable chrome items from the kitchen in greasy dish water. If you do, the next time the items get hot during cooking, the grease is likely to burn on. Trying to remove burnt-on grease is a thankless task.

1 To begin with, use **washing-up liquid** in **warm water** first, applied with an **old toothbrush** to work into cracks and crevices. Rinse with **water** and polish to a shine with a **soft cloth**.

2 If that doesn't do the trick, use **bicarbonate of soda** sprinkled onto a **damp sponge** or **cloth**. Let the bicarbonate of soda sit on the chrome for an hour, then

rinse with **warm water**. Then dry it off and buff to a shine with another cloth.

3 Or rub down chrome with **undiluted cider vinegar** or **white vinegar** – no need to rinse. **Ammonia** can also be used – but rinse it off with water and dry completely.

Here are some other tricks for cleaning chrome:
• **Chrome oven rings** often get grimy and sticky. To shine them up, rub with a paste made from **vinegar** and **cream of tartar**.
• If a plastic bread wrapper has melted over your chrome toaster or toaster oven, dab **acetone** or **nail polish remover** on the melted mess, then buff with a **soft cloth**. Keep the remover well away from plastic parts.
• Rub a chrome surface with **half a lemon** dipped lightly in **salt**. Or use **white vinegar** and **salt** on a **soft cloth**. Rinse well with **water** and buff to brilliance with a **dry cloth** or **paper towel**.
• For chrome trim on taps and kitchen appliances, apply **baby oil** with a **soft cloth** and polish to restore lustre. If hard water has left deposits on taps, use a product like *Flash Bathroom Spray*, which will help to shift limescale.
• To rid chrome of rust spots, especially on car trim and bumpers, crumple **foil** into a wad and rub hard on the shiny side. This technique also works wonders on golf club shafts.

Polish off rust spots on chrome with a ball of crumpled-up aluminium foil.

Clocks

When cleaning wind-up clocks, what you don't do is as important as what you do. The most important aspect of cleaning a mantelpiece, wall, grandfather or other nice mechanical clock is careful maintenance of the internal mechanism to prevent wear and tear.

To take care of the inner workings it's best to entrust your clock to an expert to have it cleaned and oiled. Clocks are too easy to damage if you do it yourself. Get the mechanism serviced every two to three years. Remember that time may be your worst enemy, but dirt in any timepiece comes in a close second.

Cleaning and oiling the inner workings of a clock is possible if you're careful. The first step is to wipe the inner workings with a **dry, soft cloth** to get rid of the worst of

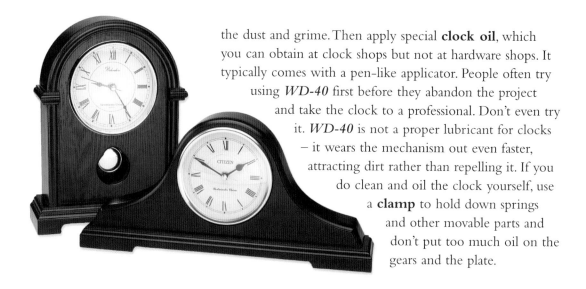

the dust and grime. Then apply special **clock oil**, which you can obtain at clock shops but not at hardware shops. It typically comes with a pen-like applicator. People often try using *WD-40* first before they abandon the project and take the clock to a professional. Don't even try it. *WD-40* is not a proper lubricant for clocks – it wears the mechanism out even faster, attracting dirt rather than repelling it. If you do clean and oil the clock yourself, use a **clamp** to hold down springs and other movable parts and don't put too much oil on the gears and the plate.

Cleaning the exterior of a wooden clock is done as you would do with any other fine piece of furniture. Use a **furniture oil** to feed the wood – **lemon oil** works well and smells pleasant. To dust a clock case, use a **dust remover**, such as *Lemon Pledge*, sprayed onto a **soft cloth**, not on the clock itself.

Wipe the piece covering the face – whether it is clear plastic, glass or acrylic – with a **clean, soft cloth**. If you know the cover is glass, you can use a window cleaner, such as *Windolene*, but never spray it directly on the clock. Spray it on the cloth and wipe very gently, so that there is no chance of excess liquid getting onto the clock face.

Coffee grinders

Wake up and smell the coffee. Whatever you do when cleaning out an electric coffee grinder, don't take it swimming. Immersion in water can ruin your grinder.

Grinding uncooked white rice will give a grinder a clean.

Clean a coffee grinder after every use. Unplug the unit. Brush out the grinder with a **pastry brush**, **old toothbrush** or **special coffee grounds brush**, sold at gourmet kitchen stores and some coffee shops. This doesn't have to be a big job – just make sure you leave the stainless steel inside the grinder shiny, so that tomorrow's batch of beans won't be sullied by stale grounds from yesterday's pot. Wash the plastic lid with a **sponge** in **washing-up liquid** and **warm water**; rinse and dry with a **soft cloth**.

Two more methods you can try:

1 Dampen a **paper towel** and swab the inside.

2 Run a small handful of **uncooked white rice** through the coffee grinder, especially if you use it for grinding anything other than coffee beans and need to totally remove traces of say, nuts, before you enjoy your next drink. Most coffee experts advise against using your machine for grinding dry spices, by the way, since the smells from grinding ingredients such as cinnamon sticks and dried basil are nearly impossible to get out.

Coffee makers

The harder the water, the more deposits it will form on the inside of your coffee maker. To keep your coffee maker perking along, clean it at least once a month – if you use the maker every day – to rid it of this whitish scale, or every two months if you brew a pot less often.

Failing to clean your coffee maker's inner workings will lengthen heating and brewing time and will adversely affect the taste and aroma of your coffee. Always check your owner's manual before embarking on any of the following cleaning methods. In general, no electric coffee maker should be immersed in water.

To clean an electric drip coffee maker

• Fill the water reservoir, half with **cold water** and half with **white vinegar**. Place a **clean paper filter** in the basket. Run the coffee maker through its entire cycle. Repeat the brewing cycle two more times, using **plain water** each time to flush out the remaining grains.

• Fill the reservoir with **hot water** and add a **denture tablet**. Run the machine through its complete brewing cycle, and then run it once more using **plain water**.

• Wash the coffee carafe in **hot water** with **washing–up liquid** and rinse with water. Then remove any other removable parts and do the same. You can wash these pieces in the top rack of the **dishwasher**, but their colours may fade. If you do, buff them with a **soft, dry cloth**.

Cleaning a home espresso machine mainly

involves keeping the steam wand and froth head clear. Get into the habit of turning off the machine, removing the

Expert advice

Brew your own cleaning solution

Starbucks coffee expert Chris Gimbl suggests brewing your own coffee maker cleaning solution. He uses lemon juice instead of white vinegar because the smell is more pleasant.

Fill the reservoir half full with water, then to the top with pulp-free lemon juice. Use a ready-to-use juice, such as *Jif*, to save time.

Run the coffee maker through its entire cycle. Discard the solution in the coffee pot and then run the brew cycle two or three more times with plain water until you don't smell lemon anymore. Wash all removable parts in hot, sudsy water, then rinse and dry.

froth head, then rinsing it under **warm water** every time you use your machine. Wipe the steam wand with a **damp cloth**. Turn the power back on and set the selector control to the steam position briefly. The shot of heat will clear any milk remaining in the steam wand. Every so often, run **water** through the unit with the filter in place, but with no coffee. If the filter holes do get blocked, use a **nylon washing-up brush** to dislodge tiny, stuck pieces of coffee.

Coins

If you are thinking of cleaning a coin you suspect might be valuable – don't. Cleaning coins at home is not a good idea if you think they may be worth something. On the other hand, if you don't like grubby spare change dirtying your pocket or your children want to make their piggy bank collection sparkling, there's no reason not to wash it.

To clean a valuable coin – or just one that you think could be valuable – take it to a professional coin dealer or conservator for a careful face-lift that will remove normal wear and tear. A coin spruced up by an amateur develops an oddly dull, sometimes scoured look, rather than bearing the blush of normal oxidation and handling.

To clean ordinary coins, give them a warm wash in a **lidded jar** that's half full with **warm water** and one or two drops of **washing-up liquid**. Check the lid is on tight, then shake. Rinse with running water and pat dry with **paper towels** or a **clean rag**. Never use abrasives either, as they'll scratch the surface.

Combs

To clean any comb, first remove any hair still clinging to the teeth. Then disinfect it in a bowl of warm water with a generous dollop of medicated shampoo. Rinse in clear water. If you want something more potent, add one cup of *Dettol* or a similar disinfectant, to a basin of warm water.

Submerge the comb in the liquid and soak for 10 minutes. Use a **small, stiff-bristled fingernail brush** or **old toothbrush** to loosen up hair oils and grime clinging to the teeth. If you're still concerned about your comb, the best way to disinfect it is to rub the teeth with a **cotton ball** saturated in neat *Dettol* (wear gloves to do this). Air dry, then rinse thoroughly before using.

To clean a baby's comb, wash it in the baby's **bath-water**. Alternatively, swish it in a solution of **1 teaspoon bicarbonate of soda** dissolved in a basin of **warm water**. Rinse with **fresh water** and air-dry.

To clean a fine-toothed metal comb used to rid a child's hair of lice and their nits or eggs, you need to take extra care. Here are three solutions:
• Soak the comb in a solution of **1 part chlorine bleach** to **9 parts water** for 15 minutes, rinse and air-dry. (If you don't dry it thoroughly, a metal comb will rust.)
• Soak the comb in **hot water** (at least 60°C) for 5 minutes.
• Seal combs in a **plastic bag** for two weeks.

Compact grills

Although the grills named after boxer George Foreman are the best known, there are several makes of compact grills – but the cleaning methods apply to all of them. Make sure the unit is unplugged before you start. The grilling surface needs the most thorough cleaning and it's easiest to do when still slightly warm, before food particles harden.

If the grilling surface is not removable, don't immerse the unit in water. (Some compact grills have parts that can be safely cleaned in the dishwasher.) Use the **plastic cleaning spatula** that comes with your unit to scrape off charred food particles from the grilling surface and into the drip tray. Once you have dispensed with the larger bits of food, wipe the ribbed grilling surface with a **paper towel** to take off any major grease. You can then dispose of this in the rubbish bin. If you use a sponge, the grease is more likely to end up down the sink resulting in a possible blockage. Next, take a **damp sponge** or **cloth** – not a wet one. To tackle especially sticky stuff, put a little **washing-up liquid** on the sponge. Rinse the sponge frequently, since it will get grimy quickly. Follow the sponging step with a few swipes of a **damp cloth** – again not a wet one – to get rid of as much moisture as possible. Then deal with the plastic drip tray. Again, remove any serious grease with **paper towels**, then use **washing–up liquid** and a **wet sponge**.

To clean the outside of an electric grill, first remove the grilling surface (if it's removable) and leave it out while you clean the other surfaces. A quick wipe of the exterior with a **damp sponge** will take care of most grease splatters. As an alternative, clean the outside casing with a **waterless hand cleaner**, such as *Dettox*. First, clean up surface dirt with **dry paper towels** and then apply a little of the hand cleaner to a **clean paper towel**, rubbing the exterior in small circular motions.

Let the cleaned grill air-dry or, if you need to accelerate the drying process, use a **hair dryer** on a low setting. Make sure the grill is perfectly dry before you plug it in again.

Computers

Computers collect more than just dust, grimy fingerprints, crumbs, hair, fingernail clippings and other unidentified miniature objects. We've heard reports that they have been home for biscuits, Batman action figures, spiders' nests and, worst of all, bits of a cheeseburger.

A computer can be given a quick once-over with a **vacuum** or **dust cloth** as part of your regular cleaning procedure. But it's a good idea to give it a more thorough cleaning occasionally. Once every three months is sufficient, although you should clean the screen every month or so. First, turn off and unplug.

To clean the screen of a traditional tube monitor, dust it with a **clean cloth** or a **facial tissue**. To remove fingerprints, wipe with a slightly **damp cloth**. Special wipes for cleaning PCs, sold at office supply stores, may be used on the screen, but they sometimes leave a soapy film. Try a **glass cleaner** instead, sprayed very, very lightly on a cloth and then wiped on the screen. Avoid ammonia-based cleaners, because they may leave unsightly streaks.

To clean a new flat screen monitor, you need to use special care as the screen is less robust and can scratch easily. This also applies to the screen on a laptop. First

Watch out

• Don't use ordinary household spray cleaners on your keyboard. If the liquid gets under the keys, it can damage the keyboard by shorting the contacts under the keys.

• If you have a new flat LCD monitor – or a laptop – never use products containing acetone, ethyl alcohol, toluene, ethyl acid, ammonia or methyl chloride to clean the screen. They can damage it.

unplug the power supply, and then lightly dampen a **clean, soft, lint-free cloth** (no paper towels or facial tissues) with water. Wipe the screen gently with a back-and-forth-motion, never in a circle. Wipe the display case gently with a **non-abrasive, soft, dry cloth** to pick up dust. And take these precautions to prolong the life of your flat screen – never tap or touch the screen with your pen, finger or other object. And don't put sticky notes on your screen.

To clean the keyboard, which is a magnet for all sorts of dirt, first turn it upside down over a wastebasket and give it a good shake. Most crumbs and dust will fall right out. Then **vacuum** it with your **brush attachment**. To clean the keys, rub them and the surrounding plastic with a **microfibre cloth**. Or purchase a **special keyboard cleaner-degreaser**, sold at electronics stores.

Using a can of **compressed air**, available at camera shops, blast away hair, crumbs and dust from between the keys. Rubbing keys with a **fabric softener sheet** will keep dust-attracting static at bay.

To clean the mouse, unscrew the mouse-ball cover on the bottom and take out the ball. Wipe it down with **methylated spirits**, available at paint stores, on a **soft cloth**. Remove any dust or fluff inside the mouse-ball socket with your finger. Then, with a **cotton bud** dipped in **methylated spirits**, clean the three rollers the ball touches inside the socket.

To clean inside the computer, you can also use **compressed air**. But be aware – opening up your computer could invalidate your warranty. Don't touch anything. To open an upright computer, unscrew one side of the case. One side is usually held by screws with knurled heads that you can turn by hand, but on some models you may need to use a screwdriver.

Keep your fingers away from cards, cords and other parts. And be sure the compressed air wand is at least 12cm from the machine. Blow air into the power supply box (that is where the power cord enters) and the fan at the back of the case. Then blast a little air into the CD and floppy disk drives. Before replacing the side, wipe it with a **damp cloth**. Let it dry before putting it back on.

To clean computer equipment exteriors, simply wipe the outside surfaces with an **all-purpose cleaner,**

Cotton buds soaked in methylated spirits are ideal for cleaning the rollers inside your mouse.

sprayed on a **soft cloth**. Dust can collect in ports where you attach cables. Use the **compressed air wand** to blow the ports clean. Or give them a wipe with one end of a **cotton bud**.

To clean the printer, open the case and use **compressed air** to blow away any dust.

If you spot a toner spill in a laser printer, don't use compressed air, because toner can be toxic. Instead, wipe it up carefully with **paper towels**. Avoid getting toner on your hands or clothes because it's hard to remove.

To clean the glass bed of your scanner, use **mild soap** or an **ordinary glass cleaner without ammonia**. (Ammonia cleaners, unless they're completely wiped off, leave a film that could make scanned documents look oily or speckled.) Spray the glass cleaner onto a **soft cloth** rather than squirting it on the glass itself. If there's a metal ruler scale along the edge of the glass, avoid getting it wet. That goes for the glue holding it down, too. Never use paper towels on your scanner. Even the more expensive types can make fine scratches on optical surfaces. Use **soft, lint-free cloths** instead. An **old T-shirt** is perfect.

Concrete

Your first step is to work out what caused the stain and then act swiftly and appropriately. The longer an untreated stain stays on concrete, the more likely it is to seep in and become part of the whole. Methods for cleaning concrete vary, but cleaning up the garage floor, patio, walkway, driveway or other concrete is an essential part of regular home maintenance.

Clean concrete at least once a year Protect adjacent glass, metal, wood, plants or other decorative materials with a **tarpaulin** or a large piece of **old plastic** – the wrapper from a new bed, or an old shower curtain are both perfect. Test the method in an obscure spot to make sure it works. Never use a metallic brush on concrete, as metallic fibres can get trapped and rust.

• If concrete is old and crumbly, brush it lightly with a **soft brush**. If that doesn't work, move on to **warm water** and mild detergent, adding **white vinegar** to the water if soil and stains persist.

• Wet the concrete with **warm water** and scrub with a **soft, non-metallic brush**. Wash off the concrete with a **garden hose** fitted with a **high-pressure nozzle** and let it dry.

• If that isn't enough, add **1 measure of non-biological washing powder** to a pail of **warm water** and scrub again.

• Or use a **biological detergent**, mixed with **water** and **20ml of ammonia**, applied with a **stiff nylon brush**.

• Rent a **pressure-washing machine** to squirt off dirt that's not ground into the concrete.

Only use non-metallic brushes to scrub stains off concrete.

To remove serious stains, such as tyre marks, grease, oil and other stubborn materials, you will have to get aggressive. For fresh grease stains, first sprinkle **dry cement**, **cat litter** or **sand** on the spot, letting it sit for an hour to absorb at least some of the grease. Then sweep it up with a **broom** and **dustpan**. For more difficult grease spots, use a **commercial degreaser**, following label instructions.

Contact lenses

Always follow your optician's advice on cleaning lenses. Most suggest that you don't casually switch solutions, but stick to those recommended on your last appointment. Wear disposables and you can skip this section of course – just throw lenses out at night and reach for a new pair next day. But if you wear soft fortnightly, monthly or longer-wear lenses, cleaning is crucial.

Here are a few basic guidelines:
• Clean and disinfect your lenses once a day. Always use fresh solution to clean and store your lenses.
• Always wash and rinse your hands thoroughly before handling the lenses. This is especially so if you've been eating spicy finger foods.
• Don't use perfumed soaps or scented hand cream. Dry your hands with a clean, lint-free towel.
• Put in the plug in your sink, or at least cover the plughole with a flannel when putting them in.
• Never use water as a substitute for the store-bought lens

A special lens holder is the cleanest and safest place to store your contacts.

care system your eye care expert recommends. Water can carry a micro–organism (Acanthamoeba) that can cause serious eye infections.

• Clean your accessories (lens case, cleaning/disinfecting containers, vials for enzymatic cleaners and the like) after each use exactly as the directions advise. Typically, this involves cleaning, rinsing and air-drying.

• Throw out your lenses once a month or as often as is recommended, to reduce the chance of infection.

Get into the habit of always handling your right lens first to avoid confusion. Most modern solutions are now so stream-lined that all you have to do is put your lenses in the case, pour in the solution then open up the next day. So no rubbing or exact timing is required.

Two other important points to keep in mind are these:

• Soft lenses pick up protein deposits more readily than gas permeable types do. If your lenses start to feel grainy or your vision becomes clouded, chances are you need to use an **enzymatic cleaner** daily or weekly, according to package directions.

• Some people have allergic reactions to contact lens solutions. About 10 per cent of people are allergic to thimerosal, a preservative sometimes used in saline lens solutions. If you hit a problem with one solution, ask your optician to recommend another.

Cooler boxes

Ideally, you should clean your cooler after each use. The method for cleaning depends a lot on what you've had in it. *Diet Cokes* on ice? Easy. Just rinse it out with water. If you've had a full picnic, with meat and other foodstuffs, you're going to have to do a thorough clean.

To clean a large, rigid plastic cooler pour a couple of drops of **washing–up liquid** onto a **sponge**, then clean thoroughly. Swish out with **clean water**, and then turn the cooler upside down, so that the water drains out quickly.

To disinfect a cool box – if you've been carrying raw meat in it, for example – mix **5ml of bleach** in a **litre of**

water. Apply the solution to the cooler with a **sponge** or **rag** or pour it into a **spray bottle**, squirt it on and wipe. Then rinse with **fresh water**. Once your cooler is clean, let it air-dry with the lid open before you store it.

To remove stubborn food stains, make a paste by mixing **bicarbonate of soda** and **water** in a bowl. Dip a **clean rag** or **sponge** into the paste, rub the spot and rinse. If that doesn't work, apply a **non-abrasive household cleaner**, such as *Kitchen Power* and clean with a **rag**. Using an abrasive cleaner could scratch the interior of your cooler, giving dirt and bacteria a place to hide – and making your cleaning job harder.

To clean a soft-structure cooler, mix **mild washing-up liquid** in **water** and wipe the cooler down inside and out with a **clean rag** or **sponge**. Rinse and air-dry. Don't put it in the washing machine and don't use bleach on this type of cooler.

Copper

Copper is a metal and, while it's harder than silver, it's still softer than either brass or bronze. For cleaning purposes, it comes in two varieties – lacquered and unlacquered. Lacquered copper, which is usually on decorative items, has a finish baked on at the factory. Unlacquered copper, found mostly on cookware, tarnishes easily but will brighten with elbow grease and the right techniques.

A salt and white vinegar mix rubbed on copper cookware will remove corrosion.

To clean a decorative copper item with a lacquered finish, you only need to dust the piece with a **dust cloth** or **vacuum** as part of your regular cleaning process. If it's dirty, you might want to wipe it with a **damp cloth**. Lacquering on decorative pieces works fine until cracks appear in the finish. Then the piece must be stripped of its coating with **acetone** or **paint thinner**, applied full strength with a **cloth**. Or boil the item in a **large saucepan** or, if it's a better shape, a **jam-making pan**, using **4 litres of water** and **100ml of soda crystals**. The lacquer should peel right off. Wash with **dishwashing detergent**, rinse with **running water**,

and dry with a **soft cloth**. If you want the piece lacquered again, get it done by a professional metal finisher.

To clean copper cookware, you should first be aware of the don'ts. Never use any scratchy cleaning tool on copper. You run the risk of leaving marks. And bleach will seriously discolour copper if it stands for a few hours or more. Instead, try these natural methods:

• Sprinkle the piece with **salt** and a little **white vinegar**.
• Cut a **lemon** in half, dip it in **salt**, and rub.
• As long as the piece can stand the heat, boil it in a **large pan** filled with **water, 100ml of white vinegar** and a **50g cup of salt**.

Whatever method you use, always rinse with **fresh water**, dry well with a **tea towel** and buff with a **soft cloth**. If you want more shine, apply a **commercial copper cleaner** according to label directions.

• Crevices – where the handle joins the pot, for instance – can be tough to clean. These spots are also magnets for paste polish build-up. Use a **cotton bud** or **natural horsehair brush** and **methylated spirits** to banish the grime.
• Swab small copper items with **ketchup** applied to a **make-up sponge** or **cotton bud**. You'll be surprised by how quickly they gleam.

Cork

When cleaning a cork floor, be sparing with whatever liquid you use. Most cork floors are sealed with polyurethane to prevent them from soaking up spills and stains. But, as the seal starts to wear away, excess water can find its way into the seams between the tiles, weakening the glue and causing the edges to lift.

When cleaning a cork floor, keep it dry if you can, by sweeping up loose dirt with a **broom** and **dustpan** first. If it's still dirty, use a **just-damp mop** that has been wrung very thoroughly from a bowl of **sudsy washing-up liquid**. Towel dry – if it's easier wrap a **towel** around your broom to do this. Every year, use a **specialist liquid wax**, such as *Osmo*, to keep up the floor's waterproofing qualities. Heavily trafficked areas – the hall and kitchen, for instance –

should be coated with polyurethane every two to three years. An expert should carry out this task and floors must first be scrubbed with a special pad to rough up old sealant.

To clean cork walls, which usually aren't sealed, rub them with **putty-style wallpaper cleaner** or a **dry foam-rubber sponge**, available at hardware and paint stores. Any spots may be carefully hand-sanded with **fine-gauge (0000) sandpaper** to remove them. Cork on walls is usually only 3mm thick, so be careful not to turn your cork into an unsightly patchwork by over-rubbing.

To clean a cork or cork-backed item, such as a coaster, a trivet or a mat, wet it with **cold water** and scrub with a **pumice stone** or **pad**. Rinse with **water** and air-dry in a cool, dry place.

Crystal

Never put crystal in the dishwasher. Crystal is too fragile and soft for the dual action of dishwasher and detergent, which can etch and dull its surface. To preserve the special sparkle of crystal, always hand-wash it in sudsy washing-up water – unless it has silver or gold gilt, in which case you should use only plain, warm water.

To wash crystal, line the bottom of the sink with a **doubled-up towel** and fill the sink with **warm water** – not hot – and add two or three drops of **washing-up liquid**. Wash one item at a time. Grasp glasses by the bowl, not the stem, and wash gently. Pump the glass up and down in **warm water** to rinse. Dry upside down on a **lint-free cotton towel** or **plastic dish rack**. Better yet, put **clean thick gloves** or **cotton socks** over your hands and dry the crystal immediately with an **old linen towel**. This way, you'll leave no fingerprints or watermarks.

To remove stains, try the three-pronged approach:
• First, mix a paste of **lemon juice** and **baking powder**

and rub gently on the crystal with a **sponge**, then wash and dry. Baking powder is about as abrasive as you can get with crystal without risking damage: bicarbonate of soda, which is coarser, is too much.

• Tougher stains can be 'riced'. Put **2 teaspoons of uncooked rice** into the crystal piece, add **water**, and swirl. Repeat, if need be.

• For stubborn stains, fill the crystal receptacle with **warm water** and drop in a **denture tablet**.

Here are some more crystal-cleaning tricks worth considering:

• For extra shine, add **white vinegar** or **lemon juice** to the rinse water.

• To wash the grooves of cut crystal, dip a **frayed toothbrush** into **vinegar**, **lemon juice** or **soapy water** and scrub.

Curlers

To wash curlers that are submersible in water – plain rollers, Velcro rollers and foam-coated wire sticks – fill your bathroom sink with warm water, mix in a couple of teaspoons of shampoo or facial cleanser to create suds and let them soak.

As a general rule, if a cleaner is gentle enough for your face or hair, it is fine for your curlers. Use a **wide-toothed comb** to gently pull out any hair stuck in the curlers. Then wipe with a **rag** to remove caked-on film. Rinse with **fresh water** and either dry immediately with a **clean towel** or air-dry.

For stubborn stains, such as hardened setting lotions or gels, add **1 tablespoon liquid fabric softener** to around **50ml of water**. Use a **soft brush** – a **nail brush** is ideal – to scrub the curlers. Rinse with **water** and dry.

To clean electric curlers, which are not submersible, use a **rag** or **soft, nylon bristled brush** and the fabric softener solution described above. Rinse by wiping the curlers with a **damp rag** and then dry.

Curling irons & straighteners

Cleaning curling irons and straighteners can be tricky. You must remove the crust of singed hair and hair styling product that builds up over time. Because they are electrical appliances, you can't soak them in water. And you should not use toxic chemical cleaners, since they can leave chemical residue in your hair.

Instead, use cotton buds dipped in a solution of **fabric softener** (15ml fabric softener to 50ml of water) to dissolve the gunge. Clearly, only do this when your appliance is switched off and grown cold. Wipe clean with a **damp rag**, then with another dry one.

Curtains

Dust your curtains once a month or so as part of a regular household clean. Use the upholstery tool on the vacuum cleaner or, if you can't get on with lifting this up high, a feather duster.

Clean your curtains about once a year. First, look for the manufacturer's cleaning recommendations, which should be on a tag sewn inside the hem – or if they are homemade, make sure you keep the cleaning instructions that come with your fabric. Depending on the material, you will either machine-wash, hand-wash, or dry-clean.

If curtains can be machine-washed, use the **delicate cycle**. They may look sturdy and stable, but being continually exposed to the sun can weaken curtains by breaking down the fibres in the material. Consequently, the minute you wash them, they may begin to deteriorate. In the same way, be gentle when drying curtains in a machine. Take them out very promptly

Dust curtains using a vacuum cleaner. Use an extension tube to reach the very top.

to reduce wrinkling. High heat can set wrinkles in the fabric, especially when the cycle ends abruptly, leaving the curtains in a ball. An alternative to tumbling curtains until they are dry is to remove them from the dryer and hang them while they are still damp. This will reduce wrinkling and may help you avoid ironing them. If your curtains are not very dirty, you can skip the washing altogether and freshen them by tumbling them in a dryer using no heat.

Cushions

Keeping cushions clean is more than a matter of appearance. Dust mites, which can trigger allergies, often lurk within the folds of a dirty sofa. Flop down after a hard day's work onto your sofa's fixed or removable cushions, and you may give yourself a sneezing fit. By removing the dust regularly, you not only keep your cushions looking fresh (and keep the dust from staining them once it is ground in or moistened), but you also improve the quality of the air in your home.

To remove dust clean cushions about once a month using a **vacuum cleaner** with the appropriate attachments, such as an **upholstery brush** and a **crevice tool**. To avoid sucking out the feathers, test a spot of any cushion filled with down. If you're drawing out feathers, you'll have to restrict your cleaning to gently brushing off the dust.

To give a more thorough cleaning, or to remove stains, wash your cushions. Generally, you should do this in situ, without taking out the cushion pad. The exception, of course, is if you're fortunate enough to have machine washable cushions. First, check the upholstery manufacturer's suggestions, usually tagged to upholstery fabric. This tag will tell you whether you should use a **water-based shampoo**, a **dry-cleaning solvent** or neither of the two. Next, pick an inconspicuous spot on the cushion and pretest whatever cleaning technique is recommended. If there is shrinking or bleeding or running of colours, contact a professional cleaner. If not, proceed.

Even if you can use shampoo, use as little moisture as possible. You do not want to wet the stuffing, because it dries very slowly and can make conditions even more suitable for moisture-loving dust mites. The trick is to clean using suds only.

• The easiest solution is to use a **foaming carpet shampoo** in an aerosol can. Follow the directions on the can, which typically tell you to allow the foam to stand until dry and then vacuum it off.

• To make your own shampoo, mix a **squirt of washing-up liquid** with a **litre of warm water**. Make suds by squeezing a **sponge** in the solution. Scoop the suds off the top and apply them sparingly with a sponge to the cushion surface. Rub gently in the direction of the fabric's grain. Rather than letting them dry as you would a shop-bought upholstery shampoo, work on a small area at a time, lightly rinsing each area as you go with a clean, damp sponge. Again, avoid soaking the fabric. Be sure to remove all the suds, or the residue will cause the fabric to soil faster.

If the fabric calls for dry-cleaning only and you only want to clean a stain, you can do it yourself, using a **commercial dry-cleaning solvent** such as *Spotless*, on sale at supermarkets. Don't pour the solvent onto the stain. Instead, moisten a **clean white cloth** with the solvent and use the cloth to draw the stain out. Blot repeatedly – never rub. Rubbing can stretch or damage the texture of the fabric. Always use solvents sparingly and in a well-ventilated area. And don't use solvents on cushions filled with latex foam rubber padding, because the solvent can dissolve the padding. However, if you need to clean the entire surface of a dry-clean only cushion, have it professionally cleaned.

Cutlery

Rinse knives, forks and spoons under running water immediately after eating. You may not want to actually wash-up if, say, you're entertaining, but rinsing will remove food that might cause pitting or staining.

Be especially diligent about eggs, fruit juices, tomatoey foods, lemon, vinegar, salty foods (including butter), mustard, and salad dressings. Silver is most vulnerable, but stainless steel, despite its name, isn't completely immune to the threat of corrosion. It's fine to soak both totally stainless steel and

Simple solutions

A silver lining
To get the most out of your good silver, take it out of hiding now and then. Frequent use and buffing will enhance the patina and will give pleasure to you and its other users. Store it in a clean, dry drawer.

If you store your silver for a long time, use either velvet fabric cutlery rolls or a wooden, felt-lined chest to deter tarnish. You can also prevent tarnish by storing silver pieces in plastic cling-film, making sure to remove as much air as possible.

silver in **warm water** in a **sink** but don't soak hollow-handled utensils for long, lest it loosens the soldering.

Wash in the dishwasher along with your dishes, taking care not to spill detergent directly on the pieces, because it could pit or spot them. For a beautiful polish however, you will have to dry everything afterwards by hand using a **soft dishcloth**.

To brighten dull stainless steel cutlery: soak it in **4 litres of hot water** mixed with **1 teaspoon of ammonia**. Rinse with **clear hot water** and dry well with a **clean cloth**.

Wash plate and sterling silver cutlery by hand. Use **washing-up liquid** in **hot water**. Rinse with **clear hot water** and dry immediately with a **soft dishcloth**. Don't use abrasive cleaners or scrubbers, such as steel wool. They will dull the finish.

The sulphur in eggs and egg products (such as mayonnaise) will cause silver to tarnish – instantly. So do pollutants in the air, but they work more slowly. Tarnish is not removed by regular washing and you will have to use a **silver polish** to remove it.

Clean pewter cutlery with a drop of **methylated spirits** on a **soft cloth**. Then follow up with the hot, soapy water treatment.

For advice on how to polish silver, see **Silver jewellery** and **Silver serving pieces.** See also **Pewter.**

Cutting boards

The most effective way to keep cutting boards completely hygienic is to have several, so that you never mix one used for raw meat with a board on which you chop up cheese or fruit salad. But however many you do have, it's essential not to skimp on the cleaning that is needed to kill the germs that could give you salmonella, *E.coli* and more.

To wash a plastic cutting board, run it through a **dishwasher**, and the hot water and disinfecting ingredients found in dishwasher detergent will kill harmful bacteria.

Clean cutting boards by scrubbing them with a paste made from lemon juice and salt. Use a putty knife to scrape off any stubborn build-ups.

Wash your cutting board as soon as possible after each use, especially after preparing meat or poultry products.

To wash a wooden cutting board, it's best not to use a dishwasher because the dishwashing process may warp or loosen the glue that holds together laminated wood. Use a **scrubbing brush** to scrub the board by hand with **washing-up liquid** in **hot water** each time you use it. To kill germs, the water must be too hot for your hands to bear. So do it right and you'll have to wear **rubber gloves**. When done thoroughly, hand scrubbing is just as effective as machine-washing.

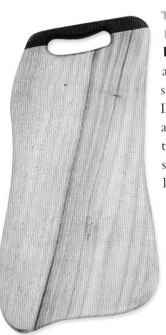

To disinfect a cutting board, mix a **teaspoon of bleach** in a **litre of water** and apply it directly to the cutting surface with a **scrubbing brush**. Do not rinse. Instead, let the board air-dry to give the bleach a chance to work. If you need the board sooner than that, let it stand for at least one minute, and then pat it dry with a **clean paper towel**.

Expert advice

STAIN LAB

Cutting board common sense

Celebrity chef Antony Worrall Thompson advises not two but three chopping boards. 'Have one for raw, one for cooked, and one for smelly foods (for example garlic and onions)', he says. With just two, whenever you make something spicy, you might be tempted to go for your 'raw' chopping board, when as part of the same meal you need to chop something bland.

d Decanters

Start with the outside, washing your decanter by hand. Never put a decanter in a dishwasher; the heat and vibration can easily break its delicate glass neck. If the decanter is an antique or made of fine crystal or cut glass, wash it in a plastic basin rather than in a hard sink to reduce the chances of breakage. Or line the bottom of your sink with a folded towel. Then just use a sponge or soft-bristled brush, warm water and mild washing-up liquid to wash the outer surface.

How you clean the inside depends on how dirty or stained the decanter is. There are several approaches. The simplest is to fill it halfway with **soapy, warm water**, hold your hand over the top and gently shake. If it is still stained, swirl a mixture of **rock salt** (also sold as sea salt, in large crystals) and **vinegar** around inside the decanter. The salt will gently scour the surface while the vinegar helps remove stains, especially lime deposits. If rock salt and vinegar don't remove wine stains, try swishing a small amount of **warm water**, **bicarbonate of soda** and **rock salt** in the bottle.

Try denture cleaner Put **water** in the decanter, drop in a **denture cleaner**, such as *Sterident* and let it stand overnight. No matter which method you use, rinse with clean, warm water.

Leave a towel-wrapped spoon or stick in a decanter to absorb moisture and prevent fogging up once the stopper is replaced.

Dry your decanter completely, so that it does not fog up after you replace the stopper. Worse than being unsightly, the moisture could harbour dangerous micro-organisms. Instead of drying your decanter by inverting it in your dish rack, which increases the chance of breakage and takes for ever, try this trick. Drain most of the water out of the decanter by holding it upside down.

To remove the last of the moisture, wrap a **paper towel** around the handle of a **long-handled wooden spoon** so that the towel extends slightly beyond the end. Put the towel-wrapped

spoon into the decanter and let it rest on the bottom overnight. By morning, the towel should have absorbed most of the condensation. If you can't wait until morning, gently blow warm air into the decanter with a **hair dryer**. Be careful as too much heat can crack delicate glass.

Decking

Think of your deck as an outdoor room, one that is exposed to sun, wind, rain and ice. To keep your deck looking its best, you need to clean it – not as regularly or meticulously as you do your indoor rooms, but well enough to maintain it for the long term. Even decks made of weather-resistant or pressure-treated wood deteriorate unless they are cared for. And, contrary to popular belief, the pressure washer is not the best way to clean wooden decking. Before you reach for the nozzle, read on.

Sweep your decking regularly to keep it free of leaves and twigs. This is the most basic step you can take. Otherwise, pollen and twig debris from trees will stain the wood surface and the piles of decomposing organic matter will hold moisture, leading to mildew and rot. Use a **heavy-duty broom** to sweep your deck regularly, taking care to keep the gaps between boards clean. If leaves or twigs get stuck in the gaps, scrape them out with a **putty knife**. The more often you sweep, the easier it will be on you and the deck, especially if the leaves are dry.

To remove dirt and mildew and brighten the colour of your decking, periodically (once a year or so) give it a more thorough cleaning. Use a **specialist decking cleaner**, such as *Thompson's* and follow the pack instructions. Using a **long-handled stiff-bristled brush** (a long handle is easier on your back and knees), scrub the deck with the solution. Rinse by washing down the deck with a **hose**.

If you have a covered or partially covered deck that is not built to withstand rain, clean it as you would an indoor hardwood floor – with a **barely-damp mop** or, on occasions, with a cleaner made especially for wood, such as *Pledge Soapy Wood Cleaner*. Do not soak the deck with water, or run the hose over it.

Leaves and twigs stuck between boards can be scraped out using a putty knife.

Cut down on deck maintenance

Cut the time spent cleaning your decking by regularly pruning any trees and shrubs that overhang it. You'll also cut down on that greatest deck enemy of all: bird droppings.

Because you will still want the deck to be a haven of flowers and scent, why not use more container-grown plants instead. Always remember to stand each container on a saucer: otherwise, each time you water, you'll create a pool of damp that will rot your wood. For total deck protection, fit 'feet' underneath your containers. You'll find these in terracotta, wood and plastic at DIY stores.

To remove stains and stubborn mildew, use a bleaching solution, made up from **40ml of oxygen bleach**, per **5 litres of warm water**. Unlike chlorine bleach, which can break down the lignin that holds the wood together and harm plants, oxygen bleach is relatively gentle and non-toxic. Simply apply it with a **mop** or **brush**. Don't scrub. Wait 15 or 20 minutes for it to soak in and then hose down the deck to remove the solution. If you use a wood sealer, such as *Thompson's Water Seal*, on your deck, you will need to reapply it after washing with oxygen bleach, which strips away sealers along with dirt and mildew.

Don't use a pressure washer Pressure washers are expensive, dangerous and harmful to the wood you are cleaning. The extreme water pressure will break up the wood fibres – exactly what you are trying to prevent – leaving the surface fuzzy, more susceptible to the weather and in poor condition for refinishing with stains and sealers. Only use them as a last resort and then be very careful. Use the lowest pressure setting available. Hold the nozzle at an angle at least 30cm away from the deck's surface.

Dehumidifiers

Dehumidifiers are are useful if you have an area of your home that is prone to dampness. They cut down on moisture as well as the mould and micro organisms that thrive in moist environments. If you don't clean your dehumidifier regularly, you may cancel out its beneficial health effects.

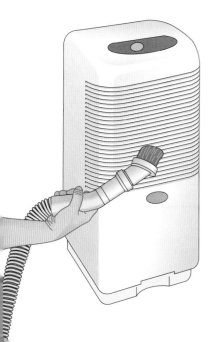

Cleaning a dehumidifier is easy Periodically dust the outer cabinet with a **damp, oil-free cloth** and clean the grill using the **dusting attachment** on a **vacuum cleaner** (left). Once a month – or more often if necessary, depending on use – scrub the drip pan and the inside of the water reservoir with a **sponge** or **soft cloth** and **mild washing-up liquid** to discourage the growth of mould or mildew. At least once a season, remove the dust and lint from the cold coils with a **soft-bristled brush**. Most dehumidifiers have an air filter in the front grill area. To keep yours working well, you should replace or clean the filter at least once a season.

Dentures

As with real teeth, dentures should be kept free of food particles, plaque and stains so that your mouth can remain healthy and attractive. And removing plaque from dentures requires the same regular brushing that real teeth need. The difference, of course, is that with dentures, you take them out to brush them.

Brush your dentures twice a day Dentures are delicate and expensive. They may break even if dropped a few centimetres. For that reason, brush them over a **folded towel** or a **bowl of water**. Go over them lightly with a recommended **denture brush** or a **soft nylon toothbrush**, using a cleanser your dentist recommends.

You can keep your dentures cleaner by also lightly brushing your gums, tongue and the roof of your mouth.

Soak your dentures for at least 30 minutes a day in a dentist-approved **denture cleanser**. Soaking will remove stains and kill germs, reducing mouth infections and odour. For convenience and privacy while you are without your teeth, soak your dentures overnight or while you're showering. Then rinse off the cleanser by lightly brushing the dentures with the **soft-bristled brush** under **cold running water**.

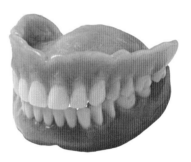

Here are some precautions you can take to protect your dentures:
• Never use a brush with stiff, coarse bristles, which can damage the materials dentures are made of.
• Don't use gritty powdered cleansers or toothpastes, which can also cause damage.
• Don't clean dentures with bleach. It can whiten the pink part of the dentures and corrode the metal framework on partial dentures.
• Never rinse in hot water. The heat could warp them.
• Never let your dentures dry out, which could also warp them or make them brittle.

Diamonds

As hard as they are brilliant, diamonds can cope with rigorous cleaning. Whenever you clean diamond rings or earings, take time to check on how secure the setting is.

Do any claws look out of line? If so, stop cleaning, put the item into a jewellery box and take it to be repaired. If you don't you'll regret it if the diamond falls out.

Assuming all your settings look secure, the simplest way to wash diamond jewellery is by soaking it in **hot, sudsy water** – **washing-up liquid** is fine. Do this in a **tea-cup** or a small bowl, never the sink. If a stone were to dislodge, you might be unable to find it and it could drain away with the water. Use an **old toothbrush** to scrub where the stone meets the setting and dirt can get ingrained. Rinse, shake dry then – if the stone is large enough, polish with a **microfibre cloth**.

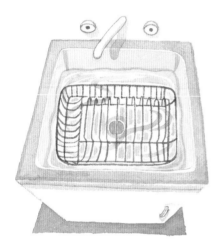

Dish drainers

Since your dish drainer is meant to hold clean dishes, a dirty dish drainer defeats its purpose.

Wash your dish drainer periodically in **warm water** with **washing-up liquid**, using a **clean sponge**. Do it separately, not while you're washing other dishes, since harmful bacteria can taint the dishes you are trying to clean. Use a **scrubbing brush** to remove stuck-on food and mould. Air-dry upside down on a **clean towel**. Disinfect the dish drainer every few weeks by soaking it in a solution of **40ml of bleach** per **5 litres of water**.

Dishes

Washing dirty dishes is a bit of a Herculean task; no matter how well you do it you always have to do it again after every meal. Here's the right way to wash up.

For everyday washing-up, fill the sink with **moderately hot water** and a squirt of **washing-up liquid**. If the plates and pans that you are cleaning are particularly greasy, then add **2 tablespoons of white vinegar** to the water.

Slide the dishes in edgewise into the water, which allows the temperature of the dish to equalise gradually. If very hot water hits a fragile dish too quickly, cracks may occur.

Once the dishes are stacked carefully in the sink, pour a little extra **washing-up liquid** on a **sponge** or **dishcloth**. Then resist the urge to scrub. Instead, wash in small circular motions. It might take longer than a vigorous scrubbing, but it will protect your china. Empty the water and fill again with **plain water** for rinsing. Put **1 tablespoon of white vinegar** into the final rinse, if you have some glass items.

When using the dishwasher:
• Load dishes so that they are separated and face the centre of the machine. Put glasses and cups between prongs, not over them.
• Don't position large dishes (or pots or pans) so that they block the spray arm, the spray tower, or the flow of water to the detergent dispenser.
• Use only **dishwasher detergent** in your machine – never soap, laundry detergent, or washing-up liquid. Follow the label directions for the amount. Less is needed if your water is soft (or artificially softened), more if it's hard.
• Use a **rinse agent** to speed drying if your water is hard, but skip it if you have soft water.
• Don't pre-rinse moderately soiled dishes under the tap. Just scrape off any food.
• Use the hold-and-rinse cycle when you haven't got enough dishes to use the machine right away – or the noise of the dishwasher means you prefer to do it overnight or when you're out. A quick rinse stops odours building up.

To hand-wash delicate china, see the section on **China.**

Dishwashers

It's all there in the manual: after each use, take the time to empty grunge from cutlery baskets, filters and check the spray arm. Skip this and you're washing the next load of dishes in the food residue from yesterday's load.

• When rinsing out the cutlery bucket, use the power of water and turn it upside down under a fast tap. This way, you'll propel dirt and food bits back out the way they came. Use a **tooth pick** to get out tiny particles of food that get trapped in the spray arm.
• Every month, run the dishwasher on empty – but with a full supply of **dishwasher powder** or **tablets**.

Give new dishes the dishwasher test

In an ideal world, all dishes would go into the dishwasher. But if you have a set that you're not sure about, why not try this test. Buy an extra item in the range – something inexpensive like a saucer – that's made in your pattern.

Put it in the back of the dishwasher and forget about it for a month while you use the machine normally. At the end of the month, take a look. If there's no change in its appearance, you'll know it's safe to use the dishwasher for the rest of this set. If it's faded, give yourself a pat on the back for being cautious about it.

• To keep the dishwasher smelling fresh if you're not going to use it for a while, slosh in **100ml of white vinegar**.

Dolls

Whether it's a child's plastic fashion doll, an expensive collector's doll or an heirloom from your grandmother, all will benefit from careful cleaning and maintenance.

To wash a doll's clothing, begin by stripping the doll. Then make sure its clothes can be washed – do a test on an inconspicuous spot on the clothing. Using an **eyedropper** or a **small syringe**, put a drop of **detergent** where it won't easily be seen, such as on a seam or a hem. If you can't see it after it dries, you should be safe. Place the doll's clothing in a lingerie bag (or use the tiny white mesh bags that come with laundry tablets) and put it in the **washing machine** on the **delicate** setting. Don't dry the clothes in the dryer as they may shrink. If the weather is good, hang them to dry on an outside clothes line for a fresh smell. In bad weather, lay the pieces on a towel to dry.

To clean the doll itself, remember that a **damp cloth** will remove a lot of the grime a doll picks up in the attic, or just from being loved. If the doll needs a bath, fill a sink with **warm water** and mix in a large squirt of **baby bubble-bath**. If the doll's body is all plastic or rubber, you can submerge it, much as you would a real baby. You might even invite your child to give baby a scrub with a **face flannel** made soapy with a little **bubble-bath**.

Saliva mixed with anything – dirt, biscuits, sweets – can set like cement, so for the extra-tough dirt that comes with dolls your children have played with a good deal, a gentle scrub with a **soft toothbrush** may be necessary. If you need a little extra cleaning power, dip the toothbrush in a solution of **5ml of hydrogen peroxide** and **50ml water**. Just make sure you rinse everything well before you return the doll to your child.

To clean a collector's doll, also begin by stripping the doll. Never use a damp cloth on a porcelain collector's doll, because it might etch the paint. Instead, use a **dry, soft cloth** to remove surface dirt from the 'flesh' surfaces. For detailed areas – around the eyes or fingers, for instance – use a **natural bristle artist's paintbrush** to remove trapped dirt and dust. This should be all you need to do, because, luckily, collectors' dolls don't tend to pick up serious stains.

If the clothing is old or delicate, you can remove the musty smell that comes with age by hanging the clothes out in fresh air. If the clothing is not fragile, you might want to consider washing it using the method described above for modern doll's clothes – but be sure to do the eyedropper test first. For clothing stains that you don't want to wash, a **household spot remover** might get them out. Check the label for the safest application procedure. Or you might try a solution of a **teaspoon of lemon juice** mixed with **100ml of water**. Dip an **absorbent cloth** or a **paper towel** into the solution and dab – don't rub – at the stain. It should lighten up right away.

Doormats

Yes, doormats are supposed to get dirty – it's their job. But at some point, your doormat will have absorbed all the dirt it can take. Then it simply becomes the bridge over which dirt travels into your house.

First, knock out the dirt Go outside – well away from your house if any windows are open. Grab two adjacent corners of the doormat and shake hard. The loosest dirt will come off easily. Then, wearing **glasses** or **goggles** to protect your eyes from dust, drape the mat over a **post** or a **clothesline** and use a **stick** – or **cricket** or **rounders bat** – to beat it. After you've beaten out all the loose dirt, take a wire brush and dislodge the stubborn stuff. If there is any gooey mess like wax or chewing gum still clinging to the mat, press an **ice cube** against the offending lump until it's brittle enough to scrape off with a **spoon**.

To remove serious stains on a doormat made of rubber or rope, use an **aerosol spot remover**, such as *Vanish*. If you think it needs a more thorough cleaning, wash it in the **washing machine** on a **gentle cycle**.

If you have wooden doormats that are seriously stained you may need to strip off the coating, sand right down and then revarnish.

See the section on **Wood**.

Doors

Doors collect dust and dirt just as walls do. So whatever you use on painted walls is just right for painted doors. Treat wooden doors as you would furniture made from the same material. Few doors are as flat as walls, though, so you have to be equipped to attack beading and crevices to get them really clean.

To remove surface dirt, dust down the door with a dry towel. Then tie a **soft, old towel** over the bristle end of a **broom** and brush into the angles and crevices where dust mounts up. If there's a lot of detailed moulding on the door, use a **soft toothbrush** to get into the tightest corners.

Wash the door once you've cleaned off all the surface dust and dirt. If you have a stained wooden door, use **soapy wood cleaner** and mix it with **water** according to the directions on the label. For painted doors, **all-purpose cleaner** is the quickest and cheapest option.

If you are feeling very particular, **sugar soap** (from DIY stores) is a more expensive and highly effective way of removing grease and surface dirt from paint. Use a **sponge** and wash from the bottom upward to avoid run marks. So beginning at the bottom of the door, scrub with the sponge in small circular motions. Rinse the sponge often and thoroughly to avoid putting dirt back on the door. If you keep the solution clean, you won't have to rinse.

To clean door hardware – knobs, handles and knockers – use **light masking tape** around the fitting, then use the **cleaning solution** that is appropriate to the material of your handle such as *Brasso* for brass handles. With glass or ceramic doorknobs, a few wipes with a **rag** dampened with **methylated spirits** should be sufficient.

Down

Check the care label of down jackets and sleeping bags and most will say machine washable. The only thing that makes them any different from the rest of your machine wash is that you need to make an extra check that all the down is securely inside your item before you start. Otherwise, a little spot where you nicked your jacket on a bramble bush can flood your washer with feathers. When you're sure all items are secure, put it into an empty washing machine and follow the care label for maximum temperature and spin (some may advise no spin).

To dry a down item, it's fine to use a **dryer**, but be sure to do it at the low temperature setting. Some people throw in **trainers** or a **tennis ball**, because the action of a small, dense object rattling around the drier stops your large, bulky item from getting tangled. Halfway through the cycle, take the down item out and give it a shake. Down can take longer than you'd think to dry so be patient.

Drains

When a drain becomes slow moving act fast. Yes, you could go on this way for a few weeks perhaps. But tackling the problem right now is more likely to avoid the whole episode ending with a plumber's bill.

If you have a slow-moving drain, it means sludge is building up in the pipe. When that happens, pour **100g of salt** into the drain, followed by **100g of bicarbonate of soda**. Then pour a **full kettle of boiling water** down the drain. The abrasive salt and bicarbonate of soda will break down the clog. If the problem is congealed grease, the clogging will loosen immediately. Don't turn on the tap for several hours, if possible. The longer you can go without diluting your work, the better.

If matted hair wedged down the pipework is the problem, you'll need a stronger solution. This one will work: dissolve **30ml of** *Dri Pak Soda Crystals* in a **litre of water** and pour it slowly down the drain. Let it work for 10 minutes; then run **hot water** until the drain seems clear.

If it is the waste-disposal unit drain that is slow, it is probably blocked with food particles. To cure the problem, first pull out the drain trap (the little basket–like object that sits in the drain hole at the bottom of the sink). Hold it inside the kitchen rubbish bin and tap it to loosen the debris trapped inside it. Replace the drain trap, twisting the knob to the closed position and fill the sink with **warm water** to a depth of 10cm. Add **100ml of bicarbonate of soda**. Turn on the waste disposal unit and let it run for a couple of seconds before you twist the drain trap knob to

Simple solutions

THE GREAT STAINGO

Blast away blocked drains

Pre-empt blocked drains by giving them an effective – and dramatic – flush through once a month.

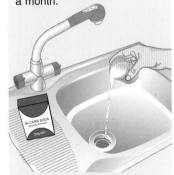

BI-CARB SODA

Pour 50ml of bicarbonate of soda down the kitchen sink. Don't turn on the water yet. Instead, follow immediately with the same amount of white vinegar, then stand back and watch the fireworks. The mixture will fizz and bubble (but don't worry – it's harmless). Wait 30 minutes. Then flush with cool water. This will keep your drains clear and prevent unwanted clogging.

the open position. The water pressure will push any remaining food particles through the drain trap and give the waste-disposer a good scrubbing at the same time. Turn on the tap for running water and let the disposer run until you get a free-spinning 'all clear' sound.

See also **Waste disposal units.**

Drawers

We all have junk drawers – which act as receptacles for hundreds of objects that have no other obvious home. There are treasures in there we'll need one day (if we can ever find them). So they deserve a regular cleaning, too.

Empty the drawer onto a table top that you have first covered with old newspaper. Then sort through and throw away everything you no longer want.

Next, clean the drawer
• For wood, use a little **soapy wood cleaner**, mixed according to directions, or mix a **litre of warm water** with **2 tablespoons of washing-up liquid** in a large bowl.
• For laminated plastic, use **30ml of white vinegar** mixed with a **litre of warm water**.
• For metal drawers, put some **bicarbonate of soda** in a small bowl and add just enough **water** to make a paste.
   Thoroughly soak a **sponge** and squeeze well, then wipe away at the drawer, inside and out. You can let the drawer air-dry, but if you're in a hurry to put your bits away again – only the must-keep stuff – dry it with a **paper towel**.

Dust

More than 5000 different materials, including skin flakes, pet hair, human hair, food bits, pollen grains, spores, insect parts, sawdust and clothing fibres combine to make the dust that settles on every surface in our homes. But when it comes to clearing up, dust is dust.

Many methods of dusting simply push dust around, which is why we try not to recommend them, unless for a specific task. Feather dusters are great, for instance, for cleaning

Dust busters Here are some no-fuss tricks to try when you want to do some spot dusting:

- To clean woodwork (except for painted surfaces), put a tea bag in hot water and let it cool. Then dampen your cleaning rag or sponge with the cooled tea and run it over the woodwork.
- To clean blinds, which can get filmy with dust, wipe the slats with a cloth dampened with vinegar, which disinfects as it cleans. This is a good trick for chandeliers, too.
- To remove dust, lint, or hair from fabric upholstery or an item of clothing, wrap masking tape or packing tape around your hand and then press your hand over the surface of the item. Unwanted fuzz, dust or lint will stick to the masking tape.
- To get rid of all the dust trapped in a pleated lampshade, use a small, medium-bristled paintbrush. This works for figurines, too.

blinds – as long as you make sure to shake the duster outside frequently. But basically, a dry dust cloth just moves the dust or suspends it. But if you use a **just-damp duster** the dust will cling to your cloth and disappear for sever when you wash it in the washing machine.

To dust a room and cut down on the time dusting takes, **vacuum** everything first – furniture, walls, windowsills, upholstery, the coffee table. Vacuuming removes a lot of dust without creating a dust storm in the process. Follow up with a **damp cloth** and your room should be dust-free for a while.

Naturally, you want to truly remove the dust, rather than kicking it up into the air. **Microfibre cloths** are great at holding onto the dust, because they have so many extra fibres. Generally, a little **water** on your **just-damp dust cloth** is all it takes. But if you're up against a great deal of grease, for example, you'll move faster if you spray on a dot of **multi-purpose surface cleaner**, provided that you just use it on the hard surfaces of your home that are listed as 'safe' on the cautions panel of your cleaner.

Dustbins

Being scrupulous about only putting items inside your dustbin that are themselves inside securely tied plastic bags does a lot to lessen how often you'll need to clean your dustbin. If you don't use sturdy sacks – or if you get a split – you'll need to disinfect your bin each week, after it's been emptied by your council rubbish contractor.

Hosing out the bin is the easiest option, but if that's too much of a hassle for just one item, use an old **watering can**, marked clearly as not being suitable for watering flowers anymore. You can direct the flow of water needed to clean more easily than simply pouring it in from a bucket.

First, take your dustbin to an outside drain: you won't want to tip foul-smelling water onto your drive or flower-beds. Fill the watering can with a mix of **40ml bleach** to **5 litres of water** and use this to rinse around the bottom and side of the bin. Empty down the drain and repeat. Wash the lid with the same solution, then invert both to dry. Later that day, when you next need to put a sack out in the dustbin, you can put your clean bin back together again.

Duvets

Check the care label before you start – and get out the bathroom scales at the same time. Many synthetic double duvets are washable, but they may weigh more than the capacity of your washing machine, which will mean a trip to the launderette.

Single, synthetic duvets shouldn't be a problem and are a simple machine wash and tumble dry job. Feather and down duvets are best professionally cleaned. In truth, it's not the washing that is the big problem – your feather duvet may indeed be up to machine washing. But the drying can be near impossible. It is no exaggeration to say that it can take days to dry a quality feather duvet.

For this reason, when accidents happen – a child or pet wets the duvet or you spill coffee – it is best to restrict your washing to that section only.

Take the duvet to the bath and using a solution of **hand-washing detergent** in the sink or bath (whichever is more appropriate) immerse the soiled section only. Rinse with **fresh water**, then blot off as much water as you can by putting the duvet between **two dry towels**. Finish spot drying with a **hair dryer**. For urine or other related accidents, follow the instructions on getting rid of the smell on pages 67–69 to avoid it becoming ingrained.

d

DVD players

The more mechanical parts your DVD player has, the more likely it is to accumulate dirt and dust. Portable models are even more susceptible. Dirty discs or lenses lead to mistracking, skipping, irregular speed and poor reproduction quality. When your player displays any of these symptoms regularly, give it a careful cleaning.

Keeping discs clean is the first step in maintaining a DVD player, because they can carry dirt into the player's interior. Always hold them by the edges. Rid discs of dust with a shot of **compressed air**. Then wipe with a **soft, dry cloth**, starting at the centre of the disc and moving out to the edge. Don't use solvents or household cleaners. Always store a disc in its case to keep it dirt-free and keep discs out of direct sunlight and away from heat sources.

Cleaning the player's lens is the next step. Don't open anything that requires a screwdriver. Most warranties become void if you open the casing. Instead, press the button to open the mechanical drawer where the DVD sits. Spray a gentle blast of **compressed air** inside the opening to force out any dust or lint. It's not a bad idea to spray the disc tray, too. Be careful to hold the can perfectly level to avoid getting any liquid near the DVD player. And don't hold the can any closer to the player than the distance recommended on the can – generally at least 10cm away. For less power, take your can further away from the player before you aim.

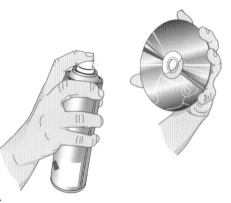

Try a blast of compressed air to rid your DVDs of surface dust.

You can buy special lens-cleaning discs that will keep the laser lens good as new. Just open the drawer that holds the DVDs and place the **cleaning disc** in the tray. When you close the tray and hit Play, the cleaning action begins. Some cleaning discs, such as *Maxell*'s, use an angular brush made of ultra fine synthetic fibres containing copper. Such discs not only clean the DVD player's lens, but also dissipate static that will attract dust.

To clean a player's exterior, a simple wipe-down with a **soft, dry cloth** is usually all that's needed. If the cabinet is extremely dirty, mix some **washing-up liquid** in water and get your cleaning cloth just barely damp before wiping it down. Avoid cleaning solvents (for example, alcohol), since they could damage the casing.

Elastic

Because it gives shape, support and comfort to clothes, elastic is found in everything from underwear to high-fashion jeans and tops. Lycra – the trade name for spandex – doesn't need special care, in that the rest of the garment material will determine how you wash it. But there are a few precautions worth following.

Body oils on elastic will cause it to break down in time. So it's important to wash items with elastic in them promptly. If the item ever needs bleaching, only use an **oxygen bleach**, such as *Ace*.

To maintain the life of elastic, tumble dry on a low setting and don't over-dry. You don't want your stretchy stuff to become crunchy.

Wash a swimsuit after ever wearing Chlorinated swimming pool water needs to be thoroughly rinsed out and salt water can fade a swimsuit. As well as the water you also need to get rid of the body oils, sweat, sun protection creams, sprays and lotions that your suit absorbs. Always do up the straps on bikinis that tie with a metal fastener, otherwise this can snag on other garments that are in the washing machine.

Many fitness clubs have a machine that wrings the water from swimsuits. Typically, you place your suit in it for 15 seconds and it emerges without drips. Whilst these are handy, such extreme spinning won't prolong the life of your swimwear. If you use them, put your swimsuit in so that its straps are lying at the bottom of the spinner and count how many seconds you spin it for. Don't guess.

Electric shavers

To keep your shaver in proper running order, brush it after each use to dislodge hair, dead skin and other stuff that's clogging the works and damaging the blades.

Many shavers have a removable head cover Pop it off and brush the underside, avoiding the delicate screen. If you've lost the tiny brush that came with your shaver, use an old **small toothbrush**. Then gently brush the cutting mechanism itself. A blast from a can of **compressed air** (from camera shops) will also dislodge any embedded dirt that stands in the way of a smooth shave.

If you use a shaving stick – a compressed powder product that dries up perspiration and facial oils to give a smoother shave – the powder can gum up electric shaver blades. To cure this, dip a **cotton bud** in **methylated spirits** and wipe the blades.

If your shaver requires more cleaning, go commercial. Some manufacturers of shaving goods sell an **aerosol spray cleaner and lubricant** for electric shavers. In general, you spray the shaver with the cleaner and run it for several seconds. Follow the package directions.

To clean the exterior, unplug your shaver and wipe the surfaces with a **damp flannel**. If anything clings to the outside, use a little **methylated spirits** to wipe it off.

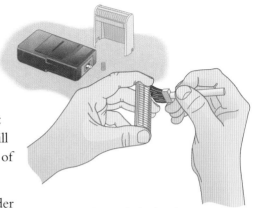

Brush underneath the head cover of your electric shaver regularly, to remove whisker dust and flakes of skin.

Enamel

Enamel is a baked-on coating for metals that doesn't rust or react with acids or chemicals and is usually easy to clean. Enamelled steel or enamelled cast-iron cookware can be a little more of a challenge because of the heat-meets-food factor.

To clean enamelled surfaces, such as appliance surfaces, dissolve **2 tablespoons of bicarbonate of soda** in **1 litre of warm water**. Wipe the surfaces with a **cloth** or **sponge** dipped in the solution and rinse with **fresh water** on a **clean cloth** or **sponge**.

To remove cooked-on deposits, see **Ovens.**

Simple solutions

Burnt-on food

Despite your best efforts, one day you'll probably burn something onto your enamel cookware. Here's what to do.

Cover the stuck-on food with bicarbonate of soda and let the pan sit for several minutes while the powder absorbs the acids and oils. Then wash as usual. If the food still won't budge, add 1 litre of water and 2 teaspoons of bicarbonate of soda to the pan, simmer for 15 minutes and wash again.

Take care with cleaners

Worn enamel can get pitted by the wrong cleaner, particularly those that are acidic. So always check the label to read 'safe for enamel' before you proceed. This is especially true with larger items that attract a fair bit of wear – your bath, perhaps or an enamel range cooker. Sometimes, you can use an everyday cleaner, but just far more dilute. *Kitchen Power*, which goes on neat on wortops, must be diluted to 1 part *Kitchen Power*, 20 parts water for enamel and washed off very quickly.

To clean enamelled cookware, let the pot cool first. Wash in **hot water** with **washing-up liquid**, rinse in **running water** and dry. Pots with metal or plastic handles may be washed in the **dishwasher**, but pots with wooden handles should not. Never use an abrasive cleaner or metal scouring pad. A **plastic** or **nylon scourer** is fine.

To care for enamelled cookware, remember:
• Keep the cooking heat on low or medium except when boiling water.
• Never subject an empty pot to high heat.
• Use non-scratch wooden or plastic cooking tools.

Erasers

The simplest method for cleaning the felt erasers used on chalk boards is to get two together, go outside somewhere well away from any open windows and clap them together. Keep your arms outstretched – there's bound to be a lot of dust.

Wash white board erasers with suds and scrub thoroughly before allowing to dry.

Erasers used on white boards will be full of washable pen, not chalk. So getting them clean again is a simple **bowl of sudsy water** job. Remember to rinse and leave them to air-dry.

To clean a pencil eraser, you're really taking off the top, dirty surface to reveal a new pristine one. Simply rub an **emery board** or piece of **glasspaper** over it until the black part is gone. This method will also help rejuvenate an eraser that has become hard and brittle. The newly exposed rubber will be clean and soft.

Extractor fans

Hold a tissue up to the grille where the air enters the fan in your bathroom or kitchen. Turn on the switch. The tissue should stay tight against the grille. If the tissue flutters, your fan isn't working effectively. Dirt is often the problem, particularly if it's been more than six months since you last did a clean; so here's how to solve it.

To clean an extractor fan

1 Turn the switch off. Unplug the fan.
2 Remove the grille and wash it in **warm water** and **washing-up liquid**. Rinse and dry.
3 **Vacuum** the housing and fan blades with the **crevice attachment**. Then wipe them off with a **damp cloth**.
4 Clean the motor and other dusty parts with a **stiff paintbrush**.
5 If you notice bad wiring or if the fan doesn't work, call an electrician. Don't attempt to fix it yourself.

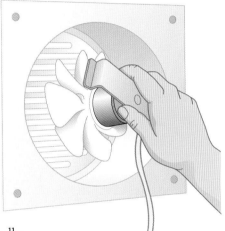

To clean fan blades, first unplug the electrical cord, then remove the fan and motor.

Wash the filter in a cooker hood extractor fan every month or two. This filter, usually made of aluminium, is designed for catching cooking grease. Remove it and wash it in the **dishwasher** or in a **solution of hot water** and **washing-up liquid**.

Range hood fans that recalculate the air, rather than venting it outside, have a **charcoal filter** that must be replaced about every six months. Check the instructions that came with your fan for how to do this.

Exercise equipment

Wipe the perspiration off the equipment after you've finished using it, because the salt from sweat is highly corrosive. This goes for all machines, especially those with metal parts. Wipe down control panels to keep moisture from seeping into them and ruining the sensitive electronics. To make it easier, keep a roll of paper towels handy in the room at home where you exercise.

Every once in a while, wipe down the equipment with a **sponge** or **cloth** moistened with a **bleach solution – 40ml of bleach** to **5 litres of water** should kill any lingering germs.

To clean a treadmill and keep it running properly, use your **vacuum cleaner** to clean under the machine every other week. Every three months, vacuum around the motor casing. Most people don't realise it, but dirt is the biggest killer of treadmill motors. Along those lines, here are two tips from a personal trainer:
• Don't wear the same shoes on your treadmill that you wear outside. Instead, keep a fresh, indoors-only pair for treadmill training.
• Consider putting your treadmill on a rubber mat instead of directly on the floor or carpet. All that friction causes a build-up of static electricity, which will attract motor-clogging dust and carpet lint.

Follow both tips and you'll have to clean less often and have a longer lasting treadmill.

To clean an elliptical trainer – the machine that combines the exercise of climbing stairs with that of riding a bicycle – wipe it down with a **moist rag**. To keep an elliptical machine from squeaking and skipping, clean and lubricate the machine's rails and wheels. Follow the manufacturer's recommendations or wipe with a **cloth** moistened with **silicone spray**.

To clean a weight machine, treat it like a car. The painted metal parts are similar to your car's painted metal body. Once a year, use a **car cleaner** (available at motor supply stores), diluted according to the package directions, to clean the grime off the paint. Rinse with a **clean wet towel** and dry with a **dry towel**. Wax the machine with a good **car wax**, again following the package directions. This will prevent scratches, reduce grime build-up and bring out a warm shine.

Periodically clean and lubricate the weight machine's guide rods to keep the weight stack from sticking. Clean the rods with a **dry paper towel**. Wipe them with a **cloth** moistened with a **silicone spray**. Don't overdo it, because too much lubrication can also make them stick together.

To maintain a stationary bike, the most important thing to do is to clean and lubricate the chain every three months or so. Clean the chain by carefully holding a **dry rag** on it and slowly turning the pedals to run the chain through the rag a few times. Next, lubricate the chain with a **Teflon** or **silicone spray lubricant,** available at bicycle shops. To avoid splattering, don't jump on and pedal immediately; let the lubricant dry, which should take only a few minutes.

Have your equipment professionally serviced every year or so to keep it working safely.

Fans

Ceiling fans have propeller blades that need regular cleaning. Use a lamb's wool duster and a stepladder or step stool and give the blades a quick dusting. Other types of fans have grilles that protect the blades. Clean the grilles and other housing regularly using a vacuum cleaner with a small brush attachment.

Do a more thorough cleaning every month or two during times of heavy use. First, disengage the circuit breaker for a ceiling fan and unplug others. Remove the grilles. Then get together the following: a **solution of water with a little washing-up liquid** and a **sponge** or **brush**. Dampen the sponge and wipe the blades. Rinse the sponge in **clear water** and wipe again. Then dry with a **clean cloth**. Be careful not to bend the blades, because that may upset their balance and make the fan wobble.

If the grilles have accumulated a lot of grime, it may be simplest to take them outside and wash them under a **hose**. Use a **stiff brush** to clean off caked-on dirt and grime.

Fibreglass (glassfibre)

You'll find this synthetic covering material used for cars and boats as well as baths, sinks and shower bases and their surrounds. It's not glass at all, but a reinforced plastic. Unlike acrylic, any colour is only on the top layer. If you scratch glassfibre, you may lift off the colour. So always use nonabrasive cleaners and scrubbers.

After you shower, rinse the shower walls with **water** and wipe them down with a **squeegee** or **chamois cloth** to avoid a build-up of water residue and soap scum. Once a week, wash with a little **mild washing-up liquid** and **warm water**, applied with a **sponge**. Always rinse cleaners off with clear water.

To attack mould and mildew, mix **bicarbonate of soda** with enough **water** to make a paste. Wet the glassfibre with water, dip a sponge in the paste and rub gently. Rinse with **clear water**. This also works for general cleaning.

To remove soap scum, mix a solution of **1 part ammonia** to **4 parts water**. Or use a cleaner such as *Flash Bathroom Spray*, that is designed to shift soap scum. Rub on with a **sponge** or **clean rag** and rinse immediately and thoroughly with **clear water**.

Hard-water deposits can also be removed with **boat cleaners**. (Many boats are glassfibre, after all.) Look for these cleaners at hardware or boating stores and follow the package directions.

To remove glue, tar, or oil-based paint stains, put a little **acetone nail polish remover** or **paint thinner** on a **clean cloth** and lightly rub until the spot disappears. Then wash with **washing-up liquid** and water. Finally, rinse with **clear water**.

To help preserve the finish of glassfibre, take a tip from sailors. A couple of times a year, use a **white polishing compound** from a car supplies shop, such as *Turtle Wax Colour Magic White Polish* on any dull or scratchy areas. Then apply a light coat of **white paste wax**, also from car supplies shops. Buff with a **clean cloth**. The surface will be slippery, so use on walls only, not on floors. This treatment will also protect glassfibre outdoor furniture.

Filters

Anything designed to catch dirt should be cleaned often. Filters fit the description. Plus, dirty ones don't just not work very well, they also cost more money, because their motors will use more energy to pass air or water through dirty filters than clean ones.

Cleaning air filters is usually simple. You throw out the old one and install a new one. So follow pack instructions and it's not a cleaning job at all. Air conditioner filters, which may be disposable or washable, also need monthly attention. If the filter is washable, remove it and **vacuum** up as much dust as you can. Then rinse it under **warm**

Your filtered drinking water is only as fresh as the filter that cleans it. Change it frequently.

running water or swirl it around in a solution of **1 tablespoon of bicarbonate of soda** and **1 litre of water** – don't use soap. Rinse and dry.

Home water-filtering systems often use activated carbon filters that extract chemicals from the water. The activated carbon usually comes in cartridges that need to be replaced when they no longer work. The tricky part is figuring out when they've stopped doing their job. Sometimes you can tell by the taste of the water if the filter is designed to remove chlorine, for example. But a more reliable way is simply to mark on a calendar each time your three or six monthly filter change is due.

Fireplaces

Ironically, fireplace cleaning is simpler during the wood-burning season and more of a project off-season. During the fire-burning season, cleaning will usually consist merely of removing some of the ashes periodically. The fireplace will actually work better when a thin layer of ash remains.

Use an ash shovel to remove ashes, then tip them into a metal bucket with a tight-fitting lid. Leave the ashes in the bucket for a few days before final disposal.

Many fireplaces have an ash pit, which is a receptacle underneath the area where you build a fire. If yours does, open it and push excess ashes into it. Or use an **ash shovel** to deposit the ashes in a **metal bucket with a tight-fitting lid**. Store the ashes outdoors in the tightly covered can for two days before final disposal, an important precaution because 'dead' ashes containing live embers have started many a fire.

During the off-season, do a more thorough cleaning. Use a **rubber eraser** on any smoke streaks that have crept up the exterior of the fireplace. If your fireplace has warm-air circulators, clean the ducts thoroughly with a **vacuum cleaner**.

You may also want to remove the black layer of creosote, a highly combustible residue created by burning wood, on the inside of the firebox. (The firebox is where you build your fire.) Remove the screen, irons and grate and sweep up all the ashes with a **dustpan and brush**.

Use a wire-bristled brush for the first attack on the creosote. If you want the firebox to be cleaner, use **50ml of soda crystals** (from supermarkets) in **4 litres of water** and apply it with a **sponge**. Brush with a **stiff-fibre brush** and rinse with **clear water**. Wear **rubber gloves**, since washing soda is caustic.

The off-season is also the time to have the chimney cleaned. This is a job for a professional chimney sweep, who will check the flue for leaves, bird's nests, cracks and soot build-up.

See also Brick, Chimneys and Fireplace screens & tools.

Fireplace screens & tools

Your entire fireplace arrangement may dazzle you with charm in the evening but, in the harsh light of the next day, your equipment may look rather battle weary.

Clean the fireplace screen with a **vacuum cleaner** as part of your regular cleaning routine in the room. A screen catches more than the sparks that want to go flying into the room. It also catches a lot of dust. Periodically, give it a more substantial cleaning with **soap** and **water**. Pick a sunny day and work outside. Make a sudsy solution of **warm water** and a few squirts of **washing-up liquid** and scrub the screen with a **stiff-bristled brush** dipped in the solution. Then rinse it off with the **garden hose**. If you're working inside, rinse with a **sponge** dipped in clean water. Allow the screen to dry thoroughly. If it has brass parts, clean them with a **brass polish**.

Clean fireplace tools (shovels, pokers, tongs), as well as irons and grates, with the same brush and soapy solution. Use **extra-fine (000) steel wool** on rust or stubborn dirt. Dry the tools with a **soft cloth**. Give them a light coat of **vegetable oil** with a clean cloth; then wipe them dry with another cloth.

If rust is a problem on your screen or tools, you can renew the finish with a coat of **high-temperature black spray paint**, sold in hardware stores.

After removing rust, a coat of high-temperature black spray paint will renew the finish of your fireplace tools.

Clean glass fireplace doors with a touch of caution
(see Watch out, left). But there is one certain guideline:
doors should be cleaned only when they're cool, never
when they're hot. Common glass cleaners, such as
Windolene, don't work very well on black creosote deposits.
A solution of ammonia and water will clean them up, but
the solution also may strip your doors of their heatproof
coating. Instead, try this:

1 Dip a **damp rag** in ashes from the fireplace and rub the
glass with that. Then wipe dry with a **clean cloth**. Or dip a
cloth in **white vinegar** and wash. Dry with newspaper.
2 If you're still seeking perfection, try rubbing with **white
polishing compound** from a car supplies shop.
3 Try a speciality cleaner, like those from the *Stovax* range,
to shine up any glass doors or surrounds.

See also **Brass.**

Fishing rods

The biggest enemies of fishing gear are sand and salt,
which are abundant at many favourite fishing spots (unless
you fish only in fresh water lakes and rivers). Clean up
after every outing. If you put equipment away wet, slimy
and salty, its performance will suffer.

To clean your rod, mix **1 teaspoon of washing-up
liquid** in **1 litre of water**. Dip a **cleaning cloth** in the
solution and wipe the rod. Rinse the soap off with **running
water** and wipe it dry with a **clean cloth**.

If mud or other dirt has built up around the line
guides, scrub them with an **old toothbrush** dipped in the
soapy solution. Use the same treatment on dirt around the
reel seat that can't be wiped off.

Don't use oil to shine your rod, as it can destroy the
protective coating and eventually loosen the line guides and
reel seat. Bamboo rods are an exception – polish them with
a **cream-type furniture polish**.

To lubricate the joints of the ferrules (the metal
connector sleeves) and keep them clean and smooth, dab a
little **petroleum jelly** on one joint and slide the two pieces

together and apart several times. Use a **cotton bud** to wipe off the petroleum jelly and dirt. If the ferrules have become rusted, you may be able to clean them with **fine steel wool (00)** or **glasspaper**, but be careful not to spoil the fit and end up with a rod that flies apart when you're casting. It may be best to send the rod to a repair specialist.

To clean the rod grips, use the same cloth and soapy solution. Cork demands careful handling, because rough treatment can cause pieces to break off. A very dirty or damaged cork grip is another candidate for a professional repair job. Allow cork grips to air-dry to avoid mildew.

Fishponds

One way to clean your manmade fishpond would be to turn the job over to a great blue heron. Herons eat lots of fish and too many fish make a fishpond dirty. Fish urine, like that of other animals, contains toxic ammonia. If you don't want to be that dramatic, the best approach to the problem is to work with nature rather than against her.

Even a small pond is a complex ecological system and the right mix of two plant groups – submerged plants to oxygenate the water and floating plants to provide shade – will help control algae. The mix must be in the right proportions to work effectively. A good book on creating ponds will tell you how to do it.

Routine pond maintenance consists mostly of removing debris such as dead leaves from the water. Use a **long-handled swimming pool skimmer net**. Don't expect your pond to be vodka clear. The water should be a pale green. Environmental balance takes a long time to establish, so don't be too quick to upset it by emptying and refilling the pond.

A major pond cleaning is called for when there is a lot of muck or too many fish in the water. The pond may have been overstocked, or the fish may have multiplied. In either case, you may have to find new homes for some of your scaly friends. A rule of thumb is that each fish in a pond should have about a barrel of water. The best time – and many experts say the only time – to clean a pond is in

Not reel simple

It is a big challenge to take a reel apart for cleaning and get it back in working order. You can postpone the job by washing the reel after every outing. Use water or a teaspoon of washing-up liquid in a litre of water. Scrub with a soft-bristled toothbrush. Wash your tackle, including any used lures. Rinse well and dry with a clean cloth.

After every couple of outings, strip out the main drive gears and the pinion gear and soak them in a strong degreaser, such as methylated spirit. Then wash with warm water and dry well.

Periodically, a reel will need to be taken apart, cleaned and oiled. If you want to do the job yourself, make sure you have the internal diagram and parts list that came with the reel, and follow the directions. However, this is really best left to a professional. Check with your local angling shop.

early spring, when cool temperatures provide a less stressful environment for the fish and plants. Even so, always keep the fish and plants that you remove from the pond in the shade to avoid stressing them.

Here's what to do:

1 Begin by removing the edge plants and then the floating ones, pot and all. Put them in the shade.

2 Use a **bucket** to draw water off the top (the cleanest part) of the pond.

Place a **children's paddling pool** in a shady spot and fill it with the water, which will be the right pH and temperature to hold the fish. Save as much of the rest of the pond water as you can in extra containers, unless it is really disgusting.

3 When the pond has been half drained, remove the fish with a **net** (top) and transfer them to the paddling pool. Cover it with a **mesh screen**, to stop any aspiring flying fish.

3 Start removing the remaining water with a **pump** or **siphon** (right). As the water level drops, remove the submerged plants and put them in the paddling pool, too.

5 While there is still water at the bottom of the pond, clean the sides with a **soft-bristled scrubbing brush**. Continue to drain until the bottom layer of dirt is in sight. Then stop pumping and remove the bottom debris with a **dustpan**.

6 Rinse the sides of the pool with a **hose** and then remove the pump and rinse. Gently scrub the bottom (right).

7 Replace the plants before you begin refilling. Use a **water conditioner**, available at pet or aquarium stores, to neutralise chlorine in the new water. Return the water that you have saved in the paddling pool and other containers to the pond and let the pond warm up slightly before returning the fish.

Simple solutions

A cleaner home for your fish

To keep a pond cleaner, an aerator of some kind (any device, such as a fountain that mixes air into the water) will help, as will freshwater snails, which will eat algae and unwanted plant growth

Flags & banners

Most flags have colours that, if each were the colour of an individual item in the laundry basket, you'd separate and wash in different loads. Banners, often with appliquéd designs and depicting seasonal or whimsical themes, also often use contrasting colours.

To keep the colours pure, first check the box or bag that your flag or banner came in – if you still have it – to see whether it has directions for cleaning. If instructions aren't available, try to determine what kind of fabric the flag or banner is made of. Most newer flags are usually cotton, nylon or polyester.

Washing a nylon or polyester flag or banner is usually safe. Put it in a **washing machine** on a gentle cycle in **warm water** with a **mild detergent**. You can hang it out to dry on a clothesline or dry it on low in the dryer.

Dry-cleaning a cotton flag or banner is usually necessary – especially if you value it highly – because it is likely to bleed if washed. A wool flag or banner should always be dry-cleaned.

Simple solutions

Keep it flying proudly

To extend a flag's life, take it down when it rains, snows or is very windy. If a flag does become wet, let it dry thoroughly before you fold or roll it. Otherwise, you're inviting mildew to take up residence.

Floors

Not all floors are created equal. Even among general categories such as wood, stone or tile, there are vast differences between specific examples. Maple isn't pine, marble isn't granite and quarry tiles are not glazed.

Still, all floors are subjected to dirt and wear, so some basic cleaning techniques apply universally. The Floor Cleaning Pyramid on page 216 gives general floor cleaning methods. When you've exhausted those, try the recommendations under the following headings for specific floor types.

To clean wood floors you will have to get down on your hands and knees. You can't swab water all over the floor – it must be used sparingly.

When damp mopping isn't enough to shift grease or serious dirt, try one of these general-purpose cleaners:
• Mix **100ml cider vinegar** in **4 litres of warm water**.
• Brew some tea using **2 tea bags** per **1 litre of water**.

You can clean up grout nicely by scrubbing it with a toothbrush dipped in a solution of vinegar and water.

Dip a **soft cloth** or **sponge** in the solution, wring it out and wipe the floor. Then to finish, buff with a **soft, dry cloth**.

Caring diligently for wood floors will save you having to re-sand them regularly which can be time-consuming, expensive and messy. And it removes from your floor not just the old finish but a layer of wood. Each time you sand, you're working your way towards the day when you'll need thin, worn-out floorboards replaced.

Determining a wood floor's finish will help you to work out how to care for it. If the floor was installed or last refinished before the mid 1960s, the finish is probably varnish or shellac. These finishes rest on top of the wood, are often waxed and require a whole-floor sanding before a new finish can be applied. Later finishes may be polyurethane, which penetrates the wood, should not be waxed and can be touched up by new urethane applied to the worn places.

You can tell one from the other by scratching the surface with a coin in an inconspicuous place. If the finish flakes, it is probably shellac or varnish. If the finish does not flake, it is probably urethane.

To check for wax, put a couple of drops of water on the floor. Wait 10 minutes and check to see whether white spots have appeared under the water. White spots mean the floor has been waxed. If there are no white spots, it hasn't.

On varnished or shellacked floors, a **solvent-based liquid wax for wood** works well. It removes dirt and most of the old wax, prevents wax build-up and leaves a thin coating of new wax. You can apply the cleaner with a **soft, dry cloth** attached to a **long-handled wax applicator**, but you will do a better job on your hands and knees. You can also use an **electric polisher**, changing the pads frequently. In any case, you must buff afterward with a **clean cloth**. Never use water-based self-polishing wax on wood floors.

On urethane-finished floors, rub with a **cloth** containing a **little furniture oil** to give them more shine. (Read the label to make sure it doesn't contain any wax.) Be sure to use very little; too much oil will attract dirt – and turn the floor into a skating rink.

To clean stone flooring, try this low-tech method: Sprinkle **damp sawdust** over the floor, scrub with a **stiff**

Simple solutions

Payback for a heel

Have high heels left stubborn black marks on your floors?

Try rubbing heel marks with a pencil eraser first. If that doesn't work, rub a hardwood floor with a rag dabbed in a little white spirit. On vinyl flooring, smear a drop of baby oil over the mark, wait a few minutes, and wipe the mark away with a rag.

brush and sweep up the sawdust with a **broom and dustpan**. Follow up with a **vacuum**.

Many kinds of stone flooring, especially marble, need a **neutral pH cleaner** (sold by businesses that sell and install stone flooring). A **mild washing-up liquid** mixed with **water** will also work nicely. Consult the dealer who sold you the stone for recommendations for specific cleaners if more power is needed. There are also professionals who can refinish stone floors.

To clean ceramic tile floors, a quick once-over with a **damp mop** is often all that is needed. Indeed, cleaning ceramic tiles would be a breeze if the tiles were all you had to clean. It's the grout that's the real problem.

When damp mopping alone isn't enough, mix **1 capful of methylated spirits** in **4 litres of water**. Apply the solution with a **mop** or an **electric cleaner-polisher**. Rinse well with **clear water** on your mop. A commercial cleaner such as *Microshield Floor Tile Cleaner* has the added benefit of containing an anti-mould ingredient which is handy if your floor is prone to dampness.

Watch out

Acids (such as vinegar) will etch marble, and strong alkaline solutions (such as soda crystals) will break down the surface and leave it rough. The moral? Sweep and clean marble floors often, and mild products will be all you'll need.

The lowdown on wax build-up

High-traffic areas will wear out their wax sooner than low-traffic areas. This means parts of your floor that don't get walked on very often can get a nasty wax build-up. A telltale sign is a floor that is yellowed or discoloured around the edges. Removing all the wax requires harsher cleaning than usual and should be done only when necessary and no more often than once a year.

Here are two recipes for a wax stripper:
- 200ml of ammonia and 400ml of detergent in 4 litres of warm water.
- 100ml of soda crystals (available at supermarkets in the detergent section) in 4 litres of warm water.

In either case, apply some solution and scrub with a stiff brush, electric scrubber, or extra-fine steel wool (000) pads to loosen the old wax. Work on a small area at a time and mop up the solution after the wax has been softened. Repeat the process in other areas until the entire floor is stripped of wax. Rinse thoroughly with a solution of 4 litres of water and 250ml of vinegar. After drying completely, apply new wax.

If the grout needs special attention, mix **50ml of vinegar** with **4 litres of water** and scrub the grout with a **toothbrush** or **nylon scrubbing pad**. For heavy-duty treatment, scrub with a mixture of **100ml of chlorine**

The Floor Cleaning Pyramid

Most of us are familiar with the Food Guide Pyramid. You're supposed to eat more of the healthy foods depicted at the bottom of the pyramid (fruits, vegetables and grains) while eating the foods at the top (sweets, fats and oils) more sparingly. On the Floor Cleaning Pyramid, the broad bottom includes the cleaning methods that apply to all types of floors and that should be used most frequently. Frequency of use declines as you go up the pyramid and the top is reserved for specialised cleaners for different flooring materials.

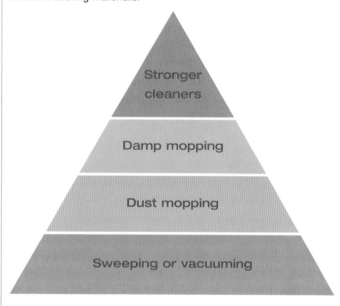

Here are other general guidelines for floor cleaning:
- Vacuum or sweep up loose dirt frequently.
- Use a dust mop – or tie a duster onto the base of a broom – to remove dust and cobwebs from corners.
- Wipe up any spills immediately.
- Clean with a damp mop or cloth (using plain water) weekly or more often. Change the water as soon as it gets cloudy.
- Use stronger cleaners only when a damp mop won't do the job.
- Rinse thoroughly after using any kind of cleaner.

bleach in **2 litres of water** (wear rubber gloves). Let the solution stand for 20 minutes, mop the floor twice with **clean water** to rinse thoroughly and wipe dry. To make future cleaning easier, it's worth sealing the grout with a **silicone sealer**, available at home stores, hardware stores or specialist tile shops.

To clean vinyl flooring that just needs touching up, use a **damp mop**. If the level of soiling requires something stronger than water, mix **250ml of white vinegar** with **4 litres of water** and apply with a **mop**. Apply a small amount with your mop, then rinse thoroughly by mopping with plain water.

To add shine, apply a thin coat of **wax** to a dry, clean floor. The one-step wax-and-clean products don't work as well as a regular wax. A **self-polishing wax** (such as *Johnson One Step No Buff Wax*) is easy to apply, but it will build up over time. A **solvent-based paste wax** (such as *Johnson Paste Wax*) is more work and must be buffed but provides superior results.

No-wax vinyl has a polyurethane finish that is intended to keep a shine without waxing. It will stay shiny for a long time if it is kept clean, but eventually the finish will dull. Follow the manufacturer's directions as to how to use a **polish** or **sealer** to renew the shine.

If hair spray has built up on the no-wax floor in the bathroom, use **shampoo** to wash it off. Mix a **squirt of shampoo** in **4 litres of warm water**, mop and rinse.

To clean laminate flooring, keep in mind that, like wood, it should not be mopped by slopping lots of water around on the floor. (Laminate is the manmade flooring that comes in tongue-and-groove planks that often simulate wood.) Don't use ammonia, solvents, abrasives, general-purpose cleaners, polishes or waxes on laminate. Despite these restrictions, laminate is very easy to clean.

Some manufacturers recommend their own special cleaner, which is usually fairly expensive. However, any **cleaner for wood floors** will be fine.

If your laminate gets scratched, you may be able to buy a **touch-up stick** from the manufacturer. In the event of severe damage, you may be able to replace a plank or two – especially if you've laid the floor yourself and have a few off-cuts put by.

Flowerpots

A beautiful flower in a dirty pot is like a beautiful cake on a food-encrusted plate. They don't go together. You don't clean flowerpots solely for aesthetic reasons, however. Plants and their soil may contain viruses, bacteria, fungi or pests, which can be passed along unknowingly to the next pot occupant.

Clean your flowerpots using the same method, whether they're made of plastic, glazed or unglazed clay, ceramic or other materials. Wash with **washing–up liquid** and **water**, as you would dishes. Scour with a **stiff brush** to remove algae and mineral deposits. Wash again with a solution of **10 parts water** to **1 part chlorine bleach**. Rinse with fresh water and let dry in the sunshine – a great natural steriliser.

Here are some more tips for cleaning flowerpots:
• If you'd prefer to avoid scrubbing, soak the pots for about an hour in a solution of **2 parts water** to **1 part white vinegar**. The minerals and algae should wash right off.
• To avoid a crusty white build-up of mineral deposits around the top inner edge of the pot, take a **candle** and rub it around the rim. That will seal the surface, making mineral build-up less likely.
• You might also heed the message that the white scaly deposits are giving. They are telling you that you're giving your plants too much fertiliser. Many indulgent plant lovers do that, so consider cutting back. Get a good book on caring for houseplants and follow its advice.
• To keep soil from spattering out of the pot when it rains or when you water the plant, put a **layer of pebbles** on top of the soil.

Discourage the build-up of crusty, white deposits on the inside rim of pots by rubbing them with a candle.

Flowers

Fresh flowers are among the cheeriest things on earth. There's not much to be done to improve on nature, other than brush off the stray piece of dirt with a soft paintbrush and coax them into lasting a long time.

Dusting artificial or dried flowers is something you need to do occasionally. Use a **feather duster** or a **hair**

dryer on its lowest, coolest setting to blow off the dust on sturdy blooms. Use **canned air** to squirt air on any especially fragile flowers. (Today most fabric flowers are made of polyester or other blends rather than silk.)

For a more thorough cleaning, try this method, which is safe for both plastic and fabric flowers. (Some people say they've used it successfully on dried natural flowers, too, but proceed at your own risk.) Draw enough water into the sink (or bath, if necessary) so that the flowers can be submerged. Add a **squirt of washing-up liquid** and slosh it around to make suds. Then put the flowers in the water, holding them down until they are covered. Gently raise and lower them a couple of times. Drain the water and rinse the flowers using the sink tap on a very slow mode or under the shower in the bathroom. Let the flowers air-dry thoroughly.

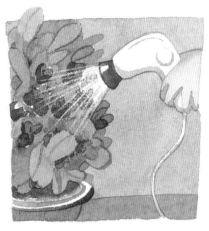

A quick and easy way to dust artificial flowers is to give them a blast of air from a hair dryer.

Here are some more flower-enhancing tricks that you might want to try:
• Use a **steam iron**, set on the lowest setting, to perk up paper flowers.
• Dried natural flowers will last longer if they've been given several light coats of **sealer** from an **aerosol spray can**. You can use **hair spray** or a **clear lacquer** or **acrylic sealer** (available at hardware stores). The flowers can be resealed after cleaning.

Making your flowers last longer

Here are some ways to slow the passage of blooms to has-beens:
- Cut off any leaves below water level.
- Wash the vase and change the water daily.
- Use a simple preservative in the water, such as 2 tablespoons of white vinegar and 2 teaspoons of sugar to a litre of water. (Sugar feeds the flowers, and vinegar inhibits the growth of unwanted mould or fungus.) Or use 1 part tonic water to 2 parts water. Or dissolve an aspirin in the water.
- Keep the flowers cool and out of direct sunlight.
- Cut off the ends periodically.

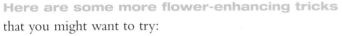

• For a final act, you might gild your lilies when they're beyond cleaning. Spray artificial or dried flowers with **gold or silver spray paint** and you'll be able to use them for Christmas or other festive decorations.

Foam rubber

The nice thing about foam rubber – whether it's the latex rubber used from the 1940s to the 1960s or polyurethane, the preferred material since the 1970s – is that it's porous. That means all you have to do to keep the foam that's in your cushions, pillows or mattresses fresh is to vacuum them. Spills are another story and will require a little more elbow grease.

To clean spills or marks on the foam's surface, first remove any covering (clean it separately); then use a **rag** dampened with **washing-up liquid** and **water** and rub the surface. Never put soap and water directly on the foam, because it will absorb the liquid. Let the foam air-dry thoroughly before you put the cushion cover, sheet or pillowcase back on.

Heavy spills that have seeped into the interior of the foam require special attention. Run **water** – only water – through the foam, then squeeze out as much water as you can. If you use soap or other cleaning agents, you'll have to rinse those out, too, or you risk creating a breeding ground for bacteria.

Bag a dirty pillow

To quickly and thoroughly clean a foam rubber pillow or cushion, all you need is a plastic bag and a vacuum cleaner.

Remove any attachment from the end of the vacuum cleaner's hose. Put the pillow in a plastic bag; then put the end of the vacuum hose in the bag, twist the top of the bag closed and hold it in place. Then turn on the vacuum cleaner. The foam will become condensed as the vacuum cleaner sucks the air and dirt out of the foam. When you turn the vacuum cleaner off, the foam will return to its original shape. This technique cleans both sides of the pillow at the same time.

To clean a deep stain from a small cushion or pillow, place the foam in the **bath** or **sink** and run **water** over it. For larger cushions, use a **shower nozzle** or **garden hose**. Don't try to do this on a mattress, which can only be surface cleaned.

Even when you're dealing with a major stain, keep water to a minimum, because it will take 24 to 48 hours for the foam to dry. There's nothing you can do to speed the process, either. Above all, don't ever rest foam near a radiator or heat source or even try to put small pieces in a dryer – it's highly flammable.

No matter how good a job you do, some odours and stains – such as pet urine – may not come out if they have seeped into the interior of the foam rubber. You may just have to replace it.

Food

Clean food – and food that's safe to eat – starts with clean hands. Follow what doctors and nursing staff do. The most important thing you can do to keep yourself healthy and prevent the spread of illness is to wash your hands frequently and thoroughly with soap and water. Once you're squeaky clean, you're ready to prepare food.

To clean fruit and vegetables, you don't need anything special. Washing with **plain water** will do. Just be sure you wash all your fruit and vegetables – even the organic ones. You are not just washing off chemical residue, but also germs that may have got onto your produce as it has been handled and stored. So whilst organic items may not have residual chemicals on them, they may have the same amount of dirt, dust and mould spores.

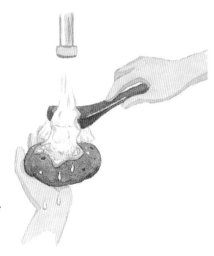

Give tough-skinned fruit and vegetables a scrub with a vegetable brush before cooking.

Here are cleaning specifics for certain foods:
• For vegetables and fruits with a firm surface, such as potatoes, celery and apples, use a **vegetable brush** to scrub the skin under **running water**.
• For leaf vegetables and fruits with a soft skin, such as peaches, strawberries and raspberries, rinse under **running water** only.
• Rinse mushrooms by holding them under **running water** or dunking them in a **bowl of water**.

How to truly get the grit

Rinsing is not enough to get the grit out of lettuce or spinach leaves. The greens need a bath. Fill a clean kitchen sink with enough cold water to cover the greens, and submerge them for 30 to 45 seconds. Swish the leaves around with your hand and then empty the water in the sink. Clean the sink to remove the sand and grit. Repeat the process. Keep washing, draining and washing until you see no more sand and grit in the sink when you let the water out.

• To dry vegetables and fruits, use a **clean tea towel** or **paper towel**. A **lettuce spinner** is a good idea for greens. If you're preparing vegetables to cook, you don't necessarily need to dry them.

• Cut away any bruised or damaged areas from fruits and vegetables with a **sharp knife**. Immediately refrigerate any fresh-cut items.

• Rinse fish quickly in **cold water** to remove ice, slime and any loose small scales you can't see.

And here are some don'ts:

• Don't use a brush on soft-skinned vegetables or fruits. You'll damage them.

• Don't use detergents or soap. The produce could absorb the residues, which you could ingest.

• Don't wash raw poultry, beef, pork, lamb or veal before using. You may think you're helping to make the meat safe, but you're not, you could be spreading germs. Cooking the meat at hot temperatures will destroy bacteria.

• Keep raw meat, fish and poultry in **containers**. Never place them directly on counters or the refrigerator shelves. Never let the juices of raw meat drip onto other foods and never use the same utensils on cooked foods that you have used for handling raw meat.

• Don't wash eggs before storing or using them. They will have been washed during commercial egg processing. Washing will just remove more of the 'bloom', the natural coating on just-laid eggs that helps to prevent bacteria from permeating the shell.

Food graters

If you're a cook who likes the freshness of home-grated cheese, citrus rind and hard spices, such as cardamom, nutmeg and cinnamon, a grater is a must-have gadget in your kitchen. It's also a difficult tool to clean because some foods get trapped in the grates or leave a residue.

To clean the grater, soak it in **warm to hot, soapy water**. Use a **pan brush** with short bristles or even an **unused toothbrush** for the smaller graters. To protect the bristles of your brush, hold the grater upside down and brush with a bottom-to-top stroke (the opposite of the grating motion). You can put a grater in a **dishwasher**, as long as the grater isn't made of tin, which can quickly oxidise when it's not dried thoroughly.

To dry your grater, place it on a **dish rack** or a **lint-free tea towel**. If you're paranoid about a tin grater not drying sufficiently and possibly rusting, let it dry for 15 minutes in the oven on a low heat.

Food grinders

Because a food grinder is often used to process meat, poultry and seafood, proper cleaning is critical to prevent transmission of harmful bacteria, such as salmonella. The best grinders disassemble completely, allowing you to clean each piece thoroughly.

To clean the grinding plates, first soak the parts in a soapy solution of **hot water** and **washing-up liquid** to dislodge most of the food. You can finish the job in a **dishwasher** (always consult the manufacturer's instructions first), set on a hot cycle.

If you're cleaning the parts by hand, one expert prefers a soak with a little salt (**1 tablespoon of salt** to **2 litres of cold water**) for about 10 minutes to dislodge the food. Then you're ready to scrub the plates and blade with a **brush** in **hot, soapy water** to kill bacteria. To help get meat or other remnants out of the holes in the plates, poke **wooden kebab skewers** through the holes.

Lay the parts on a cloth towel and let them air-dry fully. Or you can place the parts in an **oven** at a temperature of 65°C for 10 to 15 minutes. If you put aluminium alloy blades in the dishwasher, they'll quickly start to rust when they sit and dry. Once the blades are dry, rub **vegetable** or **salad oil** lightly over them to protect them from rusting.

To clean a food grinder's motor unit, never immerse it fully in water. Instead, use a spray bottle to lightly mist on an **anti-bacterial kitchen cleaner**. Or make your own: use **10ml of bleach** in **1 litre of warm water**. Wipe off with a **cloth**.

Food processors

For general cleaning, use water pressure from having the tap on at full blast to remove stuck on food from your food processor's discs and blades.

If your recipe doesn't require the use of the feed tube on top of your food processor, cover the bowl with a strong piece of **plastic wrap** before locking on the lid. This will prevent splattering on the lid and minimise cleaning.

To clean the power unit of your food processor, turn it off and unplug the unit. Wipe it with a **damp cloth**. Wipe off the safety motor drive cover and reinstall it on the unit, if necessary. Never use coarse or caustic cleaning products on the power unit or immerse it in water.

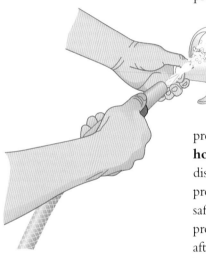

Some food can be particularly hard to clean off, especially when it's dried. For very tough jobs, a quick squirt outside with a hose may get things shifted.

To clean the attachments, put them in the dishwasher – all except the blades. Since items can shift in the dishwasher, the blades could bend, be dulled or be burned if they touch a heating element. Wash the blades in **hot, soapy water**, dry with a cloth and store for future use. Some experts also prefer to hand-wash the plastic bowl of a food processor in **hot, soapy water**. This protects the bowl from the harsher dishwasher detergent, which can make the plastic brittle and prone to breakage. On some models, the plastic bowl has a safety spring located where the bowl attaches to the food processor. It's difficult to get this spring thoroughly dry, so after you've given the bowl a quick wipe, let it air-dry before reassembling the processor. Otherwise, the spring may rust.

Fountains

Washing your fountain periodically with a solution of 1 part bleach to 10 parts water will help inhibit to algal growth. To prevent mineral deposits from forming on bowls, the motor shaft, or other parts of the pump (which could cause it to fail), always use distilled water, rainwater or dehumidified water in the fountain. If your fountain is so big that using distilled water is not practical, treat the water with a mineral deposit inhibitor recommended by your local fountain or garden centre.

To remove mineral deposits – should they develop despite your best efforts – you'll first need to know what your fountain bowl is made of.

• Some materials, such as resins and copper, are soft and should be cleaned with a **cotton rag**.

• Slate can be cleaned with a **soft-bristled brush** – but don't use soap. Slate can be porous; if it absorbs soap, your fountain could turn into a bubble bath.

• Other fountain bowl materials can be cleaned with an **abrasive sponge** and **white vinegar** or a **mineral deposit cleaner**, available at hardware stores and home improvement stores.

If your preventive maintenance is working, you may need to clean your fountain parts only once a year. If you're getting mineral deposits, you'll have to clean the parts more frequently – likewise if you're not using a water treatment product. In general, you should sterilise your fountain after you clean it and before you reassemble it by dipping all parts, including the pump, in the **mild bleach solution** mentioned above (1 part bleach to 10 parts water).

To clean the fountainhead, you will also need to know what it's made of:

• Most moulded fountainheads are cast from a polyester resin mixed with fillers such as powdered marble. These materials are strong but scratch easily, so the best way to clean them is with **warm, soapy water** and a **soft sponge**. Before using tile cleaners or other acids on a cast resin fountainhead, check it by putting a few drops of the cleaner on the bottom of the fountainhead and scrubbing it for a short while with a **toothbrush**.

• When cleaning concrete or natural stone, never use an acid cleaner. **Washing-up liquid** or **bleach** mixed with **water**, plus a **scrubbing brush**, will work fine.

• Clean slate as for removing mineral deposits.

To clean a fountain pump, first check to see how well it's working. Most pumps have some sort of inlet strainers or screens to ensure that small pebbles and other debris don't get into the pump and jam or damage it. Watch the water flow in your fountain. If you notice it's slowing down, clean the pump before it clogs entirely, overheats and burns out. (Then you'll have to replace it.)

Simple solutions

If you want to see the coins at the bottom

To combat slime and algae in a fountain, preventive maintenance will go a long way. A water treatment, such as *Fountec*, will keep algae at bay and yet is safe for birds, pets, and plants (not for fish, though). You typically add a few drops to the fountain each week. Treatment products are available at fountain and garden stores.

With indoor pumps and simple outdoor pumps, you can follow the instructions that came with the pump to learn how to take it apart and reassemble it. If your pump has an adjustable flow, note the setting when you remove the pump for cleaning, in case you inadvertently change it. Once you have taken the pump apart, clean it with **warm water**, **washing-up liquid** and an **old toothbrush**. Dip the parts in a **bleach solution** and reassemble it.

The more complex, industrial-type fountains are trickier to clean and should be entrusted to a professional cleaner.

Fountain pens

All fountain pens – whether they have a metal or gold nib – should be cleaned after they have been filled four or five times or you have used four or five cartridges.

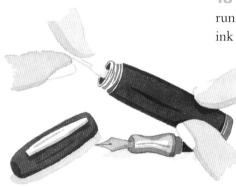

Use a cotton bud to clean inside the narrow barrel of your fountain pen.

To clean your fountain pen, flush the nib section by running it under **plain tap water** at room temperature. For ink deposits that may have stood in the pen for a long time, make one of the following three solutions. They will help the water penetrate into areas in the pen much more quickly and thoroughly:

• **1 drop of washing-up liquid** in **1 cup of water** at room temperature.

• A couple of squirts of **all-purpose household cleaner**, such as *Flash*, in **1 cup of water**.

• A few squirts (about a teaspoon) of a **bleach cleaner**, such as *Tesco Oxygen Bleach*, in **150ml of water**.

To clean self-filling pens, the kind you dip into the ink, place your cleaning solution (see above) in a **glass** and draw it into the pen, just as you would to fill the pen with ink. Then place the nib in the water and let it all soak for two hours to two days, depending on how long the ink has been in the pen. To rinse, draw fresh water into the pen and empty it a couple of times.

To clean a pen that's not heavily caked with ink, fill the pen with one of the above solutions and empty it two or three times.

Cleaning ink-cartridge pens is a little trickier because there's no device on the pen to force the cleaning solution through the very fine internal channels of the nib. Squeeze an **empty ink cartridge** to force the air out, dip it into one of the cleaning solutions mentioned above and release it, drawing the solution into the cartridge. Attach the cartridge to the nib section as if it were full of ink and squeeze the cleaning solution out of the cartridge and through the nib. Repeat the procedure a couple of times.

More tips for cleaning fountain pens:
• India ink or waterproof inks aren't recommended for fountain pens. They should be used only with the type of pens that are dipped into an inkwell.
• Avoid letting hot water, alcohol or acetone come in contact with your fountain pen, because they could damage certain parts of it.
• The barrel (the shaft that holds the ink) and cap of your pen can be washed in **cold water**. Use a **cotton bud** to clean the interior of these long, narrow cylinders.
• Dry each section of your pen before putting it back together. A **cotton bud** is useful for this task, because it can get into all parts of the pen.

Fridges & freezers

Keeping your refrigerator and freezer clean is not only important to the appearance (and smell) of your home, it's also crucial to the hygiene of your food and your family's health. There are three major aspects of keeping refrigerators and freezers clean: removing dirt, killing germs and deodorising the interior.

Cleaning the fridge is only a half-hour job, so there's no need to fret about keeping food cold. Instead, empty one shelf at a time, so food on the other shelves can stay chilled. Remove the first shelf and spray it liberally with a **disinfecting all-purpose cleaner** – *Dettol* make one – to vanquish the inevitable sticky spills. (Glass cleaner isn't sufficient.) Alternatively, a **squirt of white vinegar** in a spray bottle will cut though grease. Use **paper towels** to wipe the shelf dry, then reinsert it in the refrigerator. Repeat the procedure with each shelf.

Simple solutions

A sweet-smelling fridge
To deodorise your refrigerator or freezer, open a box of baking soda, leave it inside, and change it every few months. This tried-and-trusted method will absorb most of the odours you don't want emanating from your fridge, but it may not go far enough to suit you. Leaving an egg cup of dried coffee also absorbs odours and brings the faint aroma of your favourite drink to the fridge that you may prefer.

To clean the drawers, pull them out of the fridge one at a time, place them in the sink and fill them with **warm water** and a squirt of **washing–up liquid**. Let the water sit for 10 minutes. Then pour this out, rinse with **fresh water** and wipe dry with a **towel**.

Meat and poultry juices dripping on refrigerator surfaces are not only unsightly; they are potentially harmful vehicles for the spread of salmonella and *E. coli*. Even though a refrigerator's temperature is low, it doesn't stop the growth of all bacteria. And it doesn't kill bacteria that is already present.

So as you remove each shelf, spray the inside of the refrigerator with a **disinfecting all–purpose cleaner**. Just because it looks clean doesn't mean that it is clean.

Cleaning the freezer is simple if you have a self-defrosting model. Just put the food in the sink. Piling frozen items on top of each other will keep them cold.

Soak a **sponge** in **warm water** and squeeze out enough water that you won't create trickles that will add to your work. Wipe each rack in the freezer, top and bottom. If you have a thick, frozen spill, scrape it first with a **stiff plastic spatula** that has a thin edge (don't use metal) and then spot clean it with a **soapy sponge**.

To defrost the freezer, use your eyes to tell you when you need to do it (every three months, would be typical) and do it before there's a tremendous ice build up. If you don't, you're effectively reducing the size of your freezer.

• Switch the freezer off at the plug.
• Use a **cool box** to store frozen food. Pack it tightly, with items that thaw fastest, such as ice cream, in the centre.
• Leave the door open and put a **thick towel** tight up against the freezer in front of the door.
• Stand a **tray** under the drip edge at the base of the freezer (this is a pull out slot that will catch the thawing ice).
• Do nothing while the ice melts.
• Using more **towels**, mop up the water. When this is complete, turn on the freezer, put back the food and avoid opening the doors at all for as many hours as you can. This will help to bring the temperature down faster.
• If you really must speed up the process, stand **saucepans of hot water** inside the shelves of the freezer: this will make the ice melt faster.

Regularly cleaning the seals and door handles is perhaps the most important aspect of fridge cleaning. When you're preparing food it's best to wash your hands each and every time you handle raw meat. That's easy to forget in the midst of cooking however and when you transfer that contamination to the door handles, another family member who uses the refrigerator could pick up the germs. The solution is to keep a box or tube of **all-purpose wipes** (*Dettol* do some) near the refrigerator and make it a habit to wipe off the handle frequently.

Furniture

Working out what type of finish your furniture has should be the first order of business. If your furniture has an oiled finish, you should only dust and re-oil it. If it has one of the more common hard finishes – such as varnish or lacquer – you have more options.

Oil finish or a hard finish? Here's how to tell the difference. Put a few drops of **boiled linseed oil** on the wood and rub it in with your finger. If the wood absorbs the oil, you have an oil finish. If the boiled linseed oil beads up, you have a hard varnished or lacquered finish.

To clean oiled furniture, dust with a **dry cloth**. Don't use a dust-attracting product on the cloth and make sure the cloth is soft and free of buttons, zips and anything else that might scratch the wood. Then apply **oil** to the wood (boiled linseed oil, teak oil or an oil recommended by the furniture's manufacturer). Rub the oil in with a **clean cloth**. Do this an average of once a month. If you've been neglectful, re-oil your furniture every two weeks for a couple of months to allow it to catch up on missing oil.

To protect oiled furniture, never put cloth items or water on it. Cloth items will absorb the moisture from the oil and dry out your furniture. Unfortunately, oil offers the least protection of any finish – get any water on it and it's spoiled – yet it requires the highest maintenance.

To clean varnished or lacquered furniture, dust first with a **soft rag** or **stick duster**. It's all right to add a little dust-attracting product, such as *Pledge*, to the rag or duster but not straight onto the furniture. Let it dry before you dust. If necessary, you can clean hard-finished furniture with a **damp cloth** and **washing-up liquid**. Now you're ready to polish.

To polish a hard finish, apply an **aerosol furniture polish**. First, mist the surface of the furniture and use one area of a **rag** to spread the polish, wiping in a circular motion. Turn the rag over and wipe off the excess polish. Avoid polishes that consist mostly of silicone and paraffin wax, because these tend to build-up and eventually soften or ruin a finish.

To clean varnished or lacquered kitchen furniture, you'll need to take a different approach, because it is exposed to grease and cooking oils. Use a **cloth** that has been barely dampened with **washing-up liquid** and **water** to remove the oily substances. Follow up with a cloth dampened with plain water and then polish. Every three months, clean it using the **white spirit method** described in the next paragraph.

To give a hard finish a thorough cleaning and remove built-up wax, you'll need a few **very soft rags**. Soak one rag with **white spirit**. Wipe your furniture thoroughly, flipping the rag frequently. Thoroughly go over

---

A nutty cure for watermarks

Is a white water spot ruining the finish on your dining room table? Peanut butter can be a surprising cure. Rub smooth peanut butter into the finish with a soft rag, over and over in a circular motion. If scratches appear, reapply, following the grain. The oils and abrasion from the peanuts will have a renewing effect on the finish. Next, take a dry cloth and wipe well. If the area now appears shinier than the rest of the surface, apply the car wax with a mild cleaner in it, such as *TurtleWax*, to the spot. Then polish your furniture.

The peanut butter method works miracles, particularly with hazy-white water spots. Solid white water spots and the more severe black water spots probably require the attention of a professional restorer.

all areas several times with the rag. Now dry the surface completely with a **soft, dry rag**. Repeat this wiping and drying process at least three times using a fresh rag.

Once the furniture is clean, you can polish. Spray the **polish** on the wood and rub it in with a **rag**, going in a circular motion. Now use another **clean, soft rag** – or flip the polishing rag to a dry spot – and wipe with the grain of the wood to remove excess polish. Carved wood should be cleaned in the same way, regularly with polish and once a year with **white spirit**. The only difference is that you'll need a **soft toothbrush** to get into the intricate details.

If a finish has become sticky, this usually means it has failed – the result of too much polish build-up, exposure to oils over the years, or the finish having degraded over time. Use **white spirit** and **super-fine steel wool (0000)** to remove the old finish, rubbing with the grain of the wood. Wipe three or four times with a rag and fresh white spirit. When you're done, the furniture will have to be refinished. Talk to a professional or follow the package directions on the finishing product you choose. Don't do this to a valuable antique. Take it to a professional.

To clean painted wood furniture, dust it with a water-dampened cloth. If necessary, use a **mild, nonabrasive detergent** (such as **washing-up liquid**) and warm water. Dip a rag into the cleaning solution and wring it nearly dry. Work on a small section of wood at a time. Rinse with clear water. Dry the surface with a clean cloth quickly before continuing.

Waxes and polishes are usually not needed on painted furniture, but if you do use a wax on a light-coloured painted piece, use a **white, creamy type polish** to avoid discoloration. Never use oil, oil polishes or oil-treated cloths on painted furniture.

A very old piece with its original finish should usually not be repainted or refinished, because you run the risk of ruining its value.

To make your own furniture cleaner for removing old polish and dirt, put **1 litre of water** in a **saucepan** on the stove, add **2 tea bags** and bring to a boil. Cool the solution to room temperature. Dip a **soft cloth** in the tea and wring the cloth until it's damp. Wipe the furniture, buff it dry with a **soft cloth** and decide whether you should polish it.

To make your own furniture polish, follow either of these formulas:
• Mix **50ml of white vinegar** and **150ml of olive oil**.
• Mix **3 drops of lemon extract** and **200ml of vegetable oil**.

You can substitute **baby oil** for the olive or vegetable oil. Rub the polish into the surface with a **clean rag**, using circular motions.

Here are some more tips for dealing with special situations involving your wood furniture:
• **Removing candle wax** from furniture is risky because you can cause further damage. Use **ice** directly on the wax to get it as cold as possible and immediately wipe up excess water. Once the wax is very cold, try carefully inserting a **butter knife** under the wax to see whether it will pop off. If this method doesn't work, don't attempt anything else. Consult a professional.
• **If you have a fresh paint stain** on your furniture, remove emulsion paint with **water**; remove gloss paint with **white spirit**. To remove a dry stain, saturate the spot in **boiled linseed oil**. After the paint softens, lift it off carefully with a **putty knife**. Alternatively, wipe with a cloth dampened in the boiled linseed oil
• If paper is stuck to your wood furniture, dampen the paper thoroughly with **salad cream**, wait five minutes and rub along the grain with **super-fine (0000) steel wool**. Wipe dry.

See also **Antiques, Bronze, Chrome, Fibreglass, Glass, Marble, Upholstery** and **Wicker**.

Furs

There is plenty you can do to preserve fur. But the actual cleaning is really the realm of professional furriers. If you try to clean – or even brush – your fur yourself, you are likely to damage it. The advice here applies whether your fur is the real thing or a quality fake.

Have fur, will travel Excellent for keeping out the
cold, fur is a surprisingly fragile material. So you'll need to
take care to keep it intact.

- Don't pin jewellery on your fur, and avoid sharp necklaces
or bracelets that could snag your fur. Use shoulder bags
sparingly, because they will wear off the hairs and give your coat
a bald spot.
- Consider wearing a scarf around your neck to protect the collar
of your fur, which can quickly become matted.
- Avoid insecticides, mothproofing and other chemicals near your
fur, including perfume and hair spray. Once a perfume gets into
your fur, it could be there to stay.
- Get into your car carefully. Furs can be spoiled by friction or
crushing. Don't sit on it, if avoidable or at least try not to sit on the
same spot consistently. When you get out of your vehicle, shake
out any crushed places on your fur.
- Check out the cloakroom at a restaurant. If it looks
overcrowded, keep your coat with you. Fold it neatly on a chair at
the table and cover it with a napkin.
- To prevent your coat from getting crushed on a plane, leave it
on your lap or fold it loosely, lining out, and place it in an overhead
bin near you. Find a bin that's already nearly full and put your coat
on top of the luggage.

Have your fur cleaned regularly by a fur specialist,
not a dry-cleaner. Fur should be cleaned or serviced once a
year, unless it has hardly been worn. In that case, have it
cleaned at least every other year. This is the only cleaning
you should do yourself. To give your coat a light dusting,
put the coat on a hanger, hold the neck of the hanger and
shake the coat.

When you put away your coat between uses, it
needs to breathe. Never keep a fur coat bagged. It will
eventually dry out. If you insist on some kind of covering,
use a cotton bag, which allows for some breathing.

If your fur coat gets wet, let it dry on its own. Don't
place it by a radiator or attempt to blow-dry it. The skin
will burn and it will get hard and stiff because the oils in
the skin will be drying out too. Fur will easily stand up to
snow or light rain, but if your fur gets totally soaked, take it
to a professional furrier right away.

Games

Most games makers these days know that their main customers are children and so make their games as indestructible as possible. That means lots of easy-to-clean plastic parts and surfaces. When game boards are made out of paper, however, cleaning gets trickier.

To clean plastic or rubber game parts, wipe them off with a **sponge** or **cloth** dampened with a solution of **mild washing-up liquid** and **warm water**. Rinse by wiping with a **clean, damp sponge** or **cloth**. Air-dry completely in a **dish rack** or on a **towel** folded on your kitchen worktop.

To clean paper-coated game boards, first try wiping with a **cloth** or **sponge** dampened only with **water** (wrung out as much as possible beforehand). You should avoid soaking the paper, which could damage the board or cause it to buckle. If the game board's colours begin to bleed, stop. If you need more cleaning power, try wiping with the **soapy solution** mentioned above for plastic parts. Pat the board dry with a **clean white cloth**.

Sprinkle clean, dry cards with talcum powder every so often to keep them smooth and grease-free.

Garden furniture

Wooden chairs and tables need to be sealed at the start of each season. Use teak oil or, if you want to change the colour, a wood stain, to do this. *Ronseal* do a wide range. Metal furniture that has been poorly stored in the winter may have developed rust spots. Use very fine grade glasspaper to get these off, then apply a coat of clear varnish to protect.

Plastic resin furniture tends to need just a good clean. Avoid bleach-based spray cleaners as they will pit the surface and – on greens particularly – you may suffer instant colour fade. Instead, make do with sudsy water from **washing-up liquid**. Use a **large sponge** or **bundled rags** to wipe down, then dry or leave out in the sun.

During the summer keep on top of the cleaning by keeping a pack of **multi-surface wipes** in the area where you store your tables and chairs. These are an effective and hygienic way to clean off the inevitable bird-droppings. You'll minimise clean-ups by taking the extra minute each evening to tip chairs up against the table, so that the seats are protected from rain and dirt.

Garden ornaments

To clean or not to clean – that is the question when it comes to garden ornaments. Just as one school of thought in the antiques world supports leaving original finishes intact, some people feel that a little algae, plus a bird dropping or two, give an ivy-tucked concrete cherub a more natural look. We'll let you decide. But if the decision is to clean, here's what you can do.

To clean garden ornaments, remember that much of what you'll be cleaning is actually alive. Organic matter, such as algae, moss, mould and mildew, all make damp stone their host – in fact, they'll go anywhere there is moisture and warmth. Add to that dust and dirt, dead organic matter and bird droppings and you end up with quite a mess (or a lovely patina, if that's your view).

You can get rid of the organic matter and remove the rest with a simple, inexpensive solution of **100ml of bleach** to **4 litres of water**, with a squirt or two of **washing-up liquid** thrown in and worked into suds. Wear **gloves** to apply it with a **long-handled brush** and gently scrub until clean. Rinse with the **garden hose**. This works for most materials used for garden ornaments and statues, including concrete, stone and polyester resins.

Because bleach can damage the plants in your garden – and most noticeably the lawn – move the ornaments to the driveway or a path for cleaning. For anything too large to move, use the cleaning agent sparingly and rinse with a **sponge** and **bucket** of **clean water** instead of the hose.

Don't ever use chlorine to clean a pond that contains fish. If you clean a birdbath, be sure to flush out the cleaning solution completely.

To clean mirror balls, use a window-cleaning solution. Mix **100ml of white vinegar** in **4 litres of warm water** and add a squirt of **washing-up liquid.** Apply it with a **spray bottle** or a **clean cloth.** Gently scrub until clean and either rinse with a **hose** or dry with a **dry towel** or **newspaper.** If the ball is stainless steel, wax it with **car wax** once a year to renew its shine and give it a protective coating. And wipe out scratches with an car scratch remover.

See also **Birdbaths, feeders & birdhouses.**

Garden trellises

Trellises make attractive additions to a lawn or garden, but all those cracks and crevices provide a wealth of places for dirt and grime to hide.

To clean trellises with no plants attached, use a **hose** with a nozzle that sends the water out in a tightly focused stream. Use a **stiff-bristled nylon** or **fibre brush** to scrub dirty spots. If the trellises are wood, use the brush sparingly; you can use a freer hand on trellises made of plastic, glassfibre or metal. You could also use a power washer, available at tool-hire shops.

To attack the green mouldy-mossy stuff that grows in shady spots, mix a solution of **4 litres of water** and **300ml of chlorine bleach** in a **bucket.** Scrub the solution on with a **brush.** Rinse with **plain water.**

Simple solutions

Plants in your way?

To clean trellises that are supporting plants, wash them in the early spring. Prune climbing plants back to about 15mm – most climbers can easily take it – and remove the rest of the plant material from the trellis.

Gemstones

Don't make the mistake of assuming that all stones are like diamonds. Some are so soft that brushing – and certainly cleaning in soapy water – is enough to dull and damage them for ever.

The softest stones, such as amber, opals and coral should merely be wiped with a silk cloth to restore their shine and lustre. Harder stones – rubies, emeralds and topaz – can be immersed in **warm, soapy water**, before being rinsed and air-dried. The heavyweights of the gemstone world – sapphire, cubic zirconium and diamond – are up to hot washing in **soapy water** and, if needed, you can scrub around the facets of the stone with a **toothbrush** to get out any ingrained dirt.

Glasses & sunglasses

For general cleaning of spectacles, wet cleaning is better than dry cleaning. Most of us have grabbed a tissue or pulled a handkerchief out of a pocket to wipe our glasses, but that can smear dirt around and scratch the lenses. Dirt particles are hard, whereas lenses are soft and getting softer. Almost all lenses today are plastic and plastic lenses are especially susceptible to scratching.

For daily cleaning, pass the glasses under **running water** and dry them with a **tissue** or a **clean microfibre cleaning cloth** made especially for glasses. Get them from your optician or at chemists. Packaged **single-use towelettes** made for glasses are also good cleaners and are convenient when you're on the move.

To remove oily smears from your glasses, pick up a specially formulated **lens cleaner** at a chemist or supermarket and follow the package instructions. Using water alone will not remove oils. Even mild dishwashing detergent can damage coatings over time and harsher cleaners (including anything with ammonia) can damage them immediately. So though lens cleaners may seem like an unnecessary expense, they will help to keep your lenses from getting cloudy and scratched and prolong the life of your glasses. The best lens cleaners even leave behind a thin film,

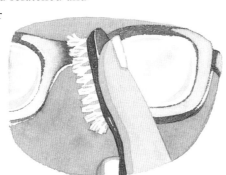

Use a soft toothbrush to give your grubby frames a gentle scrubbing.

Simple solutions

THE GREAT STAINGO

Got a screw loose?

Next to dirty lenses, the most annoying glasses problem is having a screw loose in the hinge – which then allows the lens to fall out of the frame.

There are special repair kits with tiny screwdrivers that can tighten the screw. But if it comes loose repeatedly, you need something more than a screwdriver.

Try welding it together with a drop of clear nail polish. Just put a drop on the screw, then turn it as usual. Once the nail polish hardens, it will have extra strength.

a kind of instant coating, which further brightens the lenses. There's one exception; if you have an anti-reflective coating on your glasses, you'll need to get a specialist cleaner from your optician.

To clean the frames of your glasses, mix a few drops of **washing up liquid** in a **jug of water**. Dip a **clean, soft toothbrush** into the solution and gently scrub around the frame, the nosepiece and the earpieces, avoiding the lenses as much as possible. Rinse under **running water** and dry with a **clean cloth**.

Glass furniture

Glass furniture creates a real sense of space in your home. But you need to clean very regularly to make sure it looks its best. Imagine that you're cleaning a horizontal mirror and you'll get the general idea for cleaning glass-topped tables and similar items.

Apply your cleaning solution – **1 part white vinegar, 4 parts water** from a spray bottle directly onto your cloth, then rub into the glass. Take care not to hold onto the table as you clean, in order to avoid fingermarks.

Apart from smearing, the other issue with glass is breakage. So the most important time for your glass furniture is not when you clean it, but when you move it to clean the carpet. Glass is amazingly heavy, so this may turn out to be a two person job. Clearly, because you'll need to touch it to lift it, you should clean glass furniture as the final stage of your room clean.

Glassware

Anyone can clean a glass. Just use hot water and washing-up liquid. But to get rid of streaks, spots and unappetising rim stains – and make your glassware really sparkle – you have to know how to dry them properly.

Clean glassware first when you're washing dishes by hand, since glasses are usually less dirty than pots, pans, plates and utensils. (If you don't clean the glasses first, then change the dishwater before you get to them. Otherwise, the glasses will end up dirtier than they were when you started.)

Use **washing-up liquid** mixed with **hot water**. Wash with a **soft, clean sponge** or **dish cloth**. Don't use an abrasive pot scrubber as it may scratch glass. Rinse with even **hotter water** – as hot as you can safely stand. Hot water not only helps cut grease, but it also beads up and steams off (the first step toward good drying is to dry fast). Avoid excessive suds, which make glasses harder to rinse and slippery to handle, which will increase the chances of their breaking or chipping.

No matter how well you've cleaned glassware, if there is slow-drying water left on your glasses, chances are it will leave streaks or spots. Fogging causes some of the worst spotting. To avoid the 'greenhouse effect' – when glasses placed upside down on their rims fog up inside – dry glasses upside down on a **drying rack**. If you don't have a rack, put them upright on a **towel** and make sure air can circulate inside the glass for rapid drying.

To remove the lime build-up on glassware that occurs when it is washed in the dishwasher, use a **commercial rinse agent** (such as *Finish Lemon Rinse Agent*) during the washing cycles. This helps water stream off while the glass is drying inside the foggy dishwasher. Or fill a large plastic bowl with **white vinegar** and give each glass a 15-minute bath. Then rinse with running water and allow to air-dry.

To remove food-colouring stains left in glassware by the dyes in powdered soft drink mixes and other beverages, fill the glass with a solution of **2 tablespoons of household ammonia** in **1 litre of hot water**. Let it stand for 30 minutes and then rinse with **clean, cool water**.

Hand-washing is best for fine glassware, even if you'd prefer to use the dishwasher. To avoid scratching the glasses, remove rings, watches and bracelets, especially those with diamonds. Swing the tap head out of the way, so there will be no chance that you will accidentally smack any precious items against it.

Using both hands, clean one piece at a time in **hot, soapy water**. Gently wash with a **soft cotton cloth** or **clean sponge**. For stubborn dirt, scrub gently with a **soft**

Rules of the game

Handling glassware safely

1 Put a rubber pad or heavy folded towel in your sink (or use a plastic bowl). In a divided sink, also put a folded towel over the ridge.

2 Wash in hot water and washing-up liquid. Avoid too many suds. Rub stuck-on food gently with bicarbonate of soda but never anything more abrasive.

3 Handle glasses by the bowl, not the stem.

4 Rinse glasses in a sink or bowl of hot, clear water.

5 Air-dry upside down on a dish rack. Or arrange the glasses upright on a towel. Never stand them upside down on a flat surface. This will lead to fogging and spotting.

6 For a special dinner party sparkle, buff the dried glasses with a soft, linen tea towel.

toothbrush. Rinse twice, first in a sink full of tepid water with a **capful of vinegar** mixed in and finally under a gentle shower of **tepid water** from the tap.

To clean really fine glassware Wearing **gloves**, use a solution of equal parts of **methylated spirit,** and **water**, then add a **few drops of ammonia**. Water and the ammonia do the cleaning, while the spirit helps the glass to dry up very quickly. Apply the solution with **cotton wool**. Don't use this technique on glass with decorative gilt, as it could lift it off.

Gloves

Cleaning gloves can be tricky for a couple of reasons. First, in addition to stains and soil on the outside of gloves, you have to remove the dirt and oils left by your own skin on the inside of gloves. Second, gloves are complicated, full of cracks and crevices caused by the shape of our hands. There is a trick, though, that makes cleaning gloves simple and it's to wear them as you wash.

This way you can position each glove exactly as you'd like it, while scrubbing with the other hand. Mix up a **mild, sudsy solution** of **warm water** and a **drop of washing-up liquid**. When you've finished washing, remove the gloves and rinse them in a sink full of clean water, emptying the sink and repeating until there is no more soap residue.

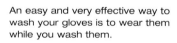

An easy and very effective way to wash your gloves is to wear them while you wash them.

To dry gloves, roll them up in a **dry towel**. After unrolling them, blow them back into shape and lay them out flat on the towel at room temperature. Never squeeze or wring gloves and don't dry them using a heat source, such as a radiator or hair dryer. If you need to iron them, lay them between the folds of a **clean towel** and pass the **hot iron** over the top layer of the towel.

See Leather or Suede if your gloves are made from either of those materials.

Gold jewellery

The whole point of gold is to shine. While it does not tarnish like silver, gold will over time develop a dingy, oily film from lotions, powders, soaps and the oils secreted by your skin. And gold that has been alloyed with other metals – copper, silver or nickel – can tarnish and smudge. To revive your gold's lustre, clean it regularly.

Here's the mildest method for cleaning gold – and also the easiest and most economical. Mix a bowl of suds using **warm water** and a **little washing-up liquid**. Soak the gold briefly and then gently scrub crevices and design details using a **soft toothbrush** or **eyebrow brush**. Place the jewellery in a **wire strainer** and rinse under warm running water. Pat it dry with a **chamois cloth**. (Any clean, white, soft cotton cloth will do at a pinch.)

For a stronger cleaning solution, mix equal parts of **cold water** and **ammonia** (cheaper than a commercial jewellery cleaner). Soak the jewellery in the solution for 30 minutes. Gently scrub with a **toothbrush** or **eyebrow brush**. Rinse with water and dry on a **soft towel**.

Having gold professionally cleaned is the safest and most effective method. At a jeweller's, ask if they can put it through their **ultrasonic cleaning machine**. Some may do this for free. Jewellery is dipped into a container of liquid and when high-frequency vibrations are sent through the liquid, the dirt and grime drop off. You can buy these machines for home use, from *Argos* or *Lakeland* from around £20, but you'll need to have a lot of jewellery for it to be worth the investment.

Watch out

• Chlorine can cause gold to deteriorate over time. Wedding rings are solid enough to be safe from its effects. But if you swim a lot, you might want to remove fine chains and delicate earrings.

• Don't clean gold with toothpaste, even though some jewellers recommend it. Some toothpastes contain harsh abrasives, such as silica (found in quartz), which can dull a glossy gold finish.

Place your jewellery in a wire strainer and rinse under warm running water.

Gore-Tex fabric

This brand-name membrane, found in rain jackets and other outerwear, is renowned for its ability to be simultaneously waterproof and breathable. You'll improve both functions by keeping your Gore-Tex fabric clean – not hard as Gore-Tex is both washable and dry-cleanable.

To clean a Gore-Tex garment, follow the cleaning instructions on the label in that garment. Typically, the instructions will be to put the garment in a **washing machine** with **warm water** and a **standard detergent**, but no fabric softener or bleach and then tumble in a **dryer**. If the garment calls for dry-cleaning, tell the cleaner you want a clear, distilled solvent rinse.

To preserve a garment's water resistance, you need to reapply a **water-resistant coating** occasionally, because multiple washings (or a single trip to the dry cleaner) will remove the fine water-resistant layer. (The sign that you've lost the water resistance is when water no longer beads up on your garment's outer shell, but instead sinks into the fabric.) The actual Gore-Tex layer will be safe, but the outer shell will need a new application of its coating, called **durable water repellent (DWR)**. Gore-Tex sells an easy-to-use spray-on durable water repellent called *Revivex*. You should be able to find it at camping stores or high-performance bicycle shops.

Granite

Some worktops and other architectural stone sold as granite may have only the appearance of granite. When it comes to cleaning, knowing whether the material is genuine granite is important, because some cleaners considered safe for granite may react negatively with your stone. The acid in vinegar, for instance, eats away at calcium, which is not usually present in granite but may be in the stone used in your surfaces.

There are also different types of surface finishes to consider, from raw stone to highly polished stone to chemically sealed stone. That may sound complicated, but cleaning the stone should not be. The best approach is the simplest.

Before you attempt to clean any granite surface, find out what sort of surface finish it has to avoid problems.

To care for granite, keep it free of sand and dirt, especially on flat surfaces, where it can be ground down by shoe soles or boots. The grit can scratch the stone. For walls, floors and other such surfaces, use either a vacuum cleaner or a dry dust mop. For worktops and tables, dust with a clean, dry rag. Wipe up spills immediately to avoid staining.

To clean granite worktops in kitchens and bathrooms, first try using only **warm water**, and wiping with a **soft cloth** or **sponge**. Let caked-on food soak for a while before wiping. You should be able to remove spills, crumbs, sauces and other substances this way. If not, then add a little **washing-up liquid** to the water. Rinse well with plenty of **clean water**. Too much soap can leave a film or cause streaking. Avoid stronger cleaning products, such as bath and tile cleaners or scouring powders, which can stain or scratch.

To remove difficult stains, keep it simple and be patient. Most stains consist of solid residue that has jammed in between the crystals of the stone after the liquid that carried it has evaporated. The trick is to put the solid back into solution so it can be removed. First, determine whether your stain is **water-based** (for example, from spilled fruit juice) or **oil-based** (salad dressing).

• **If the stain is water-based,** pour **hot water** (from the tap, not the kettle) on the stain and let it stand for a few minutes. Wipe away the excess water. Then stack **1cm of paper towels** on the stain and saturate with **hot water**. Cover with a piece of plastic (**plastic wrap** will do) and a flat, heavy weight, such as a book (be careful not to ruin the book). Let it stand for about 10 hours. (Do it overnight and you won't have to worry about anyone moving it.) Next, throw away the paper towels and the stain should go with them. Let the spot dry and then observe. If some of the stain is still present, repeat the treatment.

• **If the stain is oil-based,** follow the same procedure, only instead of water, use **acetone** (but do not heat). After the 10 hours is up, throw away the paper towels and rinse the spot with clean water. If necessary, repeat. Acetone can be found in chemists, sold as nail polish remover.

Greenhouses

Think of your greenhouse as a hospital – the cleaner it is, the healthier the plants housed there will be. Dust, debris and clutter are magnets for insects, diseases and harmful microorganisms. Dirty windows also block the sun, so can mean your plants will grow less well.

Dust your plants to remove fungal spores (such as grey mould and powdery mildews) and mites (such as the omnivorous spider mite). Most people hose off their plants, which is fine but tends to unsettle and spread the dust. An easier – and more effective – method is to vacuum them. Use an extension lead and your ordinary **vacuum cleaner** with a **dusting attachment**. This works best on sturdy leaves that you can hold in your hand while you quickly whisk the brush over the surface. Once a year is enough to halt the growth of the plant predators mentioned above.

Cut down on clutter in your greenhouse. Piles of dead plants, stacks of dirty pots and sacks spilling over with potting soil can all be places for insects and microorganisms to spend the winter. Remove all of these things – and any other clutter – regularly. Try not to pile them right next to the greenhouse. Either get rid of them or store them in a shed, garage or basement. Dead plant material is the worst offender. Purge dead plants and pick up dead leaves.

Keep your greenhouse weed-free to get rid of yet another source of food for insects and bacteria. Weeds also boost a greenhouse's humidity level, which will make conditions even riper for disease and pestilence. Keep a sack of **hydrated lime** on hand (but don't clutter up the greenhouse with it). Sprinkle it under benches and in corners to deter weed growth. It lasts for a long time and is non-toxic to humans. You can buy hydrated lime at your hardware store or the local feed and seed store. Never use herbicides in your greenhouse.

Wash the greenhouse windows at least once a year. Do it when you have the least amount of living plant material in your greenhouse – so before you bring in those new seeds or seedlings to get growing for spring transplanting. For most people, window-washing time is during the autumn. Your goal is to keep the glass or polyurethane as clear as possible, as well as to kill any harmful microbial growth on the inner surface. Use a **mild washing-up liquid**; it not only loosens dirt but also has ingredients that break up proteins and fats – and rupture the membranes of bacteria and fungi. Depending on the size of your greenhouse, either put the washing-up liquid in a **hose end sprayer** or mix it with water in a **clean spray bottle**. Rinse by spraying with the **garden hose**.

Gutters & downpipes

Water is your home's worst enemy and guttering and downpipes are an important line of defence. You need to keep them clean so that they can work properly. A blocked gutter will force water down the side of your house, where it can cause serious damage.

Clean out gutters any time they are blocked. But be on the look out for this in autumn, as leaves fall. Wear **heavy gloves**, as thorns and roof nails often end up in gutters and use a **ladder** tall enough to reach the gutters safely. This is a two person job. Make sure someone else is holding the bottom of the ladder. Each time you move it to a new section, stop and check you have anchored the ladder securely and safely and that the rungs are square-on with the house before you begin your climb.

Make your own scoop using a **large plastic milk carton**. Cut the top off and you have a handled container with a wide opening (see box) – just right for scooping out rubbish and easy to throw away afterwards. After you've removed all the debris, sluice it out with a hose.

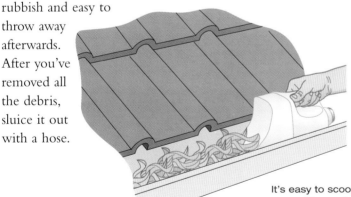

It's easy to scoop up leaves in your gutters using a plastic milk bottle with the bottom cut out.

Simple solutions

THE GREAT STAINGO

Make your own gutter bucket

A gutter bucket is a handy tool to help with cleaning gutters and it's easy to make.

Take a plastic bucket with an all-metal handle. Using wire cutters, make a cut in the middle of the handle. Bend each end of the handle into a hook shape, turn the hooks toward the same side of the bucket and hang the bucket from the gutter. Put the leaves and such from your gutter into the bucket, rather than dropping the mess into the shrubbery below. When the bucket is full, climb down and empty it on your mulch pile. Soggy leaves are good for adding richness to the soil.

To clean the outside of gutters:

Mix a solution of **100ml of trisodium phosphate** and **4 litres of water** and, wearing **gloves**, use a rag to wipe over the guttering. This is purely a cosmetic job: it won't make your guttering last any longer, but will make it look shinier.

Hairbrushes

Most of us don't clean our hairbrushes often enough. When we finally get around to it, we often spend more time untangling the balls of hair than we do on the cleaning job itself. Clean more often using the following tips and you'll save time in the long run.

Before cleaning your hairbrush, first remove all of the trapped hair using a comb.

To clean a hairbrush, first pull out any loose hair from the bristles. Then make your own economical and effective cleaning solution by mixing **2 teaspoons of shampoo** and **60ml of vinegar** in a sink filled with **warm water**. Soak the brush in the solution for several minutes. Pull a **clean, wide-toothed comb** down each row of bristles to remove any remaining hair.

By now, the solution should have loosened any build-up of oil, dirt, gel and hair spray on the brush. Scrub the brush clean with a **nailbrush** (hold it down in the sink to contain the splatter) and rinse with **warm running water**. Let the brush air-dry.

To clean a makeup brush, avoid using commercial makeup brush cleaners, which often contain harsh chemicals. The chemicals aren't good for the sensitive skin of your face and can dry out a makeup brush, which can be quite expensive – especially the ones made of real animal hair. For a safe, non-drying alternative, mix **2 parts water** with **1 part gentle fabric wash**, such as *Woolite*. Dip the tip of the brush into the solution. Don't dip the wooden or metal handle, because water can cause the bristles to fall out. Rinse in **clean water**. Repeat until the brush is clean (no makeup colour is visible) and free of the wash solution. Dry the brush gently with a **towel**, being sure to move the towel 'with the grain', or direction of the hair.

Hair dryers

Modern dryers require minimal upkeep. But some maintenance is essential. A dryer with a debris-choked filter can overheat. It will perform poorly, possibly even damaging your hair. To keep it blowing properly, plan to clear the filter every three months if you use it daily.

Dryers work by fanning the surrounding air, directing it through the appliance's heating mechanism and blowing it out through the nozzle as a stream of hot air. But the dryer pulls in dust and lint along with the air and those particles lodge in a screen that filters the air before it hits the heating coils. Enough debris can accumulate in the filter to block air from flowing through. That's when the dryer may start to overheat. You may detect a warning odour like that of burning hair.

When a dryer overheats, its thermostat attempts to cool things down by tripping the heating coils off and on. You feel alternating hot and cold air blowing out, which won't provide the styling effects of consistently warm air. Extreme blockage may trigger the dryer's non-resettable shutdown device and ruin it completely.

A hair dryer's filter needs to be cleaned regularly to prevent overheating and possible damage.

To clean your dryer filter, first unplug the dryer. Top-quality dryers have a filter cover that lifts off, giving easy access for cleaning. Scrub the filter with a **dry, soft-bristled brush** or **toothbrush** to get out the lint, dust and hair. Or use your **vacuum** with a **crevice attachment**. Pull out any stubborn bits with **tweezers**. If your dryer doesn't have a filter cover, you'll need to brush, vacuum or tweeze the filter from the outside.

To clean the dryer body and accessories, just wipe with a **damp rag** (not a wet one, which could drip water into the heating element). Even the stickiest, slipperiest hair products are generally water soluble, so a damp cloth should remove them.

Hammocks

Hammocks are all about relaxing – which you can't do if you're reclining amidst grime and mildew – not good for either you or your hammock. Rot is another threat, caused by strong sunlight and detergents wearing away at a hammock's natural-rope fibres.

To make your hammock last longer, you need to keep it not only dirt free but as dry as possible. So a good dose of prevention is called for.

• Before use, spray your hammock with a **fabric guard**, such as *Lakeland Waterproof Fabric Protector* following the instructions. Renew treatment every three to five months.

• Don't hang the hammock in full sun, as the rays will fade synthetics and weaken cotton.

• Find a dry indoor spot to store the hammock in bad weather or whenever you won't be using it for a while.

A good universal approach is to mix **30ml of mild washing-up liquid** with **8 litres of water**. Spread the hammock out on a large, clear, hard surface, such as a deck or patio. Keeping the wooden spreader bars dry, scrub one side of the hammock with a **soft cloth** or **sponge**, then flip it and clean the other side.

A soft-bristled brush will let you gently scrub dirty areas. Rinse well with **clear water** and hang the hammock to air-dry, preferably in a low-humidity breeze but not in direct sunlight. Quick drying keeps the fibres strong and discourages mould and mildew. The hammock should be fully dry in two days. Other cleaning approaches depend on the fabric and construction of your hammock.

To clean white cotton or cotton-polyester rope, just spot-clean dirt using **1 part gentle fabric wash**, such as *Woolite*, to **8 parts water**. If there is mould or mildew, fill the bath with water and a **mild bleach solution (1 capful of chlorine bleach per 1 gallon of water)** and soak the hammock in it for 30 minutes.

To clean synthetic fabrics such as polyester and acrylic, bind the hammock so that it won't tangle – if it is a model that has no spreader bars, such as a Mayan-style hamaca. Fold the hammock in half, bringing the two end rings together. Bind it with twine just below the rings, then at the fold and finally in the middle of your bundle. This keeps the hardware out of the strings and saves them from becoming a tangled puzzle.

Drop the bundle into a pillowcase and tie it closed. Put it in the **washing machine** on the gentle cycle, using **non-biological detergent**. After washing, unbind and spread the hammock out to dry for a couple of days.

You can also hand-wash it in a solution of **1 part gentle hand-washing detergent** to **4 parts water**.

If the yarn is solution-dyed, meaning the dye was added when the synthetic was still liquid, you can rid it of mildew and stains by hand-washing it in a **bleach-and-water solution**. Don't go any stronger than a 50-50 mix. Use **rubber gloves** and test for colourfastness on an inconspicuous corner.

To clean coloured rope, fabric, or quilted fabric hammocks, scrub using **1 measure of laundry detergent** in **10 litres of warm water**. Test for colourfastness first. Treat mildewed areas with the mild bleach solution suggested above for cotton-rope hammocks.

Spot-wash hammock pillows using a **mild washing-up liquid solution** and a **soft-bristled brush**. Avoid soaking the batting inside.

If your hammock has wooden spreader bars, they will come covered with a protective coating such as marine varnish, which you can replenish every six months. You'll find **boat varnish** at hardware stores and boat supply stores. Follow the directions on the label. If your hammock is suspended on a wooden frame, touch up the frame with linseed oil every three to six months.

Handbags

Most handbags are home to a host of essential items as well as attracting all sorts of dust and clutter. All will last longer and look better if they are cleaned properly.

Before cleaning any handbag, first empty the bag of its contents. Brush away loose dirt – inside and out – with a **soft white cloth**, or **vacuum** it using an **upholstery attachment**.

If your bag is so deep that you can't see what is inside, secure a piece of **nylon mesh** (from a pair of old tights) over the end of the suction tube of your **vacuum** (don't use any attachments). Dust and dirt will go through, but not jewellery and coins dropped in the bottom of your bag. Next (with the exception of suede), wet a soft cloth in a **cleaning solution** appropriate for your bag's construction material. (See page 250.) Wring the cloth nearly dry and rub the bag inside and out, taking care not to dampen it any more than it takes to clean it.

How you clean a handbag depends on what it is made of, so check before you buy or apply any products.

As well as visible dirt, you will wipe away skin oils, hand lotion, makeup and perspiration. The handle, clasp and straps are typically high-grime spots on the exterior. Inside, wipe the liner – especially the bottom – and interior hardware, such as zips.

To clean a leather bag, use **saddle soap** or a **cream leather cleaner/conditioner**, available at shoe repair shops. Follow the label instructions. Always follow saddle soap with a **solvent-free leather conditioner**, to avoid drying out the leather. Then buff with a soft cloth.

To clean a fabric bag, use ½ **teaspoon of a gentle fabric wash**, such as *Woolite*, in **60ml of lukewarm water** for all-over cleaning of sturdy fabrics. Use it full strength for spots. For delicate fabrics, use **barely damp baby wipes**.

To clean patent leather, use a **cream cleaner conditioner** if it's real patent leather. Be gentle – patent leather scratches easily. On imitation patent leather, use **washing-up liquid** or a **car interior vinyl and plastic cleaner**, such as *Turtle Wax*, available at car supplies shops.

To clean plastic, vinyl, or polyurethane, try a plastic cleaner, such as *Turtle Wax*, sold in car supply stores. Wipe softer synthetics with a solution of **washing-up liquid** or a **gentle fabric wash** and **water**. Alternatively, use **baby wipes** or a **car interior vinyl and plastic cleaner**. To restore the shine to shiny plastics, spray them with **silicone wax spray** after cleaning. Then buff.

To clean a straw bag, use **1 part liquid hand soap** to **3 parts water**.

To clean a suede bag, brush the nap with a **natural-bristle shoe brush** to remove surface dirt. Otherwise, have it professionally dry-cleaned. Use protectant sprays sparingly, since some can attract dirt.

Oops!

Dye-hard duo

Never stack a leather handbag on top of or directly under a plastic one. The dye from the leather bag will leach and be absorbed by the plastic.

Hats

To keep a fur, felt, velour or beaver hat clean, regularly brush the dust and dirt from the surface with a nylon or horsehair brush. It's important for a hat to be dust free because once the hat gets wet, the dust becomes much harder to eliminate.

With fur and felt hats, always brush with the nap (in the direction of the material) and use separate brushes for light and dark hats. To deal with more extensive stains or soiling, take your hat to a professional for cleaning and shaping. It's a job specific to the hat and is based on fabric and the type of soiling that has occurred that only a professional is equipped to handle. Avoid the temptation to use stain removal products. There's a good chance you'll damage your hat further and create stain rings.

You can give new life to a felt hat by simply brushing it over the steam of a boiling kettle.

If you spill something on your hat, blot it immediately with a **soft, absorbent cloth** to prevent it from seeping into the hat. If your hat gets spotted with mud, let it dry first. Then lightly brush it off with a **nylon** or **horsehair brush**.

To clean a straw hat, brush it with a **brush** or **dry cloth** to remove dust and loose dirt. Beyond that, these hats are not really cleanable, even by a professional. With time, most straw hats naturally turn yellow and there's nothing you can do about it.

To clean a wool hat, use a **sticky fabric roller** designed to remove hairs and lint from clothing or a **new paintbrush**. Firmer brushes are too rough to use on wool hats.

If a hat has faded in spots and you're ready to hang it up for good, here's how to get a little more life out of it:
- **For a white hat**, apply **talcum powder** using a **dry sponge**. (A makeup sponge works well.)
- **For coloured hats**, grind down a **crayon** that matches the colour, mix with the **talcum powder** and apply.

Expert advice

Take the inside out

If the satin lining of your hat is removable, you can wash it. Fill a sink with cold water and add a couple of drops of washing-up liquid. Place the satin lining in the water and rub it with a stiff scrubbing brush. To rinse the lining, hold it under cold running water until the soap is gone. Let it air-dry. If you want to remove creases, expose it to the steam from your steam iron – without actually touching the iron to the lining.

Hearing aids

Hearing aids need daily attention to remain in top working order. Wax and moisture are common causes of hearing aid malfunctions – wax on hearing aids that fit inside the ear and moisture from perspiration on hearing aids worn outside the ear.

To clean an in-the-ear hearing aid, start by washing your hands to avoid contaminating the device. Then, using a **brush** (either one supplied by your hearing care provider or a **clean toothbrush**), remove any wax on the exterior of the hearing aid. Do this daily if you get a lot of wax or every other day if you don't. Another option is to wipe the surface with a **dry cotton cloth** (an **old T-shirt** works well) or a cloth lightly dampened with **alcohol**. If you use alcohol, wipe only the shell of the unit, not over the microphone or receiver, which can be damaged by moisture.

Cleaning a behind-the-ear hearing aid is a two-part operation. To clean the ear mould that fits inside the ear, use **water** and **soap** (*Pears*, for instance) or a **germicidal soap** such as *Carex*. Put the soap on a **cotton cloth** dampened with **lukewarm water**. Wipe the ear mould clean, giving it a good rub. Rinse with **lukewarm water** and dry with a **towel**. To clean the hearing aid itself, use just a **brush**: a **toothbrush** is fine.

Every three months, take the hearing aid to your hearing care specialist for a thorough clean. He or she should have the appropriate tools for cleaning more deeply into the interior of your hearing aid.

The special tools and accessories that go with your hearing aid need cleaning, too. In-the-ear hearing aids have wax guards or wax sceptres, that protect the receiver from getting clogged with wax. Clean them with a **brush**. Behind-the-ear hearing aids can be fitted with a sleeve jacket that covers the component behind the ear, protecting it from moisture. Wipe the sleeve clean with a **cloth**.

Like a computer, a hearing aid has an electronic chip in it. Water is its enemy, so watch the amount of liquid you use when cleaning. It's also a good idea to keep your hearing aid in a dry place when you're not using it – for example, in the bedroom while you're taking a shower, instead of in the bathroom.

Simple solutions

THE GREAT STAINGO

Put it in dry dock

Keep your hearing aid working longer by storing it overnight in a dry-aid kit, which absorbs moisture. You can purchase a dry-aid kit, also called a dehumidifier kit, from your hearing aid supplier.

To make your own dry storage container, find a jar that has a good seal. Then check around your house for a desiccant bag – one of those little packets of moisture-absorbing crystals that come with new camera equipment and other products.

Put the bag and your hearing aid in the jar and close it up. A desiccant bag will last for six months. Desiccant bags can also be bought wherever you buy hearing aid equipment.

Hoses

Hoses require little cleaning other than the removal of dirt by spraying water from the hose onto itself.

Always start cleaning garden hoses with the least abrasive method and work your way up. If you need some extra cleaning power, dampen a **rag** in **warm water** and add to it some **biodegradable soap** (available at camping stores). Rub it over the hose and use **clean water** from the hose to rinse. If you still have some dirt stuck on the hose, use a **vinyl cleaner** on vinyl hoses or rubber hoses that are coated with vinyl. Follow the manufacturer's instructions on the packet.

If your hose is blocked up but there are no kinks in it, you may have a build-up of calcium deposits from minerals in the water. Bend the hose back and forth along the entire length to break up the build-up. If there's a nozzle on the business end of the hose, remove it and then turn on the water. This will help to flush out the loosened deposits.

Give your garden hose a long and happy life

To increase the life expectancy of your hose, here are some more things you can do:

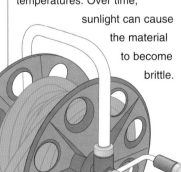

- Although most hoses have UV retardants, it helps to remove your hose from strong sunlight and freezing temperatures. Over time, sunlight can cause the material to become brittle.

- While your hose isn't in use, store it on a reel to prevent it from forming kinks or knots. Place the reel out of the sun or on the east side of the house (so it only gets the morning sun).

- For winter storage, drain the hose and store it indoors. To drain it, first detach the hose from the tap. Starting at the end of the hose, pick it up so that the water runs through the hose ahead of you. Make large loops over your shoulder as you go. When you reach the end, all the water will have run out. If you have a hose that's too heavy to loop over your shoulder, make loops around a bench or on a raised patch of ground.

- At the end of the summer, place the hose out in the sun for two days to thoroughly dry it.

- Store the hose flat in large relaxed loops. If you hang your hose, you'll get bends that may freeze and damage the material.

- Never walk on or drive over a hose. Hoses aren't designed to withstand that much external pressure.

Hot tubs

Hot tubs are a bit of a luxury. But if you're lucky enough to have one, how often should you clean It? That will depend on how often you use it.

• If two people use it three nights a week, clean it thoroughly and drain it every three months.
• If you have a lot of children and the family uses it up to six nights a week, clean it every two months.
• If your hot tub is an occasional luxury, clean it as needed. You should still test chemical levels weekly.
• If you aren't keeping track of your use, here's a good rule of thumb: Don't keep the water in longer than three months – six months maximum. You won't need a calendar to know when you've waited too long. The water will be cloudy or foamy, or it will smell like a science experiment.

Cleaning your hot tub's filter is important because a dirty, worn-out filter will fail to trap spa contaminants and will put undue strain on your tub's pump motor and heater. Rinse your filter weekly with **water** to get rid of coarse dirt and debris. Take a **garden hose**, apply the stream at a 45 degree angle and give it a pressure washing inside and out. Allow the filter to dry. Next, remove any fine particles of dirt carefully with a **brush** or by applying a **stream of compressed air** (from an air compressor or from an aerosol can, available at supermarkets as well as camera, computer and discount stores) to the filter's outer surface.

If algae, suntan oil or body oils still leave a coating, soak the filter overnight in a **degreaser cleaning solution** from the hot-tub dealer. Some experts recommend that you soak the filter monthly in a degreaser. If it's still clogged, check your water chemistry and adjust, drain and clean the tub or buy a new filter cartridge. Replace the filter annually.

Every three months, drain the water and clean the acrylic shell inside and out with a **non-soap-based cleaner** – most bathroom cleaners are detergent based, so use one designed for an acrylic bath. Spray it on the tub, let it sit for a minute and then wipe off any scum or stains or rub with a **sponge**. Refill the tub right away – or wax it after cleaning with an **aerosol wax**. You'll find that **old, clean cotton T-shirts** make great buffers. Be sure not to spray the cleaning solution and wax into the jets.

h

If you're still getting cloudy water, your jets aren't working properly or gunk is appearing on the water, you may have clogged pipes and you'll have to use a **spa cleaning agent,** available from your hot-tub supplier.

To clean hot-tub covers, use a **cover cleaning product** or a **general vinyl cleaner**, sold in car supply stores to clean soft-top cars. Applying a **paste wax** to your hot-tub cover is a good idea, because it creates a barrier between the cover and the sun, slowing down the sun's fading action.

When the cleaning is done, refill the tub with **cold water**. It will take about an hour. Then do your water tests and add the amount of chemicals and disinfectants recommended by your hot tub's manufacturer. Start the hot tub. It will take 6 to 12 hours for the water to reheat.

House plants

Your plants need more than regular watering. To maintain their ability to grow, they do need cleaning. Remove dust and dirt with a shower. This is important, because grime is the enemy of photosynthesis, the process in which leaves absorb sunlight and carbon dioxide to make food for the plant. The shower will also help remove insects.

Just like humans, house plants will be re-invigorated after a shower to remove dust and dirt.

First, prepare the plant's pot Put the pot in a **plastic bag** and tie the bag tightly around the base of the plant without damaging it. You want to be sure the plant doesn't get over-watered in the shower. If your plant has multiple stems, lay extra plastic bags between the stems. Put the plant in the **shower** and set the water temperature to tepid – neither hot nor cold. Let the shower sprinkle the plant for a few minutes.

Sometimes minerals in the shower water will build up on the plant's leaves, making them look dull. To clean the minerals off hard-surfaced (not hairy) leaves, wipe with a **dry, clean rag**. Support each leaf with your free hand as you wipe. Or gently scrape the minerals off with your thumb.

Cleaning plants with hairy leaves is a little trickier. First give them a gentle dusting with a **feather duster** and then put the plant in the shower, as above.

After the plants have had their shower, allow them to dry thoroughly in the shower stall or set them on **paper towels** or **old newspapers** until they're not dripping any more. If you return them to direct sunlight while they're still wet, the light may burn the leaves.

Now check your plant's surroundings Make sure the window where it sits is clean so that the plant will get maximum sunlight. White mineral deposits can be toxic to your plants, so gently scrape them from the soil surface and the inner rim of the pot. If you have an extreme case of mineral build-up, put the pot in a sink where it can drain freely and run a lot of water through the soil to remove the minerals. (Don't do this during times of low light or dormancy, however. Plants should be actively growing; otherwise they may develop root rot.)

Cleaning a cactus requires a gentle touch – not only to prevent skewering yourself, but also to protect the waxy coating that helps the plant to conserve moisture in desert climates. Stick to misting your cactus with a **spray bottle** filled with **water** and even then only clean the areas of the plant that are showing dirt or dust. Make the cleaning quick and gentle and let the cactus dry before putting it back into direct sunlight. Or use **long tweezers** to carefully pick off any dust particles.

To clean succulents with fuzzy leaves, use a **soft paintbrush** or **feather duster** to remove dust. The fuzziness protects the plant in arid conditions and washing can be hazardous to the leaves.

Keep your cactus clean to allow it to look its best and stay healthy.

Humidifiers

A humidifier is a blessing if you suffer from winter dryness of your nose, throat, lips or skin. The air it dampens will also alleviate static electricity, peeling wallpaper and cracks in paint and furniture. But humidifiers can encourage the growth of dust mites and mould, so proper care and cleaning is essential.

If you use a humidifier, plan to clean daily with a more thorough cleaning every three days and regular disinfecting. If this seems like a lot, remember that mould begins to grow after 48 hours.

To clean a portable humidifier, first turn it off. Empty the reservoir (the tank where the water sits) every day and wash it out with **hot, soapy water**, using a **brush** or other scrubber to remove mineral deposits or film. Rinse well under **running water**, taking care that no water gets into the motor. Wipe all surfaces dry with a **clean cloth** and fill the reservoir. **Distilled water** is preferable because you'll avoid the build-up of mineral deposits, but tap water will suffice.

Every three days, clean your humidifier more thoroughly. Begin as you would the daily cleaning. After rinsing, wipe the reservoir with **white vinegar** (diluted with water, if you wish) to break up mineral deposits. Wipe off the mineral deposits, rinse again, wipe dry and refill the reservoir with water.

Disinfecting your humidifier will reduce spore growth. Mix a solution of **20ml of bleach** with **3 litres of water** and add it to the humidifier's reservoir. Run the humidifier until it starts to mist or steam. (Be sure to do this in a well-ventilated area and don't stand near the steamed bleach – it can injure your lungs.) Turn off the humidifier and let the bleach sit for a couple of minutes. Empty the reservoir into a **sink** and rinse the reservoir with **running water**. Fill it again with **fresh water**, run the system for two to three minutes and then turn it off. Empty the reservoir and rinse again. Repeat the cycle until you no longer smell the bleach.

Note: if the manufacturer's instructions don't recommend bleach, don't use it. They may recommend instead a **3 per cent solution of hydrogen peroxide**, which is fine but does not work as well as bleach.

If your humidifier has a filter, check it every third day. If it's grey, replace it. The filter can't be cleaned.

At the end of the humidifying season, clean the humidifier following the bleach method above. Make sure all parts are dry and store the unit in a dry location. When it's time to use the humidifier again, clean the unit again and wipe up any dust on the outside with a damp cloth.

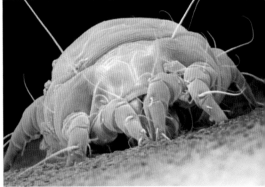

Dust mites in humidifiers can cause and aggravate allergic reactions such as asthma.

Iron

Wrought iron, as defined metallurgically and by the process used in working the metal, is not produced any more except for restorations. (Real wrought iron is worked white hot, hammered and twisted into shape.) Today the term is often used, incorrectly, to include decorative iron, 'mild steel' or cast iron.

Indoor iron pieces – such as bed frames, lamps and chandeliers – are dust magnets. If your item has a black-satin finish, you might as well be shining a spotlight on the dust – everyone will see it.

The easiest and quickest way to clean indoor pieces is with **compressed air** (buy it in cans from camera shops). It simply blows the dust away and is especially good for all the edges, corners and crevices of detailed iron, which defy the reach of a conventional cleaning rag. Or try carefully dusting intricate ornamentation with an **unused, soft-bristled paintbrush**.

Use a dry wire brush to scrub off remaining rust before applying touch-up paint.

To clean a smooth piece of wrought iron, wipe first with a **soft cotton rag**, to remove dust and then wipe with **furniture polish** sprayed onto a clean section of the rag. If there's dirt stuck to the wrought iron, the furniture polish may help lubricate and remove it. Water isn't recommended. It will collect in areas that can't be reached by a drying cloth, leading to rust. Furniture polish, on the other hand, provides a protective coating that repels water and resists dust.

To clean outdoor furniture that has a rusty finish or patina, let your item reach the desired rusty brown before you clean. Wipe off loose rust, dust or dirt with a **rag**. Then coat the piece with a **clear lacquer paint** (available at hardware stores) to protect it from the elements and to prevent further rusting.

Outdoor furniture that isn't supposed to rust needs to be cleaned only when it looks dirty or has mud or grime caked on it. Remove dirt by spraying with a **garden hose**. Periodically check the piece for rust, which may start around areas such as bolts. If you see minor oxidation, gently

How to season cast-iron cooking pots

When you buy a new piece of cast-iron cookware, you need to season it. Seasoning is a process that will protect your new pot from rust and give it a natural nonstick surface.

First, clean the new pot with dishwashing detergent and warm water to remove oils and debris from the manufacturing process. Fill the pot about two-thirds full with water. Add 80ml of white vinegar per 4 litres of water and boil for one hour. Let it cool and then pour away. If the pot is rough, scour the inside with fine-grit wet/dry glasspaper or steel wool.

Wash the pot inside and out with plain water. Apply a light coating of vegetable oil or lard on the inside and outside surfaces. (Using a spray cooking oil is fine.)

Heat the pot in a moderate oven for an hour and then turn off the oven and let the cookware cool with the oven door closed. When the item has cooled, wipe off any excess oil. The seasoning is complete.

The more you cook, the better the seasoning gets. With proper care, your pot should not rust. But if it does, repeat the seasoning process.

---

use a **dry wire brush** to remove the rust. Wipe off any dust particles you create. Before applying **touch-up paint** to the surface, wipe the area clean with **acetone** or **paint thinner** on a **cotton cloth**. This will make the paint adhere better by removing oils that have transferred to the iron from your hands. It also will dissolve any remaining paint in the rusty area. Let the paint thinner dry before painting. Wear **gloves** and **goggles**, as acetone and paint thinner can be quite harsh to the skin and eyes. If your wrought iron is very rusty, you may have to take it to be sandblasted.

To clean cast iron, the kind that is poured into a mould at a foundry, use the same cleaning methods used on wrought iron. Cast-iron items typically include doorknobs, railings and fences. Hose down the item and then inspect it for rust. If you find rust, clean it off with a **wire brush**. Then wipe away any dust that your cleaning has produced, before putting on a **rust–preventive paint**, such as those made by *Dinitrol* (see *www.rust.co.uk*). Spray and paint-on versions are available.

Cleaning well-seasoned iron cookware requires very little effort. Generally, all that's required is a little **boiling water**, light scraping with a **wooden spoon** and a quick wipe with a **clean cloth**. Dry thoroughly and lightly oil again. For badly burned-on food, use a **copper wool scouring pad**. For extreme cases of burned-on food and grease, use any **common oven cleaner** according to the package directions. Rinse well. Then, unfortunately, you'll have to season the item as if it were new. (See box above.)

Watch out

Don't use soap, detergent or the dishwasher with your cast iron cookware. And never pour cold water into hot cast iron – that could break it. Extensive cleaning with soaps or detergents will remove the seasoning and you'll have to repeat the process.

Store pots with the lids off to prevent condensation and keep your cookware clean, dry and oiled. A **wire brush** is best for removing rust. Really bad cases of rust may require **glasspaper** or **commercial rust removers**.

Irons

Generally, these tend to need cleaning when you've had a minor mishap – for example, you've tried to iron synthetics on too high a heat and some of the fibre has stuck to the soleplate of the iron.

To remove stuck on fibres, heat the iron until the fibres liquefy. Then, on nonstick and aluminum or chrome soleplates, use a **wooden spatula** or **flat stick** (for instance, an ice lolly stick) to scrape off the fibres. Never scrape with plastic, metal, or anything abrasive. Run the iron over a **terry cloth towel** or some other rough material that the remaining fibres will be able to stick to.

If you don't know what's stuck on your soleplate and the mark doesn't liquefy when you heat the iron, use any **hot iron cleaner**, available at fabric shops and hardware stores.

If the stain still remains on an aluminum or chrome soleplate, your next option is to make a paste of **bicarbonate of soda** and **water** with the consistency of toothpaste. Rub it on a **cool iron** with a **soft cloth**, then wipe it off with another **damp cloth**. Don't use this method on nonstick soleplates.

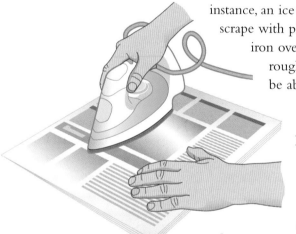

Iron over a newspaper to get rid of the waxy stain on the soleplate of your iron – the newpaper will absorb the hot wax.

On Teflon or metallic-coated nonstick surfaces, a **damp cloth** should wipe off any water marks and a **wooden spatula** should remove any fibre stains. Should any marks still remain, rub a **nylon scouring pad** on the iron's soleplate when it's cool.

Here's how to clean specific substances from your iron:
• **To clean sticky, oil-based residue** from an aluminum or chrome soleplate, use an **all-purpose cleaner** on a cold iron. Spray the cleaner onto the soleplate and rub with a

soft cloth. Remove the cleaner by rubbing with a **wet cloth**. (Never rinse the electrical appliance in water.) Before using the iron again, heat it and rub the soleplate on a **terry cloth rag** to remove any traces of the cleaner and residue.

• **To clean acetate or nylon** that has melted and hardened on the soleplate, use **acetone** on a **cloth** and rub the affected area of the cold soleplate until the melted residue is gone. Don't get the acetone on the plastic shell of the iron, because the acetone will melt it.

• **To clean a waxy stain** (from a crayon, for instance), heat your iron as hot as possible and iron a completely dry **newspaper** until the wax is gone. Rest assured that the print won't come off on your iron.

• **To remove small bits of burned lint**, use your iron's 'burst of steam' feature as directed.

• **To prevent stains from forming** on the soleplate (so you can avoid having to clean as above), use a **pressing cloth**, a lightweight pure cotton cloth, which will act as a barrier between the iron and your clothing. A pressing cloth – and this can be a bit of old, white cotton sheeting – will prevent synthetic fibres or starch from attaching to the iron.

To clean the iron's steam chamber, check the manufacturer's guidelines about whether to use distilled or tap water. Generally, newer models use **tap water** – the minerals actually help in the steaming process. With the cord unplugged, fill the iron with **water**. Then plug in the iron and, depending on your model, either turn the iron to its cleaning mode function (most manufacturers recommend using the self-cleaning feature once a year) or to the steaming feature.

Hold the steaming iron over a sink, with the soleplate face down, until the steam stops. Unplug the iron and leave it in the sink for another half hour to fully dry.

Or place the iron face down on a **heatproof cooking rack** while it steams. The steam will remove lint, dirt, dust and mineral deposits that have built-up in the steam vents. Finish by wiping with a **dry cloth**.

If you haven't steamed your iron for a while, you may find that the water or steam looks rusty. This is actually burned lint, which can stain your clothes. So it's important to clean your steam chamber and vents every couple of months.

Unbend a paperclip and use it to unclog and clean the vents on the sole plate of your iron.

If the steam-cleaning technique described above doesn't remove the mineral deposits from the steam chamber, try using **vinegar** if your manufacturer's instructions allow it. Pour **white vinegar** into the steam chamber and steam it through the vents. Rinse out the vinegar and refill the chamber with **water**. Let the water steam through the iron to remove all the vinegar. If you're not careful about removing the vinegar, it may stain your clothes the next time you use the iron. The acidic nature of the vinegar may also etch and damage the interior of the iron if left inside the steam chamber.

If the steam vents on the soleplate become clogged, unbend a **paperclip** and push it into the holes to reopen the vents before steaming the iron.

Cleaning the iron's outer shell is simple. Just wipe it with a **damp rag**.

Always dry and cool your iron before putting it away and store it in an upright position on the heel rest.

Ivory & bone

Treat ivory and bone with care. Whether you're cleaning a figurine or a beaded necklace, the condition and fragility of the item will determine your approach.

True ivory comes from the tusk of an elephant or mammoth. Today, the tusks of other mammals, such as walruses and certain whales and some synthetics are considered ivory as well. Ivory is chemically similar to bone and antler, but ivory has no blood vessels, whereas bone does. Bone is fragile and porous, but ivory is dense. Ivory and bone are both sensitive to heat, light and moisture.

If your ivory item is fragile, take it to an expert to be cleaned. Because ivory readily absorbs oils and stains, wear **white cotton gloves** while working with ivory, or, at the very least, wash your hands thoroughly with **soap** and **water** to remove oils and dirt.

If your ivory or bone is sturdy and stable, clean off the surface dust or dirt with a **barely damp cotton cloth** or **cotton swabs**. To dampen, use a solution of **mild washing-up liquid** and **water** or use just water. Too much

Watch out

All of these factors could damage your ivory or bone:
- Display areas exposed to sunlight or a spotlight.
- A closed display case with light bulbs inside, heating the interior.
- Nearby ventilation or heating ducts, the tops of appliances or other sources of heat or cold.
- Sulphur in rubber-based storage materials, adhesives and paint (the sulphur in rubber can discolour ivory).

moisture may cause surface fractures to appear on the ivory. Wipe the surface of your item with a **dry cloth**, and apply a **second cloth** or **cotton bud** dampened with white spirit to remove any soap residue. Wipe with a **dry cloth**.

Never rub the surface of ivory and bone You may inadvertently remove the original surface coats or any pigments or patinas.

To remove wax or oil from ivory, use a **cloth** or **cotton bud** barely dampened with **white spirit**. If your ivory or bone has scrimshaw (engravings or decorations) on it, test an inconspicuous part of the scrimshaw to see whether it will withstand the cleaning technique. If it doesn't react well to the test, don't try to clean the scrimshaw yourself.

If your ivory or bone is stained (a yellow stain is typical), you will have to call an expert. These stains are usually due to the oxidation that comes with age or may be caused by the oils on your hands. Sometimes, placing the ivory or bone in sunlight bleaches it and helps it to regain its warm white color. Keeping ivory or bone in the dark accelerates the yellowing associated with ageing. But do not expose ivory or bone to long periods of intense sunlight or heat, because that will dry it out and cause it to crack.

Store ivory and bone in a carefully controlled environment, ideally 45 per cent to 55 per cent relative humidity and about 20°C, in low light. Conditions should be kept constant. The most severe damage to ivory and bone is caused by fluctuations in relative humidity and temperature. Low humidity will cause ivory to dry out, causing shrinkage and cracking. High humidity and changes in temperature can cause your ivory to expand and contract.

k Kennels

If your pet has a kennel outside, you don't have to change the bedding as often as you change your own sheets. But at least once a month isn't too often to keep fleas and mites and other kinds of pests at bay and make it a clean and comfortable haven for your dog to sleep in.

Start cleaning a kennel by treating it like you would a teenager's bedroom. Get everything out. If you use straw, throw it away. If your dog likes to curl up in blankets, put them in the washing machine. Hose down the kennel, inside and out. You might need to lift one end to drain all the water. Then get ready to scrub.

When washing a kennel, don't use anything that you wouldn't want your pet to lap up. Chemical household cleaners will make a home sparkle. But dogs aren't as particular about the way their home looks as they are about the way it smells. A pine-scented habitat might smell deliciously clean to you, but your dog might disagree. Instead, use a **plastic-bristled brush** to apply an **organic cleaner** or use a homemade solution of **4 tablespoons of lemon extract** or **lemon juice** with **4 litres of water**. Alternatively, mix **100ml of vinegar** to 300ml of water.

A sprinkle of bicarbonate of soda on your pet's clean bedding will absorb odours and keep them fresher for longer.

Replacing the bedding is the last step If your dog likes to lie on straw, put in some fresh straw and sprinkle it with **bicarbonate of soda** to make the freshness last longer. If your pet prefers blankets, let the washed blankets dry in the sun for extra freshness; then sprinkle a little **bicarbonate of soda** on them.

Kitchen cabinets

To routinely clean the cabinet exteriors, dust with a clean cloth regularly and wipe with a damp cloth periodically. (In terms of frequency, the meaning of regularly and periodically will depend on your specific cabinets and frequency of use of the cabinets.) Never use abrasive cleaners or scourers on kitchen cabinets. Also avoid using your dishcloth, because it may contain grease or detergents that can add streaks and smears.

To wipe away the stains around handles on doors and drawers – you'll need to use a heavy-duty cleaner, because those stains will probably be the most troublesome, being a mixture of skin oils, food smears and softened finish. On cabinets made of plastic laminate, metal or glass, try a **strong all-purpose household cleaner**. Spray it onto a **cloth** or **sponge** and apply to the dirty areas. Let the cleaner sit for a few minutes and then wipe it off with a **rinsed-out cloth** or **sponge**. Wipe again with a **dry cloth**.

To clean wood cabinets, first try a little **washing-up liquid** applied directly to a **cloth** or **sponge**. Rub into the dirty areas around the hardware. Then wash the entire cabinet with an **oil soap solution**. Use **60ml of oil soap** (such as *Pledge Soapy Cleaner* for wood and laminate surfaces) to **4 litres of water**. Apply with a **cloth** dipped in the solution and wrung out. Then go over the cabinets with a cloth dampened in **plain water**, followed by a **dry cloth**.

To protect the surface of the cabinets, apply a wax suitable for your cabinets' material. **Car wax** or other **paste waxes** work well on wood. Once a year, apply thinly to a clean surface with a clean cloth and then buff.

To clean cabinets that have windows, wash the glass with a **cloth** or **paper towel** sprayed with a little **glass cleaner**. Don't spray cleaner, or even plain water, directly onto the glass – it can drip down and damage the surrounding wood.

To clean the shelves, use the same methods as for the exterior surfaces. Shelves should need thorough cleaning only once or twice a year – assuming you clean up any spills as soon as they happen. To remove an old spill, sprinkle with **bicarbonate of soda** and wipe with a **damp cloth**.

Knick-knacks

If you swoosh away the dust from your glass menagerie or curios frequently, it won't have a chance to turn to greasy grime that will require a more intrusive cleaning job.

To dust a whole rack of knick-knacks, use a **hair dryer** or **feather duster** every couple of days – if you're of the swooshing school. Or wipe them, one at a time, with a **clean microfibre cloth** once a week. Either way, you'll probably rarely need to wash them.

To wash your knick-knacks, mix a little **washing-up liquid** in **warm water** in a **plastic bowl** and immerse the knick-knacks, assuming they're made of china, glass, plastic or metal. Use a **clean, thick cotton sock**, worn over your hand, as a cleaning mitt. That will get into most crevices. Use an **old toothbrush** on places that your hand can't get to. Rinse the items well with **fresh water** and dry with a **clean cloth**.

For an even speedier wash, run your knick-knacks through the **dishwasher** on the gentlest setting.

To clean cloth items, try the **vacuum cleaner** first, using the **brush** or **crevice attachment**. If that isn't enough, put the articles in a **paper bag**, add **2 tablespoons of bicarbonate of soda**, shake and then shake some more. Remove the items from the bag and brush or vacuum off.

Watch out

Don't use soap and water – and especially not the dishwasher – to clean hand-painted or antique knick-knacks. If a prized piece needs cleaning, as opposed to just dusting, wipe it lightly with a damp cloth. The same gentle touch applies for wooden knick-knacks.

Knives

Do you want a bright and shiny knife at all times? Then choose stainless steel. The problem with stainless is that when it loses its edge, it doesn't take well to sharpening. Or do you prefer a really sharp knife, one that you can easily sharpen? Choose carbon steel. The downside is that it's difficult to keep bright and shiny.

Wash knives immediately after use in a little
washing-up liquid and **hot water** with a **cloth** or
sponge. Rinse with **hot water** and wipe with a **dry cloth**.

To remove stains from a carbon steel blade,
try a paste made of **salt** and **vinegar**. Rub it on the blade
with a cloth. Or dip a **slice of lemon** into **salt** and rub
that on the blade. Some stains will respond to a **nylon
scrubber** or **steel wool**.

To shine the blade, use **silver polish**.

To protect the edges of knives, store them in a
rack or, if in a drawer, cover the blades with **cardboard
sleeves**. You can make a sleeve by cutting a piece of
cardboard (from a cereal box, for example) the length of
the blade and twice as wide. Fold the cardboard in half
lengthwise. Use **tape** to seal the side and one end. Insert the
knife in the open end.

To clean a pocket-knife, open all the blades – and in
a Swiss Army-type knife, all the other accessories as well.
Wash them in **hot, soapy water**. Remove dirt from the
little slots with a **toothbrush**. Rinse in **hot water**, dry with
a **clean cloth** and leave the knife open for a while to allow
the slots to dry thoroughly. Lubricate the hinges periodically
with a little **sewing machine oil**, available at fabric shops
or sewing machine suppliers.

To clean a hunting knife, use the same method as for
a **pocket-knife**. After using your knife in the field, rinse it
off in a stream, or wipe it clean with leaves or grass.

Life on the edge A sharp carbon steel knife edge has lots of practically invisible
'teeth', which get bent out of line during use. Keep them as straight as possible by
using a honing steel before each use.

1 Hold the steel in your left hand (if you're right-handed).
2 Place the knife against the steel at a 20 to 25-degree angle.
3 Draw the knife across, heel to tip, so that the entire blade passes over
   the top of the steel.
4 Repeat with the other side of the knife on the bottom of the steel.
   Continue for about a dozen strokes.

Eventually, the blade will get so dull that honing will no longer be effective. Then it's time for
sharpening, a process that removes some metal and leaves a new edge. Many hardware, kitchen,
or department stores offer sharpening service.

Lace

Lace is usually an extremely delicate material, so you shouldn't be surprised that there is a long list of cautions to observe when you are trying to clean it.

• *Don't* use the washing machine, dryer, your usual detergents or soaps, chlorine bleach, lemon juice or salt.
• *Don't* rub lace or lift it by itself while it's wet.
• *Don't* send it to a dry-cleaner, except for recently made lace that specifies dry-cleaning on the care label.
• *Don't* clean lace that is fragile, old or valuable, yourself. Give it to a professional conservator. You should wash only sturdy lace – for example, a tablecloth of no great value.

Make sure the pins you use on your lace are stainless – rust marks can appear very quickly and spoil all your hard work.

To clean lace, place a **clean white towel** in the bottom of the **sink** or **bathtub**. Lay the lace cloth on the towel. Mix **1 teaspoon of** *Orvus WA Paste* per **4½ litres of warm water**. (*Orvus*, a pH neutral detergent used as an animal wash, is available from sewing and quilting suppliers.) Make enough of the solution to cover the cloth. Soak for 15 minutes and then agitate by gently lifting and lowering the towel.

To rinse, use room-temperature **distilled water**. Keep changing the water until it is totally clear. Drain. Use the towel as a sling to lift the lace.

To dry, first blot up as much water as possible with **dry towels** and then lay the lace flat on a **clean, dry towel** and allow it to dry completely.

Lacquer

Lacquer is eye-catching because of its mirror-like finish and also because that finish often belongs to furniture, such as a dining table or piano, that is the focal point of a room. Keep your lacquer at its shining best with these tips.

To dust a lacquered surface, use a **large, folded piece of cheesecloth** slightly moistened with **water**. Don't wipe in a circular motion – that could leave 'whirlpools' on the finish. Wipe in only one direction, the one in which the piece was originally polished, if you can determine that.

To clean when dusting isn't enough, mix a little **washing-up liquid** in **tepid water**, dip in a **soft cloth** and wring it out. Wipe the surface down. Wipe again with a **rinsed-out damp cloth**, then again with a **dry cloth**.

To polish a dulled surface, use a **non-silicone paste wax**. Silicone will cause problems if the piece ever needs to be refinished. Apply the wax with a **soft cloth** in one direction and buff the same way. Don't overdo the buffing, because rubbing creates static electricity, which will attract dust particles.

Lamps

Cleaning your lamps doesn't make them just look good, they will work more effectively too: any dust on a light makes it shine less brightly.

To remove dust from a lamp, use a **microfibre cloth** regularly. The **vacuum cleaner** with its **brush attachment** may work better on some materials, such as unglazed pottery or wood. The more often you dust, the less often you'll have to do more intensive cleaning.

Include the light bulb in your routine – that's where the money-saving comes in. Dust build-up reduces bulb efficiency, wastes energy and raises your electricity bill.

To remove dirt, first unplug the lamp and remove the shade and the bulb. Start with a **clean cloth** or **sponge** dampened with **plain water**. Wipe all parts of the lamp, starting with the base and working up. Don't wet the socket or the plug.

To avoid dulling the finish, buff the lamp immediately with a **clean, dry cloth**. To attack more stubborn dirt, try about ½ **teaspoon of washing-up liquid** applied directly to a **cloth** or **sponge**. Wipe the dirty areas, scrubbing gently if necessary. Rinse the cloth or sponge in **clear water** and go over the surface to remove the detergent. Follow with the **dry cloth**. Polish the lamp occasionally with a polish suitable for the material the lamp is made of.

Watch out

• Don't use solvents, waxes, polishes, or harsh cleaners of any kind on old lacquer. Modern finishes are tougher, but test any cleaner or polish on a small, inconspicuous area before applying it generally.

• To avoid scratching, nicking or dulling a lacquer finish, don't place objects on the bare surface. During use, dining tables should be well protected with a tablecloth or place mats.

To wash glass globes or chimneys, clean with a **cloth** or **sponge** and a solution of **hot water** and a little **washing-up liquid**. It's safe to immerse those parts as long as they don't have electrical connectors. Rinse with a solution of **hot water** and a dash of **ammonia** and wipe dry with a **clean cloth**.

Lamp shades

A lamp shade can set the mood in a room by directing and softening light. Whatever its colour or style, it will do this most effectively when it's clean.

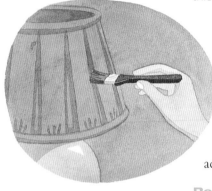

A soft brush is perfect for dusting as it can be gently worked in between the pleats on a fabric lampshade.

To remove dust before it turns to grime, go over the surface – inside and out – with:
- a **vacuum cleaner** with the **small brush attachment** for sturdy cloth shades;
- a **microfibre cloth** for glass, plastic, paper, or metal shades;
- a **soft-bristled horsehair paintbrush** for silk, acetate and pleated shades.

Regular dusting will help you avoid higher-impact cleaning, which can be messy for you and dangerous for your lamp shade. Water can dissolve glue, for example, causing the shade to fall apart.

To remove serious dirt, the safest cleaning method after dusting is to use a special **sponge** that's intended to be used dry. Ask for a **dry-cleaning sponge** at a hardware or DIY store. Use it like an eraser to rub away dirt. Try it on any shade, but be sure to use it instead of water on paper shades and those with glue.

To clean fabric shades that are stitched rather than glued, wash them in the **bath**. And while you're going to the trouble of doing one, it makes sense to do all your shades that need it. Metal and plastic shades can also be cleaned in the bath at the same time. To wash the shades, begin by drawing around **6cm of tepid water** into the bath. Add **1 tablespoon of washing-up liquid** and swish it around. Lay the shade on its side in the bath and gently roll it in the water. Metal and plastic shades can stand a little more vigorous cleaning, with a **cloth** or **sponge**. Change the water when it becomes dirty and wash again.

To rinse, drain the wash water and draw clear water. Again, roll the shade in the water and change the water when it turns grey. Metal and plastic shades can be rinsed under **running water** and wiped dry with a **cloth**.

To dry a cloth shade, use a **towel** to press out as much water as you can. Finish with a **hair dryer**, tipping the shade upside down frequently so that no water settles in the bottom of the shade, where it could leave a water stain. Drying quickly is important, because the metal parts of the shade can rust and stain the fabric.

To clean a glass shade, fill a sink with **warm water** and add **1 or 2 teaspoons of ammonia**. Immerse the shade in the water and wash it with a cloth. Use a **toothbrush** to get into crevices. Rinse and dry with a **clean cloth**.

Lawn mowers

Take good care of your power mower and it will take good care of your lawn. Good care means keeping the mower clean and maintaining it regularly.

To clean the underside, make sure the engine is off and can't start accidentally. Remove the spark plug wire (or in the case of an electric mower, make sure it is unplugged). Prop up one side of the mower on a **block** – don't turn it completely over. Use a **garden hose** to wash off loose grass and dirt. Then remove the remainder with a **putty knife**, followed by a **stiff-bristled brush**. If you do this every time you use the mower, you will never get a caked, muddy grass build-up again.

On the mower's exterior, keep the engine free of dead grass, leaves and grease (which is a fire hazard). To keep the mower running well, brush off the air-intake screen and the cooling fins on the engine with a **stiff brush** to keep them free of debris.

Turn the lawnmower on its side or prop it using wooden blocks but don't let it tip upside down.

Attend to a petrol mower's air filter after every 25 hours of use. Replace a disposable paper filter (available where lawn mowers are sold). A foam-type filter has a removable sponge that should be soaked in **warm water** and then dried. Follow by putting a few drops of **clean engine oil** into the sponge and squeezing it to distribute the oil. Then reinstall the sponge.

An annual professional tune-up for your lawn mower will save you a lot of trouble. It should include a carburettor adjustment and a cleaning of belts, cables and switches. It also can include sharpening the blade and changing the oil, spark plug and air filter if you prefer not to do those things yourself.

Simple solutions

A kitchen solution to a garden problem

To prevent grass and dirt under the deck of your lawn mower, use spray-on vegetable cooking oil. Squirt it on when the mower is new. If it's too late for that, clean the underside and then apply the oil on the metal after it dries. This will make it easy to clean the mower after each use.

Leaded glass & stained glass

The lead in leaded glass does not refer to the glass or to lead crystal. It refers to the material used in the cames, which are the grooved metal rods that hold the panes of glass together. Today, some cames are made of copper or zinc, but it's still referred to as leaded glass.

Stained glass is associated mainly with churches but many Victorian and Edwardian properties still retain elaborate glass in their doors and upper window panes. The following directions for windows can also be applied to less hefty objects, such as lamp shades, boxes, light (or sun) catchers and more.

To clean leaded or stained glass, use **plain, warm water**. Wash each pane individually with a **clean cloth** dampened in the water. Don't use a spray bottle, because the water will drip into the cames. Wipe dry with a **clean, soft cloth** or **chamois cloth**. Never apply much force when washing such windows, because you can actually bend them, especially if the cames are lead, which is a very soft metal. Use only the damp cloth for cleaning the cames.

For more cleaning power, use **1 teaspoon of methylated spirits** in **1 litre of warm water** and follow the same procedure outlined above. If dirt or some kind of old finish remains, leave it alone.

Watch out

● When cleaning leaded glass, never use common household glass cleaners or home concoctions with vinegar, lemon, or ammonia. Never use any kind of abrasive cleaner.

● If the glass has painting on it, don't clean it at all. Even water might damage or remove fragile paint. Painted parts of a window are usually recognisable as something like a bird or a face applied onto the glass, rather than an integral part of it. House numbers are also sometimes painted on, but otherwise the stained glass in houses is less likely than that in churches to have been painted.

Leather

Leather means any skin or hide that has been tanned, but after that the similarities end and the differences begin. Two main categories of leather require different cleaning techniques.

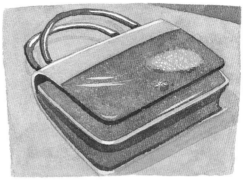

Natural leather has little surface protection and is highly susceptible to staining. It is not dyed with pigments, has no finish coat of polyurethane and is recognisable by its rustic, natural appearance. Even water or treatments suitable for other kinds of leather, such as saddle soap, may mar its surface.

Putting a small pile of talcum powder on greasy spots will often help to absorb a stain.

Coated leather is recognisable by its pigment-dyed surface treated with a polyurethane coating. Most – but not all – leather garments, upholstery, purses and shoes are coated leather.

A few guidelines apply to both kinds:
• Follow cleaning directions from the manufacturer.
• Test any cleaning method on an inconspicuous area before using it generally.
• For any valuable leather article or serious cleaning problem, consult a professional, such as a dry-cleaner who specialises in cleaning leather.
• Avoid harsh cleaners and even excessive water, which can leave stains and remove dye and lubricants.
• Never dry wet leather near a heat source.

To clean natural leather, rely on frequent dusting with a **soft cloth**. You could try removing dirt with a new **art rubber**, available at stationery and art supply stores, but even that might leave a smudge. There is little more you can do without making a problem worse.

See also **Suede.**

To clean coated leathers, dust regularly with a **cloth**, occasionally with a **dampened cloth**. Wash every six months or so with **saddle soap**, which is available at tack shops, sporting goods stores, some shoe stores and hardware stores. Here's how:

1 Remove loose dirt with a **stiff brush** or **damp cloth**.
2 Rub a damp cloth on **saddle soap** and work up a lather.

3 Rub the **soapy cloth** on the leather using a circular motion and wipe away the excess with another damp cloth.
4 Allow to air-dry.
5 Buff with a **clean, soft cloth**.
6 Finish with a **protective leather cream** recommended by the manufacturer or a general-purpose one sold by leather retailers.

To treat spots on coated leathers, try these methods – but don't forget to test on a patch first:
• Apply **unscented talcum powder** to greasy spots and let it absorb the grease. Wipe off with a **cloth**.
• Rub with a **cotton swab** dipped in **surgical spirit**.
• Make a paste of equal parts **lemon juice** and **cream of tartar**, work it into the spot (including scuff marks) with a **cloth**, let it sit for an hour or so and wipe clean.
• Treat ugly white stains on shoes and boots caused by water and road salt with a 50-50 mixture of **water** and **white vinegar**. Dip a cloth into the solution and blot.
• On mildew, use a 50-50 solution of **methylated spirits** and **water** on a cloth. **Saddle soap** also may work.

See also Shoes.

Light fixtures

How do insects and spiders manage to sneak into a ceiling light fixture that has no visible gaps? Whatever their secret, now and then you will want to remove their dried-out little bodies – and clean the fixture too.

To clean a wall or ceiling fixture, first turn off the switch and plant a sturdy **stepladder** nearby. Remove any grilles, shades, shields, globes, light bulbs or light tubes. You may have to hold onto a globe while you remove screws and balance yourself to keep from falling.

To wash the removable parts, fill the sink with **hot water** and add a little **washing-up liquid**. Lay a **towel** or **rubber mat** on the bottom of the sink to prevent damage. Immerse the pieces – except for the light bulbs or tubes – and clean with a **soft cloth** or **sponge**. Rinse and dry well with a **soft cloth**. Wipe the light bulbs or light tubes with a **damp cloth**, avoiding the ends that go into the sockets.

To wash the fixed parts, use a **cloth** or **sponge** dipped into the same cleaning solution and squeezed until it's barely damp. Wipe the fixture, being careful not to get any moisture in the socket or on the wiring. Rinse the sponge or cloth in clean water and wipe the fixture with it again. Wipe everything dry with another cloth and reassemble the fixture.

Litter trays

How, and how often, you clean your cat's litter tray depends on the kind of litter and the box – and, especially, on how fussy your cat is.

Here are the basics:

• **To clean a litter tray**, remove solids daily – and don't forget, or your fastidious cat may find another spot.

• **With clumping litter**, remove the faeces and urine clumps with a **slotted scoop** available at pet and discount stores. Clumping litter should be dumped and the box washed about every two weeks – sooner if your nose or eyes say it's time.

• **For non-clumping litter**, remove the solids daily with a **scoop** and change the litter and wash the box at least once a week or more often if needed.

• **To clean self-cleaning boxes**, which can include motors and other moving parts, follow the manufacturer's directions carefully.

To wash the box, use a little **washing-up liquid** and **water** and scrub with a **stiff brush**. Avoid using any cleaner with a strong smell, such as scented detergents or ammonia, which could turn up a sensitive feline nose. But do disinfect with a solution of **1 part chlorine bleach** to **10 parts water**. Rinse thoroughly with **plain water** – your cat may stop using the tray if it smells of washing-up liquid – and if possible dry in the sunshine – it's a natural disinfectant.

Oops!

Don't perfume the litter tray

You had the best intentions in the world sprinkling a deodorising powder on the litter tray, thinking your cat would appreciate the scent as much as you do. But alas, cats' noses are extremely sensitive – and unpredictable. Some cats take offence at even such a mild, inoffensive substance as baking soda.

If your cat suddenly stops using its litter tray and has substituted something else – such as the dining room rug – scent may be the problem. Switch to a different litter and see if that helps. If not, buy a new box. A lingering, if faint, urine smell embedded in the plastic could also be why your cat is going to the toilet elsewhere.

Or wipe dry with a **clean cloth** or **paper towels** before adding fresh litter.

To stop any footprints emanating from the box area, put a piece of carpet or a rubber mat at the spot where your cat leaves the box.

Locks

You may never have given a thought to cleaning a lock. But when turning the key becomes difficult or impossible, dirt may be the problem.

To clean the lock exterior, wipe with a **damp cloth** or **sponge**. For more power, use a little **washing-up liquid** applied to the cloth. Rinse the cloth before rinsing the lock parts. Wipe dry with a **clean cloth** and buff.

To achieve more shine, apply a **polish** appropriate to the metal, or an **all-metal polish** such as *Peek*, available at hardware stores.

To clean the inside of a door lock, give it a good dousing with a **penetrating lubricant** such as *WD-40*. Take the tiny tube that comes with the lubricant and fit it over the spray nozzle. Poke the other end of the tube into the keyhole and spray for 10 seconds while holding a piece of **kitchen roll** underneath

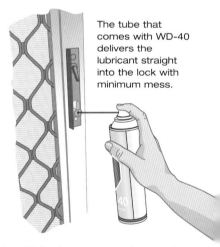

The tube that comes with WD-40 delivers the lubricant straight into the lock with minimum mess.

to catch excess lubricant. This will flush out any grime and will not attract dirt. Don't use conventional oil inside a lock, as dust will stick to it and gum up the mechanism.

To clean a lock that no longer works, first take it apart. Wash the inside parts with a **degreaser**, following the directions of the cleaner's manufacturer. Then lubricate the parts with a **multipurpose lubricant**. Both are available at hardware and motor supply stores.

Louvres

Louvre doors can be real magnets for dust. Remember that frequent dusting will postpone the day you have to tackle any heavy dirt build-up.

A soft paintbrush is all you need to dust between the slats on louvres. Flick the bristles to clean off dust.

To dust louvres, you have several options. Use these tools separately or in combination:
• the **brush attachment** of a **vacuum cleaner**
• a **soft paintbrush**
• a **clean, white cloth** wrapped around a **ruler** or **putty knife** or other flat object
• a **lamb's wool duster**
• a **special slotted duster** – from Lakeland stores or *www.lakeland.co.uk*

Dust from top to bottom, using a gentle wiping action, not a flicking one that will send dust back into the air. Shake the duster outside, not in the house.

To clean dirt from painted louvres – or louvres that have been coated with varnish or polyurethane – wipe with a **damp cloth**. For any grime you can't remove that way, rub with a little **washing-up liquid** applied directly to the cloth. Rinse the cloth in **plain water** and wipe again.

Some alternatives:
• Scrub with a **clean paint pad with a handle** – this should fit between all but the most tightly spaced louvres.
• Dampen a **cotton glove** in **water**, squirt some **washing-up liquid** on it, put the glove on and slide each finger between a different slat. With this method, you can clean several louvres at the same time. Rinse with another **damp glove** or a **damp cloth**.

To clean wood louvres with an oil finish, wipe with a **cloth** dampened with **boiled linseed oil**, **mineral spirits** or **turpentine**, all available at hardware and paint stores.

Simple solutions

Cleaning glass louvres

To clean louvred windows:

1 Mix a solution of 200ml of vinegar in 3 litres of water.

2 Open the window to its fullest extent so the slats are perpendicular to the window frame.

3 Take a thick white cotton sock and dip it into the solution; wring.

4 Put the sock over your hand like a mitten and clean the slats on both sides, one at a time, starting at the top.

5 Use a clean, dry sock to dry the slats in the same manner.

Luggage

Space-age technology has improved the materials used in today's luggage, making everything from flight bags to briefcases more durable and easier to clean.

To clean soft-sided luggage, use a **mild, all-purpose cleaner** mixed with **water**. Mix **1 part all-purpose cleaner** to **7 parts water** and use a **brush**, **cleaning cloth** or **sponge** to scrub dirt or spots with a circular motion, working your way outward. Most soft-sided luggage is made of tough nylon materials backed with plastic to repel water and it is easily cleaned.

To clean hard-sided luggage, use a little **washing–up liquid** in **warm water**. Wipe with a **sponge** or **cloth** that's been dipped into the solution and wrung out. Then rinse and dry. You can brighten the piece by waxing with a **silicone-based car** or **furniture polish**, available at hardware stores. Follow the directions on the package. Don't use a combination cleaner-polish.

To clean leather luggage and briefcases, determine whether the leather is natural or coated and follow the directions in the Leather entry on pages 273–274.

To clean aluminium cases, wash with a **cloth** dipped in the **washing–up liquid solution** described above. Never use ammonia-based cleaners, as they will darken the metal. For a good shine and protection, polish with *Peek* **multi–purpose metal polish**.

Simple solutions

For the infrequent flyer

To eliminate a musty, mildewy smell from luggage, wipe it with a solution of 200ml of white vinegar in 1 litre of water. Then wipe with a cloth dampened in plain water. Leave the luggage open to air-dry for a few days.

To avoid such smells, store luggage where it won't be subject to extremes of temperature or humidity and air it out periodically.

Lunch boxes

Food can be a potent source of germs and disease. Make sure you clean your lunch box thoroughly so any remains from yesterday's meal are not allowed to fester.

To clean metal or hard plastic lunch boxes,
wash with a **clean sponge** or **cloth** in **hot water** and a
little **washing–up liquid**. Rinse and dry. Always do this
after each day's use.

To clean soft-sided lunch boxes and bags,
wipe the inside with a **damp sponge** or **cloth**. For spills,
use a sponge dampened in **hot, soapy water**. Allow to air-
dry thoroughly.

To clean a grimy old metal lunch box,
begin by removing any loose dust or dirt with the
brush attachment of your **vacuum cleaner**. Use
as little abrasion as possible on the lithograph
design when you clean and polish it.

   Wash the box using **hot water** with a
little **washing–up liquid**. Mix it in a
separate container – not in the lunch
box itself. Wash with a **sponge** or **soft
cloth**, never with anything abrasive and rinse
the sponge under running water frequently.
Scrub tough grime gently with a **toothbrush**,
which is also useful for cleaning the handles. Rinse
in clear, warm water and dry with a **soft cloth**. Leave
the box open for an hour to let it dry thoroughly. Any wet
areas will be susceptible to rust.

To protect and polish the surface, apply a
nonabrasive car polish with a **soft cloth**, followed by a
buffing with another **clean, soft cloth**. Use a **chrome
polish** on the metal hardware, being careful not to get it on
the lithograph. Car and chrome polishes are available at
hardware and motor supply stores.

Marble

Although marble is a heavy stone that may seem indestructible, it is actually extremely porous, prone to staining and far from impervious to harsh treatment.

Watch out

Never use lemon, vinegar or any other acidic ingredient on marble. Acids will eat through the protective finish and damage the stone. Avoid ammonia as well. Abrasive powders should not be used either, since the grit can scratch and dull the marble finish.

Clean marble with a **gentle liquid soap** that does not have a grease remover. The safest course is to take it easy. Mix about **2 tablespoons of mild liquid soap** – *Ivory*, for instance, in ½ **gallon of water**. Using a **soft sponge** or a **sponge mop** if you're cleaning a marble floor, wipe the marble clean. Follow with two to three water rinses, depending on how soapy the cleaning mixture is. Then dry with a **soft cloth**.

Clean marble floors regularly, before dirt and grit have a chance to scratch the surface. Wipe up spills immediately. As with a wood surface, avoid putting drinks glasses directly on marble, which can cause water rings. Water should bead on the marble. If the surface appears to be absorbing liquid, it's not sealed properly.

Reseal your marble floor annually at least – it's as easy as waxing a floor. Buy a **stone sealer** from a DIY store. Take a **sponge**, **sponge mop** or **rag** and cover the entire marble surface, including corners. There's no need to strip the floor before you seal.

To clean surface stains, use a **marble polishing powder**, such as **tin oxide**, which is available at DIY stores. Follow the product's directions to the letter. If the marble item you're cleaning is stained but not of great value, you can try removing them with a thick paste made of **baking soda** and **water**. Apply the paste to the stain. Cover the paste with a sheet of plastic to keep the paste damp and let it sit for 10 to 15 minutes before wiping it off. Rinse with **warm water** and dry. Repeat the procedure if the first application doesn't fully remove the stain. If stains still remain, you will have to call on the expertise of a professional marble restorer.

Marble floors should be resealed annually to maintain their stain resistance.

Mattresses & box springs

If you never give a thought to cleaning your mattress, here's a wake-up call: dust mites are almost certainly feasting on dander in your neglected bed and mould spores may also be multiplying.

Dust mites, tiny organisms that feed on the microscopic flakes of dead skin we all shed, can cause allergic reactions in some people, particularly those with asthma. Washing your sheets with **hot water** and occasionally **vacuuming** the mattress will help keep mites under control.

Periodic care and cleaning of a mattress will prolong its life even if you don't have allergies. Here's how:
• **Every six months,** rotate your mattress end to end and vacuum the exposed surface. Run the **brush attachment** over the entire mattress, including the sides. This will remove not only dust mites, but also mould spores. Empty the vacuum cleaner bag or cylinder outdoors after cleaning or, if the bag is disposable, throw it away.
• **Once a year,** flip the mattress over and vacuum it again. Remove the mattress and **vacuum** the box springs with the **brush attachment** as well. If you have the type of box springs with exposed springs, use a **bottle brush** to reach in there and lift away dust.

Removing stains from your mattress can be tricky, because moisture can be very harmful. Clean with **upholstery shampoo,** following the package direction. Or you can lift the stains out using **dry suds,** which are made by whipping a **grease-cutting washing-up liquid** or **clothes detergent** in water. Keep mixing until you have lots of suds.

Using a **clean cloth, soft brush** or **sponge** dampened with **warm water,** apply the suds in a circular motion to the stain. Then draw out the moisture with a **clean, dry towel.** Repeat the procedure if necessary, then wipe the area with a **clean cloth** dampened with **clear water.** Again, press a **dry towel** against the spot to draw out the moisture. The key is to leave as little water on the mattress as possible, because moisture in the mattress filling can lead to mildew and mould growth.

Simple solutions

Accidents will happen

If bed-wetting is a problem in your household, invest in a waterproof mattress cover. But never totally enclose your mattress in plastic. Mattress covers allow the mattress to breathe because the sides are made of cloth and the bottom part stays uncovered.

Urine smells and stains are difficult to remove from a saturated mattress. Sprinkle dry borax power (available from *Wilkinson's*) directly on the wet spot. Rub it in, let it dry, and brush away or vacuum up the borax.

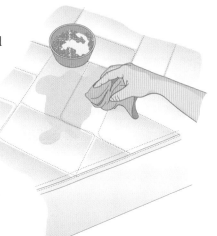

Use the frothy suds rather than the liquid beneath to clean your mattress.

To speed drying, blow an **electric fan** toward the mattress or take the mattress outside and let the sun do the job. If you've cleaned the entire mattress (one small section at a time), you may want to use a **dehumidifier** in the bedroom to draw out even more moisture.

Medicine cabinets

Experts recommend an annual review of the contents of medicine cabinets and urge consumers to get rid of expired prescriptions, leftover antibiotics, cough syrup that has separated and sterile gauze in broken packages.

Begin your review of medicines by examining the expiry date on each bottle or package and inspecting the contents for signs of deterioration. Pour expired liquids down the drain and throw expired pills straight into the rubbish bin to keep them out of the mouths of children and pets. If you can't find an expiry date, it is probaby old enough to retire. At the least, expired medicines are ineffective. At worst, formulations that have degraded over time can create new problems when ingested. So when in doubt, throw it out.

Developing an annual clean-out habit works best if it's tied to some other event, such as spring cleaning.

Cleaning the medicine cabinet itself is simple. Use a **sponge** and mixture of **mild washing-up liquid** in **warm water** to clean the interior and shelves. Or remove the shelves and put them in the top rack of your dishwasher.

See also **Mirrors.**

Expert advice

Keep your medicines high and dry

A steamy bathroom may not be the best place to store your medicines. Most medicines are best kept in a cool, dry place, since heat and humidity can affect their potency. Store medicines on high shelves in cupboards, out of the sight and reach of children, rather than in bathroom medicine cabinets.

Microwave ovens

Microwave ovens have revolutionised everyday cooking and fast preparation isn't their only virtue. Compared to conventional ovens, microwaves are very easy to clean.

To clean fresh food splatters before they have had time to dry, simply wipe down the microwave's interior with a **sponge** or **paper towel** dipped in a mixture of **washing-up liquid** and **water**. Follow with a **clean water rinse**. Use the same method for washing removable trays or turntables in the sink.

To remove dried-on food, heat a bowl of water inside the microwave before cleaning. Heat **2 cups of water** for three to five minutes on high power. The resulting steam will soften the dried food. Then wipe down the interior with a **sponge** or **soft cloth**.

To get rid of odours in your microwave, wipe the interior with a solution of **1 cup of warm water** and **1 tablespoon of baking soda**. Rinse with warm water. Or combine **1 cup of water** with ½ **cup of lemon juice** in a bowl and heat it on high for three to five minutes. Let it stand in the microwave for five to ten minutes before removing.

To remove stains from the microwave's ceramic floor or turntable, make a paste of **baking soda** and **water** and apply it to the stain. Let it sit until the stain disappears, then wipe it off and rinse with a **wet sponge** or **cloth**.

Clean the microwave door with **paper towels** and **glass cleaner**.

Heating a container of lemon juice and water on 'high' is a very effective way to rid a microwave of odours.

Mirrors

You want the reflection that stares back at you from the glass to be as crisp and bright as possible. A variety of low-cost cleaning methods will produce sparkling mirrors that reflect a streak-free image.

When using glass cleaner on a mirror, make sure you spray the **glass cleaner** on a **lint-free cotton cloth** or **rag** rather than directly on the mirror's surface. Not only do you use less cleaner, but you also prevent excess cleaner from running down the mirror's edges, where it can cause the mirror's silver backing to oxidise, turn black and brittle and eventually flake.

Old newspapers can do a good job of cleaning glass. Wear **rubber gloves** if you choose this method, to keep the

Watch out

Never clean mirrors using abrasive or acidic cleaners. Mirrors are composed of reflective layers of tin, silver and copper, backed by a layer of paint. Abrasive cleaners can scratch the glass. Acidic solvents can damage and corrode the reflective layers.

A little glycerine will keep a bathroom mirror mist-free after cleaning.

printer's ink off your hands. Begin by mixing equal amounts of **vinegar** and **water** in a bowl. Crumple the **newspaper** into a ball, dip it into the mixture and thoroughly wipe the mirror. Follow by rubbing with a **dry newspaper** or **cotton cloth**, to eliminate streaking. For extra shine after the mirror is dry, wipe it with a clean **blackboard eraser**.

To remove caked-on hair spray, wipe it off with a little **surgical spirit** on a **soft cloth**.

Motorcycles & motor scooters

Motorcycle mania isn't just for Harley-riding bad boys any more. Anyone who relishes the freedom and sense of adventure that a motorbike can give will ride a little taller when the bike is gleaming. It's not hard to make your motorbike look its best, so get out the garden hose and get ready to add some shine.

To keep water out of cables and controls, cover the handlebars with plastic before washing the bike. The **plastic sleeves** that catalogues are delivered in cover handlebars well. Put a piece of **plastic tape** over the ignition keyhole to keep water out of the lock.

Before washing spray the bike with a garden hose If the bike is badly caked with mud and road grease, you'll probably need to use high-pressure water. But take care to not let the pressurised water hit the instruments, ignition keyhole, carburettor or brakes. They could be damaged if water were to get inside.

Motorcycle shops sell a variety of **wash sprays** that remove oil and road grime, such as *S100* cycle care products. Use such a spray on the engine and wheels, wipe with a **clean cloth** and rinse immediately.

Next wash the bike's painted areas You'll find that car wash solutions work well and a **cotton towelling mitt** will allow you to get into tight spots without cutting your fingers. Don't use laundry or dishwashing detergents – they're much too harsh and can take off the wax and leave streaks. Rinse the bike well with fresh hose water before any solution-coated areas have time to dry.

Watch out

● Remove all rings and bracelets that could scratch the bike.

● Wait about an hour after riding before cleaning it. Never clean a hot engine, because the exhaust pipes can burn your skin if they haven't had time to cool.

● Make sure you clean the bike on level ground; otherwise the side stand could slip and cause the bike to fall on you.

Dry the bike to prevent water spots **Cotton towels** will work, but a **synthetic chamois** is best because it sheds less. Ride the bike within an hour of washing it, to get rid of any water drops that have collected in the engine, handlebars and controls. This also completely dries the brakes, which can be damaged by corrosion.

When your bike's finish starts to look dull, give the painted surfaces a coat of **wax**, applying it with a **dampened sponge**. Cleaner waxes and polishes are fine for older bikes. But on newer bikes, use *Carnauba Wax*, a natural wax that doesn't contain cleaners. Cleaners can literally take off the top layer of paint on a bike that is less than six months old.

Musical instruments

A clean instrument produces a clearer sound and periodic cleaning will actually extend an instrument's life. You can cut down on real cleaning with a little preventive maintenance: habits as simple as washing your hands before playing and returning the instrument to its case whenever it's not being used go a long way to keeping dust and grime at bay.

Clean a brass instrument regularly after using it. If you don't, the sound quality will suffer. All that blowing pushes saliva down into the horn's bore, where it reacts with zinc in the metal to produce lime deposits. The gradual buildup of lime will cause the bore of the horn to get smaller and smaller, which will start to affect the quality of the sound. After each use, you'll need to perform the following routine maintenance.

Empty water from the horn Then open each water key and blow through the instrument. Work the valves at the same time so excess water will be blown out. Wipe the outside with a **clean, soft cloth**, paying special attention to the area your hands have touched. Use a **mouthpiece brush** to clean the rim of the mouthpiece. Always store the instrument in its case, but make sure it's completely dry before putting it away.

Clean a brass instrument thoroughly every month or so, depending on how frequently you play. The process takes about an hour. Start by taking the instrument apart. If the valve caps or slides are stuck, don't try to force them. Instead, forget the home cleaning and take the instrument to a professional repairer. (To find the name of a good repair person, consult your music shop or ask your music teacher or band leader.)

But if you're able to take the instrument apart easily, put the valves, caps and slides aside, keeping the valves in their proper order. (Each valve is numbered, with number 1 corresponding to your index finger.) Fill a **sink** or **bathtub** with **lukewarm water** (hot water can damage the finish) mixed with a squirt of **washing-up liquid.**

Submerge the body of the instrument and the slides and swish the water around. If you have a **cleaning snake**, run it through each part. Rinse all the pieces in **clean, warm water** and dry them with a **cotton towel**. Place the parts on a **clean, dry towel** so the insides can dry. Clean the valves and caps by rinsing them with **warm water**, being careful not to get the felt at the top of each valve wet. Wipe them dry and let them air with the other parts.

When all the parts are dry, lightly lubricate each slide with **slide grease** and reinsert it. Use **valve oil** to lubricate the valves and then reinstall them and the valve caps in their proper order.

To clean your drums, use a **soft, damp cloth** to snare any dust that has collected. Wipe off the head and outside of the drum.

Clean your drums thoroughly once a year. Remove the heads and hardware. Mix **1 teaspoon of mild washing-up liquid** in **500ml water**. Dampen a **soft cloth** in the solution and wipe down the drums, heads and hardware – taking care to keep the springs from getting wet.

The tension rods may need extra attention. If they're black and coated with old grease and grime, give them a quick bath using **grease-cutting washing-up liquid**. Use **old rags** to wash and dry the rods, because the stains left behind on the cloth are tough to remove. Rinse by wiping all parts with a **cloth** dampened only with water. Then dry each piece individually with a **clean cloth**.

When cleaning cymbals, it's best to simply dust them with a **dry cloth** and leave more rigorous cleaning to the

Expert advice

STAIN LAB

Of temperature and tempo

Extreme temperature shifts in a short time pose a hazard to drum shells and their finishes, says Los Angeles drummer Dan Grody. As humidity and temperature change, the changing moisture content can cause the shells to expand, contract, warp, or even crack. Drums are safest when stored in a temperate climate – the same kind that feels comfortable to you.

professionals. Cymbals are usually coated with a lacquer designed to prevent tarnishing and cleaning solvents can eat through the coating.

Clean a stringed instrument regularly and you'll never have to fret. Each time after you play the instrument, wipe the fingerboard and strings with a **clean, dry cloth** or **chamois**.

Every month or so, clean the instrument's body, which will increase the life span of the finish. Use a **soft cloth** dampened lightly with a **suitable cleaner** − which will vary depending on whether you're cleaning a guitar, violin, or cello − and apply evenly, following the grain of the wood. It's very important not to flood the instrument or allow cleaner to soak into seams or peg holes. After a good rubdown, go over it again with a **dry cloth**.

Remove the grime that builds up on a violin fretboard when you change the strings.

When you replace strings, it is a good time to clean the fret board. Usually, the built-up gunk − perspiration from fingers or rosin from a bow − can be removed with a **soft cloth**. But if necessary, give it a very light brushing with **steel wool (000 or 0000)**.

The metal tuning mechanisms will corrode over time and should be polished when they start looking dirty. Consult a music shop with a repair department for product recommendations.

Older, valuable instruments should be professionally cleaned once a year, since the varnishes are tricky and can be ruined by inexperienced hands.

Maintaining a woodwind instrument is important, although a thorough cleaning should be left to a professional. Serious players should have their instrument cleaned professionally every year. Every other year will suffice for casual players.

For regular maintenance, take these steps every time you play:
• **Remove the reed** (unless you have a flute or piccolo, of course), which will warp if left on the instrument. Dry it with a **soft cloth** and return it to its reed case.
• **Swab inside each section of the instrument** with a

Simple solutions

Face the music
Guitar strings are easy to clean with pre-moistened face wipes The pads contain alcohol, which helps with the cleaning and they're just the right size to wrap around the string and slide up and down.

cotton handkerchief after each use. For flutes, you'll need to buy a **cleaning rod** from a music shop (or you may still have the one that came with the instrument when it was new). To use a cleaning rod, thread a corner of a **cotton cloth** through the eye of the rod, wrap the cloth around the rod and insert it in the flute body, rotating it to soak up moisture. Then withdraw the rod. Each time you finish playing your flute, dry the pads with a **folded, clean paper towel**. Don't close the pad down and pull the paper towel away, because pad skins are delicate and more likely to tear when wet. Just press the pad down on the paper towel to remove moisture on the surface, release and then remove the paper towel.

• **Take special care with the pads** that cover the tone holes on a flute and other woodwind instruments. They're usually made of a felt covered with a very thin, treated animal skin. When wet, they're easily torn. You can maintain the life of the pads by drying them after each use. Take a **clean, absorbent paper towel**, place it between the keys and the body, close the keys and let the paper absorb the moisture. Don't pull the paper towel out while the key is closed, which can tear the skin. Instead, open the key and remove the paper.

• **Wipe the body of the instrument** with a **soft, clean cloth** to remove all fingerprints.

Clean the mouthpiece weekly, either with a **mouthpiece brush** or, on larger instruments, by pulling a **handkerchief** through the mouthpiece.

Every month or so, take an **artist's sable brush** and brush out any dirt that's built up in the ribs (the body of the instrument where the keys are attached). You need to prevent dirt and grease from getting into the pads and mechanisms. Stay away from polishes, which can remove the top layer of metal on an instrument.

Make sure the instrument is completely dry before putting it back in its case.

See also Pianos.

Needlework

Cleaning needlework isn't as simple as it may sound. Techniques will vary according to the age of the item and the fabric on which it's embroidered. If you are unsure of a piece's age or fabric, consult a professional, particularly if the item is a family heirloom with sentimental value. Asking at a shop that sells wools is a good place to start.

To clean needlework less than 15 years old that's embroidered on cotton or wool, follow these steps:

1 Use care in taking the item apart, whether it is cross-stitch in a frame or needlepoint on a cushion. If the piece has cut edges that might unravel, zigzag the edges on a sewing machine before cleaning. Measure the piece so you'll be able to return it to its original size.

2 Fill a clean sink with **slightly warm water** and a squirt of **washing-up liquid** that *doesn't* have a grease-cutting formula. (If you're unsure whether the threads are colourfast, use cold water. Red threads in particular are notorious for bleeding when warm water is used.)

3 Gently work the soapy water through the fabric, squeezing and agitating the piece. For stains, use a **spot remover** made for cotton or wool, or pre-soak the piece for at least 30 minutes in the washing-up liquid solution.

4 Rinse the item several times in **clear, cold water**, making sure you get all the detergent out so that it doesn't turn the whites yellow.

5 After you've thoroughly rinsed the piece, place it on a **cotton towel**, roll up the towel to remove excess water and unroll.

6 Using a **blocking board** pin the piece facedown at its original measurements so that it will return to square as it dries. (Check your work with a T-square.) Make your own blocking board by using a **cork notice board**. Cover it with **muslin** and secure the muslin with **staples**.

Watch out

Dry cleaning isn't the best choice for cleaning needlework, because dry-cleaning fluids contain chemicals that may damage the piece. This is especially true if you're unsure of the type of fabric you're cleaning. In addition, the steam machines used by dry cleaners will take the sizing out of the piece, making it extremely difficult to block again.

Treat your needlework with care. After a gentle wash, pin it face down onto a blocking board so it will dry to its original shape.

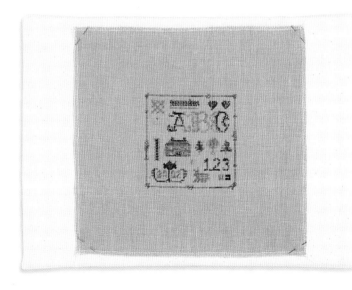

Office equipment

Fax machines, printers, scanners, photocopiers and answering machines in the home office need dusting regularly to stop dirt building up.

But if you work from home and so 'shut off' that room during your non-work time, it's easy to forget that your work environment needs a clean too. It's all too easy to spill coffee into your computer keyboard.

Use a **microfibre cloth** to lift dust off your equipment. For crevices in keyboards, telephone keys and other keypads, use a **clean cosmetic brush** to lift up dirt.

Keeping keypads clean Fingers leave lint and grime all over keypads. Dip a **cotton bud** into a small amount of **methylated spirits**. Press the bud onto a **paper towel** to eliminate excess alcohol. Dab each key lightly. For larger surfaces, use a **cotton ball**, dipped in methylated spirits, to get rid of unsightly dirt.

Simple solutions

Keep your work clean!

Generally, when machines develop a problem from dirt, it isn't because of the outer case, but rather as a result of dirty documents that have been fed through them. So give a shake or a dry dust to any paper that looks particularly suspect before you run it through your fax.

Outdoor toys

Cleaning at the start of each spring isn't just about keeping the rust down on your equipment. It's about safety too – because at the same time as you check the swing and climbing frame poles for wear and tear, you'll also tighten up any bolts that have become loose or moved out of the ground.

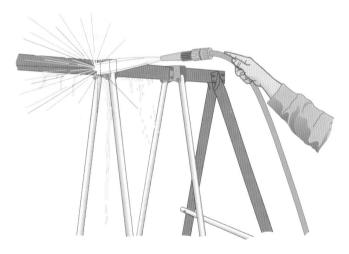

A quick rinse with a hose every couple of weeks will keep your children's outdoor play equipment free of built up grime.

Cleaning the frames is a simple bucket of sudsy water and a sponge job. Most play equipment is made from aluminium or steel (if metal) or toughened plastic. Both respond well to basic cleaning.

Shift stubborn stains – bird droppings, mould from leaves that have pooled in crevices over the winter – using **concentrated washing–up liquid** on a **pad**. Dry off thoroughly, using **old towels.**

During the summer, keep a pack of **multi-purpose wipes** in the shed, so that you can regularly clean stains from the fabric tops of climbing frames and swing seats.

Ovens

Proper cleaning improves your oven's efficiency, extends its life and, most importantly, reduces the risk of fire. Read on for ways to remove oven deposits that don't involve hours of backbreaking scrubbing. Even if you have a self-cleaning or continuous-cleaning oven, neither of which is entirely self-sufficient, some of the tips that follow will help you to clean it properly.

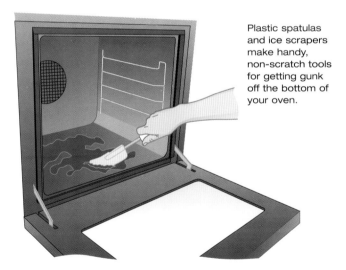

Plastic spatulas and ice scrapers make handy, non-scratch tools for getting gunk off the bottom of your oven.

Wipe the exterior surfaces of your oven to remove food spills every time you wipe down worktops. All you need is a **moist sponge**. Make it a habit and you'll save time in the end, because even the exterior surfaces get warm enough to bake food on very quickly.

To clean the interior, start by removing all oven racks and grill pans. Wash them by hand in the sink. Use a solution of **warm water** and **washing-up liquid**. Scrub with a **nylon-bristled brush** or other **gentle, non-metal scrubber**. Anything abrasive, such as steel wool, will scratch the metal's finish, which can lead to rusting and will make food stick even more the next time.

To loosen baked-on deposits in a conventional (non self-cleaning) oven, fill a **glass bowl** with ½ **cup of full-strength ammonia**. After making sure the oven is completely cool, put the bowl of ammonia in the oven, close the door and let it stand overnight. The fumes will release the bond between the crusty food and the oven interior. The next day, open the door and let the fumes dissipate. Then remove the bowl and wipe away the loosened food with a cloth or sponge.

To remove stubborn food that remains after the ammonia treatment, try scouring with a **nonabrasive scrubber** dipped in a solution of **warm water** and **washing-up liquid**. As with the racks and grill pans, avoid scratching the oven's finish. On flat surfaces, such as the door glass, try scraping with a **plastic ice scraper** – the kind you use on your car windshield.

A commercial oven cleaner is a last-ditch solution when cleaning a conventional oven. Follow the directions carefully and wear protective **rubber gloves** when applying. These products are strong and harmful to humans. Never spray a commercial oven cleaner on a hot oven, electric elements or oven lights. Heat can make the cleaner even more caustic.

Help your self-cleaning oven by doing a little preparatory work. Self-cleaning simply means that it will break down food spills with temperatures as high as 480°C. But the high heat doesn't reach all parts of the oven and in areas such as the frame around the oven opening and the edge of the door outside the gasket, the self-cleaning cycle can actually bake food on even more. So clean those parts first with a **nonabrasive scrubber** dipped in a sudsy solution of **hot water** and **washing-up liquid**. Rinse well using a **sponge** and a **bucket** of **clean water**.

Simple solutions

Grease guard for your oven

No matter what kind of oven you have, you can retard grease build-up by periodically wiping the interior of the oven with a vinegar-soaked cloth.

Once the self-cleaning cycle is complete and the oven has completely cooled down, wipe out the ashy residue with a **damp sponge**.

Give your continuous-cleaning oven a human touch. The interior of this type of oven is coated with a chemical mixture that lowers the temperature at which heat will dissolve foods. So whenever you bake or roast at a temperature above 180°C (350°F, gas mark 4), you are breaking down food that has splattered on the walls or bottom. But major spills, especially those involving sugar, can cancel out the effect. So clean up all big spills at once.

Wipe out the entire oven occasionally using a **nonabrasive scrubbing pad** and **warm water**. Then run the oven empty for an hour or two at 240°C (465°F, gas mark 9) to break down any grease or food that the oven's normal cooking and cleaning cycle has not dealt with. Never use abrasive cleaners or cleaning tools in a continuous-cleaning oven.

Cleaning Aga and range cookers is even simpler – because the cooker is always on, you can only totally clean them whilst they are turned off for their annual service. What you can do in the meantime is to be scrupulous about keeping the enamel front and top clean. Use a **non-abrasive cleaner**, such as *Astonish*, that is safe for enamel. Take even more care of the steel tops: a **microfibre cloth**, just dampened, is best. For the cooking plates, use a **stiff wire brush** to scoop off burnt food.

Each year, when the oven is serviced and so gets cold, clean out the inside using a cloth dipped in a **sudsy washing-up liquid solution**.

Watch out

- Never use commercial oven cleaners in a self-cleaning oven. When heated to those high temperatures, the chemical residue grows dangerously caustic.
- Never use commercial oven cleaners, cleaning powders, or metal scrubbers to clean a continuous-cleaning oven. These products may ruin the chemical mixture that allows the oven to clean itself.

Paddling pools

Since small children – and generally small children with muddy or grassy feet – are the main users, paddling pools tend to get dirty fast.

After each day's use, empty the pool and hose it out to prevent it from incubating germs. Store it under cover, upside down, or propped on its side, so that there is no risk of rainwater filling up inside – and creating a potential drowning hazard in your garden.

To remove scum from the sides, clean with a sponge or cloth dipped in a solution of **60ml bicarbonate of soda** in **4 litres of warm water**. Or wash with a solution of **1 tablespoon of washing–up liquid** in **3 litres of water**. Rinse with a **hose**.

Painted surfaces

Paint is not only decorative – it's also a protective coating. But even though paint is made to stand up to considerable wear and tear, you must take care when cleaning it.

Strong chemical cleaners or too much scrubbing to remove greasy fingerprints can dull the paint's finish, creating an uneven patchiness that will clearly show up. In bad cases, over zealous cleaning can remove paint altogether. Since touch-up painting, even with a colour match, tends to look splotchy, a cleaning mistake could lead to a complete repainting, which is not what you want to happen.

Dust painted surfaces regularly, when possible, to keep dirt and grime from staining the surface when smeared or moistened. For painted furniture, shelves, door and window trim or knickknacks that are coated in a gloss paint, use a **clean dust cloth**, either dry or slightly dampened with water. Dusting – especially wet dusting – entire walls is not feasible, since many walls are covered with emulsion-based paint, which wet dusting could actually remove.

To remove stubborn stains from gloss paint, first try wiping gently with a **cloth** dampened with a **sudsy solution** of **warm water** and **washing–up liquid**. If that doesn't work, try an **all-purpose cleaner**, but only after

Cleaning up after toddler accidents

Sooner or later it will probably happen, despite your best efforts at prevention. Even small amounts of faecal matter can easily sicken children if the germs get into their mouths, so for anything more than a wee, you'll need to get everyone out and clean up at once.

1 Tip soiled matter into a bucket and flush it down the toilet.

2 Wash the pool with a solution of 40ml chlorine bleach to 5 litres of water.

3 Allow to air-dry.

Take these precautionary steps to minimise the risk of transmitting illness:

● Don't let children use the pool if they have diarrhoea, open sores, or rashes.

● Have children go to the toilet before using the pool.

● Make the kids take frequent trips to the loo whilst they're using the pool, especially if it's a hot day and you're providing plenty of drinks.

testing the cleaner on an inconspicuous corner of your painted surface. Clean from the bottom up so that your cleaning solution doesn't drip down, pick up grime and leave dirty streaks.

Rinse with a clean, moist cloth or **sponge**. Dry well with **clean towels** to prevent water from damaging the paint or what's beneath it.

To remove marks from surfaces, such as walls, that are coated with emulsion, first try rubbing with a **white rubber**, the kind you'd find at an office supply store for rubbing out pencil marks. If that doesn't do the trick, try gently wiping the marks with a **water-moistened cloth**. Blot dry soon afterward with a **clean towel**. But be forewarned: water can stain or even remove emulsion paint.

Painting equipment

The best painters will tell you that a good clean-up at the end of the day is essential. Not only does it keep their tools in good shape, which means easier application and cleaner lines, but it also prolongs the life of rollers, pans and paintbrushes.

On the other hand, the professionals will also be the first to tell you that there are times when you don't have to completely clean your gear and in these special cases (see below) that will save you valuable time and energy. If you dread dealing with the messy aftermath – the paint-smeared rags, the cloudy water or turps, the matted paintbrushes or rollers – read on to discover a simple, environmentally friendly clean-up technique.

Start by putting the excess paint from roller trays back into the paint container. Squeeze as much paint as you can from your brushes (wrap them in **newspaper** and press with your hands) and scrape paint off your rollers with the **curved scraper** on a **5-in-1 painter's tool**, available at paint and DIY stores. Then wipe off as much of the remaining paint as possible using something disposable, such as an **old rag**, **newspaper** or **piece of cardboard**. Let the rag or paper dry and then throw it away.

Simple solutions

For supple bristles

To keep the bristles on a clean oil brush soft, rub a little petroleum jelly into them. Before using the brush, rinse it in paint thinner or turpentine. Never rinse out an oil brush in water. Water tends to make bristles turn dry and brittle.

Use a two-bucket system to keep things tidy
Whether you're using water-based or oil-based paint, use
2 large buckets (**plastic 15 litre buckets** work well) to
contain your mess: one for washing and one for rinsing. The
system is economical (because you can reuse solvents), it's
friendly to the environment (you reserve rather than throw
out paint or used solvent) and it's neat.

Use one bucket for washing If you're cleaning up
after using water-based paint, mix **warm water** with a
squirt of **washing-up liquid** in the bucket. If you've been
using oil-based paint, put a small amount of **paint thinner**
or **turpentine** into the bucket – 6cm in the bottom should
be enough. Immerse the brushes then, wearing **disposable
latex gloves**, use your fingers to gently work the paint out
of them. Use a **brush**, **comb** or an **old fork** to clean
between the bristles.

**To remove paint from the metal band on the
handle,** scrub gently with a **wire brush**. Use a **roller
spinner**, available at paint shops, to remove paint from the
rollers, either spinning it in the wash bucket or, better yet, in
a third, empty bucket. (The paint will really fly around.)
Wash the roller pans over the wash bucket using a **soft-
bristled brush**. Leave the dirty water or solvent in the
bucket, cover the bucket with cardboard or newspaper to
prevent evaporation and let it stand.

For short stops during painting or
overnight, wrap your brush tightly
in plastic wrap to prevent it
drying out.

Use the second bucket for rinsing, after you've
removed the bulk of the paint from your brushes or rollers.
For cleaning up water-based paint, use **clean water**; for
cleaning up oil-based paint, use **fresh paint thinner**. When
the water or solvent squeezed from the brushes or rollers
comes out clear, you'll know you're finished. As with the
wash bucket, cover the rinse bucket containing water or
solvent and let it stand.

Let the paint solids settle to the bottom of the wash
and rinse buckets overnight. The next day, carefully pour
the water off the top of the solids. Using a **putty knife** or
paint stirrer, scrape the paint off the bottom of the buckets
onto **newspaper** and discard it. Paint thinner or turpentine
can be reused. Carefully pour the relatively pure liquid on
top back into its original container. (Never store solvents
in plastic, because solvents will damage plastic containers.)
Again, scrape the solids up and discard.

If you are using oil paint again the next day, you don't need to thoroughly clean your brushes and rollers. Just give your brushes and rollers a cursory cleaning (squeeze and scrape off the excess paint) and then wrap them tightly in **aluminium foil** or **plastic wrap**. This will keep them from drying out – and will save you the hassle of cleaning up twice. You can save the thorough two-bucket clean-up routine for the end of the project.

If a water-based brush or roller just won't come clean, it may be because many of today's water-based paints contain resins, similar to those used in oil-based paints, to improve adhesion, gloss and durability. After cleaning and rinsing the brush or roller in **water**, try a second rinse in paint **thinner** or **turpentine** to completely clean it. Then wash with **clean, soapy water** to remove the thinner.

Panelling

Panelling comes in two main varieties: real wood and simulated wood. Real wood panelling, made of walnut, oak, maple or other kinds of woods, is hardly different in quality from the fine wood furniture in your home.

It is usually either sealed with a hard surface coat, such as varnish or polyurethane, or it contains a penetrating stain or oil finish. Simulated wood is a manufactured product made to look like real wood and it is often coated in plastic. Understanding these differences is crucial when deciding how to clean your panelling.

To remove dust from raised moulding, carving or other features on either type of panelling, vacuum regularly using your **vacuum cleaner's brush attachment**, or wipe with a **cloth**. For simulated wood, you can use a **moistened dust cloth**, but avoid using water on real wood. Moisture can damage wood.

To clean real wood with a surface coat, such as polyurethane, you may have to use water, but begin by trying a **spray-on furniture polish**, such as *Pledge*. These products remove dirt and dust while adding a hard wax finish. For heavier cleaning, try a **cloth** lightly dampened with a **neutral cleaner**, such as *Pledge Soapy Cleaner.*

To clean real wood with a penetrating finish, such as oil, use a **cloth** just dampened with **methylated spirits**, which will cut through the grease. Wipe gently back and forth in the direction of the wood grain. But work quickly and with care: methylated spirits will lift dirt and grime but will also remove the oil finish, so when you've finished cleaning, you may well need to touch up – or reapply – the panelling's oil or stain finish. So only use this as last-resort cleaning. If you regularly wipe over with a **just damp cloth**, you should avoid needing to take this more drastic step.

Clean simulated wood panelling the same way you would a glossy painted surface. Its plastic coating, while not impermeable, means you can wipe it down with a cloth using a solution of **warm water** and a squirt of **washing-up liquid**. If you need something stronger, try an **all-purpose cleaner**, but only after testing the cleaner on an inconspicuous corner of the hardboard.

Rinse the hardboard panelling with a **clean, moist cloth** or **sponge**. Once the surface is clean, dry well with **clean towels** so that the water won't damage the compressed wood beneath the coating.

Patios

Patios end up stained by grease drippings from the barbecue, rusty metal furniture and decaying leaves. The good news is that as they are outside, you can use heavy-duty cleaners – and, if worst comes to worst, blast the dirt off with a power washer.

To reduce staining, sweep the leaves and other debris off your patio regularly. Use an **outdoor-quality bristle broom** or a **rechargeable leaf blower**.

Give your patio a more thorough cleaning, using a cleaner that is biodegradable and won't harm plants, such as *Swarfega Patio and Drive Cleaner*. Use a **stiff-bristled brush** (a long-handled one will be easier on your back and knees) to scrub. Rinse with a **hose**.

Simple solutions

Give rust a drink of lemonade

To remove rust stains wet the patio area and cover it with a solution of 1 part lemon juice to 4 parts water. Take care not to get the surrounding area wet – lemon can bleach out coloured paving slabs. Cover your solution with a piece of plastic sheeting (to prevent the moisture from evaporating) and hold it down with something heavy. Let it stand for 10 minutes or so. Scrub with a stiff-bristled brush and rinse with the hose. Repeat if necessary.

To deep-clean a stone, brick or concrete patio, use a **pressure washer**. Take care not to etch your patio material or injure yourself and never hold the jet too close to the patio surface. If you rent a power washer, be sure it comes with detailed safety instructions.

Pearls

Unlike hard, crystalline gemstones, pearls are as sensitive as they are beautiful. Perfume, cosmetics and hair spray can stain them. The acids in your perspiration can eat away at their fine coating – known as nacre. And since a pearl's value is largely determined by its colour, lustre and the thickness of the nacre, cleaning your pearls is essential to maintain their value.

Fortunately, cleaning is also easy and harmless to the pearl, as long as you stick to the following simple methods.

Wipe off your pearls after each wearing Use a **barely damp, very soft cloth**. (Chamois is best.) This removes harmful substances such as perspiration, perfume and makeup that can penetrate the pearls' porous surface. As a preventive measure, always apply any perfume, makeup and hair spray before you put on your pearls.

Occasionally clean pearls more thoroughly to restore their natural finish and lustre. Use a **mild bar soap**, such as *Pears* and **lukewarm water** to create **light suds**. Dip a **soft cloth** in the suds and gently wipe the pearls. Rinse with **clean water** and dry with another **soft cloth**. Never soak your pearls to stop the string from getting wet.

When drying pearls, here are some things to keep to in mind:
• To make sure the pearls and string are dry, lay them on a **slightly damp cloth**. When the cloth is dry, the pearls will be too.
• If you wear pearls when their string is wet, the string may stretch and attract hard-to-remove dirt.
• Never hang pearls up to dry, since that may also stretch the string.

Watch out

Pearls can be harmed by many common cleaning substances and methods including ammonia, commercial jewellery cleaners with ammonia, ultrasonic cleaners, steam cleaners, detergents, bleaches, powdered cleansers, baking soda, vinegar, lemon juice and most washing-up liquids.

Pet equipment

Keep your pet's things clean: their bedding and bowls, toys and sweaters (if they wear them). Cleaning will prolong the life of the equipment, keep your pet healthy and reduce pet odours.

Wash food and water bowls daily to avoid the growth of bacteria. Put them in the **dishwasher**, if they are dishwasher safe. You can include them with your own dishes – the high dishwasher temperatures will disinfect everything. Or hand-wash using **hot, soapy water**. (Do this separately from your dishes.) Keep two sets of dishes for your pet and rotate them. Stainless steel bowls are usually easiest to clean.

Non-leather collars and leashes can be washed.

Clean leads periodically to remove dirt and salt, which can corrode the metal parts. Soak non-leather leads in a **sink** full of **warm water** with a squirt of **washing–up liquid** and a dash of **liquid fabric softener** (to keep the lead soft, not stiff). Rub clean with a **sponge**. Rinse in a sink full of **clean, warm water**. Don't wash leashes in the washing machine, because they could get tangled and the metal clasps could dent your machine. Hang up to dry.

See also **Leather.**

Hand-wash dog coats using the same care you'd use on your own clothes – unless the care instructions say otherwise. Most are made from the same materials as human sweaters – wool or acrylic. Fill a **basin** with **lukewarm water** and add a **gentle fabric wash**, such as *Woolite*, or a squirt of **mild washing–up liquid**. Soak and then gently rub out any stains. Rinse thoroughly in **clear, lukewarm water**. Gently wring the sweater out. Wrap it in a **clean towel** to remove moisture. Lay the towel out on a flat surface and work the sweater into shape with your hands. Let it dry.

Wash pet toys regularly to keep them clean and bacteria free. Wash rubber and plastic toys in a **sink** full of **hot, soapy water** with a dash of **bleach**. Scrub with a **nylon-bristled brush**. Stuffed toys and rope toys can go in the **washing machine** and tumble dryer. When they fray, or the stuffing starts to escape, throw them away and get your pet a new toy.

To wipe unsavoury dribbles off the Frisbee (or rubber ball) you've been throwing for Spot, use a **wet wipe**. Take along a **portable travel carton of wipes** when you play fetch in the park with Spot – or any other time you're away from a garden hose.

See also **Kennels & doghouses** and **Pests**.

Pewter

Did you know that pewter is the fourth most precious metal after platinum, gold and silver? A tin alloy, pewter has long been prized for its lasting value. It does not rust and tarnishes only slightly or not at all (depending on the alloy's metal content).

Antique pewter, which is usually high in lead, can look dark and dull, but that patina is part of its appeal and value as an antique. Before cleaning pewter, first determine whether your pewter piece is an antique or of more recent vintage.

Use ultra-fine steel wool on pewter to avoid scratching.

To remove dirt and grime from antique or newer pewter, wash it in a **sudsy solution** of **warm water** and **washing-up liquid**. Gently wipe the surface with a **sponge** or **soft cloth**. Rinse with **clean water** and then drip dry in a **dish rack** or on a **folded towel**. Never put pewter in the dishwasher. If your piece is an antique, stop here. Because of its metal content, polishing it won't necessarily make it shine – but it may decrease its value.

To make bright, modern pewter shine, use a **silver or brass polish** or a **mildly abrasive scouring powder**, such as *Ajax* and a **soft cloth**. For severe corrosion, try applying the **metal polish** with **ultra-fine steel wool**. Use grade 0000 only. Any coarser steel wool will scratch the finish. Buff with a **soft cloth** after using the steel wool.

Photographs, slides & negatives

Photographs, slides and negatives are easily damaged and your options for cleaning them are quite limited. So keeping them out of harm's way is your best bet. How much you're willing to do for a photograph probably depends on whether it's a family heirloom or just one of a mountain of snapshots from last year's holiday

The ultimate protection for a photograph is a glass covering and a frame. This way, the only thing that gets dirty is a hard surface that's easy to wipe clean. A frame will enhance the photograph's value and help it last longer. But don't hang the photo where direct sunlight will reach it.

To clean the framed photo, take it off the wall and lay it flat. Spray some **glass cleaner** onto a **soft, clean cloth** and wipe off the dust. Never spray directly onto the glass – the cleaner could drip behind the frame and damage the photo.

For valuable unframed photos, acid-free paper and plastic envelopes and acid-free storage boxes offer good protection; another good storage option is an album made of high-quality materials.

Try to use white cotton gloves to handle your negatives; it will prevent them being ruined by fingerprints.

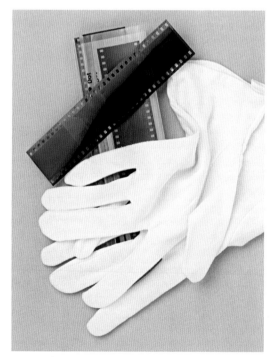

Remember that high temperatures, high humidity and direct sunlight are all damaging to photographic materials.

Handle photographic materials very carefully The salts and oils from your skin can damage them easily, so never touch the image area directly. Ideally, handle photographic material while wearing **white cotton gloves**. If you must use bare hands, handle your photos, slides and negatives by the edges only.

If your photograph has dirt on the surface, see if it will come off with the gentle swipe of a **soft brush**. If not, stop there – anything more will put the photo at risk. You'll have to take it to a professional lab to be washed.

If your photo has finger marks around the edges or on an unimportant part of the image, you may be able to wipe it away. Dip a **cotton bud** in **distilled water** and wipe at the mark very gently. Don't go over the mark again and again, because you'll soften the emulsion and damage it. Let the photo dry before you store it.

To clean dust from slides and negatives, buy a can of **compressed air** from a camera shop. Test the can by spraying your skin first. If the can has been exposed to high temperatures or has been shaken, water may spray out with the compressed air – not something you want to get on your photographic materials. Wearing **white cotton gloves**, hold your slide or negative by the edges and position the nozzle to the side, 9cm from the film surface. Spray in several quick bursts to remove any dust.

An antistatic cloth can remove dust from slides and negatives – provided you use a light touch. Buy an **antistatic cloth** at a photographic shop. Hold the slide or negative by the edges in one hand. With the other hand, fold the cloth around the film so that it touches both sides. With as little pressure as possible, draw the cloth down the surface, moving only in one direction. The more pressure you apply, the more likely that you are to drag the dust across the surface and scratch it.

To protect your negatives from dirt and dust, slip them into the **sleeves of clear plastic sheets** that are sold at photographic shops. Do this the moment you get the negatives home. These sheets fit into ring binders and are an excellent way to mark and catalogue your negatives.

Rules of the game

Protect your photos

1 Handle photos, slides and negatives only by the edges, preferably using white cotton gloves. Never touch the image area.

2 Frame important photos under glass, using acid-free matting.

3 For removal of serious dirt, take your photographic materials along to a professional lab.

4 Limit exposure to heat, humidity and sunlight.

5 Use acid-free storage materials (envelopes, sheathes, album pages and boxes).

Pianos

Restraint is the name of the game when it comes to cleaning a piano. It's not an easy task and most professionals recommend that do-it-yourselfers limit their input to the basics.

A thorough cleaning is needed every three to five years and it's best to get a professional to come to your house to save you the trouble and expense of transporting such a large instrument. The smaller jobs you can tackle yourself include polishing the exterior, vacuuming the keyboard, cleaning the keys and dusting the soundboard.

If your piano's casework is covered with a high-gloss, black lacquer finish, it needs only dusting with a **soft, dry cloth**. Give it some extra elbow grease if you're buffing away fingerprints. (See Lacquer for more details on caring for this finish.)

To brighten mahogany pianos, wipe with **non-silicone furniture polish**. Put the polish on a **soft cloth** very sparingly – just enough to remove that last bit of dust clinging to the wood.

To clean the piano's keyboard, go over it with a **vacuum**, using the **brush attachment**. To clean plastic or ivory key tops, mix a solution of **mild washing-up liquid** and **water**. Dip a **cleaning cloth** into the solution and wring it out thoroughly. Clean each key individually and dry it immediately. As you clean, make sure that no liquid drips down the sides of keys. Both plastic and ivory key tops can warp and pop off when wet. Rinse with a **barely damp cloth** and dry off with a **clean towel**.

Ivory keys, which yellow with age, can be cleaned with a **cloth** dampened with **methylated spirits** – but remember the yellowing of ivory is natural and can't be completely whitened. As an alternative, dab some ordinary (non-gel) **toothpaste** on a **damp cloth** and rub the keys. Wipe the toothpaste off and buff with a **dry cloth**. **Sunlight** also helps whiten real ivory keys, so try to position your piano so that it gets some sun (but not direct sunlight) and leave the cover open. (Sunlight has the reverse effect on plastic keys – it yellows them – so for plastic, leave the cover closed.) To protect your tuning, don't place your piano against a poorly insulated outside wall.

Cleaning the soundboard is the trickiest task in cleaning a piano. Grand pianos, with their open lids, collect a lot of dust. Use the **bare hose** of your **vacuum cleaner**, held just above the soundboard but not actually touching it, to suck away dust and dirt. You can cut down on dust by

Use a barely damp cloth when cleaning the keys of your piano.

shutting the lid when the piano isn't being used or by placing decorator's felt (available from piano shops) over the soundboard.

On an upright piano, cleaning the soundboard requires removing the bottom panel, which is heavy and therefore requires extra care. A spring that releases the panel is usually found beneath the key bed. Before vacuuming, look for small parts that may have fallen out of the piano or into the piano cabinet – a broken hammer, for instance. Again, the vacuum hose should hover above the soundboard and strings, never coming into direct contact.

Pillows

Pillows can be a big source of sneezes – particularly for allergy sufferers. Dust, body oil, perspiration and dead skin particles gather on (and inside) pillows. That combination is bad enough, but pillows also harbour dust mites, microscopic organisms that many people are allergic to.

And if you have goose down, dust and dirt act as abrasives and shorten the life of the down. So give your pillows – which are usually stuffed with either a synthetic fibre, goose down or feathers – a good cleaning at least twice a year.

Most fibre-filled pillows can just be put in the washing machine. While you should always follow the instructions on the pillow's care tag, generally you can use the **cold-water cycle** for fibre-filled pillows and tumble them in the **dryer** on **low heat**. Or you can dry it on a **clothes line**. Hang the pillow in the sun by one corner. Make sure it is completely dry before using.

Down and feather pillows should be machine-washed or dry-cleaned depending on the manufacturer's suggestion. Some recommend dry cleaning only, claiming that machine-washing down and feathers reduces their natural resilience. If you do decide to dry-clean your pillows, take them to a cleaner with experience of cleaning down. If there are

Simple solutions

For fluffy pillows

A quick way to freshen pillows is to tumble dry them on low heat for 10 minutes. It's much easier than a complete washing, and it removes some dust. Do it twice a year, in between washings.

any lingering dry-cleaning solvent fumes, air the pillows until they are all gone.

If you machine-wash down pillows, the big problem is drying them afterwards. Most are fine in the machine – as long as you have checked the care label – but it is not very safe to dry them in the tumble dryer as it could overheat. Also, it's expensive: it may take four hours of tumble drying to dry a pair of pillows. Waiting for a hot day and drying them outside is your best option. However, it's still such a lengthy chore, that you may simply prefer to give your pillows a fixed life, then throw them out and buy some brand new ones.

Plastic containers

Plastic is the miracle product – tough, resilient, easy to clean. That is, until certain foods, most notably tomato-based sauces, etch their way into its pores and cause what seem to be permanent stains. But don't give up hope. Where there is a cleaning will, there is a way.

Nearly all plastic food containers are dishwasher safe. This includes the *Tupperware* brand. You also can hand-wash them in **hot, soapy water**, using a **sponge** or **nylon-bristled brush** to scrub away stuck-on food.

To remove stains, mix a paste of **bicarbonate of soda** and **warm water** and scrub with a **nylon-bristled brush** if the stain is light. For heavier stains, try one of the following techniques:

• Scrub with a solution of **60ml dishwasher detergent** mixed with **250ml warm water**. Rinse well. Wear gloves – dishwasher granules and powder are an irritant.
• Soak in a solution of **50ml bleach** mixed with **1 litre of water**. (Wash in **soapy water** afterward and rinse well.)
• Let the container stand in direct sunlight for a day or two.

To clean large plastic storage containers not meant for food, wipe out with a moist cloth. For stubborn stains, scrub with a **sponge** or **nylon-bristled brush** in a solution of **warm water** with a squirt of **mild washing-up liquid**.

Plastic sheeting

When it comes to cleaning plastic sheeting or toughened acrylic, don't use commercial window cleaners. as most of them contain ammonia, which will eat into acrylic. So whether you're cleaning acrylic windows, garden furniture or napkin holders, follows this advice.

To clean acrylic plastic, use a solution of **washing-up liquid** and **lukewarm water** and apply it with a **soft cloth**. Avoid dry dusting, which can grind dirt into the acrylic's surface. If the surface is extremely dirty, let the soapy solution loosen the dirt and then rub gently with the cloth, turning it and rinsing it often.

Pool & billiards tables

Despite their bulky size, pool tables are precision instruments, with finely balanced slate tops and smooth felt coverings. You don't want to damage your table, even when armed with the good intention of cleaning it. Fortunately, there's not much you need to do to keep a pool table clean.

Dust the wooden legs and rails as you would fine furniture. Follow the pool table manufacturer's recommendations for the type of finish that's on the wood. When in doubt, tread lightly, using a **dry dusting cloth** or a **feather duster**.

Brush the felt top after each use Use a soft **horsehair** or **nylon-bristled brush** specifically designed for billiard felt. They're available at billiards suppliers. Brush in one direction only – the direction in which you usually break. This keeps the nap in good condition.

Simple solutions

Pool table protocol

Here are two hints that will help keep your pool table in game-playing condition:

● Keep a lint roller handy for picking up particles from the tabletop while you're using it.

● Keep your table covered when not in use. This will keep dust off and reduce the amount of cleaning you must do. Use a plastic or vinyl covering.

Use a specially designed brush to keep your pool table felt in top condition.

Dust the felt top periodically using your **vacuum cleaner** and a **brush attachment**. This picks up chalk and other dust from beneath the cloth, which can damage the felt fibres over time. But be very careful not to use a nozzle that will pull the cloth from the bed.

Porcelain

Fine, dainty and often almost translucent, porcelain is one of the most fragile of all ceramics. Fired at very high temperatures, it is glass-like, so treat it with care. How you clean depends on which finish your porcelain has – a bisque, or unglazed, finish or a glossy glazed finish.

To wash porcelain, use a **washing-up bowl** or a sink lined with a **towel** or **rubber mat** to protect against breakage.

To remove dirt and grime from either type of porcelain, first try a mild solution of **warm water** and **washing-up liquid**. Wipe with a **cloth** or scrub gently with a soft, **nylon-bristled brush**. A **toothbrush** is useful for nooks and crannies. Rinse well using **clean water**.

If that doesn't remove all the stains, try something stronger, such as an **all-purpose household cleaner**. Always rinse immediately and completely. These cleaning compounds can stain or etch porcelain. Air-dry in a **dish rack** or on a **folded towel** on the worktop.

To remove coffee or tea stains from the inside of porcelain cups or a porcelain teapot, scrub gently with a **cloth** or **soft-bristled brush** and a paste made from **bicarbonate of soda** and **water**.

To remove dirt from hard-to-reach crannies, such as inside porcelain flowers or in the folded hands of a figurine, use a **toothbrush** and **soapy water** on glazed porcelain and a **spray-on bleach-based kitchen cleaner** on the unglazed variety.

Pots & saucepans

Cast iron and copper pans should not be put into the dishwasher. Manufacturers of non-stick cookware also advise against washing them in the dishwasher as well, where hot-water spouts and spray rinses are far harsher on pots than soapy water and hand care in the sink.

Besides, dishwasher detergents generally rely on alkaline-heavy cleaners to cut grease and extremely alkaline cleaners can mar cookware just as badly as acidic cleaners can.

Hand-wash pots and saucepans that can't be put in the dishwasher much as you would dishes. Scrape out any food residue with a **wooden spoon** or **rubber spatula**. Fill the sink with **moderately hot water** and add a squirt of **washing-up liquid**. As soon as the pot has cooled sufficiently, slide it into the soapy water and let it sit for a minute. Then gently scrub in a circular motion, using a **sponge**, **brush** or **dishcloth**. Many non-stick surfaces – especially older ones – are easily scratched, so pay attention to the manufacturer's directions for cleaning. Clean the saucepan inside and out, sides and bottom. You'll know it's come clean when it's smooth to the touch. Rinse in **clean, hot water** and dry with a **kitchen towel**.

Removing burned-on food can be done without working up a sweat – but you do need lots of patience, lots of hot water and washing-up liquid. Squirt some **washing-up liquid** in the pot or pan, fill it with **hot water** and leave the kitchen. Nothing removes burned-on food like a good two-hour soak in hot, soapy water.

See also **Copper, Dishes** and **Iron.**

Pottery

There is everyday pottery, such as jugs, plates, flower vases and garden containers. And then there is the kind of pottery that belongs in an art gallery or museum. One is utilitarian; the other is precious and requires a light touch – and possibly a professional's care.

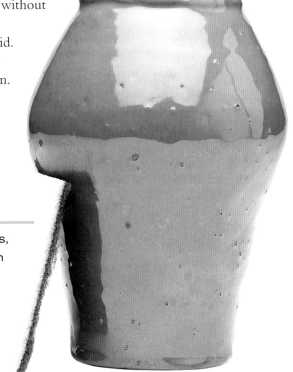

In the former category, there are two types of pottery: glazed and unglazed. The rule of thumb is: the thicker the glaze, the easier the pot will be to clean. You can get tougher with glazed pottery.

To clean glazed pottery – such household items as plates, mugs, serving trays and flower vases – proceed much as you would with your dishes. These items have been fired at up to more than 600°C, meaning they can stand up to any heat they will encounter in your dishwasher. Hand wash fragile or expensive pieces in the sink with **warm water** and **washing-up liquid**, so they don't run the risk of getting chipped in the dishwasher. A **scrubber sponge** will be fine for most hand washing, but the glaze will even stand up to the abrasion of a **steel-wool pad** such as *Brillo*.

To remove heavy dirt and grease, first dampen a cloth in **methylated spirits**, wipe it over the glazed pottery and then wash as usual in the dishwasher or sink.

To clean unglazed pottery – such as terracotta flower pots – just wash in the sink with **warm water** and **washing-up liquid**. Unglazed pottery is porous, meaning it will soak up water. It may take a day or two for the pot to dry out, but the water won't hurt it.

Fine antique or museum-quality pottery should be cleaned delicately if at all. If nothing is flaking loose on the surface, you can dust with a **soft brush**. If more cleaning is required, wipe gently with a **damp cloth** or a damp cloth with a little **washing-up liquid** added. Inspect the piece first. If the pottery has been repaired in the past, such cleaning could damage the repair job. For more extensive cleaning, consult a professional conservator.

Power tools

If you don't clean your power tools periodically, they'll get you back – by going into permanent retirement. Dust, sawdust and rust can seep into the motor and accumulate, eventually bringing the tool to a standstill.

How frequently you clean your power tools depends on how often you use them and how carefully you store them.

In general, give them a good cleaning any time you notice a build-up of residue such as saw dust, oil or grease. To keep everything running smoothly, don't store your tools where weather can affect them. And remember, if you don't clean them often enough, simple dust clogs can render built-in safety features useless.

To clean your power tools, first unplug your tool or remove the batteries and wipe out the battery compartment with a **soft, dry cloth**.

Do not, under any circumstances, spray anything liquid into the motor of any tool you're cleaning. Instead, use the professional gadgeteer's favourite cleaner – a **can of compressed air** (which can be bought at a camera shop). Hold the can level before you point the extension straw and hit the spray button. If you don't hold the can perfectly level, you may end up spraying liquid into the motor and that would be disastrous. Spray a blast of air into the air vents. If you see a cloud of dust puff out of the motor, you know you've waited too long to clean your tools.

If you're fussy about your tools' appearance, don't use abrasive cleaners. Simply squirt some **glass cleaner** onto a piece of **kitchen paper** and wipe away the grime.

Pressure cookers

Pressure cookers are tricky. When they force hot air out, food particles can get trapped in the pressure gauge (the device that rattles when the cooker is doing its job). Clean the gauge after every use to keep stray food particles from turning into bacterial debris.

Keep the rubber gaskets on your pressure cooker clean and supple.

For cleaning out the pressure gauge, the best tool is a **large safety pin**. (Even though a toothpick would do quite nicely, it could break off in the little hole and wreck your cooker.) Work at the little hole from both sides. You'll be amazed at the dirt that you can force out.

Also give regular attention to the gasket, the rubber ring that seals the space between the cooker and the lid. If you don't keep it clean, food build-up can result in bacterial build-up. Remove the gasket, pour a little **washing-up liquid** into your hands, hold them under the tap until you have **suds** and then massage the gasket until you're confident you've removed anything that might breed bacteria. Be careful not to stretch the gasket unnecessarily while you wash it.

With repeated washing, the gasket can stretch and lose its shape. And a gasket that doesn't fit properly is as good as no gasket at all. It can also get crunchy with wear, so after you wash and dry it, rub the gasket with some **oil – olive or vegetable –** anything but corn oil, which can get sticky and actually attract debris.

It's a good idea to keep an extra gasket on hand. (If you have trouble finding one for your cooker, order one from the store where you bought it or call the manufacturer for a list of places that sell the kind that fits your model.)

To clean the inside of the cooker, nothing works better than **washing-up liquid**, **hot water**, a **plastic scrubbing sponge** and a little muscle power.

Printers

First, remove any paper from the paper feed tray and, if the tray comes off, remove it from the printer. Using a dry cloth, wipe off the sides and bottom of the tray to get rid of dust, pet hair, pollen and general dirt. Never use even a slightly damp cloth: you don't want water anywhere near the printer innards.

Clean the paper rollers to prevent paper from sticking to them. There are two kinds of rollers, plastic and rubber. Clean plastic rollers with **cotton buds** dipped in **white spirit**. For the rubber variety, use **latex paint remover** – available from DIY stores. Avoid getting the remover on plastic parts, because it will damage them. Don't touch the printing mechanism unless your owner's manual gives cleaning advice on this.

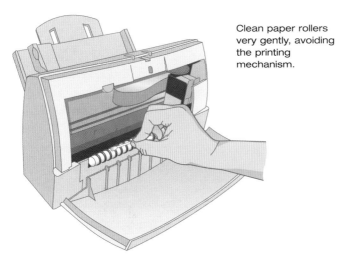

Clean paper rollers very gently, avoiding the printing mechanism.

Cleaning the printer's insides shouldn't be necessary. Many printers work using a laser system and moving things inside can damage this permanently.

If you spot a toner spill in a laser printer, don't ever try to clean it with compressed air – toner can be toxic, so you don't want a cloud of it billowing up in your face. Instead, wipe it up carefully with **paper towels**.

Cleaning the outer casing is a simpler matter and can be treated like any toughened plastic. Use a **damp cloth**, tightly wrung after dipping it into a solution of **sudsy washing-up liquid**.

See also **Computers.**

Quilts

New quilts are almost always washable – just check the care label and follow instructions. But old or handmade ones need special care. Those that have been handed down have character that comes from having been cherished. Unfortunately, that character often appears in the form of water rings, dye bleeds, stains of unknown origin and tears – all of which will dictate how you wash it.

Even with meticulous care, you shouldn't expect your hand-me-down or heirloom quilt to look like new. Instead, embrace the flaws, the water rings, the colour bleeds, the rips and the mystery stains.

Test first, wash later When you're dealing with a vintage or heirloom quilt, there are many uncertainties. How was it stored? Has it ever been dry-cleaned? Are the fabrics colourfast? Depending on the quilt's history, there may be stains, tears and deterioration that require special care. To avoid a catastrophe:

Test the fabric strength
- Some fabrics are so fragile that they tear like tissue paper. Depending on the quilt's age and how much it was cherished or neglected, some pieces of the fabric may deteriorate simply when touched. If you have such a weak patch, tack the area with needle and thread or consider replacing the patch altogether.

Test the dyes
- You could have a mix of cotton, velvet, acetate or silk, all in one patchwork quilt. Each piece of fabric and each dye need to be tested for colourfastness.

To test, mix 1 tablespoon each of ammonia and liquid laundry detergent per 3 tablespoons of water. You may have to fiddle with the proportions, depending on how hard or soft your water is. You need just enough soap to eliminate friction and not enough to generate lots of suds.

Dampen a white towel with the solution. Be sure not to wet the testing cloth too much, or you could do exactly the damage to the quilt that you're seeking to avoid. Touch – don't press – the damp cloth or towel to an obscure corner of the quilt. Leave it on for 30 seconds. Then lightly blot the spot with a dry part of the cloth.

Did any of the fabric colour bleed onto the cloth? If not, go for stage two, which is a slightly more aggressive version of what you have just done.

Go to another part of the quilt, a colourful one that you suspect might bleed. Find a dry spot on the white cloth and dampen it in the solution. This time, press harder on the quilt and wait a whole minute before blotting.

To make absolutely sure, take a third run at it. Go to another part of the quilt, press harder with the damp cloth so that the quilt actually absorbs a little of the cleaning solution and lightly rub. If your white cloth is still white or has picked up no more than a trace of the colour from the test spot, it's safe to wash your quilt.

After you've tested your quilt for bleeding and deterioration (see 'Test first, wash later' opposite), it's time to wash. The more colourfast your quilt is, the warmer the water you can use, but don't go much warmer than tepid. If the quilt has weak spots in the seams or fabric, put it in a **mesh laundry bag** and use a low or non spin programme.

If you're worried about machine washing, use your **bath**. Fill it with enough water to cover the quilt with 6–10cm to spare. (Don't put the quilt in yet.) Add **detergent**, choosing one that contains bleach if your quilt is yellowing. Swirl the water to mix. Then lay the quilt in the water, spreading it as much as possible. Stay by the bath-side for 10 minutes, swishing, smoothing and squeezing with your hands (wear rubber gloves) to release the dirt. If you notice that the colour is starting to run, drain the bath immediately and rinse the quilt with **cold water**. But if all goes well, you can leave the quilt in for up to an hour.

When it's time to rinse, pull out the plug and push the quilt to the other end of the bath. Bunch it up here until all the water has drained from the tub. Then squeeze the quilt to force out the excess water. Rinse by agitating the quilt just as you did in the washing step. If the rinse water becomes discoloured, repeat the drain-and-rinse process. If you used bleach, rinse it twice. Squeeze the quilt again.

To dry the quilt, try tumbling it in the **dryer** with cool air, if you think the quilt can stand it. If not, hang it on a **clothesline** to dry.

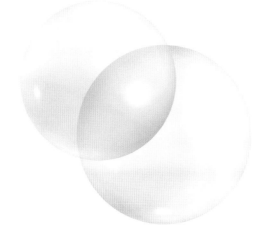

Radiators

A dusty radiator can be worse than ugly – it can be costly. Layers of dust can compromise the ability of a radiator to do its job and because heat attracts dust, your radiator will be dustier than most other things in the room. A weekly dusting with a feather duster or a dust cloth will keep accumulation down. Twice a year is often enough to do a major radiator cleaning, unless your environment is particularly dusty.

The best times to do this are in the spring or early summer, when you're no longer using it and in the autumn, before you turn it on again. That way, there will be no danger of burning yourself.

First, remove as much of the surface dirt as possible using a **hand vacuum** or the **brush attachment** of your **vacuum cleaner**. The brush can actually go some way toward getting in between the tubes. But the **thin nozzle attachment** goes further. You won't get everything out with a vacuum, but there are more effective ways to clean inside the crevices.

To reach the dust trapped between tubes, use a couple of common kitchen items. Wrap a sheet of **paper towel** around the broad end of a **kitchen spatula** and secure it with a **rubber band**. Then slide the spatula up and down both sides of each tube of the radiator. For resistant substances and especially sticky spills, spray some **all-purpose cleaner** on the paper-swathed spatula and have another go at it.

Deal with rust spots as soon as you see them. You can get the larger chips off with a **wire kitchen brush**, followed by some **medium** and then **fine-grade glasspaper**. Be sure to get rid of all the rust so the corrosion will stop after painting. Once you've smoothed the surface and there is no visible rust residue, spray the spot with special **radiator paint**, available from DIY stores.

To clean a portable electric radiator, unplug it and then follow the directions given above for cleaning traditional steam radiators. (You won't need the de-rusting and painting steps.) When you put your electric radiator away for the summer, store it in a plastic rubbish bag so that it doesn't get dusty.

Records

With CDs having made records obsolete, it's increasingly hard to track down old copies. Clean the records that you still have, to make them last longer and sound better.

Velvet record brushes are the favourite of many who do clean their records. They have a handle for gripping and a velvet-grained fabric on the bottom. They come with a liquid, which is mostly water with a dash of mild soap. Harsher chemicals will damage record vinyl. Ask for them at specialist music shops and follow instructions.

Wipe your record extremely gently with a barely damp cloth as it spins around.

If you don't have a velvet record brush, you can use a **very soft cloth** with a fine weave to clean your records. Don't use anything that creates lint – that's what you're trying to get rid of. Make a mixture of **99 per cent water** and **1 per cent baby shampoo**. Barely dampen the cloth – make sure it isn't wet – and hold it lightly on the record as it spins on the turntable. Be careful not to touch the record with a fingernail.

Paint on a cool tin roof

The biggest problem with maintaining a tin roof is keeping it painted. Paint often sheds from tin roofs in sheets. Then you've got big problems, mostly with rust.

Choose a sunny but cool day to paint a tin roof. Wash it first, using a soapy solution in your garden sprayer. Rinse well. Allow it to dry. Then paint with a rustproof, oil-based paint.

If you have heavier, sticky grime on a record, try again with the **baby shampoo mixture** and a little more pressure on your cloth. If that doesn't work, take the record off the turntable, holding it only by the edges. Rest one edge against your body and hold the other in one hand. With your free hand, wipe the record with the cloth, moving back and forth in the direction of the grooves.

Roofing

Moss, algae and mildew all adore your roof. They literally feast on shingles and burrow beneath them, causing the shingles to blacken and thin.

Embark cautiously on do-it-yourself roof cleaning. In fact, unless you are very confident about working at height, it is much better to leave this job to a professional. When you combine a steep pitch with the use of ladders and cleaners that make the roof slippery, you have a recipe for potential disaster hanging over your head. Clearly, falling from a roof can be fatal. So the roofs that we suggest cleaning here are likely to be those on a shed or single storey extensions.

To clean asphalt roofs as well as cedar and other wood roofs, first go to a DIY store and pick up a **cleaner for treated-wood decks** – one that contains **oxygen bleach**. (Don't use chlorine bleach.) On a cloudy day, when

the roof is cool, mix the cleaner according to the package directions and squirt it on the roof with a **garden sprayer**. (High-pressure sprayers will damage the roof.) Let the cleaner sit for half an hour. Then give it a scrub with a **broom** or **brush**. Rinse thoroughly with a **garden hose**.

Tile roofs can attract moss and other growth, too, but cleaning them yourself is not recommended because wet tiles are delicate and extremely slippery. Always let a professional do the job.

To create an inhospitable environment for growth on your roof, apply **zinc strips** close to the top (or comb) of the roof. Rainwater reacts with the zinc and drips down the roof, discouraging growth. You can get these strips from a roofing supply company.

Several kinds of metal roofing, including painted steel and copper, need little maintenance. Although costly to install, such roofs will last many years.

Rugs

The best way to keep a rug looking fresh is to keep it from getting dirty in the first place. Remove outdoor shoes when entering the house and you'll cut down on 80 per cent of the dirt tracked inside.

Give rugs a good, regular shake outside
Vacuum them often, front and back, against the nap to pick up ground-in dirt. Rugs in high-traffic areas need a more thorough cleaning at least once a year; those in out-of-the-way places, less often.

To shampoo a small rug

1 **Vacuum** the rug.

2 Mix **100ml of mild washing-up liquid** or **rug shampoo** with **2 litres of cool water** in a **clean bucket**. (Don't use harsh detergents, sudsy ammonia, or regular ammonia on your rugs.)

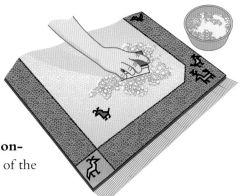

3 With a **long-bristled, soft brush** or a **firm, non-shedding sponge**, brush the pile in the direction of the nap. Don't scrub. Wet thoroughly.

4 Wash the fringe of the rug, if it has one. If the floor under the rug is wood or otherwise easily damaged by water, place a **plastic** or **rubber dust sheet** under the fringe. Then put a **clean white towel** on top of that (still beneath the fringe). Using a **brush** or **sponge** moistened (but not sopping) with the cleaning solution, brush the fringe from the knots out to the end. To rinse, replace the first towel under the fringe with a **dry towel** and blot the fringe with yet another towel dampened with **warm water**. Allow the fringe to dry on a third dry towel.

5 To rinse the main part of the rug, wet **clean rags** with **warm water** and press them against the rug.

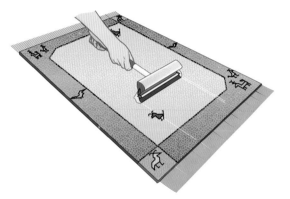

6 Squeeze out excess moisture. (A **window squeegee** works well.) Squeegee the pile in the direction of the nap until no more water comes out. Use more **towels** to mop up any excess.

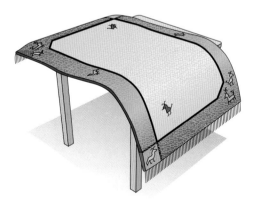

7 If there is plastic underneath the rug and it has become wet, replace it with dry plastic. Lay down **dry towels** and lay the rug flat on the towels to dry thoroughly on one side. Then turn it over to dry the other side, replacing the towels

again if need be. Or dry the rug on top of a garden table in the shade outside.

8 If the pile feels stiff once it has completely dried, vacuum or brush it gently.

To remove a stain on a rug

Several important rules of thumb apply. Attack the stains in this order:

1 Blot stains, using **clean cloths** or **absorbent white kitchen roll**.

2 Scrape up whatever solids you can, using a **kitchen knife**, **spatula** or **putty knife**.

3 Work from the stain's outer edges to its centre. This is important, because doing it the other way round could spread the stain.

4 If the stain has penetrated the entire rug, place a **clean cloth** underneath the rug to absorb what seeped through.

5 Dilute the stain by blotting with a **cloth** dampened in clean **water**.

6 Try a **carpet stain remover** – *Vanish* or *1001* are both very effective.

7 If this doesn't work, mix **1 teaspoon of mild washing-up liquid** with **250ml warm water**. Blot with a **white towel** dampened with **clear water**. Don't saturate.

8 **Shaving cream** can also work wonders. Moisten the spot with **water**, work in the shaving cream and rinse with a **clean cloth** dampened with **cool water**.

9 Mix enough **powdered laundry detergent** with **water** to make a paste. Be sure the detergent has no brightening or whitening agents – choose one that's designed specially for colours like *Ariel Colour*. Let the paste sit for 10 minutes and then remove any residue with a **wooden spoon**. Blot with a **clean towel** and rinse with another **towel** wrung out in **warm water**.

See also **Carpeting.**

Saddles & tack

How often you clean saddles and tack depends on how often you use them. At a minimum, clean and condition them at least twice a year – more often, if you're caught in the rain or often ride out when it is cold and damp, which can leach natural oils from leather and cause dry rot.

To clean a saddle, use **saddle soap**, a **sponge** and **warm water** to work up a foamy lather. Stirrups, stirrup leathers and fenders attract the most dirt, so pay particular attention to those, wiping them on both sides. If dirt is really ingrained, let the foamy saddle soap sit to soften it. Rinse the soap off thoroughly. (If you leave soap residue on the leather, it will attract rather than repel dirt.) Use **toothpicks** to lift out dirt on deeply tooled leather.

Allow the saddle to air-dry overnight, but during the day don't leave it out in the sun for hours, where it could dry out too much. Once it's dry, condition the leather lightly. Use a **leather dressing**, applied with a **soft cloth**. Then buff with a **clean, soft cloth** to bring out the leather's natural shine.

To clean your tack, use the same general technique as with saddles, but be sure to take it apart first. Bits must be taken off the headstall and reins, for instance. Brush off any loose dirt with a **rag** or **soft brush**.

Storing your saddle and tack is also important.
• Store a saddle on a **rack** with air circulating freely.
• Hang bridles and halters on a rack shaped like a horse's head. (Simply hanging them onto nails or hooks on a wall can cause leather to bend out of shape and weaken.)

Watch out

If your saddle seat is suede, don't use soap and water on it. Instead, clean it with a stiff-bristled suede brush.

Satin

Cleaning satin is tricky because this shiny fabric shows grease and other stains so easily. The techniques differ according to the material your satin is made from.

If you get a greasy stain on satin of any kind – be it on blanket binding, satin sheets, pillows, holiday decorations or other items – try blotting (not rubbing) the stain first with a **clean white rag**. Then cover the stain with **flour** or **unscented talcum powder**. Let it sit for an hour. The powder should absorb most of the stain. Then gently brush the fabric with a **soft-bristled brush** and launder a washable item according to the instructions on the fabric care label. If a blanket is washable, its binding will be too. Treat stains first with a **pre-wash stain remover**. If an item is not washable, take it to a dry-cleaner.

Satin sheets are a little trickier to care for because there are several types.
• **Woven acetate or silk satin sheets,** should be dry-cleaned or washed in the **bath** or a **large bowl** in water at room temperature using a **gentle fabric wash** such as *Woolite*. Hand-wring gently, wrapping up the sheet in an **absorbent white towel** and hang to dry.
• **Polyester and nylon satin sheets** are more durable. You may machine-wash them, but hand-washing will keep pilling to a minimum. If you are putting them in a washing machine, use warm or cool water and very little detergent. Never use bleach. Put in the dryer on the lowest setting. Never line dry nylon sheets in the sun.

To clean satin pillows, vacuum them using the **soft brush attachment**. Give greasy stains the **flour treatment** described above. If stains persist, launder a satin pillow only if it has a removable cover.

Watch out
● Shield sheets made of silk and nylon from the sun. Never line-dry nylon satin sheets, for the sun is nylon's public enemy number 1. If your bedroom is sunny, choose acetate or polyester satin.
● Never dry woven acetate sheets in a dryer.
● Be especially careful when wringing silk satin sheets – silk is usually thin and tears easily.

Scissors

To keep scissors cutting smoothly, it's important to clean them. Keep scissors for different tasks strictly segregated: a pair for cutting paper and craft projects, others for working with fabric or snipping toe nails.

To keep your scissors cutting smoothly, wipe the blades after each use with a **soft rag**. This stops lint and other material from getting caught in the blade pivot area, where it can interfere with the performance of your scissors.

Oil scissors occasionally at the pivot area (around the screw head and between the blades) using a **penetrating lubricant**, such as *WD-40*. Never use vegetable oil or any other oil that will attract dirt and get gummy. Gently work the blades a few times to force the lubricant into the joint.

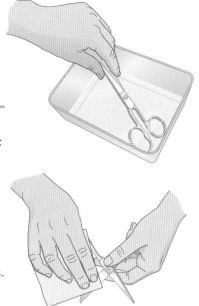

Soak rusty scissors in white vinegar, then sand them gently until they are smooth again.

Simple solutions

Keeping shears in the pink

Prolong the life of pinking shears by being sure there is always fabric between the blades when you cut. Never open or close the blades without fabric in between.

If your scissors get dirty, wash them in **washing–up liquid** and **water**. Dry scissors thoroughly with a **soft cloth** before storing them.

If your scissors get rusty, soak them first in **white vinegar**. Then use **fine glasspaper** on the handles and blades, being careful to avoid the cutting edges. Always store scissors in a dry, cool, clean place.

To keep the blades sharp, some scissor makers recommend using sharpeners. Most experts, however, suggest that you take them to a professional.

Sewing machines

If you have a modern, computerised sewing machine, follow the directions in your owner's manual. If you have a traditional style electric or mechanical machine, here's what to do to keep it running smoothly.

Watch out

Never oil a computerised machine or use any kind of liquid anywhere near it. (Oil and liquids can irreparably damage circuit boards.) Use a hair dryer to blow away lint. If you're unsure about how to clean your computerised machine, take it to a sewing machine repair shop.

For a mechanical sewing machine, be sure you use the right oil. Use **sewing machine oil**, available at fabric stores and sewing machine shops. Other lubricants, such as *3-in-One* oil and *WD-40*, dry too fast and will eventually cause the machine to seize and stop. Put no more than one or two tiny drops of sewing machine oil in each of the 30-odd holes that pockmark your machine.

Remove dust and debris to keep it running smoothly. Slide the edges of a **thin piece of muslin** between the tension discs (the metal pieces the thread passes through). Be sure the presser foot is up to slacken the tension springs. (If you have no muslin, gently slide a **credit card** between the discs to loosen dust and dirt caught between them.) Remove the machine's cover. Using a **can of compressed air** (available from camera shops) or **hair dryer**, blast movable parts with a stream of air, from back to front, to remove any loose threads, lint and dust.

Take off the throat plate (sometimes called the needle plate), paying close attention to how it is removed and replaced. On some models, it screws in. On others, it is spring-loaded. The same goes for the bobbin, bobbin case (also called the shuttle) and hook race – watch what you're taking apart or you may not get it together again. Use **compressed air** (available from camera shops), a **hair dryer** or a **small stiff-bristled nylon brush** to clean these parts. At a pinch, a **pipe cleaner** will extract small fibres from moving parts. So will a **dental pick**. Don't use toothpicks – they're too flimsy and could break and get stuck in the machine.

Dust the outside with a clean cloth (**Microfibre cloth** works well.) A **mild household cleaner** will get rid of grimy fingerprints. Spray first on a **cloth** and then wipe. If the case is metal, **sewing machine oil** or *WD-40*, sprayed first on a **rag**, will give it a shine.

Cover your machine when you're not using it. Ready-made **plastic covers** are sold at sewing machine shops. Or make a cover yourself from an old pillowcase. Keep the machine away from heat, light and open windows.

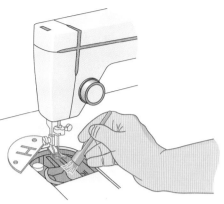

Clean out dust and lint from your machine regularly.

Sheets

Cleaning sheets is an easy job for the washing machine. Simply read the care labels on cotton and polyester-cotton sheets to find the maximum temperature of the wash.

For best results, wash as part of a mixed load: a pair of sheets plus two hand towels and flannels will fill most washing machines. When drying, to minimise (or hopefully avoid) ironing, remove the sheets when still just damp and fold into eighths. Store in the airing cupboard. If you're doing a turnaround on one set of sheets, you'll need to dry them fully and then iron.

Shells

Even the most beautiful seashells can smell awful if you don't remove decaying matter stuck inside. Seashells come in myriad sizes and varieties, but they're mainly characterised as either dead or alive. Dead seashells have no animal tissue inside. You should never remove shells from beaches or rockpools if the creature inside is alive.

To clean empty seashells, soak them in a 50-50 solution of **bleach** and **water**. How long you do this depends on the kind of shells you're cleaning, as well as how many you do at once. Soak first for 30 minutes, longer if you want shells bleached white or if they're really grimy. Before you remove them from the solution, make sure that the periostracum – the leather-like, flaky covering on some shells – is gone. Rinse with **fresh, warm water**.
• If barnacles and other clingy materials persist, use a **dental pick** or **ice pick** to remove them.
• If the lip of a seashell gets chipped, use a **rotary grinder** or **file** to smooth out rough edges.
• If you like your shells to shine, coat them with a light layer of **vegetable oil** or **baby oil**.

To clean seashells still containing residual decayed matter, you have a choice of cleaning methods:
• **Bury the shells 45cm deep in your garden** for a month or two. Insects, bacteria, worms, larvae and other tiny organisms will eat everything that you want to remove from the shell.
• **Give them the deep freeze treatment.** Place the shells in a **waterproof bag**, add enough **water** to the bag to cover the shells and place them in the **freezer** for a few days. Then let them thaw to room temperature. You should be able to grab the remaining tissue inside and remove it.
• **Boil water in a large saucepan** and submerge the shells for five minutes. Using tongs and being careful not to burn yourself remove one shell at a time and, grasping it with gloves or a towel, pull out the tissue inside.
• **A smelly but no less effective way** to clean shells is to 'cook' them in the microwave. (The time will vary depending on the oven's power and the strength of the shell.) Start with 30 seconds and increase the time in 10-second increments. Use tongs and special care as you remove

the shells and grab whatever decayed animal tissue remains. Should tiny pieces of tissue remain, put the shell outdoors and allow insects to feast on what's left. Once all the flesh is gone, treat the shells as described above for dead shells. Give them a **bleach bath** and rinse completely.

Shoes

To protect new leather shoes, spray or rub them with a water and stain repellent such as *Scotchgard* before wearing then. Use one designed especially for leather. Then polish them before stepping out. Leather shoes are usually malnourished and dry when they come out of the box and the extra layer of polish will protect them.

Petroleum jelly will help to keep your patent leather shoes shiny and supple for longer.

To give leather shoes and boots a shine:

1 Remove the laces.

2 Brush off loose dirt with a **stiff brush** or **cloth**.

3 If the shoes are especially dirty, clean them with **saddle soap**, following package directions.

4 Rub a **clean cotton cloth** in **polish** and then onto the shoes. Let the polish dry for 10 minutes.

5 Buff with a **clean cloth**.

To clean patent leather shoes, first remove any scuff marks with a **clean rubber**. Then shine with **baby oil**, **furniture polish**, **petroleum jelly** or **cream leather cleaner/conditioner**, available at shoe repair shops. Buff with a **paper towel** or **clean cloth**. Be gentle – patent leather scratches easily. At a pinch, rub leather or patent shoes with **hand cream** and then buff. On imitation patent leather, use **mild washing–up liquid** or a **car interior vinyl and plastic cleaner** from motor supply shops.

To remove salt stains from leather shoes, rub with equal parts of **water** and **vinegar**, applied with a **cotton pad**.

To clean white shoes, wipe them with a cloth dabbed in **ammonia**. (This works well on canvas, too.) Remove scuff marks with a dab of **white (non–gel) toothpaste**. Then buff.

To protect suede shoes, apply a **stain repellent** designed for suede or nubuck. Use a **rubber–tipped** or

Simple solutions

When you don't have time to polish

For an instant shine, use baby wipes. This technique will dry out the leather over time, so follow up with polish later on.

plastic brush to brush the nap and remove dirt. If you get a stain, remove it immediately with a **solvent** made for either material. An **oil-absorbent block**, made especially for suede shoes and available at shoe shops, will also wick away the stain when held against it. Or you can blot an oily stain with **baby powder** or **chalk dust** (which you can pulverise from a **piece of chalk** inside a **sealed plastic bag** using a **small hammer** or **rolling pin**). Allow the powder to sit overnight. Then brush it off.

To erase scuff marks on smooth leather shoes, rub the marks with the cut edge of a **raw potato** and then buff.

Showers

How can the shower – the place where you clean yourself – get so dirty? Nowhere, except for the kitchen sink, does a home show grime more than in the shower. Soap, shampoo and dirt combine to make an unsightly scum.

To keep your shower sparkling, try these tips.
• **When you shower, clean the shower** straight afterwards. Steam from a hot shower will loosen grime and make the job easier.
• **With tiled shower walls and floor,** if you don't want to use a **multi-purpose bathroom cleaner** (the easiest option) you can use **dishwasher detergent** (either powder or liquid will do). Mix **60ml dishwasher detergent** with **500ml warm water** in a **small pump spray bottle** and shake to dissolve the detergent. Spray liberally on walls, let it sit for two or three hours and then scrub with a **sponge**. (Dishwasher detergent is an irritant, so wear **gloves** and don't get it on your skin). Use a **sponge mop** to scrub high spots and the floor.
• **To clean tile grout,** make a paste of **bicarbonate of soda** and **bleach** (add bleach to the powder until it's a thick goo). Wear **gloves** and smear the paste on with a **spatula**. Air-dry for an hour and then scrub with a **toothbrush** and **water**. (Never use ammonia nearby, since ammonia and bleach don't mix.)
• **To prevent water spots,** rub the shower walls and doors with a **squeegee** right after you have taken your shower. Or try one of the **daily shower cleaners**. Mist surfaces right

after you shower, while the walls are still warm and wet. The cleaner will prevent deposits from forming and will wash down the drain the next time you shower.

• **If your shower sprouts mould,** try this trick. Wipe down the walls with a solution of **1 teaspoon water softener**, **1 tablespoon ammonia** and **1 tablespoon vinegar** in **200ml of warm water**. Rinse with **fresh water**. Buff dry.

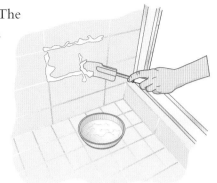

To clean your shower doors, follow these pointers:

• Wash them with **white vinegar** to banish soap scum.

• Or take **leftover white wine** that's rapidly turning to vinegar, empty it into a **trigger spray bottle** and squirt it on your shower doors. Rinse well with **water** and dry with a **soft cloth**.

• Wipe down the doors with **fabric softener** on a **damp cloth**. Buff with a **clean, dry cloth**.

• Another way to keep soap scum at bay is to wipe down the shower doors with **lemon oil**. **Baby oil** works too, as does **furniture polish**, buffed with a **soft cloth**. (This also works on tiled showers, but don't put these slippery substances on a shower floor.)

• Scrub shower door runners with **white toothpaste** and an **old toothbrush**. Brush with **vinegar** to rinse. Or dip a **stiff-bristled paintbrush** in **vinegar** and scrub thoroughly.

• To keep runners from growing a bumper crop of mildew, run the head of a **small sponge paintbrush** along the bottom runner channels when you've finished showering.

Cleaning tile grout

1 Liberally smear a paste of bicarbonate of soda and bleach onto the grout with a spatula.

2 After about an hour, scrub the tiles clean using an old, soft toothbrush.

To remove soap film on a plastic shower curtain, place it in the washing machine with two or three **large bath towels**. Add **100ml of vinegar** and wash, removing it before the spin cycle. Hang it up immediately to dry. If the mildew is out of control, use **180ml of chlorine bleach** instead. To avoid a soapy build-up on the bottom of the shower curtain, rub it with **baby oil**. Always keep a shower curtain unfurled to give mould and mildew a less inviting place to grow.

See also Baths and Tiles.

Shutters

Used to add character and cut down on strong sunlight, and now often used as a smart alternative to blinds and curtains, shutters can become more unsightly than decorative if you let the dust and grime accumulate.

Regular maintenance will keep your indoor shutter-cleaning chores to a minimum. Dust every month on both sides with the **soft brush attachment** of your **vacuum**. In between sessions with your vacuum, touch up the shutters with a **microfibre cloth** or **feather duster**.

To clean indoor shutters, remove the shutters from their hinges and put them somewhere level – a **workbench** topped with a **white towel**, for instance. Spray the shutters with a **gentle all-purpose cleaner**, taking special care to penetrate the cracks and crevices. Allow the cleaner to sit on the shutters for five minutes. Wearing **rubber gloves**, start cleaning at the top of shutters and work toward the bottom. Clean the slats with a **towel**, your **rubber-gloved fingers** or a **small soft-bristled brush** for nooks and crannies. Use a **trigger spray bottle** filled with **warm water** to spray away dirt and other grime from the slats. Using a **dry cloth**, dry the slats one at a time. Reach hard-to-dry areas with a **rag** wrapped round the handle of a **wooden spoon**.

Cleaning outdoor shutters is basically the same operation – with a few refinements. Remove the shutters from the outside walls and lay them flat or prop them against a secure support. Wet down the shutters with an **all-purpose cleaner** or a **spray bottle of water** with a squirt of **washing-up liquid** added. Leave the cleaner on for a few minutes. Then use a **screwdriver**, wrapped in a **towel**, to attack hard-to-reach spots. Rinse with a **garden hose**, using as much water pressure as your hose can muster. Dry the slats with a **towel**. Let them finish drying in the sun.

See also **Louvres.**

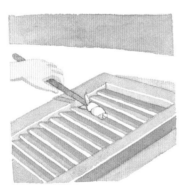

A rag wrapped around a wooden stick or spoon will get into the awkward crevices between slats.

Silk

Take care when cleaning silk – many silk garments are washable if you are careful, but don't assume that they are. Check the fabric care label carefully to avoid disaster.

Treat stains from spills and other marks before you wash silk. (See below for special ways to treat perspiration and deodorant stains.) On a hidden spot, apply a paste of **powdered laundry starch** such as *Dylon In-Wash Starch* and **cold water**, to make sure the silk is colourfast. If it is, apply the paste to the stain, let it dry and brush it away.

Roll delicate garments in a white towel to remove excess moisture.

To wash a silk garment, you can either do it by hand or use the delicate cycle and cool or warm water in your washing machine. A **mild detergent**, such as *Woolite*, works best. Carefully roll the garment in an **absorbent white towel** to blot up excess moisture. Then either lay the garment flat to dry or hang it on a padded hanger.

To iron silk, use a low setting and iron on the inside of the garment only.

Perspiration and deodorant stains can discolour and weaken silk. (The salt in perspiration and aluminium chloride and other chemicals in deodorants and antiperspirants, can stain silk.) Dry-clean or wash perspiration-stained garments as soon as possible.

　　To treat perspiration or deodorant stains on washable silk garments, try one of these remedies, but first test it on a hidden spot to see whether the fabric dye holds.

• Soak the perspiration stain in **warm water** and a paste of **table salt** and **white vinegar**.

• Make a paste of **cream of tartar** and **warm water** and apply it to the stain. Allow the paste to dry, then brush it off and launder the garment as usual.

• Apply a mixture of **warm water** and **water softener** to the stained area and then rub with a bar of **laundry soap**. Brush it off and then wash.

• Dissolve **2 aspirins** in **100ml of warm water** and apply it to the stain. Let it dry for hours, brush it off and launder.

See also **Satin.**

Watch out

When cleaning silk, always keep these precautions in mind:

● Never use chlorine bleach, because it can irreparably damage the fabric.

● Never dry silk in sunlight, because it will fade.

● Never wash silk ties; both the silk and its lining are prone to shrinkage. (The lining will usually shrivel first.) Instead, take them to a dry-cleaner.

● When you're dressing, apply hair spray, makeup and other beauty and grooming aids before putting on anything made of silk. The alcohol in them could cause dyes to bleed.

Simple solutions

Avoiding deodorant stains

Deodorants and antiperspirants can leave stains on clothing as easily as can perspiration itself. So always apply your deodorant and then make sure that it has dried before you dress. Excess deodorant will rub off onto garments, eventually staining them.

● When you're cleaning silver pieces that are decorated with semi-precious or precious stones, avoid using anything remotely abrasive near the stones.

● Don't soak silver pieces set with semiprecious or precious stones for longer than a few seconds, since water can dissolve the glue that holds them in place.

● Silver hates chlorine, so take off silver jewellery before jumping into a swimming pool.

Scrub stubborn tarnish with an old toothbrush after overnight soaking.

Be especially careful with silver candlesticks, candelabra and knife handles filled with paste or wax. If you rub too hard or rinse in hot water, they could soften and bend.

Silver jewellery

Air and light are the two biggest enemies of silver jewellery. So how you store your silver makes a big difference to how much it will tarnish.

Always store clean silver in a cool, dry place, wrapped separately in a **soft cloth** and then enclosed in a **resealable plastic bag** to prevent the pieces from getting jostled about and scratched by other jewellery.

Clean your silver once a month if you wear it frequently. The best cleaner is **silver paste** or **liquid polish**. Apply with a **soft cloth** according to the package directions and then buff with another cloth. Rinse the piece gently in warm water, if needed.

Another method is to rub with a **soft cloth** dipped in **bicarbonate of soda**, using a **frayed toothbrush** to get into hard-to-reach areas. Rinse well in warm water and buff dry with another cloth.

Or line a **small bowl** with **aluminium foil**, with the shiny side towards you. Fill the bowl with **hot water** and mix in **1 tablespoon** of **bleach-free powdered laundry detergent** (not liquid) – try one especially for colours. Put the jewellery in the solution and let it soak one minute. Rinse completely and air-dry.

To clean badly tarnished or dirty silver jewellery, fill a **small plastic bowl** with **warm water** and add a few drops of **dishwasher powder**. Soak the jewellery in the solution overnight. Should the dirt persist on your silver after its overnight soak, clean the piece with an **old toothbrush**. Then rinse and dry carefully with a **soft cloth**.

Specially treated anti-tarnish cloths, available at most grocery and hardware stores, may also be used to touch up silver jewellery.

Silver serving pieces

Though most people save them for best or let them sit on a sideboard, silver serving dishes, whether plated or sterling silver, actually benefit from being used frequently. Rotate your pieces so that they will age uniformly.

Clean your silver twice a year following this tried-and-tested method. Use a **high-quality silver polish** and a **soft cloth** to apply the polish in a circular motion and warm water to rinse.

If there is candle wax on your silver, don't scrape it off – you could scratch the surface. Instead, soften the wax in a **warm oven** or with a **hair dryer** on low and then peel it off. Or dribble on a little **turpentine** or **methylated spirits** to dislodge the wax.

To clean ornate silver pieces, sprinkle on **bicarbonate of soda** and rub gently with a **soft cloth**.

To wash silver, do it by hand in **mild washing-up liquid** and **warm water** and dry immediately with a **soft cloth**. Water left on silver can pit and corrode it.

As a general rule, don't wash silver in the dishwasher; it's simply too soft to withstand the jostling and abrasion. If you must use the dishwasher, keep silver pieces well away from metals such as copper and stainless steel. They will mark each other if they touch.

To restore the shine between cleanings, use **polishing gloves** and **cloths** or a **jeweller's rouge cloth** (flannel treated with a red polishing powder). These items are sold at hardware stores and many department stores.

To store a silver serving piece, slip it into an **anti-tarnish bag** or **cloth**. **Acid-free tissue paper**, sold at craft shops, also works. Then place it in a **plastic bag**. (Don't use newspaper, because its carbon can eat into silver.) **Silica gel packets** placed inside will keep moisture at bay. Don't use rubber bands to close the bag – they contain sulphur, which damages silver. Store away from sunlight.

A rub with a silver cloth or rouge cloth will restore a shine to cutlery between cleanings.

Sinks

With all the soap and water that flow through your sink, you'd think it would be clean all the time. But soapy deposits, food stains, rust and water spots have a way of accumulating quickly and creating a dirty scum.

For general cleaning of any sink, use a squirt of **washing-up liquid** and scrub the sink with a **soft sponge**. Rinse away residue. Don't use an abrasive cleaning

Rub a freshly cut lemon around a porcelain sink to remove stains.

agent or applicator, because it will scratch. A non–abrasive cleaner, like *Astonish* or *Chemico* will work on more stubborn staining.

For a lightly stained porcelain sink, try one of these treatments:
• Rub a **freshly cut lemon** around the sink to cut through the grease. Rinse with **running water**.
• Sprinkle **bicarbonate of soda** around the sink and then rub it with a **damp sponge**. Rinse with **vinegar** or **lemon juice** to help neutralise the alkaline cleaner and then rinse with running water.
• Make a paste the consistency of toothpaste with **bicarbonate of soda** and **water** and gently rub the sink with a **sponge** or **soft nylon brush**. Polish with a **paper towel** or **soft cloth**.

Never use **scouring powders** or **steel wool**, because they will scratch.

To remove rust from stainless steel or iron sinks, wipe *WD-40* on the rust mark with a cloth and rinse thoroughly.

To remove water spots from any sink, use a **cloth** dampened with **vinegar**.

For a sparkling white ceramic sink, place **paper towels** across the bottom and saturate them with **household bleach**. Let it sit for 30 minutes and rinse with running water. Note: do not use bleach in coloured porcelain sinks, because it will fade the colour. Clean these sinks with **mild liquid detergents**, **vinegar** or **baking soda**.

For a sparkling metal sink, use a **specialist chrome and metal cleaner**. Apply then polish dry using a **tea towel**.

Stains in Corian-type sinks can be removed with **toothpaste** or a paste of **bicarbonate of soda** and **water**. Gently scrub the paste on with a **white scrubbing pad**. Your last resort is scrubbing very gently with **very fine wet–or–dry glasspaper**. Scrubbing too hard could wear a groove in the Corian. Polish the cleaned spot with a special polish made for Corian surfaces.

Water spots that have etched themselves into a sink's porcelain are extremely difficult to remove. Buff such spots out with a **polishing compound** as soon as you notice the spots. Use **rouge** with porcelain sinks.

To cover a chip or scratch on a white porcelain surface – including sinks, tubs and appliances – pick up a container of **white enamel paint** at DIY stores. Following the package directions, paint over the mark with a **small artist's brush**, let it dry, rub with **fine glasspaper** and paint again. Repeat the process until the painted area is even with the surrounding surface. If you want to get fancier, buy a **porcelain repair kit**, which will include filler, hardener, cleaning spray, glasspaper and more.

Skylights

What better way to let natural light into your home – while maintaining your privacy – than with skylights? So you don't have to look up into a dirty sky, do some simple maintenance to preserve your view. The materials depend on whether you have glass or acrylic skylights.

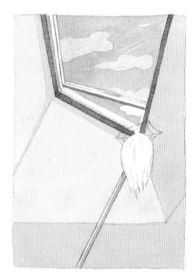

Remove dust and cobwebs from a skylight easily and effectively using a cobweb brush or a barely damp mop.

To clean the exterior of your glass skylights, treat them as you would any other window cleaning task. But remember to use extra caution as you are far higher up. Using a **long-handled squeegee**, it will be possible (though you'll need some dexterity) to clean the outside of your skylight. Use a **commercial window cleaner** that doesn't need rinsing or drying off. You don't want be at an awkward angle for any longer than necessary.

A twice-a-year cleaning of your skylights and frames is sufficient; more often and you may wear out the silicone seal around the skylight and cause leaks.

The interiors of glass skylights can be cleaned monthly – or less if the skylight is difficult to reach. Wooden frames can be cleaned with a **furniture polish** if you can reach them. They'll also need to be finished, painted, or stained every three years to protect the wood against damage from ultraviolet rays.

If your skylight is made of acrylic, take care as strong cleaning solvents can easily scratch and damage the acrylic. Even using glass cleaner on acrylic can be a problem. So to clean the inside and outside of your acrylic window safely, mix **1 tablespoon of washing–up liquid** in **4 litres of warm water**. Dip a **soft cloth** into the solution, wipe over the window and rinse well. If stubborn stains remain, use any **plastic cleaner**. Spray the cleaner on a cloth and wipe over the acrylic pane. You can also use the plastic cleaner to remove marks on vinyl frames.

If your skylight has a screen, you will need to remove it to clean the inside of the window. If this is too difficult, open the window and clean the inside at the same time that you clean the outside. To clean the screen, **vacuum** it using the **brush attachment**. If the screen is really dirty and you can remove it, wash it with a **soft brush** dipped in a solution of **washing–up liquid** and **warm water**. Then rinse thoroughly.

Slate

Whether you have slate flooring, a slate mantel or a slate kitchen counter, light cleaning is a simple task, especially if you have sealed the slate carefully beforehand.

To remove dust on slate, just **vacuum** or wipe it with a **damp cloth** or a **damp mop**.

To remove floor dirt, mix **100ml of ammonia** in **6 litres of water**. Apply the cleaning solution with a **sponge mop**. If you dust weekly, you can do a thorough cleaning with ammonia once a month or every other month.

To protect slate floors from staining, apply a **stone sealer** – either gloss or satin – after it's installed. Slate is especially susceptible to oil stains (from salad oils, for instance). So sealing a slate floor in a kitchen or eating area may be a good idea. If you wish, follow the sealer with a **wax finish** that can protect the sealer and make it last longer. The sealer and the wax work together to make slate easier to clean.

A sprinkling of flour or cornflour will help absorb an oil stain on a slate worktop.

To clean a slate worktop, scour the surface using a **multi purpose cleaner** and a **damp sponge**. Do not use abrasive pads, which may remove some of the stone and change its appearance.

To clean up oil stains, sprinkle a liberal amount of **flour** on the surface and let it sit for 10 minutes. Then scrub the surface with a **grease-cutting cleaner**, such *Flash* or use **warm water** with a squirt of **washing-up liquid**.

To protect a slate kitchen work-top, oil it with a 50–50 mixture of **boiled linseed oil** and **turpentine**. Wipe the solution on the slate with a cloth and then buff the slate with a **soft cloth**, **towelling rag**, or **old bath towel** until it's dry. Oil will darken the slate and give it a satin finish while creating a protective barrier. Oil your kitchen worktop once or twice a year. Oil other non-floor surfaces – mantels or hearths, for instance – every two years.

Sleeping bags

Sleeping bags come with one of three types of insulation: natural (down or down and feather); synthetic fibres, usually nylon; or fleece. But whatever type of sleeping bag you have, if you use it only a couple of times a year and treat it well, you might be able to go for 10 years without giving it a thorough cleaning.

To keep a sleeping bag in good shape, here are some guidelines:
• Use a washable cotton liner or always wear nightclothes when you're using the bag.
• Spot clean after a trip with a **sponge** and **soapy water**.
• After a camping trip, air your sleeping bag for a couple of hours or place it in the dryer for 10 to 15 minutes to get rid of any moisture.
• Store your bag in a **large breathable storage sack**, not in the stuff sack or in a plastic bag.

To hand-wash a sleeping bag – the most careful way to do it – fill a **bath** with **warm water** and just a little soap. For down bags, select a **down liquid soap** (available from camping supplies stores). You can also safely use a **mild detergent**, such as *Woolite*. Don't use any detergent containing bleach on a down bag (but it's safe for nylon bags). Check the package directions to determine the amount of detergent to use. Remember that using too

Watch out

Dry cleaning is not recommended for down or synthetic sleeping bags. It can strip the natural oils in the down and take the silicone coating off the synthetic-filled bags. You can probably dry-clean a fibre-filled sleeping bag, but check the manufacturer's recommendations first.

Gently knead the sleeping bag in the soapy water to loosen dirt and grime.

much will mean more rinsing later on. Gently knead the bag to help the soapy water penetrate the material.

If your sleeping bag has a waterproof outer shell, turn it inside out before you immerse it so the soapy water will be able to penetrate.

Rinse your bag twice – several times if necessary – with **clear water**. Don't cut corners on this step, particularly if you're working with down. It's very important to remove all soap before the down has dried. Do not wring water from your sleeping bag. Instead, squeeze out the water by rolling up the bag tightly and carefully.

To machine-wash a sleeping bag, you may want to use a **self-service laundry** if your bag is heavier than your machine's total load weight (or can't fit easily within the drum). Follow care label advice for the correct wash programme.

Drying is the key to preserving your sleeping bag. If your bag is not dried thoroughly before you store it away, the matted lumps that formed when it was wet will stay that way. The bag will no longer offer optimum insulation and may develop mildew. For these reasons, it's often better to dry your bag at a self-service laundry, where you can use a large dryer. In a home dryer, the sleeping bag will take up so much room that it won't tumble well. Consequently, the clumps of down or synthetic fibres will not be broken up during drying.

If you decide to wash your sleeping bag at home and then dry it at a self-service laundry, put it in a **plastic bag** for the trip to the laundry. Use the **largest dryer** set to

Simple solutions

The squeeze play

When hand-washing a sleeping bag, try this simple trick to prevent the compartments formed by baffles (those stitched partitions that keep the fill evenly distributed) from inflating and floating to the surface. Keep the bag in its stuff sack and immerse both bag and sack in the tub of water. You've already forced the air out of the bag when you put it in the stuff sack. Once both are immersed, you can remove the sleeping bag from the sack and work the soapy water into the bag.

high heat. Melting the nylon shell is not a danger because the bag has room to tumble, but if you're in doubt, use a lower setting. Once the nylon shell is dry, set the dryer on medium heat so that the interior feathers can dry. Throw in a couple of **clean tennis balls** to help break up clumps of down. Remove the bag as soon as it's finished tumbling.

Even if your bag feels dry, the down insulation may not be. Check for lumps – a sign the down is still wet.

After drying a sleeping bag with fibre-pile insulation, gently fluff up the fleece with a **comb** or **brush**.

Slide projectors & screens

Cleaning electronic gadgetry is not rocket science. It merely requires know-how (supplied by this book) and patience (supplied by you). If you try to do it too quickly, you may damage your projector.

To clean a slide projector, start with the outside of the unit (wait until it is completely cool). Separate and set aside the optical assemblies – the lens, which is easily removable from its track and the lamp, which slides out the back of the projector. Use an aerosol can of **deionised compressed air** to blow any dust or loose dirt off the projector casing. (If it's really dirty, walk outside to spray it, so that you won't have another mess to clean up inside.) Spray any openings inside the casing to loosen dust. With a clean, ideally unused **3cm bristle paintbrush**, dust all the nooks and crannies, making sure to clean around the gate area, which catches the dropping slides and the exhaust grill, where dirt tends to collect. Once again, blow compressed air on the case to remove any remaining dust. Spray a **multi-purpose surface cleaner** (or a **lens cleaner** from a **camera shop**) on a clean, **lint-free cloth** and wipe the exterior surfaces to remove fingerprints and grime.

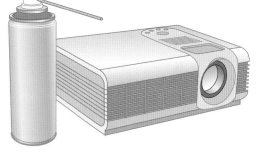

Use compressed air to dust the projector case, the lens and the lamp.

To clean the projector's optics – which you removed and set aside – be extra careful not to scratch the lenses. Use the **compressed air** to first dust the projection lens. Place a couple of drops of **surface cleaner** on both the front and rear of the lens and, with a **lens tissue**, rub gently in a circular motion to remove dust or water condensation marks. No matter how tempted you may be don't try to clean the internal lens. These are very sensitive parts. Among other things, unskilled fingers can disturb the finely calibrated focusing mechanism. (Every five years or so, have the projector serviced by a professional, who can clean and lubricate the internal systems.)

To clean the projector's lamp, set the cleaned projection lens aside and locate the lamp, which is typically next to the exhaust fan and tends to get really dirty. Again, remove dust with the **compressed air**, loosen dirt with the **paintbrush** and give the lamp a final canned-air 'rinse'. Using the **lens tissue** and **surface cleaner**, gently wipe the mirror that accompanies the lamp. There should be a clear condenser lens bracketed in front of the lamp. Unscrew the bracket, gently remove the lens (holding it on the edges only) and clean it as you did the other lenses. Reattach it to the lamp assembly. If the condenser lens is tinted green (as it often is on models made more than a decade ago), take even more care when handling it. Don't touch the lens with bare fingers (handle it with a clean cloth or tissue) and if you must set it down, do so on a **cloth**. This time, don't use the cleaning solution; wipe it very gently with the **lens tissue**.

After reassembling the projector, turn it on. You may smell a strange smell, generated by the dust disturbed during the cleaning. The smell will stop after the dust has settled, so if the machine still smells after 30 minutes, it may need professional attention.

Cleaning the projection screen is the easy part. Although there are different screen materials, the cleaning techniques are the same for nearly all. Make a solution of **mild washing-up liquid** and **warm water**. Gently wipe away dust and dirt with a **sponge** dipped in the solution. Rinse by wiping with a **clean, wet sponge**. Blot dry using a **clean cloth**. That's it. Never use solvents, such as acetone or paint thinner and never use abrasive cleaners.

If you have a glass bead screen or a screen with a delicate surface, don't clean it with water and soap. Instead, simply brush away dust using a **soft-bristled brush** or a **clean, lint-free cloth**.

Watch out

Don't clean the aluminium frames in direct sunlight or very hot or very cold temperatures, because the cleaning solution may dry too quickly and streak the surface. If that happens, it could be difficult to restore the aluminium to its original appearance.

Sliding doors

The sliding glass door to your patio or deck provides a nice view but can also collect a lot of sand, dust and debris in its tracks. How you clean the door depends on its frame – wood, aluminium or, more common in newer construction, vinyl.

Vacuuming the sill tracks is the first step in cleaning any sliding door. Run the **vacuum** over the tracks at least once in the spring and autumn, then weekly in summer, when you use the door frequently. When you do your general room vacuuming, paying extra attention to the carpet just in front of the door will help to reduce the amount of dirt that gets dragged into the tracks.

Vacuum the sill tracks regularly to keep them free of grit and dirt.

To keep your door sliding smoothly, spray **silicone** on a **soft, dry cloth** and wipe it onto the track. Don't allow the silicone to come into contact with wood surfaces or the weather strip. Lubricate rollers with **light oil** such as *3-in-One*.

To clean the outside of a vinyl frame, use a **mild washing-up liquid solution** – just a couple of squirts to **3 litres of hot or warm water** is fine and apply this with a **soft sponge** or **cloth**. Rinse with **clear water**. Make sure you clean the frame before you wash the window so that you won't get your sparkling window wet and smeary again. Start at the top of the frame and work down.

To clean the inside of a vinyl frame, wipe with a **damp cloth** at the time that you clean the window. Don't use abrasive cleaners, abrasive scouring pads, or glasspaper in an attempt to buff or shine the vinyl frame or to remove marks. You'll simply create scratches.

To clean wood-framed sliding doors, fill a **misting bottle** with **warm water** and a squirt of **mild washing-up liquid**. Very lightly mist the sliding door frames and wipe off any dirt with a **soft cloth**. Finish by gently drying with another soft cloth. Never use a hose or any high-pressure washer on the door, because you may also saturate the wood. Likewise, if your wooden door frame is painted, never use abrasive cleaners, as they can soften emulsion paint. A few will even soften oil-based paint. If stubborn grime won't come off with water or a mild detergent, consider lightly sanding it and then refinishing.

It's important to make a thorough inspection of your wooden door frame at least once a year – more regularly if you live near the coast. That's because wood is highly susceptible to attacks by fungi and other deterioration.

To clean aluminium-clad sliding doors, again, use **washing-up liquid** and **water**, made up as above and applied with a **sponge** or **soft brush** from top to bottom. Rinse immediately. Air-dry or wipe with a **soft, dry cloth**. For a protective coating, apply **car wax** to the aluminium. All exterior aluminium frames should be cleaned annually.

Next, clean the glass, inside and out. (See Windows for cleaning solutions and techniques.) Any **window cleaner** will be fine for this job, but avoid getting the cleaner on the window frames, because ingredients in some glass cleaners will damage the frame materials.

Skirting boards

Skirting boards take a huge amount of punishment. Though they're usually gloss-painted to be hard-wearing, they are kicked by children and bashed with the vacuum cleaner on a regular basis. Scuff marks can be tough to remove, so follow these tips to keep skirtings pristine.

To clean gloss-painted skirting boards, remove scuff marks and dirt with a **sponge** and a **grease-cutting all-purpose spray cleaner**. Spray the cleaner on a cloth not the skirting board, to prevent streaking. For really tough stains, test an inconspicuous corner with **scouring powder** and a **plastic scrubbing pad**. If it doesn't affect the finish, you can apply the method to the entire surface. A general cleaning rule of thumb comes into play here: use the least aggressive cleaner initially and then resort to more aggressive tactics as the scuffs dictate. Skirting boards that are painted with stain or emulsion paint require the gentlest cleaning method (water, washing-up liquid and a flannel).

To clean vinyl or rubber skirting – more properly called cove moulding – spray on a **wax stripper** and let it soak in for a few minutes to loosen old wax and grime. Scrub with a **nylon brush** and rinse.

Prevention can save you a lot of work. Whilst you may think it's the kids who are kicking the skirting board, it's more likely to be the vacuum (check the bumper at the front is always in place) or when you mop the floor (avoid mops that have sharp swivel heads). And if you use a strong cleaner on floors, quickly wipe away spills and splashes that could discolour your skirting board.

Smoke alarms

You'll already know to check and test the batteries in your smoke alarm each week. But did you know that you should also clean them every other month? Cobwebs, dust and even spiders can cause your smoke alarm to become less sensitive and so work less effectively.

Clean the outside and inside of the alarm using a **vacuum cleaner** and a **brush attachment**. Flip open or unscrew the casing to get inside. If you can't reach the alarm with your vacuum's extension tubes, stand on a ladder. A can of **compressed air** (available from camera shops) can also be sprayed on the casing and inside the alarm to clean it.

Test your alarm, once you've cleaned it, to see that it's working properly. Stand by the alarm, light a candle or strike a match and then blow it out. The smoke should activate the alarm. Or, if your system is activated by light (it should say so on the box), shine a flashlight into the alarm to set it off. Simply pressing the button on the alarm casing is not a test. That only indicates the horn is working, not the detection mechanism.

Vacuum your smoke alarm every couple of months to ensure it functions properly.

Cover the alarm whenever you're doing major work in the house that could send dust into the air. Don't forget to remove this covering promptly after you've finished. You should also protect the alarm if you're painting around it – never paint the alarm casing.

Sofa covers

Removable covers on your sofa are a fairly straightforward machine wash job (but check the care labels first). It's taking them off, then stretching them back on again that can be so time-consuming.

To remove dust and debris, give the covers a going-over while they're still on the furniture with your **vacuum cleaner**, using the **upholstery attachment**. For cushions, use the **vacuum nozzle** without any attachments.

To clean sofa covers, remove them and give them a good shake outside. Most can be washed, with the exception of rayon, which often requires dry cleaning. Consider washing curtains at the same time if they're made of the same fabric, so if they fade slightly, it will be consistent and not noticeable.

Covers will sometimes shrink the first time they're laundered, but it shouldn't be by very much. If hard to get out stains mean you decide to wash them twice, remember to put the curtains through a second time as well.

To dry sofa covers either hang over a **drying rack** or put them in a **dryer**. Some people feel that machine-drying is too harsh. If so, don't peg them out on the line: the wet weight of the cover is so great that it may pull the fabric out of shape. Instead, dry flat. Put some **old dry sheeting** on a **garden table**, then lay the slip cover on top, holding it down with a couple of **books** or **bricks** (wrapped in **clear plastic**) so that it doesn't blow off.

You're ready to get them back onto the sofa while they are still marginally damp. (Too dry and it will be impossible to fit them back on again.) Pull all seams and cording into place before you start. Save your hands and nails by using a **wooden spoon** to help tuck the corners of the cover back into place.

Simple solutions

Take Eeyore for a spin

For a quick and easy way to dust and freshen plush toys, toss them into a dryer and tumble on the fluff setting for 10 minutes. To remove odours from a stuffed animal, add a scented dryer sheet when you tumble them in the dryer.

Soft toys

Stuffed animals tend to spend a lot of time on floors snuggling with loving children, who unintentionally rub whatever food and grime they have on their hands into the fake fur. Because of the variety of stuffing materials and accessories, such as clothing and ribbons, cleaning them can be trickier than simply throwing them in the washing machine.

Periodically dust stuffed animal toys using the **vacuum cleaner brush attachment**. Be sure not to suck up any loose buttons or clothing accessories. Preen fake hair with a clean **hairbrush** and then vacuum again to lift whatever the brush has loosened. (So that you won't get dirt and hair-product residue on the toys, buy a brush that you use only for this purpose.) To remove pet hair and lint, use a **lint roller**.

To remove light dirt, just lightly clean the surface. Wipe with a **damp cloth**, trying not to get moisture into the stuffing. Follow up by preening with a **hairbrush**.

To remove juice and other spills on stuffed animals, do what a live animal would do if you doused it with liquid: shake. Shake the toy, outside or in a **bath**, to keep the liquid from splashing onto anything else. This will remove some of the liquid without smearing it into the fur – or worse, the stuffing. Blot up as much remaining liquid as you can with **kitchen roll**. Never rub. Wet with a **cloth** or **sponge**. Blot again. Rinse the cloth or sponge. Repeat until the spill is gone.

For deeper cleaning, start by reading the care tag sewn into the seam. Machine-washing is safe for some stuffed animals, such as those filled with most synthetic fibres, but it can ruin others, such as those that have cardboard stiffeners. The same goes for drying: for some stuffed toys, a dryer is fine, but other toys are stuffed so tightly that they will mildew or will never dry out.

If your toy isn't machine washable, surface-clean using a solution of **warm water** and **mild washing-up liquid**. Rub gently with a **cloth** or **sponge** dampened in the solution, being sure not to soak the filling. Rinse by wiping with a **cloth** or **sponge** dampened with clear water. To maintain a consistent look to the surface, clean the whole animal and not just one spot. Air-dry and then preen with a **hairbrush**.

If the tag says it's OK to wash, tie the stuffed toy up in a cloth bag, such as a laundry bag or pillowcase (but

not a mesh bag), to protect the fur. It's OK to put several toy animals in the bag, as long as they fit loosely and aren't too big for the washing machine. Wash in cold water using a mild detergent on a gentle cycle. Don't use bleach or fabric softeners. Put the whole bag in the dryer and tumble on the machine's gentlest setting.

Sports equipment

Luckily, most sports equipment is made of tough materials and can stand getting dirty and scuffed. In fact, over-cleaning can be as much of a problem as under-cleaning, since rackets, balls, skis and other sporting goods often contain finely calibrated, high-tech materials. The trick is in knowing how and how often to clean sports gear.

To keep archery gear clean, wipe off your bow and the shafts of arrows after each use with a **clean, moist cloth**. To remove stubborn dirt, wipe them with a mild solution of **washing-up liquid** and **warm water**. Rinse with a **water-soaked cloth**. Dry with a **clean towel**. Don't use solvents on bows or bowstrings.

To keep the bowstring from drying out and breaking, wax it monthly using **string wax**. Most compound bow pulley systems are self-lubricating, so there is no need to lubricate wheels and cams. Wipe off the metal limb bolts (which hold the compound parts together) with a **silicone-soaked rag**, available at stores that sell hunting and fishing gear. Periodically spray arrow feathers with an **arrow waterproofing spray**.

To keep darts clean, there's not much you have to do as long as you keep your darts out of your beer. Keep the points free of burrs by turning them gently in the concave part of a **round sharpening stone** (available where darts are sold). Every so often, remove the number ring from the dart board and rotate it, so that the wear is distributed evenly. Ideally, as you get ever better at darts, you'll have to do this more often, as only the centre and board under the 20 will get the wear.

To care for a football, which is usually made of synthetic leather, keep it dry. If your football gets dirty, wipe it with a **moist rag**. If it gets very wet, air-dry it. Don't ever use a heat source such as a hair dryer or a radiator to dry a football.

To keep golf clubs clean, wipe the dirt and mud off them after each day of golfing. Use a **cloth** and **plain water** or a very mild solution of **washing–up liquid** and **water**. Rinse by wiping with a **wet cloth**. Dry well with a **dry cloth**. Try not to get the leather grips wet. Large deposits of dirt can hurt your game, so keep a moist cloth handy while playing to spot-clean after digging up divots.

To clean a synthetic golf bag, wipe it with **plain water** or the same **mild, soapy solution** recommended for clubs. **Vacuum** out the bottom and the pockets occasionally. To clean a leather golf bag, follow the instructions for coated leather in the **Leather** entry.

Every so often, vacuum out the bottom and pockets of your golf bag to get rid of dust.

To keep hockey gear in good working order, the most important thing is to allow it to dry properly – which means letting gear dry naturally, not with the help of an additional heat source. Proper care also means taking gear out of the car boot and stick bag as soon as possible. After each game, dry and store pads (hanging them, if possible) in an upright position. The same goes for the stick.

To get the most out of skates, rotate the wheels as soon as you notice that they are wearing down. Switch the most worn with the least worn. Switch from one skate to the other. Since wheels wear faster on the inside edge, turn the less worn side inward. If the bearings get wet, remove them from the wheels and wipe them dry as soon as possible, using a **clean, lint– free cloth**. Don't lubricate the outside of the bearing – that will attract dirt.

Clean bearings that have removable outer shields. You'll know they need cleaning when they spin slowly or make a noise while spinning (the sound of dirt inside). After following the manufacturer's instructions for removing the shields, clean the bearings by inserting a **stick**, **pen** or **pencil** through their doughnut-shaped casing. Taking great care and wearing **rubber gloves** and **eye goggles**, dip the skates into a **shallow bowl** of **white spirit** and slowly spin them in the liquid until the dirt is

To clean the bearings, spin them in a solution of mineral turpentine or kerosene until the dirt is gone.

gone. Lay the bearings on a **paper towel** to dry, or blow them dry with a **can of compressed air** (available from camera shops). Finish up by lubricating them with **bearing lubricant**, available at skate supply shops or sports shops.

To maintain a skateboard, keep in mind that most skateboards are made of laminated wood and shouldn't get wet. Dry them if they do. To clean dirty decks, scrub the grip tape with a **soft-bristled brush** dipped in **clean water**. Rinse by wiping with a wet cloth or sponge. Dry well with a clean cloth as soon as you've finished rinsing.

As with skate wheels, skateboard wheels should be rotated when you notice they are wearing down. Switch the most worn with the least worn. If the bearings get wet, remove them from the wheels and wipe them dry as soon as possible using a **clean, lint-free cloth**. Don't lubricate the outside of the bearing, because that will attract dirt. If your bearings have removable outer shields, you can clean and lubricate them. Follow the instructions described above for cleaning and lubricating skate bearings.

To clean your tennis racket – or squash or badminton racket – wipe it with a **damp cloth**. Don't get the strings wet, as moisture can ruin them. Try not to wet the leather grip either, as moisture can take away the grip's tackiness and make it slippery. Wipe perspiration off with a **dry cloth**. If your overgrip (the material you can wrap around or slip over the grip) gets dirty, replace it.

To clean skis and poles, wipe them down with a **moist rag** and then dry with a **dry rag**, or use a sudsy solution of **warm water** and **washing-up liquid**. Rinse and dry well. Wax your skis every few times you use them. Each time you wax them, clean the bases either by using a **spray-on/wipe-off base cleaner** (available at ski shops) or by putting on **hot wax** with an **old iron** and scraping it off with a **plastic scraper** before it has dried. (Scrapers are available at ski shops, or at a pinch you can use a **plastic windshield scraper**. Once you've used an iron for waxing, never use it on clothes.) After you ski, always dry your skis and poles with a cloth to keep them from rusting.

To clean ski boots, wipe them off with a **damp cloth** – if they are the hard-plastic variety – and remove the inner boot after each use so that both will dry properly. Wipe leather boots with a **damp cloth,** but avoid getting them very wet. Let them air-dry, but never near heat, which will dry out and crack leather. If your leather ski boots do get wet, remove the insoles and stuff single sheets of **newspaper** in them. Keep leather boots coated with a leather waterproofing product, available at sporting goods and shoe shops.

To clean a snowboard, follow the instructions for cleaning and waxing skis described above. Every time you snowboard, dry your board afterward with a **cloth** to keep it from rusting.

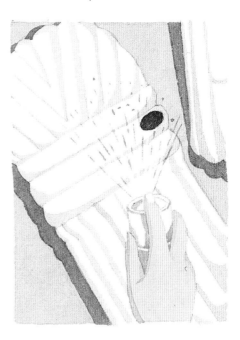

A spray-on fabric guard will keep pads clean and waterproof.

When washing outfits for any sport, promptness is key. Don't let sweaty outfits remain in lockers or balled up in gym bags. Wash them in your **washing machine** without delay. Tumble dry on low: too high a heat can make screen-printed numbers and names on uniforms crack.

If you need to clean pads and protectors for sports such as cricket, hockey and football, surface clean them with a **cloth** and **plain water** or a very mild solution of **washing-up liquid** and **water**. Rinse by wiping with a **wet cloth**. Don't submerge pads or protectors – the water might remain in the padding and lead to bacteria growth and odours. Spray pads with a **fabric waterproofing product**, such as *Scotchgard*, to help keep them clean and less susceptible to moisture.

Sprinklers

Your lawn sprinkler system will let you know when it needs cleaning by spraying in an bizarre pattern – or not at all – when it gets jammed by sediment or mineral deposits. Clean it once at the beginning of the watering season and once at the end and you can reduce the misfiring.

Remove sprinkler spray heads (if possible) and rinse in a **bucket of water**. Look for any sediment that may be clogging the nozzles. Scrub lightly with a **toothbrush**. Use your **hose** to force high-pressured water back through the holes. Since most sprinklers these days are made of plastic parts, don't use soaps, oils or solvents, which can create a build-up or degrade the plastic. If all else fails, try to loosen the sediment by gently pushing a **wire** into the nozzle as water flows out. If you have a mineral build-up, wipe it with or soak in a solution of **1 part vinegar** to **3 parts water**.

Take the valves apart and clean them the same way you would the spray heads, first using **water** and a **toothbrush** and then, if that doesn't work, **vinegar** and **water**. Rinse any clogged screens in **clean water**.

Unclog a sprinkler spray head by gently probing the nozzle with a fine wire.

Stainless steel

Stainless steel is hardy and rust-proof, but that doesn't mean you don't have to clean and care for it. Without attention, stainless steel will dull over time and pick up oily fingerprints as well as mineral spots from hard water. The biggest problem, however, is scratching. Scratch it and you remove the hard, thin oxide coating that makes it stainless. Then it will rust like any old steel.

Wash stainless steel cutlery and pots in **hot, soapy water** or in a **dishwasher**. Scrub off stubborn food with a **cloth**, **sponge** or **nylon-bristled brush**, but avoid abrasives. If you're washing it in the dishwasher, be careful not to spill powdered dishwasher detergent on stainless steel – the strong powder will cause dark spots. To remove baked-on food, scrub with a paste of **bicarbonate of soda** and **water**.

Polish stainless steel with a clean, dry cloth to remove hard-water spots. For stubborn spots, wipe with a cloth soaked in straight **vinegar**. Or use a **stainless steel polishing product** or *Peek All-Purpose Metal Polish*. Follow the label directions.

Clean stainless steel sinks and appliances with a solution of **warm water** and a squirt of **washing-up liquid**, using a **soft cloth** or **sponge**. Always scrub in the direction of the stainless steel grain. Rinse with a **cloth** or **sponge** and **clear water**. Polish dry to avoid spotting, using **paper towels** or a **cloth**. For more cleaning power,

Watch out

● To avoid corroding stainless steel, rinse acidic, salty or milk-based foods off stainless steel utensils that won't be washed right away.

● Never use abrasive scrubbers, such as steel wool, on stainless steel. They will dull the finish and may even cause it to rust.

use a solution of **1 part white vinegar**, **3 parts water** or scrub with a paste made of **bicarbonate of soda** and **hot water**.

Stairs & steps

You're vacuuming away, getting through room after room and then you hit the stairs, which can be a cleaning roadblock, especially if they are carpeted. What to do?

Clean stairs from bottom to top That way, you don't grind dirt into the carpet. After cleaning the broad stair treads, use a **vacuum crevice tool** to get into the cracks along the wall and where the vertical riser meets the tread. Periodically, vacuum the carpeted risers.

Stone

Stone is one of the most durable materials on Earth. Most of it has been here for millions of years. But durable is one thing; clean and scratch-free is another. Even tough stone can be scratched by everyday grit and damaged by some of the most common household substances, including that old cleaning friend, vinegar. Take care of your stone and it will surely outlast you.

Sweep or dust stone often to remove sand and dirt from flat surfaces, where it can be ground down by shoe soles, furniture or pots and pans. The grit can scratch the stone. Dust using either a **vacuum cleaner** or **dry dust mop** (for floors) or a **clean, dry rag** (worktops and tables). Wipe up spills immediately to avoid staining.

To clean a stone worktop, first try using only **warm water**. Wipe it off with a **soft cloth** or **sponge**. Let caked-on food soak for a while before wiping. You should be able to remove spills, crumbs, sauces and other substances this way. If not, add a little **washing-up liquid** to the water. Rinse well with **clean water**, because leftover soap can leave a film or cause streaking. Avoid stronger cleaning products, such as bath and tile cleaners and scouring powders. These can stain or scratch your stone. Never use vinegar, lemon juice or other acidic cleaners on marble,

Dry mopping a stone floor regularly prevents damage from grit.

travertine or limestone. The acid will eat away at the calcium in the stone.

To remove stains from stone, keep it simple and be patient. Most stone stains are solid residue jammed in between the crystals of the stone after the liquid that carried it has evaporated. The trick is to put the solid back into solution so it can be removed. First, determine whether your stain is water-based (for example, from spilled grape juice) or oil-based (salad dressing).

• **If it is water-based**, pour **hot water** (from the tap, not the kettle) onto the stain and let it stand for a few minutes. Wipe away the excess water. Stack **1cm of paper towels** on the stain and saturate with **hot water**. Cover with a piece of **plastic** and a **flat, heavy weight**, such as a **cast-iron skillet** or a **book** (be careful not to ruin the book). Let it stand for about 10 hours. (Do it overnight and you won't have to worry about anyone moving it.) Next, throw away the paper towels and the stain should go with them.

• **If the stain is oil-based**, follow the same procedure, only instead of water, use **acetone** (but don't heat). After the 10 hours is up, throw away the paper towels and wash the stain. In both cases, let the spot dry and then observe. If some of the stain is still present, repeat with hot water or more acetone.

Sweep patio stone regularly to remove leaves and sticks, which can stain and hold mould-growing moisture. Once a year, give your patio stone a more thorough cleaning using a **patio cleaner**, available from DIY stores. Use a **stiff-bristled brush** (a long-handled one will be easier on your back and knees) to scrub the patio. Rinse the stones with a **garden hose**.

See also Patios and Worktops.

Suede

Suede, leather with a soft-napped finish, is one of the trickiest materials to clean. It can be one of the most expensive materials as well. As tough as suede seems, it you will get it dirty – and since you're reading this entry, you probably already have – there are a few tricks to cleaning it. Above all, be careful and patient.

Brush suede regularly to remove dirt and restore the nap. When you are going to put it away for a while, brush the item with a **suede brush**, available at stores that sell leather goods or shoes. Do it gently and in a slow, circular motion. If you don't have a suede brush, use a clean, dry kitchen sponge instead.

If you stain suede, blot up as much of the stain as possible and then take the item to a professional cleaner who has experience with cleaning leather and suede. Here are a couple of exceptions:

• For **grease or oil stains**, cover the stain with a small pile of **talcum powder**. Let it stand overnight. The powder may absorb the stain.

• Remove **dried water marks** by brushing lightly with a **suede brush** or **clean dry sponge**.

Watch out

Don't get perfume, hair spray or any other alcohol-based cosmetic products on suede. They can make the colours run. For the same reason, never use a liquid or solvent-based spot remover on suede

Remove oil stains from suede by covering them with talcum powder.

Swimming pools

Even if you're lucky enough to have a swimming pool, no pool is maintenance-free. These days, many pool owners use advanced pool-cleaning systems, such as automatic underwater vacuums, pumps and filters. But these automated systems are meant to keep a clean pool clean. If you let the algae and pool grime really build up and you'll end up spending hours scrubbing by hand. So the trick to keeping pool cleaning to a minimum is to stay on top of it, even if you have an automated system.

A daily scooping will keep your pool clean and help the filter work more efficiently.

Spend at least five minutes every day with your outdoor pool. Walk around it, picking up debris near the edge and making sure the water is clear and not cloudy – a sign of improper pH levels. Any time you see more than five or six leaves or sticks; use a **long pole** and **net** to scoop them up. Although an automatic pool vacuum system will pick up the occasional leaf or twig, its main job is cleaning dirt. Too many leaves can clog the system.

Keep up the chemical regime Maintain your pool with the manufacturer's recommended dosage of chlorine, which kills bacteria and germs. Use an **algaecide** – not chlorine – to reduce algae. Clean the skimmers and filters very regularly. Do it at least once a week and more often if you feel it is necessary.

Periodically 'sweep' the surface Walk around the pool's edge, scooping up debris with the pole and net as you go. Empty the net occasionally to keep leaves from falling back into the pool. When you've finished the edges, net the middle by stretching the net out, letting it fall upside down in the water and dragging it back toward you. Repeat this while making your way around the pool. Do this once a week or as needed.

Clean the sides using a long-handled pool brush Starting at the top of the pool wall, make one smooth motion downward with the brush. When you reach the bottom, bring it back to the top and do it again, only this time move the brush over one brush width. Continue until you've circled the pool once. Do this once a week or as needed.

Scrub tiles weekly to keep them clean and free from algae.

Once a week, scrub the tiles using a **pool tile cleaner** and a **tile brush**, available at pool and spa supply stores. Use as little cleaner as possible to keep the product from filling your pool with suds.

Net up any debris – once you have brushed the sides and cleaned the tiles – to remove dirt and debris. (Make sure all sediment has settled.) You'll pick up any additional debris that your cleaning has dislodged.

Table linens

Because of the food stains they so easily accumulate, most tablecloths and cloth napkins need to be, and are, machine washable. But simply throwing dirty or stained table linens into the machine may not be enough to keep them looking crisp and fresh under your fine china, crystal and silver. A few tricks of the trade will help.

Wash table linens before stains set After a spillage or big, messy dinner parties, wash them in a **washing machine** as soon as possible, following the manufacturer's recommendations on the care label. Pre-treat stains with a **commercial spot remover**. For best results, don't let the pre-treatment dry before washing.

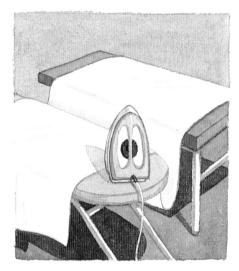

Drape a long cloth over a table to keep it clean while ironing.

When ironing tablecloths, cut down on the creasing by placing a table next to your ironing board. Let the cloth hang over the table but don't let it drag on the floor.

If your table linens have lace trim, make sure the lace is machine washable. Some lace is not and may shrink considerably when washed in water.

• If the lace is not washable, have the item dry-cleaned.
• If it is washable – and luckily, most table linen lace is – wash it gently. The safest technique is to hand-wash it in **warm water** with a squirt or two of **washing-up liquid**.
• If it is machine washable, wash it in a **mesh bag** tied at the top. This will prevent the lace from snagging.

• To keep the lace from creasing, which it will do in a machine dryer, air-dry it, laying it as flat as possible.
• When ironing, make small, gentle circular motions with your iron to avoid stretching the lace.

Tapestries

Tapestries are like fine rugs hung on walls, except that, fortunately, they are not subject to the abuse that rugs get. But tapestries still need regular care and cleaning. Antique tapestries can be extremely valuable – and fragile, since age deteriorates textile fibres. If you have an antique tapestry that needs cleaning, play it safe and take it to a professional – a textile restorer or a dealer in antique tapestries or oriental rugs who has cleaning experience.

Using a professional cleaner may be the safest way to clean and protect your tapestry.

Periodically dust your tapestry using the **upholstery attachment** on your **vacuum cleaner**. If possible, leave the tapestry hanging and carefully vacuum it in place. This will save the time and hassle of having to take it down and re-hang it. Depending on the conditions in your home (how much dust you have), do this once or twice a year.

If you need to spot-clean a tapestry, make a suds shampoo by mixing ½ **teaspoon washing-up liquid** in **1 litre of warm water**. Squeeze a **sponge** in the solution to whip up a head of suds. Test for colourfastness by rubbing a **cotton bud** dipped in the suds on an inconspicuous corner of the tapestry. If the colour holds, continue. Using as little water as possible, scoop the suds off the top, applying them sparingly with a sponge to the tapestry surface. Rub gently. Before the suds dry, lightly rinse each area as you go with a **clean, damp sponge**. Be sure to remove all the suds, or the residue will cause the textile to soil faster.

For a deeper cleaning, have the tapestry **dry-cleaned** by a professional. Make sure the dry-cleaner has experience cleaning the type of tapestry you own.

To remove wrinkles or creases, iron the back of your tapestry with a **steam iron** on a **medium setting**. If you must iron the front, lay a **thin towel** on the tapestry to protect the fibres.

Tarpaulins

We throw these up to protect lawn mowers, boats, motorcycles and other things from the elements. As a result, they often take a beating, catching bird droppings, diesel smoke, sap and dust.

There are two main types of tarpaulin:
• The heavy-duty vinyl ones that cover boats and party tents.
• The garden variety, which come in blues, greens and browns and appear to be woven.

When cleaning a tarpaulin, use a long-handled brush to save your back.

To clean heavy-duty vinyl, scrub with a **nylon-bristled brush**, a solution of **washing-up liquid** and **water** and lots of elbow grease. Lay it out on a freshly hosed driveway or clean parking lot. For stubborn stains, add vinegar: **200ml of white vinegar** per **3 litres of water** to the soapy water.

Clean polyethylene tarpaulins the same way, but expect to clean them less often. Because of their chemical makeup, these don't attract dirt as readily as vinyl.

Taxidermy

Don't pet your stuffed animals. A taxidermy specimen isn't made for manhandling. Often it contains insecticides to prevent moths, larvae and other organisms from setting up house and feasting on it.

Tarpaullnss • Taxidermy • Telephones • 359

So inspect it regularly for signs of damage from these pests. But avoid touching it. Besides leaving damaging skin oils on the piece, you might expose yourself to insecticides or even to toxic heavy metals such as arsenic and mercury, which may have been used in preserving it.

Dust is another sneaky enemy It can find its way into fur and feathers. But leaking toxins can migrate into a dust cloth or become airborne as you dust, so you shouldn't dust it at home. Experts recommend that specimens be cleaned by a professional every 10 years or so. That's the lowest-risk way to get the job done.

If you know your creature is free of these toxins, or you have decided to give it a quick once-over regardless, gingerly dust fur-bearing specimens with a **barely damp soft cloth**, following the natural direction of the fur. Wipe only the fur: even slightly dampened skin will begin to stretch and fats in the wet skin can begin to turn rancid. For birds, use a **feather duster**, working from the bill or beak back, following the natural direction of the feather pattern.

To keep the eyes bright, apply **glass cleaner** or a mix of **1 part white vinegar** to **4 parts water** to a small patch of **clean cloth** and wipe onto the glass eyes. **Baby oil**, applied similarly, will bring back the lustre of horns and tusks. In either case, keep the cleaner away from fur, feathers and skin. Avoid getting any solvents on specimens, particularly on preserved fish – they will dissolve the fish's lacquer finish.

Simple Solutions

Location is key

If you want to preserve a stuffed creature, find it a haven away from tobacco smoke, fireplaces, airborne grease and food particles, the oil from human hands and direct sunlight (which will lighten the fur or feathers the way it will fade coloured curtains). It needs to be a dry area, to ward off mildew. If possible, keep your stuffed animal in a self-contained display case

Telephones

You use it every day. So do the other members of your household. And guests. As well as finger marks, there's also the issue of germs: especially if anyone using the phone has a cold.

Simply spraying it with disinfectant won't do Your phone is an electronic instrument with intricate wiring and receiver and speaker holes that you don't want to gum up. Follow the rule for cleaning all electronics – always apply cleaner to a cloth and use the dampened cloth to wipe it clean.

To clean and disinfect a phone, use an **antibacterial product**, such as those made by *Dettol*. Spray sparingly onto your cloth, then wipe the phone.

As an alternative disinfectant, use a **strong, germ-killing mouthwash**, such as *Listerine*.

Televisions

Dust is likely to be your biggest challenge when cleaning your television. However often you clean, it seems always to come back, thicker and more static.

Unplug the television before you clean it, particularly if you need to use a wet cleaner.

To clean a TV screen, first identify the type of screen you have. Only standard tubes and plasma screens can be wiped with a **wet cleaner** as described below for the TV casing. Liquid crystal display screens, which include not only LCD TVs but also projection TVs with digital light processing (DLP) screens, should be wiped clean with a **dry, clean cotton cloth**. Consult your owner's manual. If the TV came with a cleaning kit, use its cleaner and cloths.

Rules of the game

Tube tactics

Always follow these rules when cleaning your TV:

1 Pull the plug before you start to clean.

2 Identify the type of screen you have. Some don't take well to liquid cleaners.

3 Never spray any liquid directly onto any type of television or its screen. Spray cleaner onto a cloth to slightly dampen it and then use the cloth to wipe it.

For an extra shine, buff the screen with a dry cloth after cleaning.

To clean a TV's case – or a tube or plasma screen that allows liquid cleaner – slightly dampen a **soft cotton cloth** with your chosen cleaner. (Pick a non-fraying fabric to avoid having ragged ends catch in the ventilation slits.) **Glass cleaner** makes the best cleaner, because it evaporates quickly. Or use a solution of **1 part liquid fabric softener** to **4 parts water** as your cleaner. Wring out the cloth so it's

barely damp, never dripping and wipe down the television. Never apply liquid cleaner directly to your screen or casing – the drips could damage the electronics. Buff the screen afterward with a **dry cloth**.

Some other ways to clean your TV:
• Simply wipe the screen with an **electrostatic dust cloth**.
• Dust the body of the box with a **dry cloth**, or clean it with a solution of **1 part neutral–pH cleaner** (such as liquid hand soap) to **3 parts water**.

Simple solutions

End that TV dust magnet
To reduce the dust-attracting static electricity on your television's screen, wipe it with an antistatic tumble dryer sheet such as *Bounce*.

Tents

Think how dirty you are when you return from a camping trip and then consider how dirty your tent must be. Today's high-performance tents are not cheap. By keeping your tent clean, you'll ensure that the zips stay working longer and prolong the life of the waterproof coating, among other things.

After every camping trip, shake out loose dirt and wipe the floor and door flaps. Use a **soft sponge** and **warm tap water**. Let the tent dry completely before storing. Not only is dirt unsightly, but grit and sand can also wear down the inside of the zip, causing it to stick. (If the zip starts to fail and you have two open sides of fabric behind the zip, use a **pair of pliers** to squeeze both teeth together, so you can retrace your zip backwards.)

Watch out

After washing a tent, make sure that the seams, which stay damp the longest, are dry before storing it. Moisture can cause mildew and mould to grow. Mildew can work its way in between the waterproof coating and the tent fabric, loosening and separating the coating from the fabric as it spreads.

The best tent to take on a camping trip is one that is clean, waterproof and has fully-functioning zips.

To keep zips running smoothly, run a **candle** up and down the teeth every now and again.

Occasionally clean your tent more thoroughly
Set it up outside and lightly spray it with a **garden hose**. Mix up a mild solution of **water** and a **gentle fabric cleaner** such as *Woolite* or – even better – use a **tent soap** (sold at camping stores). Use a **sponge** or **soft cloth** to gently wipe the tent clean. Rinse well, but don't saturate the tent material. Let the tent dry in indirect sunlight. (UV rays can weaken the tent materials.)

To clean mildew from a tent, wash the tent with **soapy water** (as detailed above) and then wipe it out with a solution of **1 cup salt**, **1 cup concentrated lemon juice** and **3 litres of hot water**. Don't rinse. Air-dry. To help prevent mildew, always store your tent in a cool, dry place. Instead of cramming it into a stuff sack, store it loosely in a **large cotton bag** or **box**, so that air can circulate.

If the waterproof coating starts to peel because of mildew or any other cause, reapply a **waterproofing compound**. Look for the appropriate waterproofing product at your local camping store.

To remove plant sap or tar from your tent, try cleaning it off with **vegetable oil** and a **clean cloth**.

Thermos flasks

Clean thermos flasks after each use with hot, soapy water. Scrub them with a bottle brush, if possible. Rinse well and air-dry. Try not to get water between the outer casing and the inner insulating flask.

For stubborn or hard-to-reach stains, fill the thermos with **hot water**, drop in **two denture-cleaning tablets** and let stand overnight. In the morning, rinse with **clean water** and air-dry.

If your thermos has an unpleasant odour that regular washing does not overcome, pour in a few **tablespoons of vinegar** or **bicarbonate of soda**. Fill the thermos the rest of the way with **hot water** and let it sit for half an hour. Then pour the solution out and rinse.

Ties

Ties are more complicated than they appear – and often made in special silks and elaborate weaves. It's all too easy to ruin a tie if you don't know the correct techniques.

Have a tie professionally cleaned once or twice a year, depending on how often you wear it. Clean a visibly dirty or stained tie immediately. Look for a dry-cleaner who's experienced in cleaning silk ties. Ask how they 'finish' the tie after cleaning it. Ties should not be pressed – they should be rolled and reshaped with steam. If you are trying a new dry cleaner, don't give them your best ties first.

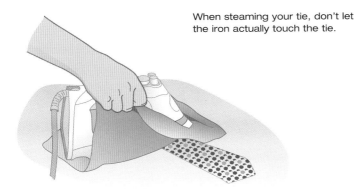

When steaming your tie, don't let the iron actually touch the tie.

If you spill something on your tie, blot away the excess using a **clean white cloth** or **napkin** and then take the tie to a dry cleaner as soon as possible. Stains, especially food stains, tend to set after 24 or 48 hours. Never try to rub the stain out. You might rub the colour from the fabric, especially if it's silk.

Tiles

While they are two dramatically different materials, ceramic and vinyl tiles are both relatively low-maintenance, easy-to-clean surfaces. Both can scratch, however, so keeping them dirt-free reduces the risk of particles rubbing against the tiling and turning into a scratch.

For regular cleaning of floor tiles – both ceramic and vinyl – sweep with a **broom** or **vacuum**. Trapped dirt and sand are highly abrasive and can cause lasting damage to

Watch out

Never put water (or mineral water or any other liquid) on a tie while trying to remove a stain. You might create a larger water mark that is hard to remove. And many of the stains normally found on a tie are oil-based stains, such as salad dressing and gravy which can't be removed with water

Simple solutions

What a heel

To remove black heel marks from tiled floors, rub with a clean white cloth dipped in methylated spirits.

matt and glossy finishes. If you vacuum, avoid using the machine's beater bar, which can permanently damage tile finishes.

Once a week, clean floor tiles by going over them with a **damp mop**. Again, this goes for both ceramic and vinyl tiles. Damp mopping removes stubborn, smeared-on dirt. Never use excessive amounts of water with vinyl tiles, since the water can seep under the tiles and damage the glue. Avoid soapy or oily cleaners, as they can leave a dull film. If anything, add a splash of **vinegar** to the mop water. Or use a **special tile floor cleaner**, such as *HG Shine Cleaner*, sold at tile stores. Follow directions on the package.

For ceramic wall tiles, wipe them regularly with a **damp sponge**. As with floor tiles, avoid soapy or oily cleaners. Add a splash of **vinegar** to the water, or use a **commercial bathroom cleaner**. Never use abrasive scrubbers or cleaning products, such as scouring powders. These can scratch glazed tile, dulling the finish and making it more susceptible to dirt.

To keep grout clean, it's best to do it regularly so that scum and mildew don't have a chance to get a foothold in the porous surface. Indeed, it's a good idea to clean grout after you shower, while it's still steamy moist and the dirt has been loosened. Running the hottest water you can will kill germs. Get out of the shower first – hold the spray into the shower. You don't want to burn yourself. Then, to get things clean, mix together **60ml of vinegar** with **3 litres of water** and scrub the grout with a **toothbrush** or **nylon scrub pad**. For more cleaning power, go over it once with a **degreaser**, such as *HG Grout Cleaner,* from tile shops, which will loosen the germ-harbouring soap scum, then rinse. Let your cleaning products do the work for you. Too much scrubbing will grind the grime in more deeply. Spray or wipe each product on and let it stand for several seconds. Wipe it down with a **clean, wet sponge** to rinse off the cleaning solution. If you must scrub, use a **long-bristled brush** that is not too stiff (you don't want to wear down the grout) or use an **old toothbrush**. Steel wool is too abrasive. If the grout is very dirty, see the box on page 160.

See also **Floors.**

Tin

Tin, silvery white with a brilliant lustre, is used as a decorative plating and to protect metals from rusting. You see it often on Mexican crafts and inexpensive kitchenware. Be careful not to scratch it when cleaning. If you do, you'll invite rust.

Dust decorative items regularly
Use a **feather duster** for pieces with lots of detail. Or wipe with a **dry or slightly damp rag**.

Wash tin items in a solution of **mild washing-up liquid** and **warm water** and a **soft cloth**. Don't use abrasive scrubbers or cleaners, because they may scratch through the tin plating.

To remove rust on tin, rub it with **extra-fine (0000) steel wool**. Once the rust is gone, wash the tin in the **sudsy** solution. Rinse well and dry completely. To prevent rust from returning, apply a thin coat of **paste wax** – a **car wax** is ideal.

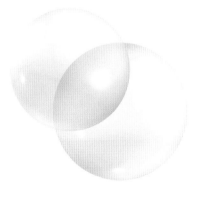

Toasters

Turn bread into toast and you're bound to get crumbs. When the crumbs fall into the toaster, you've got to get them out. Fortunately, most toaster makers are aware of this and design their appliances for easy cleaning.

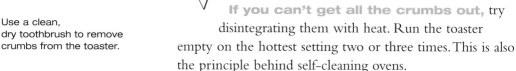

Empty the crumbs out of your toaster once every week or so, depending on how much you use it. Some toasters have slide-out crumb trays; others have hinged doors that allow you to empty the crumbs. No matter what kind of toaster you have or what sort of mechanism it has for crumb removal, always unplug the toaster before you start cleaning it.

If you can't get all the crumbs out, try disintegrating them with heat. Run the toaster empty on the hottest setting two or three times. This is also the principle behind self-cleaning ovens.

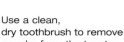

Use a clean, dry toothbrush to remove crumbs from the toaster.

For hard-to-remove crumbs, use a **clean, dry toothbrush**. Again, be sure the toaster is unplugged. Loosen crumbs with the brush and then dump them out. Turn the toaster upside down and shake. Do it gently, being careful not to damage the heating element.

Wipe down the outside of the toaster with a **damp cloth**. Wipe around the control knobs. Add a dash of **vinegar** or squirt of **washing-up liquid** to the cleaning water for more cleaning power. For stainless steel toasters, polish with a **stainless steel polish**.

Toilets

We all have to clean toilets. There's no getting around that. But most people are not very efficient at cleaning their toilets. And many are stumped by the stubborn rings that get left around the bowl.

To clean a toilet, work from the top down. Start with the tank, move to the seat, clean inside the bowl and then clean the base. Doing it this way will help you focus. Moreover, the dirtiest part of the toilet – and therefore the last place you want your rag to touch – is the base. For everything but the bowl, use a **dry cloth** and a **spray-on bathroom cleaner**. Spray the cleaner on the toilet surface and wipe it off with the cloth. Keeping the cloth dry makes it easier to wipe everything up. Wet it and you'll be chasing that moisture around and have to wring out the cloth, too. Avoid sponges, which work quite well but can absorb – and transfer – microorganisms.

Clean the bowl with a **rounded bowl brush** and cleaner. Avoid brushes with metal wire, since they may scratch the bowl. (For rings around the bowl see right.)

To clean around the hardware that holds the seat to the toilet and the toilet to the floor, use a **grout brush** or an **old toothbrush**.

Tools

In the old days, toolmakers dated their tools – carving the year into the wooden block of a plane, for example – in the expectation that the tools would last for generations. Back then, a tool would last a long time if its owner took care of it. The same is true today. Here's how.

The most basic goal with hand tools, especially those made of wood and metal, is to keep them dry. If a tool gets wet, wipe it dry. If it gets sweaty or dusty, clean it with a damp cloth and then wipe it dry with another cloth. Water can rust a saw blade and warp a wooden level.

Keep retractable measuring tapes free of dirt, sand, dust and other debris. These foreign objects can scratch the coating. Once it is scratched, the metal tape will rust. Wipe the tape clean with a **dry cloth** frequently. Don't use a wet cloth – and don't let your tape get wet. Moisture will find its way into the spring mechanism and will rust it. To remove tar and glue from the tape, use **methylated spirits**.

See also Garden tools and Power tools.

Simple solutions

Ring around the bowl

For stubborn rings around the toilet bowl, use a pumice stone, available at chemists, where it's sold to help you get hard skin off your feet. Keeping the stone wet, rub it on the ring until it's gone. This works for old rings as well. It will not scratch white vitreous china, which is what most toilets are made of, but it will scratch glassfibre, enamel, plastic and other materials. So don't try this if your toilet is made of one of these.

Watch out

Avoid oiling most tools (garden tools are the exception), since the oil may get on the handle, causing the tool to slip dangerously.

Toys

The main issue in cleaning toys is to never use anything toxic. Even if your son or daughter no longer chews on toys, hands will end up in mouths, since young children don't understand the concept of germs.

Wash toys regularly to keep them clean and bacteria-free. Wash rubber and plastic toys with **warm water** combined with a squirt of **washing-up liquid**. Wipe clean with a **soft cloth** or **sponge**. Be careful of painted-on features, such as faces, numbers or other designs. These could rub off. Dry with a **cloth** or leave to air-dry. For larger plastic toys, such as plastic sit-in cars and plastic playhouses, use a **hose**, a **bucket of soapy water** and a **soft-bristled scrubbing brush**.

Wipe down metal toys, such as tractors and cars, using a **damp cloth**. Water leads to rust, so avoid soap (since suds require rinsing) and don't submerge such toys. If a metal toy or a toy with metal parts gets wet, dry it quickly with a **hair dryer** to avoid rusting. If there are batteries, beeping sounds or blinking lights, don't wet the toy. Water will completely ruin the circuitry.

Clean wooden toys with a mild solution of a **neutral cleaner**, such as *Pledge Soapy Cleaner* and **water**. (Follow the manufacturer's directions for amounts.) Use a **cloth** or **soft-bristled brush**. Don't soak or submerge the wooden toy. Instead, dip the cloth or brush in the soapy water and wipe the toy clean. Rinse with a **clean cloth** and plain water. Dry with a **clean, dry towel**. If the toy is scratched, splintered, or chipped, or if the water has raised the grain (making the wood feel rough), lightly sand it with **fine glasspaper** once the toy has dried.

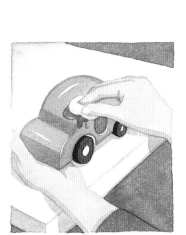

Don't saturate wooden toys with oil when cleaning them – use small amounts and wipe clean.

If a wood toy has a natural, oil-based finish, reapply **oil** to keep the wood conditioned. Since toys often end up in children's mouths (wooden baby chew toys are expressly meant for this purpose), use a **food-grade vegetable oil**. Allow the oil to penetrate for about an hour and then wipe off the excess.

It is especially important not to clean wooden toys with harsh chemicals, because wood absorbs and harbours such chemicals which could harm a child if ingested.

Clean Barbies and similar dolls by wiping with a
cloth and **water** mixed with a little **washing-up liquid**.
Wash hair with **baby shampoo**. (A drop of **hair
conditioner** will soften the hair.) Don't use any heat
source, such as a hair dryer, to dry the hair, as that will turn
it frizzy. Instead, comb the hair out gently, starting from the
bottom and working up to remove tangles. Let the doll air-
dry. For more doll-cleaning advice, see **Dolls.**

See also **Soft toys.**

Trainers

To wash or not to wash in a washing machine? That's the
main question about cleaning trainers, which can get very
dirty and smelly. And the answer is: it depends.

Most shoe manufacturers discourage machine-washing
because detergents and the machine's agitation don't agree
with many leathers and adhesives and can ruin their shape.
But some simple canvas or all-synthetic shoes can safely take
a spin in the washer.

Before cleaning any type of trainer, check the
care label. If they are older and you have no label, you have
to decide whether it's worth the risk – perhaps because they
are just too dirty without a machine wash anyway. Take out
the laces and wash these too. Put them into a mesh bag and
into the machine.

For leather trainers, it's best to use a **regular leather
cleaner and conditioner**. Don't use saddle soap. It may be
great for saddles, but it can damage other kinds of leather.

To clean canvas or synthetic trainers in a
washing machine, spray them first with a **stain removal
spray**, especially if they are grass stained. Wipe the spray
around the shoe, let it sit for a couple of minutes and then
put the shoes in the wash. Include **light-coloured towels**
in the wash. The rubbing action of the towels will not only
help clean the trainers, but will also keep them from
bouncing around.

**To clean canvas and synthetic trainers by
hand,** rinse the shoes in **clear water** and then use a **soft**

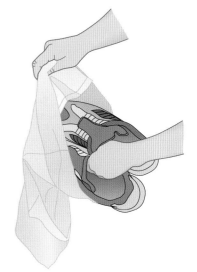

Put trainers in a mesh bag
before putting them in the
washing machine.

brush to scrub the shoes with a **neutral cleaner**, such as a **non-scented liquid hand wash**. For scuff marks, scour with a **white, nylon-backed scrubbing pad**. Rinse to remove all traces of detergent and then air-dry. Stuff the shoes with **white paper** to retain their shape.

As an alternative for canvas trainers, squirt on some **foam shaving cream**, let it sit for half an hour and brush off what remains. Then wipe the canvas surface with a **clean, damp cloth**.

To give your trainers a fresh smell, place a **sheet of fabric softener** in them overnight. Or make a **bicarbonate of soda sachet** by placing a couple of **teaspoons of bicarbonate of soda** in the centre of a **cotton cloth**. Close the cloth around the bicarbonate of soda and secure it with a **string** or **rubber band.** Put one sachet in each shoe overnight. You can reuse the sachets in any kind of shoe.

Simple solutions

Keep your tumble dryer's duct clean

If you keep your dryer's filter clean but it still isn't as efficient as it used to be, the duct ushering the air outside may be blocked. Detach the duct from the back of your dryer and clean it out. (Do this once a year as a matter of course.) Make sure the vent cover on the outside of your house is in place. (Replacements are available at DIY stores.)

Tumble dryers

When cleaning a dryer, the most important task is to clean the filter. Dryers work by heating air, drawing it across your wet clothes to sop up the moisture and pushing the soggy air outside through a vent or condensing it into water and storing this in a tank that you empty regularly.

The most modern tumble dryers have alerts to remind you to clean the filters that collect lint before or after every load of clothes. Look in your manual for how to pull out the removable metal or plastic filters. Hold it over the bin, whilst scraping the little blanket of lint off the filter with your hand. If some of the lint won't come free, you might take the filter to a sink and clean it with **warm water** and a **mild washing-up liquid** or get those bits next time around.

If you discover crayon marks inside your dryer, run the dryer empty for five minutes to soften up the marks. Then wipe them away with a **cloth** dipped in a solution of **water** and **washing-up liquid**.

See also Washing machines.

Typewriters

Many people still like to use a typewriter – the thunk of the keys is very satisfying. Like record players or telephones with dials, these have yet to die out completely. So if you don't want to enter the computer age, here's how to keep your typewriter clean so that you don't have to.

Dust your typewriter regularly Use a **vacuum cleaner** with an **upholstery attachment** to suck the dust out, or the reverse – a can of **compressed air**, available at office supply stores – to blow it out. Alternatively you can brush carefully between the keys using a **small, dry paintbrush**.

Wipe the case and body of the typewriter with a **clean, lint-free cloth** lightly moistened with a **commercial window cleaner** – the emphasis here is on *lightly* moistened. You shouldn't risk letting liquid drip into the body of the typewriter, especially if it is an electric typewriter. Wipe the key tops, buttons and bars. Fight the urge to use paper towels, since they may tear and leave little pieces stuck in the mechanism.

To clean beneath the keys, wrap the same cloth around the end of a **letter opener** and gently work it between the keys.

Wipe the black roller, known as the platen, with the same cloth. It is likely to have ink on it (especially if you have children who like to press the keys without paper in the machine). The ink may or may not come completely off. Don't worry. A little leftover ink is better than trying to remove it with an ink stain remover that contains alcohol, which will dry the platen out and make it brittle. It needs to remain soft and slightly pliable. The ammonia in the glass cleaner will help condition the platen.

Have your typewriter professionally lubricated every so often. Don't try to do it yourself. You might do more harm than good.

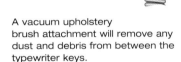

A vacuum upholstery brush attachment will remove any dust and debris from between the typewriter keys.

Umbrellas

Umbrellas don't get very dirty, which is fortunate, because they've got to be among the most awkward things in the world to clean – like trying to bathe a stork. But whilst personal umbrellas usually get along without attention, you may need to clean large patio umbrellas, especially those left permanently outside through the summer months which may collect tree pollen, wet leaves and bird droppings.

To clean a personal umbrella, just let the rain do the job the next time it showers. To prevent mould and mildew, open the umbrella and let it dry thoroughly before you put it away. If you want to clean it more thoroughly, open it up, spray it with a **hose**, and scrub gently with a **sponge** dipped in **warm water** with a squirt of **washing-up liquid**. Rinse and dry thoroughly before storing it.

To remove dirt, pollen and bird droppings from a patio umbrella – which is usually made of either vinyl or a coarse fabric – spray it with a **garden hose**. Then scrub it with a **nylon-bristled brush** dipped in a **bucket** containing a sudsy solution of **warm water** and **washing-up liquid**. Rinse by spraying the umbrella with the hose.

Protect a patio umbrella's metal rods by polishing them with **car wax**. Wax also makes the metal easier to clean in the future. Following the manufacturer's directions, lightly wax the metal. Take care not to get the wax on the umbrella covering, as it can stain fabric and gunk up vinyl mesh.

Upholstery

Upholstery poses a cleaning challenge, since it almost always covers some sort of padding – be it cotton batting or foam rubber – and because it's often not removable.

Even when upholstery material can be removed from the padding, as in the case of zip-up sofa cushions, some experts warn against removing and washing it.

Sofas sold as having loose covers are, of course different: for most, you can simply use the washing machine to clean the covers. Just follow care instructions on the labels. The danger of taking off cushion covers from fixed upholstery is that they may not fit back on the cushions. There may also be some fading, which could make your sofa arms look very dark in contrast. Assuming you're leaving everything in situ, the most basic aim with most upholstery cleaning is to clean without soaking the padding beneath.

Vacuum upholstery regularly to remove dust and dust mites. Use an **upholstery attachment** with a gentle **brush end**, so you don't damage the upholstery material. Use a crevice tool attachment for nooks and crannies. If your upholstered piece is stuffed with feathers, do not vacuum it unless it is lined with a down-proof ticking fabric. You might suck the feathers out. If you have no vacuum-cleaner attachments, brush the dust away with a **soft-bristled brush** at least once a month. Dust, when moistened or ground in, can stain upholstery.

Upholstery stain-removal basics To find out what specific solution you should use to remove a particular stain – what takes out chocolate or grease, for example – see the Stains section on pages 46–77. Meanwhile, here are some general tips for removing stains from upholstery:

1 Remove as much of the stain-causing material as you can by blotting with paper towels or scraping with a dull knife. When blotting up a large stain, always blot from the edge of the stain to the centre to contain it.

2 Avoid rubbing or pushing the stain deeper into the upholstery.

3 Since you never want to soak an upholstered cushion or piece of furniture, spray bottles are good for lightly applying water-based cleaning solutions and rinse water. You can buy one cheaply at a garden centre.

4 To dry upholstery that has been rinsed with water, lay a pad of paper towels on the spot and place a weight, such as a brick or a hardback book on the pad. (Put the brick or book in a plastic bag or on a piece of foil to prevent colour transfer to the upholstery.) Let the upholstery dry and then remove the towels.

For more thorough cleaning, or to remove stains, your upholstery will need washing. First, check the upholstery manufacturer's suggestions, usually tagged to your item. This tag will tell you whether you should use a **water-based shampoo**, a **dry-cleaning solvent** or neither of the two. Next, pick an inconspicuous spot on the upholstery and pretest whatever cleaning technique is recommended. If there is any shrinking, bleeding or the colours run, contact a professional cleaner. If not, proceed.

If shampooing is safe, use as little moisture as possible. It is important not to wet the upholstery's stuffing, because it dries very slowly and can attract dust mites and mould. Clean using suds only. The easiest method is to use a **foaming commercial shampoo** in an aerosol can. Follow the directions on the can, which typically will tell you to allow the foam to stand until dry and then to vacuum it off.

To make your own upholstery shampoo, mix ½ **teaspoon of washing-up liquid** per **1 litre of warm water**. Make suds by squeezing a **sponge** in the solution.

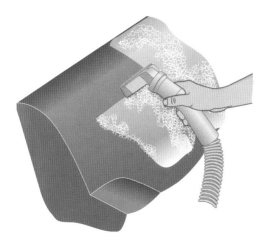

A commercial foaming shampoo should be perfectly dry before you attempt to vacuum it off upholstery.

Scoop the suds off the top, applying them sparingly with the **sponge** to the upholstery. Rub gently in the direction of the fabric's grain. Rather than letting the suds dry as you would with a commercial shampoo, work on a small area at a time, lightly rinsing each area as you go with a **clean, damp sponge**. Again, avoid soaking the fabric. Be sure to remove all the suds or the residue will cause the fabric to become dirty more quickly.

If the fabric calls for dry cleaning only and the upholstery is portable, have it professionally cleaned. If, however, you are cleaning a stain – or if the upholstery is part of a large piece of furniture – you can do it yourself, using a **commercial dry-cleaning solvent**. Don't pour the solvent on the stain. Instead, moisten a **clean, white cloth** with the solvent and use the cloth to draw the stain out. Blot repeatedly – never rub. Rubbing can stretch or damage the texture of the fabric. Always use solvents sparingly and in a well-ventilated area. And don't use them on upholstery filled with latex foam rubber padding, because the solvent can dissolve the padding.

V

Vases

Dirty vases not only look unattractive, but they also reduce the lifespan of the cut flowers you keep in them. The residue in vases, including growth such as algae, plugs up the stems and causes the flowers to dry up more quickly.

The easiest way to clean vases is to scrub them with **hot, soapy water** and a **bottle brush**. Rinse well and let them dry completely before storing.

Simple solutions

Narrow-neck vases

If you can't get to the inside walls of a vase with a bottle brush, fill the vase with hot water and dissolve a couple of denture-cleaning tablets – *Sterident* tablets, for instance – in the vase and let it stand overnight. Rinse well and dry.

Swirl a mixture of white vinegar and rock salt in a vase to remove white mineral deposits inside it.

To remove white mineral deposit stains from the inside of vases, swirl a mixture of **sea salt** and **vinegar** around inside the vase. The salt will gently scour the surface while the vinegar breaks down the deposits.

VCRs & videotapes

As with any electronic gear, the cleaner you keep your VCR, the better all the small parts will work – and the longer the piece of equipment will last. That said, don't open up your VCR for interior cleaning. You can cause more harm than good. Luckily, the insides rarely need cleaning if you keep the outside clean. The only interior part you need to keep clean is the playback head – but you can do that with a head-cleaning tape.

Watch out

Avoid video cassette-cleaning machines. Because these devices sometimes involve rewinding machines, they often damage the tape by stretching it.

Clean the front panel with a **soft cotton cloth** and **glass cleaner**. (First, turn off the VCR.) Don't use paper towels as they can tear and shed lint. Don't spray the glass cleaner directly on the unit. Instead, spray it on the cloth and gently wipe the cloth on the panel. For sensitive areas, such as around the panel control knobs and buttons, dust with a **small, dry paintbrush**. Don't apply cleaner to these areas, since it could seep into the controls. This way, you won't accidentally change your control settings, either.

To clean the chassis of the VCR – that is, the sides and top – use a **soft cloth** either dry or lightly misted with **glass cleaner**. Don't wet the cloth, since any residue left on the chassis may collect dust and lead to corrosion. Never spray anything directly on the chassis. Wipe away from the vent holes (not toward them) to avoid pushing dust into the workings of the VCR.

Dust the back of the unit, where the cables plug in, with a **dry paintbrush**. Don't use cleaner around this sensitive area. If you must remove the cables to access the back, be forewarned: many units store information for user settings, clock and timers, and this memory can be lost when the unit is unplugged from the electrical outlet.

Wipe cables down with a cloth misted with the same cleaner you used on the panels. Be careful not to pull the cables out as you wipe.

Clean the playback head periodically – once every few months, depending on use, or when the playback quality indicates a problem. If you rent a lot of videotapes, you may need to clean more often, since rental tapes bring with them dirt and debris picked up from all the other VCRs they've been played in.

Use a good-quality **dry head–cleaning cassette** – 'dry' because the liquid that sometimes comes with head-cleaning cassettes may not evaporate completely before another tape is inserted, which can worsen the situation by attracting grime from the tape to the playback head. Always read your owner's manual. If your VCR incorporates an automatic head–cleaning system, the manufacturer may recommend that you do not use any kind of head-cleaning tape.

If you need to clean a videotape's case, carefully wipe it with a **damp cloth**. Make sure you don't wet the tape itself or the tape path. Remove any labels or adhesives that are coming off. Labels that have fallen off are one of the biggest causes of tape jams.

Rules of the game

Step-by-step VCR cleaning

Clean the outside of the VCR whenever you dust. Clean the playback head every few months, depending on use – or whenever playback indicates a problem.

1 Turn off the VCR.

2 Spray glass cleaner on a soft cloth and gently wipe the front panel.

3 Dust control knobs and buttons with a small, dry paintbrush. Don't use cleaner on these areas.

4 Clean the sides and top with a soft cloth either dry or lightly misted with glass cleaner.

5 Dust the rear with a dry paintbrush. Wipe cables with a cloth misted with glass cleaner.

6 Clean the playback head with a good-quality dry head-cleaning cassette. First, check your owner's manual.

Velcro

When Velcro gets 'dirty' – meaning the two sides get clogged up with lint and fuzz balls – it stops working. When that Velcro is attached to a pair of sandals or a handbag, you might be tempted to get rid of the sandals or handbag. Don't. It's easy to freshen Velcro up so that it works the way it did when it was new.

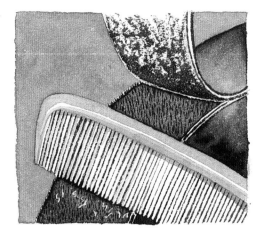

Running a fine-toothed comb along Velcro will get it looking and sticking like new again.

To remove lint from the bristly side of Velcro, use a **fine-toothed comb**. Gently comb out the lint and hair and stray threads. If possible, submerge the Velcro in water while combing.

To remove lint from the soft side of Velcro, use the **sticky side of gaffer tape** the way you would use a lint roller.

To keep Velcro fresh, seal the two parts together when it's not in use or while machine-washing. If you need to, buy extra Velcro tape from a fabric or craft store and use that to seal the Velcro.

If the worst comes to the worst, instead of throwing away the shoe or handbag, replace the Velcro. It is available from most haberdashery stores.

Vents

Located in floors, walls and ceilings, vents typically have angled louvres to keep large debris from getting into the house, whilst still allowing in air. These louvres also collect lint and dust. Fortunately, they are easy to access.

An upholstery brush attachment will pick up dust on a vent.

Vacuum the outside of the vent frequently
Make it part of your regular vacuuming routine, and you'll cut down on dust and lint build-up considerably. Use a **brush attachment**, which helps loosen dust.

At least twice a year, remove registers and returns and clean both sides of them. Try cleaning them with the **vacuum**. If that does not completely remove the dust, wipe them with a **moist dust cloth**. If you replace filters behind your returns more often than twice a year, clean the return vents every time you remove them.

Vinyl

Vinyl exterior surfaces are often advertised as being maintenance free. But that doesn't mean you don't have to do some cleaning, even if you do have a conservatory or window frames made of this tough, water-repelling coating.

To wash exterior vinyl use a **garden hose** attached to a **long-handled car brush attachment** (*Flash Power Car Wash System*, for instance). If you don't have one, make up buckets of **water**, squeezing a dash of **washing-up liquid** into each. Use a **sponge** or, for speed – a **kitchen sponge mop** and **water**. If mildew is a problem, use a solution of **50ml chlorine bleach** per **5 litres of water**, applying this with a **squeeze out kitchen mop** for speed and accurate coverage. Rinse off thoroughly.

Exterior vinyl may need to be washed every 12 to 18 months, depending on the climate and the presence of air pollutants.

For a more thorough wash, use a **pressure washer**, which you can hire from *HSS Hire Shops* for the day or weekend. Remember to wear **safety goggles**. Move methodically from side to side from the bottom up, reversing direction for the rinse cycle.

To clean articles made of vinyl, here are several cleaners to try:
• A little **liquid washing-up liquid** in **warm water**.
• For mould and mildew, a solution of **1 part white vinegar** to **2 parts water**.

To keep vinyl soft and pliable, rub a little **petroleum jelly** into the surface and then buff with a **soft cloth**. Or use a **vinyl cleaner/conditioner**, which you can buy at hardware and car supply stores.

Petroleum jelly will help to keep your vinyl items soft and pliable.

Wall coverings

The most common wall covering is washable wallpaper, which is treated with vinyl for easier cleaning. But many other coverings exist, including delicate papers; fabrics, such as cotton, linen, silk, rayon, hessian and velvet; and coverings made from grass, reeds, hemp, cork or leather. They generally are not washable, although some gentle cleaning methods won't hurt them.

Simple solutions

Smudged wallpaper

• To remove fingerprints and smudges, try an art rubber, available at arts and crafts and office supply stores.
• To remove greasy spots, make a paste of plain flour and water. Apply to the spot, let it dry, and vacuum up.
• To remove wax, heavy crayon or grease,
hold a double thickness of greaseproof paper on the spot and press it with a warm iron.

To determine whether wallpaper is washable, wet an inconspicuous area with a solution of a little washing-up liquid and water. If the paper absorbs water or darkens or if the colours run, it's not washable.

To clean washable wallpaper
• Don't flood the surface with water, over-wet the seams or edges or leave water on for more than a minute.
• Don't scrub unless the manufacturer says the covering is scrubbable.
• Don't use harsh, abrasive cleaners.

To clean other wall coverings, vacuum regularly, using the **small brush attachment**. Some people also swear by using **white bread**. Simply ball up a slice until it is doughy in your hand, then roll it onto the dirty area. This should pick dirt up off the wallpaper. Keep going, with fresh pieces of bread, but making sure an already dirty surface never touches your wall.

Walls

There are two major sources of the dirt that gets on walls: the kind that comes off people's hands and the type that comes out of thin air. How often your walls need washing will depend largely on the hands and air that touch them. If you have a smoker or a wood-burning stove or fireplace in the house, your walls will show it. If you have children – they will add their own special touches to the walls.

To dust walls, a **lamb's wool duster** works well. Or wrap a **microfibre dust cloth** or **clean white cloth** around a **broom** and dust with that. It's especially useful on the highest parts of the walls and the ceiling.

To remove spots, rub gently with a **white art rubber**, available at arts and crafts and office supply stores or with a paste of **bicarbonate of soda** and **water**. Use **white spirit** on grease and *WD-40* (both available at hardware stores) on crayon marks. Use **methylated spirits** on ink or marker spots.

Apply cleaners to the cloth, not the wall and test on an inconspicuous area first. There is a big danger that, with the alcohol, you will also pull paint off the wall. So try to go just along the stain line. You are trying to dissolve the stain – the ink – in your solvent – yet not have enough solvent left over to dissolve the painted wall beneath.

To wash down walls that are painted or covered with washable vinyl paper use:

• **200ml of ammonia**, **1 teaspoon of washing-up liquid** and **4 litres of water**.
• *Sugar Soap* cleaner, made up as directed – on sale at DIY stores.

Keep the cleaning solution in one bucket and plain water for rinsing in another bucket. To protect the floor, use a dust sheet. To keep water from running down your arms when they're raised, wrap **rags** around your wrists and hold them on with **rubber bands** or **elasticated hair ties**.

To clean the walls, wash with one of the solutions mentioned above using a **natural sponge** or a **white cloth**. Follow the guidelines in the Rules of the Game sidebar for applying the cleaning solution. Reach the high points by standing on a sturdy **stepladder** tall enough so you won't need to stand on the upper two steps.

See also **Painted surfaces** and **Wall coverings.**

Rules of the game

Start at the bottom; work your way up

Almost everywhere you clean, you're advised to start at the top and work down. However, some (but not all) professional decorators don't do this when washing walls. They start at the bottom and go up. The logic is that dirty water running down a dirty wall leaves worse streaks than dirty water running down a clean wall. Either way, if your wall is filthy, you'll still do an awful lot of mopping up. But why not give this way a go first?

1 Apply cleaning solution over a small area at the bottom.
2 Wash, using circular strokes.
3 Rinse with plain water.
4 Dry with a towel.
5 Move up.

Washing machines

Every now and then you have to give back. That is, clean the washers and dryers that do so much cleaning for you. Fortunately, it's easy to do – and these machines even help to clean themselves occasionally.

Cleaning the exterior of your washer or dryer is very easy indeed. The most common spots are blotches of spilled laundry detergent, fabric softener or bleach. They're all designed to respond best to warm water, so wipe them up with a cloth dipped in a solution of **warm water** and **mild washing-up liquid**, which will vanquish dirt and accumulated dust, too.

To clean inside your washing machine open it up and wipe down the inside of the door using the same solution of **warm water** and **mild washing-up liquid** on the cloth that you used on the exterior. Use an **old toothbrush** to clean the crevices of the moulded frame around the door. If you have a removable detergent cup, take it out to clean it. If it's built in, clean it as thoroughly as you can, using a **pipe cleaner**, if necessary. The rest of the interior of your washing machine gets a pretty good cleaning every time you use it.

To cure residual musty odours, run the machine through a wash cycle without any clothes in it. Use the hottest temperature setting available and a medium or high water level. While the washing machine is filling pour in **200ml of bleach**. As a preventive measure, follow this routine once a year.

Waste disposal units

These small, but extremely useful kitchen appliances have their own built-in scrubbing action. To keep your unit smelling fresh and running properly, all you need are a few common household items.

To keep food waste from building up inside your disposer, keep these rules in mind:
• Grind only small amounts of food at a time.
• After you've finished grinding food, run a steady, rapid flow of **cold water** for up to 30 seconds. Even if instinct tells you that hot water cleans better, stick to cold water. It solidifies fatty and greasy wastes so they will be chopped up and flushed down the drain.
• Don't pour oil or grease through the disposer.
• Don't grind large bones. (Small bones are safe and even help break up grease deposits.)
• Don't grind bulky, fibrous materials like sweetcorn kernels.
• Never put caustic soda or chemical drain cleaners into your disposal unit.

Simple solutions

Get rid of drain smells

If you won't be at home for several days, make sure no food wastes that might start to smell are left in the disposer. To flush any residue, plug the sink, fill it with around 6cm of water and run the disposer while the water drains.

To remove any fatty wastes that build up inside the disposer, periodically grind a handful of **ice cubes** mixed with **100ml of bicarbonate of soda**. Together the powder and cubes (which of course are cold) will safely scour the inside of the unit. To eliminate odours, grind **lemon** or **orange peel** through every so often.

Waste paper baskets

The details of cleaning waste paper baskets vary according to the materials they're made of. However, always take the waste out of the basket before you start any cleaning.

To clean a waste paper basket made of a natural material – such as cardboard, paper, wicker, straw or wood – use a **vacuum cleaner** with the **small brush attachment**. If the basket becomes soiled, wipe it with a **damp cloth** or **sponge**. Don't use harsh cleaners.

To clean a plastic or metal waste paper basket, wash it with a solution of **60ml bicarbonate of soda** in **4 litres of warm water**. Use a **cloth**, a **sponge** or, for more challenging dirt, a **stiff brush**. Rinse and dry with a **soft cloth**.

To clean the kitchen waste bin at the same time you're mopping the kitchen floor, just mix up your **cleaner-and-water solution** in the bin instead of in a bucket. During the 10 or 15 minutes it takes to mop the floor, the dirt in the bin will be loosening. When you pour out the mop water, give the interior of the bin a once-over with a **stiff brush**, rinse with **running water** and dry with a **cloth**.

Simple solutions

Less wasteful waste handling

Using a liner makes cleaning a waste paper basket easier. But don't always buy brand-new plastic bags to line your waste paper baskets. It's a big waste when households are awash in used but perfectly usable plastic bags from shopping and other sources. For pedal bins and bins used in bedrooms and living rooms (rather than eating rooms) used paper bags also make fine liners (except when wet items are involved).

Watches

Salt water is one of your watch's biggest enemies and your watch is exposed to daily in the form of sweat. Other contaminants include skin oils, dirt and substances such as lotions and insect repellents. Clean only the band and the outside of the watch, leaving the inner workings in the hands of a professional watch mender.

For regular cleaning, wipe the band and watch with a **damp cloth**, then again with a **clean, dry cloth**.

For more extensive cleaning, remove the band by releasing the pins on both sides of the watch.
• Clean a leather band with **saddle soap**, followed by buffing with a dry cloth.
• Wash a cloth band with a little **washing-up liquid** and **water**, rinse in **clean water** and lay flat to dry.
• Clean a metal band by soaking it in a solution of **washing-up liquid** and **water**. Use an **old toothbrush** to scrub. Rinse in **clean water** and dry with a **soft cloth**.

Check the crystal and have it replaced immediately if you notice any damage to it or to the face of the watch, which indicates moisture has entered. A jeweller can also buff out scratches in a plastic crystal.

To store your watch, keep it in an individual compartment in a jewellery box or wrap it in a piece of soft cloth.

To clean the inner workings, take the watch to a professional. Mechanical watches (the kind you wind) need an overhaul about every two years and analogue quartz watches (with hands and batteries) need one every three to five years, just about when you need to replace the battery anyway. Digital watches, which have no mechanical works, don't need an internal cleaning, although you will eventually need to replace the battery.

Water heaters

All water has some sediment in it and over time in a water heater, this can cause mineral build-up and eventually clog your heater quite seriously. So try some preventive tips.

To counteract mineral build-up, you have a number of choices:
• Have a plumber flush the heater or install a water softener.
• Buy a 'self-cleaning' water heater.
• Buy a 'tankless' water heater. It's more expensive, but it's also more energy efficient.
• Flush the heater yourself.

If you decide to do the job, here's how:

1 Turn off the heater and the cold water that runs into it.

2 Hook a **garden hose** to the drain valve (the one near the bottom of the tank). Make sure there are no kinks in the hose. Put the other end of it where you want the hot water from the tank to go.

3 Open the drain valve.

4 Disconnect the cold water inlet pipe on the top of the water heater to let air into the water heater so it will drain. After all the water has drained, close the drain valve.

5 Pour **4 litres of a food-grade delimer** (available at plumbing supply stores and hardware stores) or **vinegar** into the cold water inlet pipe. Pour only 200ml at a time and pause between each. Let it work for several hours.

6 Drain the cleaner.

7 Reconnect the cold water inlet pipe, open the valve and let water run through the heater for several minutes, flushing out the cleaner and dissolved sediment.

8 Close the drain valve and open the hot-water tap nearest to the water heater. Let the water heater fill up.

9 When water comes out of the open tap, re-open the drain valve and let the water heater rinse until the water appears clear.

10 Close the drain valve and open all the hot-water taps to remove the air from the heater and pipes.

11 Turn the water heater back on and remove the garden hose from the drain valve.

Wheelchairs

Regular cleaning and careful maintenance of a wheelchair is well worth the effort and will easily repay your hard work. Your wheelchair will run far more smoothly and last much longer.

To clean a wheelchair, wash the frame, wheels, tyres, seat and back with **warm water** and a little **washing-up liquid**. Apply with a **clean cloth** or **sponge**, rinse with **plain water** and dry with a **clean cloth**. Don't get water in the wheel or caster bearings. This kind of cleaning should be done about once a month. For daily cleaning, wiping with a **damp cloth** is usually sufficient.

To clean the caster axle bolts, remove the bolt, wipe crud away with a **cleaning cloth** and put back the bolt. This spot tends to collect hair, string and other debris that will make the chair harder to propel.

To clean the axles, remove the wheels and wipe the axles with a **clean cloth** containing a few drops of **oil** (whatever oil is recommended by your owner's manual). This area, which can accumulate mud and dirt quickly, should be cleaned once a month or more.

To clean between different users, wipe the chair with a disinfectant.

Whirlpool baths

Whirlpool baths have two distinct dimensions that require cleaning: the external surfaces and, more crucially, the unseen intricacies of the circulation system.

To clean the bath surfaces, wipe with a cloth after each use. Clean periodically with a solution of **hot water** and **washing-up liquid** and rinse. Don't use abrasive scrubbers or cleaners, which will harm the glossy finish.

To clean the circulation system, follow the instructions that came with your unit. Or do this:

1 Adjust the jets so they are not drawing air.
2 Leave the water in the whirlpool after using.
3 Add the whole of a large bottle of **white vinegar**.
4 Alternatively try **2 teaspoons of powdered dishwasher detergent** and **300ml of chlorine bleach**.
5 Run the whirlpool system, following the operating instructions, for 5 to 10 minutes.
6 Drain and refill with **cold water**. Circulate for five minutes.
7 Drain and wipe dry with a **clean cloth**.

How often you clean the circulation system depends on the recommendation of the manufacturer and how often you use the whirlpool. Recommendations vary from once every three months to twice a month or more.

Wicker, rattan & bamboo

Wicker is not a single material. It's a term for something made of any of several materials that are bent and woven together. The most common are rattan (the solid-cored vine of a climbing palm), cane (the skin or bark of large rattans), reed (swamp grasses or rattan core), bamboo (a large grass with a hollow core), willow and twisted paper fibre (the kind used in Lloyd Loom furniture).

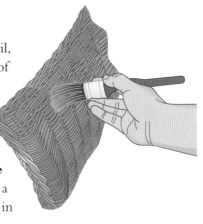

Use turpentine and linseed oil on natural wicker to prevent dryness and cracking.

Wicker comes in many finishes, ranging from natural to oil, varnish, shellac or paint. There are also synthetic versions of wicker made from resin, plastic or glassfibre. And when it comes to cleaning, the materials aren't all the same.

When cleaning synthetic wicker, you can be aggressive. This is the only wicker that should be allowed to remain outdoors. Clean it with a **garden hose** and **plain water**, using a **cloth** or **sponge** or scrub with a **stiff brush** and a solution of a little **washing–up liquid** in **water**. Rinse with the **hose** and dry with a **clean cloth**.

To clean natural-fibre wicker, keep furniture free of dirt with a **vacuum cleaner**, using the **brush attachment**. Other useful tools are a **toothbrush**, a **stiff paintbrush** and a **pencil–sized dowel** sharpened in a pencil sharpener. Wipe the wicker with a **damp cloth** or **sponge**, but undertake more extensive wet cleaning cautiously. Consult an expert before doing any major cleaning or refinishing of antique pieces. To find an expert, check with antiques dealers or on the internet.

To wash most natural-fibre wicker, use a solution of a little **mild soap** – *Carex* handwash, for example or a squirt of **washing–up liquid** – in **warm water**. Wipe with a **cloth** or **sponge** wrung out in the solution. Rinse with a **garden hose** and dry quickly – in the sun or with a **hair dryer** or **fan**. Don't sit on the furniture for two or three days, as you could stretch the fibres and cause them to sag.

There are some exceptions Don't hose down bamboo or twisted paper wicker. Clean these with a **sponge** dampened with **soapy water**, followed by a **sponge** moistened with **clear water**. Wipe dry.

To treat for dryness and cracking, use **1 part turpentine** to **2 parts boiled linseed oil** on natural-fibre wicker, except for bamboo. Apply with a **paintbrush**, using as much as the wicker will absorb. Wipe off any excess with a **cloth** and let it dry for three or four days. For bamboo, apply a thin coat of **liquid** or **paste wax** periodically.

Wigs

Wigs are made of synthetic materials, human hair or a combination of the two. Synthetic wigs are easier to care for but not as versatile in accepting styling. For example, heat, such as that from a curling iron, can ruin them. Human hair wigs can be coloured, permed and curled with a curling iron or heated rollers.

To wash a wig, follow these steps:
1 Gently straighten the hair with a **comb**.
2 Draw **water** – cool to lukewarm, not hot – into a **pan** large enough to immerse the wig.
3 Dissolve about **1 tablespoon each of shampoo** and **bicarbonate of soda** in the water.
4 Swish the wig around in the solution.
5 Rinse well in **cool water**.
6 Dissolve **1 tablespoon of conditioner** in a **pan** of **fresh water**. Swish the wig in the solution. Then rinse.
7 Lay the wig on a **towel** and roll it up to remove as much water as you can. Don't wring.
8 Remove the wig from the towel and gently shake it out. Use your fingers to loosen the fibres, but don't try to remove tangles with a comb or brush while the wig is wet.
9 Set the wig on a **bottle** or some other tall item to dry.

To clean makeup from the front of the cap or hair area, make a paste of **bicarbonate of soda** and **shampoo**. Apply it during the shampooing process with an **old toothbrush** and scrub gently.

Simple solutions

Canned air for hair

There are thousands of cleaning uses for containers of 'canned air' (which is really a compressed gas) but using it to keep a wig looking fresh is perhaps one of the most unlikely. Yet, this is just what it can do. Set the wig on its stand, hold the can upright and spray off dirt and dust.

Windows

So much has been printed about the fastest and best way to clean windows that you'd think it was an Olympic event. In fact, lots of things work: choose one that works for you.

Here are a few simple hints that apply to most windows:

• Clean the windowsills and frames before the glass. **Vacuum** to remove loose dirt before wiping with a **damp cloth**.

• Start at the top and work down to avoid dripping onto clean windows.

• Don't clean windows in direct sunlight. The cleaner will dry before you can wipe it off, creating streaks.

• Make your drying strokes go up and down on one side of the window and back and forth on the other. That way you can tell which side the streaks are on.

• Your drying technique and materials affect the final appearance more than the kind of cleaner.

Now let's move on to the contentious part.

The cheapest way to clean a window is to use **plain water** and **newspaper**. However, this method can get messy. So you may well prefer to use **paper towels** or a **soft, lint free cloth** or **pad** for the final wipe down. Apply the water with a **sponge** or **squeegee**, available at hardware stores. Dip the squeegee into a **bucket of water**, picking up just enough water to wet the window without drenching it. Then wad up the newspaper a little and rub the window until it's dry.

   Paper towels also work but are expensive and wasteful. A **chamois cloth** works as well.

Using a squeegee to clean windows is the method preferred by many people, including most professional window cleaners. If it's your choice, buy a good squeegee with a removable rubber blade so that it can be replaced as it wears. The main disadvantage of a squeegee is that it's impractical on small panes of glass – although you can buy smaller, 10cm ones at hardware shops. When using a squeegee, technique is important.

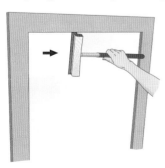

1 First, wet the squeegee.
2 Draw it across the top of the pane.
3 Start the squeegee at the bottom edge of that swath and draw it down one side of the glass to about 4cm from the bottom. Repeat this step,

Rules of the game

Cleaning windows

1 Start at the top and clean downward.

2 Apply cleaning solution with a spray bottle.

3 Lightly scrub with a sponge or cloth.

4 Wipe clean with a squeegee or polish with newspaper. Work back and forth on one side of the window and up and down on the other. You'll be able to see which side needs extra polishing to remove streaks.

5 If you're cleaning with a squeegee, keep a rag in each pocket – one for wiping the squeegee and the other for cleaning the corners.

6 When cleaning inside, lay a towel on the windowsill to catch dripping solution.

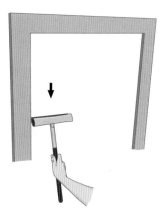
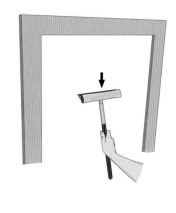

overlapping each stroke as you work your way across the whole window.

4 Draw the squeegee across the bottom of the pane.

5 Wipe the squeegee on a cloth between strokes.

6 Use a clean cloth to wipe the window edges, if necessary.

7 On very large windows, wash and dry the top half, then move on to the bottom half.

Keeping sashes spotless

Many sash windows are now made so they can be tilted inward for cleaning. But if you don't have that kind, you can still clean both sides from inside the house – provided both upper and lower windows move fully, as they're supposed to. Take care at all times: but no major leaning out is ever required. Here are instructions for reaching the outside of both windows.

1 Pull the top window all the way down. (It will be on the outside.)

2 Reach through the opening to clean the top part of the outside. Wash, then wipe.

3 Raise both windows all the way to the top.

4 Reach through the opening to clean the bottom part of the outside window.

5 Lower the inside window enough to reach the outside window and push it all the way to the bottom.

6 Now reach through the opening to clean the top part of the inside window.

7 Raise the outside window all the way to the top and lower the inside window as much as possible while leaving room for your arm to pass through the opening.

8 Reach through the opening to clean the bottom part of the inside window.

For added cleaning power on dirty glass,
here are some formulas to try:

• For grease or hard-water deposits, use **100ml of white vinegar** in **2 litres of water** plus a squirt of **washing-up liquid**. For speed, pour this into a **spray bottle**.

• For grime, grease or smoke, use **100ml of clear ammonia** in a **litre of water**.

• For tough jobs, you can add **methylated spirits**. But it will need rinsing off afterwards, so only do this if all else fails. Mix up **250ml of methylated spirits** with **40ml of clear ammonia** and a drop of **washing-up liquid** in **2 litres of water**.

• For the ultimate dirty window, get a **specialist window clean product** from a car supply shop. This is pricy and will need rubbing in, then rinsing off. So it's just for a small area.

Trouble shooting tip

• To remove hard-water mineral spots, use **straight vinegar**.

• For scratches in glass, rub a little **toothpaste** into the scratch and polish with a **soft cloth**.

• To peel off paint and stuck-on adhesives, scrape with a **razor blade**. Don't use a putty knife, however, because it's duller and can damage the glass.

Simple solutions

Car window winter wonder

One of the worst things about winter is having to scrape a layer of ice from the windshield when you're late for work. To wake up to a frost-free car windshield, coat it the night before with a solution of 3 parts vinegar to 1 part water.

Woks

A well-seasoned wok is practically non-stick and needs only light cleaning. Follow our instructions for seasoning and caring for your wok and it will last for ages.

To clean a new wok made of carbon steel
(the authentic kind), begin by removing the temporary protective coating applied by the manufacturer. Scrub the wok inside and out with **washing-up liquid** and **steel wool** and rinse with **hot water**. If some coating still remains, fill the wok with **water** and boil it until the coating dissolves. Empty the water and scrub again thoroughly with **steel wool** and **soap**.

To season a new wok, after washing it as described above, follow these steps:

1 Set the wok on a burner and heat it until a few drops of water sprinkled into the wok do a mad dance. As it heats, the wok will change colour, becoming darker.

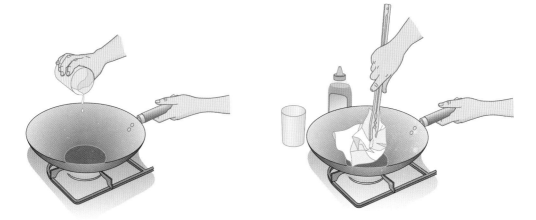

Pour in a few drops of water and heat to boiling. When the wok has turned black, using tongs, wipe round with paper towels dipped in sesame oil.

2 When it turns black, dip some wadded-up sheets of **paper towel** into **sesame oil**. Hold the wad in a **pair of tongs** and wipe the oil over the inside of the wok.
3 Turn the heat down to low and let the wok sit on it for 15 minutes. If the surface looks dry, wipe with another **thin coat of oil**.
4 Turn the heat off and let the wok cool.
5 Repeat the oiling and heating process once more before using the wok for cooking.

To clean a wok after cooking, wipe it out with a **paper towel** or **damp cloth**. Scrubbing a seasoned wok or using a detergent will ruin the carefully cultivated patina, but if you do need to scrub or wash with detergent, then simply re-season, as above. Similarly, if a wok gets rusty, just follow the steps for cleaning and seasoning a new wok.

To clean an electric wok, follow the manufacturer's directions, which will vary depending on what kind of surface the wok has and whether it is immersible in water.

Wood burning stoves

Keeping a wood burning stove clean isn't only a matter of cleanliness. It's also a vital matter of safety. Every year wood burning stoves are responsible for fires that destroy homes and kill people. One common cause of these fires is the improper disposal of ashes.

To dispose of ashes safely, remove them with a **metal ash shovel** and place them in a tightly covered **metal bucket**. Don't use plastic shovels, paper bags or cardboard boxes under any circumstances. Then take the bucket outside and let it sit for a couple of days to ensure that the harmless-looking ashes aren't harbouring any embers. For final disposal, add to garden soil or sprinkle on the lawn to use the potassium and other minerals. This is the cleaning chore that needs to be done most often during the heating season, whenever the ashes are around 10cm deep.

To clean a stovepipe, another chore you may have to perform several times during a season, disconnect it from the chimney and from the stove when the fire is out. Take the stovepipe outside and shake it into a **metal bucket** to remove the soot and creosote. If there are stubborn clumps of residue, use a **stiff-bristled brush**.

To ensure the cleanest operation of your stove, burn hardwood (maple, ash, oak, beech and birch for example) that has been seasoned for a year. Burn a hot fire for at least half an hour every week during the heating season. If you new to a wood burning stove, buy a stovepipe thermometer from a hearth shop or wood stove dealer to tell you the meaning of hot in this context.

To clean the outside of the stove, vacuum when there is no fire, using the **small brush attachment**. For dirt that vacuuming won't remove, wipe the surface of enamelled stoves with a **damp sponge**. Use **stove polish**, available at hardware stores and hearth shops, on stoves made of cast iron, plate steel, sheet metal or a combination of these materials. **Balled-up waxed paper**, used on a warm stove, also shines those finishes. Rust or other heavy dirt may be cleaned from a cold stove with **fine steel wool** and *WD-40*, available from hardware stores.

To clean glass doors on a wood stove, follow the directions in your owner's manual. A mixture of **water** and a little **ammonia** works well to remove smoke, but check your manual first to make sure the glass doesn't have a special protective coating, which might be harmed by the ammonia.

Other stove parts that need periodic cleaning are baffles, smoke shelves and catalytic combustors. These devices increase the efficiency of your stove and reduce pollution. They're often located near the spot where the stovepipe meets the stove. Your owner's manual will tell you if your stove has one or more of these parts and will explain how to clean them.

Woodwork

Woodwork usually gets dirty faster than walls because it's the edging around doors and windows that most often comes into contact with little hands and dirty fingers. Woodwork will probably need cleaning more often than walls, but fortunately there is a lot less of it to clean.

For routine cleaning, **vacuum** skirting and dado rails and casings (the framework around doors and windows) with the **small brush attachment**. Dust the top surfaces of this woodwork periodically with a **microfibre cloth**.

To wash woodwork, use a solution of a little **washing-up liquid** in **warm water**. Apply with a **wrung-out sponge** or **rag** and then rinse with **plain water**. If the gloss has been dulled, follow by rubbing with a **cloth** that has a tiny amount of **furniture polish** on it. This works on both painted and polyurethane surfaces.

To clean heavily soiled areas, apply a little **undiluted washing-up liquid** directly to the **sponge** or **cloth**. Rub the dirty area and rinse thoroughly with **plain water**.

To prepare the surface for new paint, wash with a **solution** of **sugar soap**. Wear **rubber gloves** and rinse afterwards.

To clean woodwork with a varnish or shellac finish, use a **solvent-based (not water-based) wood cleaner**, available at home improvement stores and hardware stores. It is both a cleaner and wax in one product. Apply it with a **cloth** and buff afterwards.

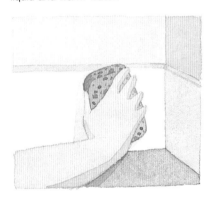

Wipe painted woodwork with a sponge dipped in a light solution of washing-up liquid and warm water.

Worktops

Keeping worktops pristine serves two purposes: your kitchen looks nicely kept and, since this is where most food preparation takes place, you're helping to cut levels of bacteria for bacteria and so reducing the risk of possible contamination and sickness.

Worktops have come a long way since *Formica*, a plastic laminate, reigned supreme. Today, the most common type is a solid-surface synthetic. (*Corian* is one popular brand.)

Other popular types are marble, granite and engineered or synthetic stone – and wood. It's worth reading the manufacturer's directions for cleaning your kind of worktop.

General maintenance calls for removing the stuff on top first, then cleaning up surface dirt and crumbs with a **soft-bristled brush** or **handheld vacuum**. Wet a **nylon-backed sponge** with **soapy water** (washing-up liquid in warm water) and use the soft side of the sponge to wash the counter, backsplash included. Let the soapy water sit on the surface a few minutes to soften any spots. Switch to the scrubbing side to remove any intransigent spots. Rinse with **warm water** and buff dry with a **clean, lint-free towel**. Or squirt with a **multi-purpose kitchen cleaner** and wipe clean with a **sponge**. Most will not need rinsing.

Plastic laminates, such as *Formica*, should not be cleaned with abrasives. Mop up spills immediately with a **sponge**, then use a **soapy sponge** or **all-purpose kitchen cleaner**. For obstinate stains, try one of these approaches:
• Sprinkle with **bicarbonate of soda** and rub with a **soft, damp cloth**. Rinse and dry with **paper towels** or a **cloth**.
• Make a paste of **lemon juice** and **cream of tartar**, spread on the stain and let sit for 15 minutes. Rinse and dry.

Laminates need a gentle touch as they age. They are susceptible to chipping, scratching and losing their shine.

Solid-surface synthetics, such as Corian, can withstand light abrasion. Wet a **scrubbing sponge** or sprinkle a **mildly abrasive cleaner**, such as *Cif* (without bleach), on a **damp sponge** and apply with gentle pressure. Rinse with water on a **sponge** and dry with a **soft cloth**.

Stone worktops, usually those made of marble or granite are rather delicate. If you are buying a new kitchen and want quick, easy cleaning, don't go for these But if you already have them in your house, here's what to watch out for. Acid etches marble and anything greasy stains granite.

To clean marble and granite, start with the don'ts: never use anything abrasive. Instead, wash with a few drops of **plain** or **antibacterial washing-up liquid** on a **damp sponge**. Rinse the surface completely with **clean water** and dry with a **soft cloth**. Or buy a cleaner formulated for stone from your supplier.

To maintain stone worktops:
• Blot up spills at once with **paper towels**. Don't wipe – that will only make it worse. Flush the spot with **warm water** and **mild soap**, rinsing several times before drying with a **soft cloth**.
• Use coasters, trivets or place mats under glassware and dishes to protect surfaces from scratching. Heat damages marble, so never set anything hot on it.
• Stone countertops are sometimes sealed with a penetrating commercial sealant. Make sure that wherever you prepare food, the sealant is non-toxic. **Vegetable oil** is an effective non-toxic and homespun coating for food preparation areas.

Engineered stone usually resembles granite but requires no sealant and little extra care. Wash with **soap** and **water** and an **all-purpose kitchen cleaner**.

See also **Granite** and **Marble.**

Wooden worktops Most will be treated with a tough laminate layer. But if you have untreated wood, go easy. To avoid scratching, do not use abrasive cleaners. Instead, use a **soapy liquid cleaner** that is especially for wood or **dilute washing-up liquid**. Always dry scrupulously afterwards. You will do the most damage if you leave wood wet. Regularly treat the wood with **wax** to prevent cracking.

Zips

There are times when you should clean a zip independently of the item it fastens – in particular those with a heavy duty function. For example, the zips in tents, sleeping bags, luggage, wet suits, fishing gear, jackets and boots may need separate attention now and then.

To clean zips in washable items, wash the item with **water** and **detergent** that is suitable for the fabric. Close the zip before putting the article into the washing machine. When ironing, protect the zip by closing it and covering it with a cloth. Excessive heat can damage or destroy nylon, plastic and polyester zips.

To make the slider work more smoothly, rub a **candle** along the zip teeth and move the slider up and down several times to work in the wax. A **white candle** works best, so you don't smear dye around. Wipe off any excess. This treatment will counteract the damage done by detergents and bleach to the factory-applied coating that keeps zips slippery.

To clean the zips on large articles – such as tents, backpacks, wetsuits, suitcases and boots – first unzip the zip. Remove any loose dirt from the teeth with a **toothbrush**. Dip the toothbrush in a solution of a little **washing-up liquid** and **warm water**. Rinse with **plain water** and leave the zip open until it has dried. Lubricate the teeth with a **candle**.

A candle is an excellent way to lubricate a sticky zip.

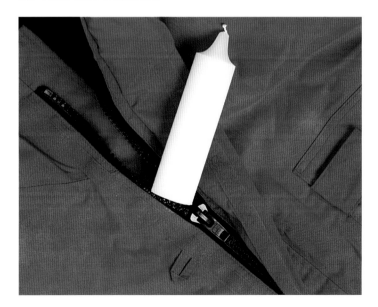

PART

3

dealing with household
cleaning
crises

Dealing with household cleaning crises

Chewing gum in your hair, fleas in your carpet, a biro leaking sticky ink in your pocket or handbag, coffee or wine pooling on a light-coloured carpet – life's just chock-full of surprises. Here's a fast-find guide to the most likely of household disasters. If something messy has just happened, don't despair – chances are we've got advice on how to deal with it right here.

Animal accidents on wood floors

Your main aim is to remove any solid matter and liquid before it soaks right through the carpet or anyone treads in it. To speed things up, if you've a pet that frequently messes, keep a crisis kit in the understairs cupboard (or somewhere that you can reach fast). Include: **paper towels**, **plastic grocery bags** (for disposing of solids and used paper towels) and an **enzyme-based cleaner** (available at pet shops). Start by removing any solids. Then blot up as much of the liquid content as possible, using paper towels. You'll soak up maximum liquid if you stand on the paper towels (in shoes) or press a weight onto them. Soak the accident site in the enzyme cleaner. Let sit for a few minutes and then blot up. Rinse the residue with water to avoid leaving smells that might draw the pet back to use the same spot.

Baby sick or nappy contents on clothes or upholstery

First try **cold water**, which may be all you'll need if these protein stains are fresh. Don't use hot water, since it can 'cook' the proteins, causing the stain to coagulate between the fibres in the fabric. Soak washables in cold water for half an hour, run the stain under cold tap water and gently rub the fabric against itself to loosen the stain. Then launder in your **washing machine** in **warm water**. For carpeting or upholstery, spray with **cold water** and blot with a **clean cloth** or **paper towels**. Repeat until the stain is gone. If residue remains, soak the accident site in **enzyme cleaner**. Wash and rinse according to product directions.

Berry stains on clothing or dish towels

Berry stains – raspberry, blackberry, strawberry and more – are considered dye stains and they're tough. For washable clothes and towels, pre-treat the stain with a **commercial stain remover**. Or apply **liquid detergent** directly to the stain. Work the detergent in well. If the stain doesn't lift out, rinse off then soak the fabric in a **diluted solution of oxygen bleach** (20ml to 2 litres of water). Clean in the washing machine, using the maximum temperature that the item will take. For dry-clean-only clothes, try a solvent. **Methylated spirits** is good at lifting off fruit stains, but you need to take extreme care, as there is also a risk that it could take the colour out of your clothes. Using a **cotton bud** with a dash of solution, dab at the stain. With a second, dry cotton bud, blot it up. Or use *Stain Devils Instant Wipes*, which are suitable for dry-clean items.

Big party clean-up

First, gather cups, bottles and glasses. As you do so, look for spills and address them right away. Empty the cups, bottles and glasses in the kitchen sink, throwing rubbish into a plastic sack and setting the glasses next to the sink. Fill your dishwasher and start the first load. Next, gather up the rest of the party rubbish, starting in the outer rooms and working your way toward the kitchen. The goal is to centralise the clutter. Dust and vacuum, again working your way toward the kitchen. Clean the kitchen last. Take the rubbish out as soon as bags are filled and tied.

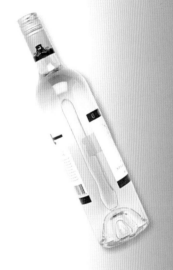

Blood on fabric or carpeting

If it's fresh, **cold water** should be all you'll need to remove this protein stain. Don't use hot water, since hot water can cook the proteins, causing the stain to coagulate between the fibres in the fabric. Soak washables in **cold water** for half an hour, then run the stain under the cold tap and gently rub the fabric against itself to loosen the stain. Wash in **warm water**. For carpeting or upholstery, spray with **cold water** and blot with a **clean white towel** (white, so there's no chance of dye transfer), repeating until clean.

Candle wax on fabric or carpeting

If the wax is still soft, blot up the excess with **paper towels**. If it is hard, gently scrape the excess with a **dull knife**. Next, lay a **plain brown bag** or **white paper towel** (no dyes or printing inks) over the wax and run a **hot iron** over the paper. The heat will melt the wax and the paper will absorb it. Continue by moving the bag or paper towel around to unsaturated sections until all the wax is absorbed. Remove residue by blotting with a **dry-cleaning solvent** such as *Spotless Dry Clean Liquid*. Be sure to test the solvent first on an inconspicuous spot.

Chewing gum on upholstery, carpeting or hair

Use an **ice cube** to remove chewing gum from a variety of places – clothing, upholstery, carpeting and hard surfaces. Simply rub the ice on the gum until it freezes and hardens. To avoid water drips, put the ice in a **plastic bag** before rubbing it on the gum. Scrape away the hardened gum with a **dull knife**. If residue remains, remove it by blotting with a **dry-cleaning solvent**, such as *Spotless Dry Clean Liquid*. Be sure to test the solvent first on an inconspicuous spot. For gum in your hair, apply a few drops of **vegetable oil** or **peanut butter** to the gum and knead until it's soft. Keep pulling away bits of gum until it's gone, then shampoo.

Coffee on clothes

For washable fabrics, soak for half an hour in a solution of **1 teaspoon of biological liquid detergent** per **2 litres of warm water**. Then put into the washing machine with the hottest water that is safe for the fabric, using **detergent**. Resist the temptation to deal with it over the sink, by scrubbing at the stain with soap. Natural soap – including soap flakes, bar soap and detergent containing soap – makes tannin stains harder to remove. To remove stubborn tannin stains, you may need to wash with **bleach**. Try a washing booster such as *Ace*.

Cooking oil splatters on hob, worktops and clothes

First, deal with the hob and worktops. Wipe oil from the worktops and the hob with **paper towels**. Then wipe surfaces with a **moist sponge** and a solution of **washing-up liquid** and **warm water** or a 50-50 solution of **vinegar** and **warm water**.

For oil on dry-clean only clothes blot the grease with **paper towels** dampened with **acetone-based nail polish remover**. (Do not use it on acetate, however – acetone will dissolve the fabric.) For washable clothes, use a **commercial pre-wash stain remover**, such as *Vanish* or a **biological liquid detergent**. Work the detergent into the stain. Immediately after pre-treatment, wash the item in **hot water** (if that is safe for the fabric and colours).

Cooking smells filling the house

Open the windows and turn on the **extractor fan**, if you have one, to get fresh air circulating. Next, take out any tea towels and cloths to the washing machine. Then, look at the work surfaces. The smell is actually clinging to the cooker and the worktop around it. So as you wipe off greasy residue, you are also wiping off the smell. Use a **multi-purpose kitchen cleaner**. If the smell is still there, clean the walls and cupboard doors close to the stove. Because heat rises and is drawn to cool areas, concentrate on wiping windows and windowsills, light fixtures and upper cabinets. If the smell is still there, you may need to wash the curtains

Or mix **60ml of vinegar** in **2 pints of water** and boil on the stove. The rising warm air will carry the odour-neutralising vinegar particles to the surfaces on which the smoke and grease have settled.

Felt-tip pen on the fridge, worktop or furniture

First, try wiping the marks off with **paper towels** or a **dry cloth**. Depending on the surface, if the felt tip is still wet, you may be able to remove the mark. If not, try wiping with a clean cloth moistened with **methylated spirits**.

Fleas in the carpet

Vacuum all carpets, concentrating on areas frequented by your pet and under seats and sofas. Also vacuum upholstered furniture in the vicinity and then empty the vacuum bag. Wash any removable rugs or pet bedding. Using a **spray bottle**, apply a **specialist flea killing product**. The most effective are those that 'fog' the room, rather than sprays that you have to direct onto areas you suspect fleas might have moved to. Treat your pet at the same time.

Glass breaking in a crowded room

Leave someone near the spot to warn others. Get a small **cardboard box**, a pair of **work gloves** and a **broom** and **dustpan** (for hard floors) or a **vacuum cleaner** (for carpets). Wearing gloves, pick up the big pieces and put them in the box or bucket. On a hard floor, inspect a wide circle around the crash site for pieces that may have spread. Check your guests' ankles – on top of shoes, trapped on trousers – for splinters of glass. Next, sweep or vacuum. Vacuum the carpet several times to make sure you have removed all tiny shards. Empty the vacuum bag when finished or tip a cylinder vacuum straight into your cardboard box. Seal the box with **sticky tape** and put it in the rubbish bin. The box will protect your hands and those of the rubbish collector.

Glue spills on furniture

Start by scraping up whatever you can using a **dull knife**. If the glue is white school glue treat it as you would a protein-based stain (page 49), which means no hot water – the hot water can cook the proteins. Spray the spot with **cold water** and blot with a **clean cloth**, repeating until clean. If it is model-making glue, blot it with a **cloth** dampened with **dry-cleaning solvent** or **methylated spirits**.

Lipstick on clothing

Lipstick contains both an oily/waxy base and dyes. You must first remove the oily/waxy part and then you can try to

remove the dye. For washable fabrics, begin by applying a
dry-cleaning solvent, such as *Spotless Dry Clean Liquid*.
Next, rub with a **liquid detergent** and scrub in **hot
water**. This should remove the oily/waxy part. Then wash
in the washing machine with a **detergent** that contains an
oxygen or **all-fabric bleach**.

Mud or salt tracked in on rug

Mud wreaks havoc on a rug. Let the mud dry first and
you'll have a better chance of getting it out. If the mud is
ground in, wait until it dries then brush it to the surface and
get up as much as you can with a **dull knife**. After that,
vacuum. If you still see muddy paw – or footprints, mix a
few drops of **washing-up liquid** in **200ml of warm
water** and blot the solution onto the rug with a **clean
white towel**. Use another **damp towel** to rinse and
remove soap residue.

For salt stains tracked in on wet shoes and boots, mix
equal parts **vinegar** and **water** and dab the mixture on
with a **towel**. Blot with **cool water** and dry.

Nail polish on wooden furniture, floor or rug

Blot up the excess with a **paper towel**. Then blot with a
cloth moistened with **acetone-based nail polish
remover**. Don't let the nail polish remover seep into a rug's
latex backing. To remove the nail polish remover, mix a
solution of **1 squirt mild washing-up liquid** (containing
no bleach or lanolin) with **1 litre of water**. Wipe the wood
or work the solution into the textile with a **clean towel**.
Draw the solution back out by blotting with a **dry paper
towel**. Rinse by lightly spraying with **clean water** and then
blot the water up with fresh **paper towels**.

Oil and grease on clothes

Blot up as much as you can with **paper towels** or carefully
scrape solids up with a **dull knife**. For clothes that can only
be dry-cleaned, blot the grease with **paper towels**
dampened with **acetone-based nail polish remover**.

(Don't use acetone on acetate, because it will dissolve the fabric.) For washable clothes, spray with a **commercial pre-wash stain remover** or use a **liquid laundry detergent**. Work the detergent into the stain. Immediately after pre-treatment, wash the item in your washing machine using **hot water** (if that is safe for the fabric and colours).

Paint drippings on floor or carpeting

Start by blotting up as much of the dripped paint as possible using **paper towels**. If it is latex paint, spray with **clean water** and blot. Repeat until you've removed as much paint as possible. If it is oil-based paint, blot with a **clean cloth** or **paper towels** moistened with **paint thinner** or **turpentine**, refreshing cloths or paper towels repeatedly. If vestiges of the paint remain on the carpet, moisten the tufts with **3 per cent hydrogen peroxide** and let that stand for an hour. Blot with clean paper towels.

Pen ink stain on your pocket

Remove the pen and throw it away. Remove the item of clothing, making sure not to smear the ink stain on anything else. Place the stain face down on **white paper towels**. (Put **plastic** underneath, to keep the ink from bleeding through and staining the surface you're working on.) Wear **gloves** and blot with a **cloth** moistened with **methylated spirits**, forcing the stain into the paper towels. If that does not work, try **white spirit**. Be careful, as these solvents are flammable. Test them first in an inconspicuous corner of the material. Rinse with **water** and machine wash.

Rotten smell from unknown source

Follow your nose. First, try to isolate the odour. Is it in a particular room? What do you think it might be? Is it a pet accident smell, a musty mould smell, a cooking odour? If it's in the kitchen and smells like rotten food, check the refrigerator and the bin. Look under cabinets or appliances for dropped food. If it's a musty odour, check the sink drain.

Here's how to handle a few common odour problems:
• For a kitchen with lingering cooking smells, see the entry **Cooking smells filling the house** on page 403.
• To get the smells out of your kitchen bin, grind up some **lemon or orange peel** and drop them into it.
• To keep the fridge smelling sweet, throw old food away (but seal it or take it outside, otherwise the bin will simply smell), wipe down the interior with **damp paper towels** and place an open box of **baking soda** on a shelf inside.

Rubbish spills on the carpet

Quickly pick up large solids and put them in a **new bag** or garbage bin. Clean up small solids, such as coffee grounds or dirt, with a **vacuum cleaner**. Blot up liquids with **paper towels**. If there are stains remaining, work out what they are and address each using the correct stain-removal technique. (See pages 46–77.) For large spills, work from the outer edge of the spill to the centre to contain the spill.

Scorched fabric

Bad scorch stains cannot be removed. Try **machine washing** using **bleach**, if that is safe for the fabric. If not, soak in **all-fabric bleach** and **hot water** and then wash.

Smoke from fireplace

When smoke from the fireplace comes into the house instead of up the chimney, first make sure there is no chimney fire. Check for a loud roaring or sparks in the chimney. If it's a chimney fire, call the fire brigade. If it's not, then chances are your chimney is not drawing well. Go outside to check the direction of any wind and open doors or windows that are on the side that is exposed to the wind.

To clear out existing smoke, open more windows and doors that will help to blow the smoke outside and use fans to circulate the air. If the smoke smell lingers, wash the curtains and clean the upholstery. (Curtains should be fine, as smoke rises.) Wipe all exposed metal in the room with a **degreaser**, since smoke seeks out cool surfaces. (The acidic soot can etch metal.)

Suntan lotion on clothing

Blot excess lotion with **paper towels** or carefully scrape the excess up with a **dull knife**. On washable clothes, spray the stained area with a **commercial pre-wash stain remover**, such as *Vanish*. If you do not have any, apply **liquid detergent** directly to the stain and work it into the stain. Immediately afterwards, machine wash in **hot water** (if that is safe for the fabric and colours). With dry-clean-only clothes, blot with a **paper towel** dampened with **acetone-based nail polish remover**. (Acetone will dissolve acetate, however, so don't use on that fabric.)

Tar on good shoes

Remove as much of the tar as possible by gently scraping with an **old spoon**. Remove further residue by blotting with clean, dry **paper towels**. Next, apply just a dash of **methylated spirits** to a wad of **paper towels** and blot or gently rub. Repeat several times using **clean paper towels** with freshly applied alcohol. If any tar remains, try wiping with a sudsy solution of **warm water** and a squirt of **washing-up liquid**. Put a small amount on a **cloth** and gently blot or rub. Rinse by spraying lightly with **clean water** and wiping dry.

Washing machine, toilet, bathtub & sink overflows

This emergency – along with bathing the dog – is why you keep old towels. First, turn off the tap. Then grab as many **old towels** as needed and place them on the pooling water to soak it up. With another towel or several **smaller rags**, contain the water by soaking it up from the outside toward the centre. Mop or use a wet vac and then let it dry, using fans and dehumidifiers, if necessary.

Water or alcohol stain on fine wood furniture

If the stain is fresh, soak up any excess water or alcohol with paper towels and then rub the spot vigorously in the direction of the grain with the palm of your hand or a **cloth** dipped in **furniture polish**. If the stain is old and dry, you'll need an abrasive/lubricant combination. Apply a **paste wax** with a very fine grade of **steel wool (such as 0000)**. At a pinch, you can even use **cigarette ashes** and **mayonnaise**. No matter what combination you use, rub gently with the grain using a **clean, dry cloth**.

Wine on carpet

Blot up what you can with **paper towels**. For large spills, work from the outside in to contain the spill. Next, lightly apply a solution of ¼ **teaspoon mild washing-up liquid** and **2 pints of water**. Work the solution into the affected area. Blot with **clean paper towels** to remove. Rinse by lightly spraying with **water**. Blot to remove excess water. Do this until all suds are gone. Then spray lightly with water and don't blot. Instead, lay a pad of **paper towels** down, put a **weight** on the pad and let the towels dry. If the stain persists, moisten the tufts with **3 per cent hydrogen peroxide**. Let it stand for an hour. Finally blot thoroughly with **clean paper towels**.

Wine on table linen

Regardless of the type of wine, if the fabric is washable, soak it for half an hour in a solution of **1 teaspoon of biological laundry detergent** per **2 litres of warm water**. Machine wash using the hottest water that's safe for the fabric. Always resist the temptation to remove wine using soap. Natural soap – including soap flakes, bar soap and detergent containing soap – makes tannin stains harder to remove. To remove stubborn tannin stains, you may need to wash the stained item with **bleach**.

PART

4

tools
of the cleaning
trade

Tools of the cleaning trade

The following is a mini-encyclopedia of cleaning compounds, solutions and utensils. We explain the uses of different types of similar products and show how to save money by making your own. We also guide you through the range of utensils available for cleaning your home, from dusters to the latest microfibre cloths and from old-fashioned brooms to the most up-to-date vacuum and carpet cleaners.

Abrasive cleaners

Imagine rubbing a wall with a piece of paper. Then doing exactly the same with some fine glasspaper. In a nutshell, that's the difference between an abrasive and a non-abrasive (that is, smooth) cleaner. Fine, scarcely visible particles – usually minerals – add friction to your cleaning. So that you can scratch off the offending grime as you rub. The finer the particle, the less abrasive the cleaner; the coarser the particle, the more abrasive the cleaner. Many abrasive cleaners – which come in powdered and liquid forms – also contain cleaning chemicals such as detergent or bleach.

If you use abrasive cleaners on a soft surface you may cause scratching. And by 'soft' that doesn't mean butter soft. Worn plastics and enamel are a classic example of surfaces that can be scratched with abrasive cleaners.

Use a full-strength abrasive cleaner – a scouring powder, such as *Ajax* – to wear off dirt, stains, tarnish and hard-water deposits. Rub across the surface of the hard-surface item with a sponge or brush and then rinse.

Use a mild abrasive cleaner, such as *Cif* cream, for cleaning sinks, tiles, showers, baths, toilets and worktops. Follow the package instructions. Be careful not to rub too hard. Even mildly abrasive cleaners can scratch and damage hard, smooth surfaces, making them rough and harder to clean in the future.

A pumice stone, the same kind of abrasive block you use to rub away hard skin on your feet, will help remove a particularly stubborn toilet bowl stain. Keep a pumice especially for this purpose.

Scrubbing pads, ranging from nylon mesh to steel wool soap pads, also work by abrasion and are a simple, quick way to clean metal saucepans that don't have a non-scratch coating.

Some common household compounds are good alternatives to commercially prepared abrasives:
• **Bicarbonate of soda** is a mild abrasive. Sprinkle it on the item to be cleaned or make a paste by adding water to a tablespoon of bicarbonate of soda until it's a little thicker than toothpaste. Use it to scour cooking dishes and saucepans, ovens without special surfaces and grill pans.
• **Toothpaste** can remove water marks in sinks and clean tarnish on silver. Coat the silver with toothpaste, run it under warm water, work it into a foam and rinse it off.
• **Salt** is very useful if you have a spill in the oven. With the oven still warm, dampen the spill lightly and sprinkle on some salt. When the oven cools, scrape away the spill and wash the area clean. Salt can also be used as an emergency damage limitation tactic, if you create a major spill on the worktop – perhaps when you're

serving up dinner and haven't time to deal with it immediately. Sprinkle over with salt – then you'll have started to work on the mess and it will come off far more easily when you're ready to clean it up.

The disadvantage of using abrasive creams and powders is that they need to be rinsed off. So using them takes longer than non-rinse spray cleaners.

Abrasives can be found in most supermarkets and DIY stores.

Absorbents

Absorbents do their cleaning by sucking up liquids or gases. They're particularly handy for wet, messy situations such as food spills, oil spills, pet accidents, vomit and blood.

Absorbents include such household products as bicarbonate of soda, talcum powder, flour, cat litter and table salt as well as commercial products. Not all absorbent products are granular, pour-on materials, of course. Paper towels and cloths do their mess-fixing magic by absorption as well.

Common absorbents and their uses include:
• **Paper towels** are the old standby for removing spills, especially from the floor.
• **Washable cotton cloths** (old cotton T-shirts for example) are also great for spills and are more economical. Microfibre cleaning cloths, which can absorb several times their own weight, are excellent for general cleaning.
• **Bicarbonate of soda**, placed in a corner of your fridge in an open pot, is a good absorber of food smells. It is also good for sprinkling on spills to absorb grease around a stove or in an oven – even for cleaning up vomit, if you need something to make it easier to lift up off the floor. Just add soda until the liquid solidifies. Then scrape off.

Don't overlook these handy absorbents:
• **Cat litter** works well on outdoor oil spills. In addition, it can be used to solidify very small quantities of paint and other liquids.
• **Sand or soil** also work well for oil spills outside or in a garage.

Absorbent products are available at supermarkets and DIY stores in the household cleaning aisles.

Acidic cleaners

Acid is the opposite of alkali on the pH scale, with 0 indicating extreme acidity, 7 neutrality and 14 extreme alkalinity. Each point that you move away from neutral pH7 is ten times more alkaline or acidic. So you don't need to go far from pH7 to reach a powerful cleaner.

Some common acids include **lemon juice** (citric acid), **vinegar** (acetic acid), **hydrochloric acid** and **phosphoric acid**.

Common uses for acid cleaners include removing rust stains, mineral deposits, stains on concrete and stains on grout, as well as unclogging pipes. Read product labels and use extreme caution when using acid cleaners. Otherwise, you risk damaging finishes and injuring yourself. Acid burns skin and the fumes can damage your lungs.

A rundown of acid cleaners at various pH levels follows:
• **Hydrochloric acid (pH0)** is the strongest acid and is used in extreme cases of hard-water deposits, lime and rust, most often in the toilet bowl. A cleaner with 9 per cent hydrochloric acid has a significant amount of acid in it and could etch surfaces and burn skin. Wear gloves and eye protection and follow directions. If the label says the product merely 'contains' hydrochloric acid, it's likely to be fairly diluted and mild.
• **Phosphoric acid (pH2 to 4)** is milder than hydrochloric and can be used on baths, sinks and tiles to dissolve mineral deposits, rust stains and mildew. Cleaning agents with phosphoric acid are safe to use on the metal trim on shower

doors and on taps if you rinse thoroughly after cleaning. Be aware that phosphoric acid doesn't really 'clean'. It etches surfaces and if you use it too frequently, you could dissolve the grout around your tiles.

Vinegar and citric acid (pH2 to 4) and other acids in this category work well for frequent cleaning. They're commonly used on glassware, coffee pots and other kitchen items. Be aware however, if you boil up vinegar, to make a concentrated solution, you are also increasing its acidity. So you will need to wear gloves and take care when using the more concentrated vinegar.

For washing clothes, add 200ml of white vinegar to the final rinse to eliminate soap residue. Pour it into the fabric conditioner drawer. Vinegar breaks down uric acid, so it's especially good for babies' clothes after nappies have leaked.

To get wool and cotton blankets fluffy, add 500ml of white vinegar to a final hand rinse.

Lemon juice is a good acid for removing stains in clothing, such as fruit juice and berry stains. It acts like bleach, which also makes it good for cleaning cutting boards and worktops. To remove a stain on a worktop, squeeze on fresh lemon juice, let it sit for 45 minutes, sprinkle on bicarbonate of soda and rub with a sponge or soft cloth. Then rinse out the sponge or cloth and wipe again.

Watch out Take these precautions when using acidic cleaners:

• Don't use vinegar if you add chlorine bleach to your rinse water. The mixture will produce a harmful gas.
• Don't use vinegar on wooden floors.
• Don't let acidic cleaners sit too long on metal fixtures, or they'll damage the finish.
• Don't use acid on stone (such as granite and marble) or concrete – both are alkaline and will dissolve with acid.

Acidic cleaners are found at supermarkets (in the food and household aisles) and at DIY stores.

Air cleaners

Air in a home can be improved in a number of ways, but the approaches fall into these two broad categories:
• **Chemical products** that attack the sources of odours or mask them.
• **Air-cleaning devices and filters** that literally 'pull' irritants out of the air.

Disinfecting cleaners don't clean the air directly, but they do eliminate the source of odours. To destroy mould or bacteria that generate a bad smell, just spray the surface where the offending microbes are growing with a traditional disinfecting cleaner such as *Dettol Disinfectant Spray*. New sprays that have hit the market (*Oust*, for instance) claim to kill odour-causing bacteria actually in the air and to neutralise other malodorous particles.

Air fresheners don't really eliminate odours – they just cover up the smell. They come in spray and time-release forms. A spray, such as *Glade*, can mask an unpleasant odour by simply using it in the area with the offending odour. A time-release air freshener that you plug in – a wick, solid cake or saturated wood block – has a longer freshening effect. Some last for 75 days. Air fresheners of either kind are commonly used in bathrooms and kitchens.

Buy chemical air fresheners at supermarkets, discount stores, chemists and DIY stores.

Alcohol

Alcohol is an effective solvent for cleaning and eliminating stains and kills germs as well. It is found (very diluted) in some mouthwashes.

Alcohol used for cleaning comes in several forms It's a colourless liquid, has a mild odour and is highly flammable. The most common is **methylated spirits**, sold principally for DIY tasks, but with a handy cleaning side-line. In particular, it's good at getting rid of stains. However, the highly unpleasant smell makes it a poor choice for general cleaning. So if using methylated spirits is suggested, this is generally as a last resort. Your cleaning tasks will be more pleasant if you're able to get satisfactory results using commercial cleaning solutions. **White spirit** is commonly used to thin or remove paint and varnish and to remove greasy smudges.

The main advantage of using alcohol-based cleaners is that they evaporate quickly. So they are especially suited to cleaning glass because they clean and quickly vanish without leaving streaks. They are also useful for cleaning telephones and the keyboards of computers, calculators and similar electronic goods. Apply alcohol to electronic items with a cotton bud.

Alcohol is also useful for eliminating oil-based stains in carpet and upholstery, for removing hair spray from mirrors and dissolving ink, lipstick, crayon and other difficult stains.

Be careful with alcohol on some finishes Alcohol can soften plastic and paint, so don't let alcohol-based cleaners remain on such surfaces long.

Watch out **A word of warning:** keep these alcohols stored safely and out of the reach of children. They are toxic. Drinking even just a moderate amount can cause blindness, unconsciousness and even death.

Buy alcohol cleaning products at DIY stores.

Alkali cleaners

Alkali cleaners are at the opposite end of the pH scale from acidic cleaners. (See page 413.) Any cleaner above pH7 (neutral) is considered an alkali. Multipurpose cleaners usually have an alkali base because alkali cleaners neutralise acid and most spills and stains are acidic.

Common uses for alkali cleaners include degreasing and removing heavy soiling. They're also good for windows and dealing with coffee and tea stains. Alkali cleaners include washing-up liquid (not the mildest ones – these will be pH neutral), mild detergents such as *Woolite* and all-purpose cleaners such as *Cif Active Gel with Baking Soda*. The more aggressive degreasers, oven cleaners, lye drain openers and wax strippers are also alkali-based products.

Here's a rundown of various alkali cleaners The higher the pH number, the more caustic the cleaner is.

• **The mildest alkali cleaners (pH8 and pH9)** include washing-up liquid and bicarbonate of soda, the Swiss Army knife of the cleaning world. In a solution with water (30ml of bicarbonate of soda per 1 litre of warm water), bicarbonate of soda cleans hard surfaces such as glass, tiles, porcelain, stainless steel, chrome and glassfibre. For heavier soiling, sprinkle bicarbonate of soda straight on to a damp sponge and rub.

• **Moderate alkalis (pH9 to pH11)** include all-purpose degreasers, such as *Cillit Bang Power Degreaser*; washing detergent, ammonia (a general cleaner, grease cutter and wax stripper); soaps; scouring powders and window cleaners.

• **The strongest alkalis (pH12 to pH14)** include lye (used in drain openers and oven cleaners), garage floor degreasers, carpet shampoos and caustic soda (for extra cleaning power for unblocking drains).

Watch out **Some cautionary notes about alkali cleaners:**

• Strong alkalis can damage skin and fabrics. They also corrode and darken aluminium. Wear hand and eye protection when handling the stronger alkalis.

• Most alkalis, except bicarbonate of soda, are toxic if swallowed.

• To remove an alkali residue from a surface you have cleaned, rinse with a solution of 2 tablespoons of vinegar in a litre of water. Then wipe dry.

Alkali cleaners can be found in supermarkets and DIY stores.

All-purpose cleaners

All-purpose cleaners are just what their name implies – they do a wide variety of cleaning jobs. Most of them are moderately alkaline, meaning they are superb grease cutters.

The big advantage of all-purpose cleaners is that you don't have to keep a lot of special cleaners round the house. Don't assume, however, that your all-purpose cleaner disinfects. Check the label if you need to get rid of germs as well.

You can use all-purpose cleaners safely on most surfaces and fabrics – counters, cabinets, walls, floors and patio furniture. They will even remove fingerprints. It's best to test an all-purpose cleaner on an inconspicuous part of the item you're cleaning before you squirt it over the entire object. Because many all-purpose cleaners have a relatively high pH, they may cause colours to run. They also can damage wood.

Citrus-based cleaners, such as *Mr Muscle Orange Cleaner* are increasing in popularity. Use them on clothes, carpets, grout, shower curtains, rubbish bins, patios and hardwood garden surfaces, toilets, the kitchen and stains. They remove gum, tar and grease. And they leave a pleasant smell behind.

All-purpose cleaners can be bought almost anywhere – at supermarkets, DIY stores, department stores. They're more economical if you buy them concentrated, because you're not paying for the water.

Ammonia

Ammonia, made up of nitrogen and hydrogen, is a gas that is suspended in water. Ammonia is an alkali booster (by itself, it's not a cleaner) that helps detergents with stripping wax, degreasing and removing soiling.

Many common cleaners use solutions that are 5 to 7 per cent ammonia. If you have a container of household ammonia, it's actually mostly water and the ammonia content is 5 to 10 per cent. Sudsy ammonia has a detergent added.

Sudsy ammonia works well on stove rings, boiler pans, floors, ceramic tiles and stainless steel. A bowl of ammonia left in the oven overnight will loosen burned-on grease and grime – just wipe it off in the morning. Ammonia is also a star ingredient in commercial window cleaners.

Watch out Take extra care when working with ammonia:

• Keep the area well ventilated. Evaporating ammonia fumes can cause nausea.

• Never mix ammonia with chlorine bleach, which creates poisonous chlorine gas. If inhaled, this combination is potentially deadly.

• Ammonia can darken and discolour some fabrics, so proceed carefully.

Ammonia isn't always easy to find. Your best option is DIY stores.

Bathroom cleaners

Bathroom cleaners are designed to eliminate soap scum and mildew on baths, sinks, tiles, showers and grout. It's a good idea to use bathroom cleaners that disinfect – that is, kill germs. To do this, you must leave the cleaner to sit for the time instructed on the label. If you wash it off more quickly, your surface may be clean but not disinfected. In general, these are tough cleaners for a tough job, so always protect your hands by wearing rubber gloves.

All-purpose cleaners, such as *Cif Bathroom Mousse,* are the best choice for cleaning the whole bathroom. Look for a product that will deal with germs and soap scum at the same time.

Acidic bathroom cleaners, such as *Bathroom Power,* are good for getting rid of soap scum. Watch out for ones that are not enamel safe, such as *Flash Bathroom Spray.* Confine these to the sink only, if you have an enamel bath. For a home-spun approach, try white vinegar mixed in equal parts with water. Apply the solution with a damp sponge or cloth and rinse thoroughly.

Commercial toilet cleaning products, such as *Toilet Duck Active Fresh* are numerous and widely available. Bleach does not remove limescale, merely whiten it. So if scale on the bowl is a problem, always choose a **limescale killing product**. Among the most effective are those you leave in overnight, such as *Harpic Power Tablets.* **Toilet wipes** are a new and speedy way to give a daily clean. Just wipe a product such as *Parazone Flushable Toilet Wipes* around the seat and rim of your bowl – then throw the used wipe into the bowl and flush.

Bathroom cleaners can be purchased at any supermarket.

Bicarbonate of soda

This venerable white powder is still the most versatile cleaning substance around. Made of non-toxic fine crystals, bicarbonate of soda acts as a chemical cleaner and doubles as a scouring powder. It also neutralises odours, keeps drains clog-free and is handy for putting out grease or electrical fires. (Sprinkle it on dry.)

The cleaning uses of bicarbonate of soda are myriad:
• **For regular cleaning on hard surfaces,** pour a little bicarbonate of soda on a damp sponge or cleaning cloth and wipe. Follow up with another clean, damp sponge or cloth.

• **To remove surface stains in the kitchen or bath**, pour out enough bicarbonate of soda to cover the stain and add just enough water to make a paste. Let the paste stay on the stain for several minutes, then scrub with a sponge and wipe it away.
• **To help remove oil and grease stains from clothing**, add 100ml of baking soda to the wash.
• **To keep your kitchen sink clog-free**, pour 100ml of baking soda down the drain each night, followed by warm water. Do the same thing for other drains in your house once a week.

The odour-killing powers of bicarbonate of soda are equally famous. First, use it dry:
• Sprinkle on carpeting, rugs and even car mats. Let it stand for 15 minutes and then vacuum.
• When you're changing cat litter, sprinkle some in the bottom of the cat box and then a little on top of the new litter.
• Pour into ashtrays to control the stench of cigarette ends.

Bicarbonate of soda also soaks up odours when it's dissolved in water. Pour 4 tablespoons of bicarbonate of soda into 1 litre of warm water. Use the solution to:
• Rinse your mouth to get rid of garlic breath.
• Deodorise a stinky plastic container. Fill it with the solution and let it sit overnight.
• Soak a washable nappy that smells strongly of ammonia.

Bicarbonate of soda is readily available at supermarkets. However, if you plan on using a lot, you can buy it more cheaply (in large tubs) at chemists.

Brooms

Whenever there's a sweeping up job to be done inside, you probably reach for the vacuum cleaner. But there are times when a broom is better. Light and easy to haul out of the cupboard, brooms can get at dust in places where there are no plugs for the vacuum.

Brooms come in two basic styles:
• **Double brooms** with a head measuring at least 45cm. These have soft bristles and are good for sweeping garages, patios and large spaces such village halls.
• **Traditional household kitchen brooms** with a compact head. These are better for interior use on hard floors.

What a broom is made of is important While most brooms today have synthetic bristles, there are still some available with natural bristles.
• **Flagged bristles** are split at the ends to make the bristles thinner and better able to pick up dirt.
• **Standard bristles** are thicker and better for sweeping up larger rubbish (outdoor garden work). Some brooms have both types of bristles – flagged bristles on the outside and non-flagged bristles on the inner row. Inside the house, softer **nylon bristles** are a good choice, because they won't scratch the floor.

If you store your broom by standing it on its bristles, the bristles may curl, giving you less-than-perfect sweeping or brushing action. Therefore, it's better to hang up your broom. Many models come with a loop on the handle for just this purpose. If necessary, drill a hole in the handle and make a loop for it, or use the hole to hang the broom on a nail. If you don't want to do that, put two large nails into the wall, around 20cm apart, so you make a horizontal line. You can now hang your broom head on these.

The best place to purchase a broom is in a DIY or hardware store. Large supermarkets may have a small selection.

Brushes

There's a special brush out there for just about anything you'd ever want to sweep away – everything from dirt to mildew, barbecue grime to worktop crumbs. They can be used dry (to remove surface dirt from irregularly shaped objects) or wet (to work in conjunction with cleaners).

Make sure the brush you're using won't damage the object you're trying to clean. Brush bristles can be made of soft hair, synthetics, natural fibres or metal (often stainless steel or brass). Brushes fall into the following main categories:

Kitchen brushes include these kinds:
• **Oven brushes** for cleaning the racks and the sides of the oven. They work best on stainless steel ovens; painted enamel and chrome ovens may get scratched.
• **Scouring brushes** for use on plates and saucepans.
• **Scrubbing brushes** for use on floors and grout.
• **Worktop brushes** which were originally used in shops to sweep crumbs from the counter. Now they are typically sold as a set with a dustpan.
• **Bottle brushes**, for scrubbing inside tight spaces.

Speciality brushes include these:
• **Car brushes**.
• **Tile brushes** which are small-headed brushes with fine bristles for cleaning tiles and grout.
• **Window brushes** for washing windows.
• **Wire brushes** for tough jobs, such as cleaning baked-on grease from barbecues.
• **Radiator brushes** for getting into narrow spaces.
• **Vacuum cleaner brush attachments** for a gentle touch when you're suctioning up dirt.
• **Paintbrushes** which can be adapted to cleaning purposes. For instance, they're great for dusting between the pleats of a lamp shade.

Personal hygiene and grooming brushes include these:
• **Old toothbrushes and nail brushes** that you've recruited for other purposes – cleaning around taps, for instance.

• **Whisk brushes** used for removing lint, dirt and dust from clothing

Brushes can be bought from supermarkets, hardware stores, DIY stores and discount retailers.

Buckets

If you're not careful when using cleaning solutions in a bucket, you can end up redistributing dirt and germs on the floor that you're trying to clean. Buy a bucket with two chambers for holding liquid, plus a wringer for squeezing your mop. Or use two buckets.

Fill one with the cleaning solution and the second with water (with a wringer compartment on the top of the bucket) so that you can wring your mop into it after each spot of cleaning, before you go back to dip into the first bucket and pick up more fresh solution.

When buying a bucket, make sure it's wide enough for your mop to fit inside and get one with measurement marks on the inside so you can tell how much water you've poured in.

You can buy buckets at supermarkets and discount retailers.

Caddies

When it's time to clean, you don't want to waste time tracking down supplies. A sturdy cleaning caddy will hold and organise your cleaning products and cloths.

The design of a caddy is something that you need to pay attention to. Look for one with dividers, so you can separate smaller items from large ones. The individual slots also enable you to separate items you use less frequently, so they will be less likely to fall out when you reach for

the most-used cleaners. Caddies with higher side walls also prevent your cleaners from falling out.

Make sure your caddy has a handle mounted in the centre and arrange your products so the caddy is well balanced. A handle with a rubber grip will make your caddy more comfortable to carry around once it is heavy.

The material a caddy is made from is worth considering. Rubber, vinyl-coated wire or strong plastic caddies are better alternatives, but avoid cheap, flimsy plastic that may crack.

Caddies can be bought at DIY stores, larger supermarkets and discount stores.

Carpet deep-cleaners

Not too long ago, buying your own deep-cleaning carpet machine was a risky option. It was easy to over-wet your carpet with them, running a risk of encouraging mildew, while some models didn't heat the water hot enough to do a good cleaning job.

Now, there are some excellent models around. But you need to be sure you have the storage capacity, before buying a bulky piece of equipment that's only likely to be used a couple of times a year.

Renting a deep-cleaning unit is economical (around £15–£20 a day), but ferrying the equipment from the hire-shop to your house and back again is a hassle and it's hard to know what condition your rental unit will be in.

If you do decide to buy a unit, expect to pay between £180–£300. The higher-end home machines, such as *Bissell Pro-Heat Pro-Tech* include such features as dials that automatically adjust the amount of cleaner dispensed based on whether you're cleaning a low or high-traffic area; an on-board heater that gets the water about 25 degrees hotter than hot tap water; and a powered hand tool attachment made especially for cleaning small spaces such as stairwells and around toilets.

Deep cleaners work by forcing a heated cleaning mixture into the carpet, then sucking about 90 per cent of the liquid back out – and with it grime and embedded dirt. (They are sometimes called steam cleaners, but they actually use hot water – not steam.) Even the most powerful vacuum cleaners can't reach the dirt at the base of a carpet, so periodic deep cleaning is important. Every 6 to 18 months ought to do it. Most deep cleaners are now upright models instead of those squat canisters with a hose.

Drying times vary from about 4 to 6 hours, depending on the thickness of the carpet and underlay.

Carpet deep-cleaners are available at retailers such as *Argos*, department stores and home improvement stores.

Car polishes

There's a big difference between polishing a car and waxing it. Polishing adds brilliance. Wax provides protection. And if you polish your car at least once a month, you'll probably eliminate the need to wax.

Before you polish, the car must be clean, or you'll rub tiny particles of dirt into the finish and create noticeable scratches. Clean the exterior with car wash solution rather than dishwashing detergent – detergents draw oil out of the car's paint, which accelerates oxidation and makes the paint look cloudy.

Once the car is clean, it's time to polish. The role of polish is to condition and nourish the paint and give it a deep, wet-look shine.

Done properly, polishing adds brilliance and makes a car as smooth as glass before you wax. The paint is rejuvenated and unlike the wax build-up you can get from over-waxing, polishing actually improves the paint finish with each application.

The key to proper polishing is using clean cloths. Have several cloths (100 per cent cotton or microfibre) on hand and constantly rotate the area of cloth you use so you're not pushing the residue you've already removed back into the paint. When there are no more totally unused areas on the cloth, change to a clean one.

Another benefit of polish is that if you've just had your car painted and you have been instructed not to wax it for three months, you can still polish, since polish doesn't inhibit the curing process.

Spray-on polishes are the easiest to apply, but there are trade-offs. They aren't as good at rejuvenating an oxidised finish and their shine does not tend to last as long.

Liquid and paste polishes require more elbow grease, but the effect is more durable. And a warning – if the label of a polish tells you to keep the product away from the rubber and plastic trim on your car, take heed. Such polishes will leave permanent, unsightly streaks on the trim.

Car polishes are widely available, but you'll find the best selection at car stores such as *Halfords*. Expect to be surprised at prices: most cost at least £5–£6.

Cleaning cloths

Cleaning cloths were once a simple proposition – you could just take some clean, 100 per cent cotton rags and get to work. But newer products and technology have made the humble cloth a whole lot better at its job.

Microfibre cloths are very efficient. Interwoven fibres that are ten times finer than silk grab and trap dust and pull it off the surface you're cleaning, without scratching. They're great for cleaning computers, CDs and television screens – in fact any surface that's especially vulnerable to scratching.

Use microfibre cloths for dusting and polishing household surfaces, or combine them with cleansers, polishes or water for an unlimited number of household tasks. Because they absorb several times their weight in fluids, they're particularly adept at streak-free cleaning.

Cleaning microfibre cloths is easy, too. Shake them out when they're filled with dry dust and machine-wash them when they look especially dirty. Remember to choose a hot wash to kill bacteria. Also available as mitts, the cloths can be used and washed up to 500 times (lasting about two years under normal use) before losing their effectiveness. When washing them, avoid using fabric softener or bleach or including softener sheets in the tumble dryer. Also avoid drying them with towels, since lint from the towels will stick to the microfibres. Some microfibres are treated with cleaning solutions and shouldn't be washed at all, such as microfibre jewellery cleaning cloths that remove tarnish and polish precious metals.

Cotton cloths are still great cleaning aids. Old T-shirts are an excellent choice. Old socks are also handy, because you can wear them like mittens and just use your hands to dust.

If you don't want to stop using your cotton cloths, just make sure you wash them between uses.

You can buy microfibre cloths in home improvement stores and car supply stores. They are more expensive and less widely available than cotton cloths. They cost about £5 for one that's around 45cm square – but compared to one-use disposable wipes, they're very economical.

Dishwashers

The whole point of a dishwasher is to ease the burden of manual washing, so it's worth finding a model that doesn't require you to spend time rinsing dishes before you load them.

Water and energy use are of major importance. Look for features that will reduce water use, such as booster heaters and smart controls and check out the machine's energy rating, which will be on display.

Energy, cleaning and drying performance are all independently rated, from A to E, with A being the most energy efficient. Each model will also give its annual water consumption. If you're on a water meter, you should choose a model that uses the minimum water.

The cost of a dishwasher varies enormously, from under £200 to more than £600. Whatever model you choose, if you want to keep it hidden behind a fake kitchen cupboard door – and so described as an integral dishwasher – you will bump up the price.

Check the noise level. Ask the sales rep to explain the decibel level of the model you are considering. More expensive models have a decibel level in the low 40s (about as loud as quiet conversation), while less expensive units are in the middle to high 50s (comparable to the noise in an average office).

What else do you get with a high-end model? A premium dishwasher brand packs a load of extra features into its new, £600 models. Three spray arms provide more thorough cleaning compared to the one spray arm in budget-priced dishwashers. And instead of an exposed heating element, there's internal heating, as it's called, which is more energy efficient and adds to the appliance's longevity (20 years compared to 8 to 10 years for lower cost units). Internal heating provides a greater range of heating temperatures, from a low of about 46°C for china and crystal to 77°C for heavy duty cleaning of saucepans. The internal heating feature also prevents the melting of any plastic parts that fall to the bottom of the dishwasher.

Dishwashers are sold at appliance stores, DIY stores, discount merchandisers and some department stores. Buying direct over the internet is often cheapest.

Dishwashing detergents

You have two choices when it's time to do the dishes. Load them into a dishwasher or wash them by hand.

Hand dishwashing products are among the gentlest detergents available and can also be used to wash everything from delicate clothing to the family dog. Washing-up liquids work by loosening grime and suspending it until it can be rinsed away. When the suds disappear, so does the cleaning action, so you'll need to add more detergent. If you buy a cheap brand that gives out quickly, you'll just have to use more – and then it's not really a bargain.

Recent innovations include hand care ingredients such as vitamin E, aloe vera and aromatherapy-inspired scents added to the liquid. Anti-bacterial washing-up liquid also has the bonus of being able to halt the growth of bacteria on sponges and cleaning brushes. Simply squeeze a little on to your sponge or brush and it should work for up to 12 hours.

Never use washing-up liquid in a dishwasher, because the suds and foam it produces can inhibit the cleaning process in the machine.

Buy washing-up liquid where you food shop.

Automatic dishwashing detergents come in three forms: powdered, gel and tablet. All are effective, although older machines may not be good at dissolving tablets.

- **Powdered formulas** have been around the longest and are generally the least expensive. The newer products – gels and tablets – offer some added benefits in certain situations, though. Powders can turn to grit if your dishwater doesn't get hot enough (60°C) to dissolve all the powder.
- **Dishwashing gels** dissolve more quickly than powders or tablets and therefore can start cleaning dishes faster.
- **Tablets** are convenient because they eliminate the need to measure, since each tablet is formulated to clean one load.

Rinse products prevent spotting and filming by lowering the surface tension of the water, so it can run straight off dishes. They also help items dry faster when left to air-dry or when you use the energy-saving function on your dishwasher. Rinse agents come in liquid and solid forms.
- **Liquids** may be used only in dishwashers with a built-in rinse reservoir.
- **Solid forms** are made to attach to the upper dishwasher rack, where they dissolve slowly during the various cycles.

Dishwasher salt is essential if you live in a hard water area and use a budget dishwasher powder. It is already included in 3-in-1 style tablets and powders.

Dishwashing detergents are available at supermarkets and discount retailers.

Disinfectants

Disinfectants are designed to kill germs on surfaces, including bacteria and viruses that can spoil food, create unpleasant odours and cause illness. Some products clean as they disinfect, so read the label if you're looking for a dual-purpose disinfectant. A product that does both will advertise that benefit.

Disinfectants contain microbe killers. Disinfecting cleaners also contain surfactants (surface-active agents) to remove soiling.

When choosing a disinfectant, checking the label is especially important. Depending on the formulation and active ingredients, disinfectants may be designed to kill:
• **Bacteria** that cause intestinal illnesses, such as *E. coli* and Salmonella;
• **Staphylococcus**, the kinds of bacteria that cause skin infections;
• **Fungi** that cause athlete's foot;
• **Viruses**, such as Rhinovirus, which is the primary cause of the common cold.

To allow disinfectants to work, follow the package directions to the letter. That usually means letting the disinfectant sit on the soiled surface for at least ten minutes to kill bacteria. Many people use diluted household chlorine bleach as a disinfectant and stain remover – that's fine. It does the job and very economically too. Make sure you follow label directions and dilute accordingly.

There's no need to disinfect your entire house. Stick to areas where you prepare food, plus other moist surfaces such as sinks and toilets. Be especially vigilant if someone in the family is sick or especially vulnerable to infection, because they are elderly or suffering from an illness, such as cancer, which reduces their immunity.

Be careful not to reinfect an area you've just cleaned by using a dirty cloth or sponge. If you clean a surface with disinfectant but then wipe with a contaminated cloth, you're simply re-depositing germs on the clean surface. Some people prefer using paper towels after disinfecting, since you throw away the contaminants. This can get expensive of course, so there's no need to shy away from cloths and sponges. Both work as well, if not better, as long as you wash them with chlorine bleach and let them dry thoroughly between uses.

Disinfectants are available from sources such as supermarkets, DIY stores and discount stores.

Disposable wipes

Disposable wipes have taken the cleaning world by storm in the last few years, generating the most growth in the household cleaning marketplace.

The appeal of disposable wipes is understandable. In terms of convenience, it's hard to beat a pre-treated product that you throw away after a single use. The popularity of wipes is driven by what's known as the three E's of consumer product value – they're effective, efficient and expedient.

Some of the latest wipe products include these:
• **Special wipes for disinfecting surfaces** such as toilets, sinks and worktops. (In such cases, disposing of germs along with the cleaning cloth is an especially attractive feature.)
• **Furniture wipes** to clean and shine wood.
• **Dry and pre-moistened floor wipes** which are attached to floor sweepers and sold as kitchen mop systems.

Dry disposable wipes rely on an electrostatic charge to attract dust. Disposable mitts, also electrostatically charged, make quick work of dusting surfaces like wood, ceramic and vinyl. The dust sticks to the mitt instead of becoming airborne.

Disposable wipes are widely available from such sources as supermarkets, home improvement stores and discount stores. Obviously, it's more expensive to use a disposable wipe that lasts for only one use. But if you're a convenience-driven consumer, you'll pay the price.

Drain cleaners

Drain cleaners come in four varieties – acids, alkalis, oxidisers and enzymatics – and their job is to get rid of blockages in drains, most commonly in kitchens and bathrooms.

Compared to mechanical drain cleaners, pouring down a cleaning solution is a simple job. However, chemical cleaners also have the potential to harm the user if instructions aren't followed exactly. Some of these drain cleaners, particularly the faster-acting ones, cause bubbling that may splash harmful chemicals back out of the drain. So stand back once you've poured the drain opener in. Never use muriatic acid (a dilute form of hydrochloric acid) to clear drain blocks. It's highly dangerous.

Oxidisers are effective on organic blockages. These chemicals react with and combine with the blocking material, breaking it up and disintegrating it (rather than dissolving it).

Enzymatic drain cleaners are slower-acting as they consume or digest waste blockages, but they're easier on your pipes than acids, caustics and oxidisers (which is more of a concern with old plumbing). They're also thought to do less harm to septic systems. However, most commercial drain cleaners are a combination of the two.

Prevent drain clog ups in your kitchen sink with this once-a-month treatment using household products. Pour 50g of bicarbonate of soda around the kitchen sink drain opening. Rinse this down into the drain with 50ml hydrogen peroxide. The bubbling and fizzing action helps to clear away the residue clinging to your pipes.

Drain cleaners can be purchased at supermarkets, discount stores, hardware stores, DIY and plumbing supply stores.

Dusters

Feather dusters and lamb's wool dusters have taken a backseat these days to microfibre dusters, which can get into cracks and crevices, attracting soil and speeding your dusting chores.

The interwoven fibres of microfibre cloths – ten times finer than silk, are good at snagging dust without scratching. For dusting, washing or spot cleaning, microfibre dusters are easy to use and can be put in the washing machine when you're finished. (Don't use bleach or fabric softener on them.)

Feather dusters still have a place in the cupboard. While they have a – justified – reputation for just spreading dust around the room, they are great for dusting in hard-to-reach areas, such as inside a lamp, in the pleats of a lamp shade and in the corners of ceilings where cobwebs collect. Feather dusters blow the dust off the object you're cleaning, allowing you to then vacuum or wipe the dust up – useful with delicate objects requiring minimal handling.

Lambswool creates a lot of static, which attracts dust. These dusters are typically good on skirtings, ceilings, ceiling fans and blinds. Lambswool is not a good duster choice for objects that are heavily blanketed with dust.

Dusters are widely available at DIY stores, discount retailers and supermarkets.

Dustpans

The marrying of dustpan and brush is a match that goes back 100 years and it's still popular. Dustpans are useful little household tools consisting of a flat pan with a tapered edge and a handle. Use the brush to sweep dust and debris into the pan.

Get a plastic dustpan If you drop a metal pan, it may scratch your floor's finish and the pan's edges are likely to bend or curl. Plastic dustpans won't rust, either.

A tight pan-to-floor seal is important. Dustpans often have a tapered, rubber edge to create a tight seal with the floor so dust won't go underneath the pan when you brush dirt into it. Some other styles have a plastic edge. Both types work well, the rubber edge will give a tighter fit to the floor but may not last as long as the plastic.

Even with a good pan-to-floor seal, it's doubtful you'll be able to collect all floor dirt with a single sweep. Even if no dirt escapes under the dustpan's edge, the finest dirt often collects in a line along the edge. This is easily remedied by sweeping, moving your dustpan back by a couple of centimetres and then sweeping again.

Use dustpans indoors and out, although you might want to keep one for each area. You wouldn't want to set a dirty outdoor dustpan down on a clean indoor floor. Dustpans for outdoor use are larger, with metal and plastic pans.

If you don't like bending down, choose a dustpan on a long handle Dustpans often come with a brush, but if yours doesn't, make sure the brush you buy is shorter than the width of the dustpan, so you won't be sweeping dust around the sides of the pan instead of into it.

You can buy dustpans in supermarkets, hardware stores, convenience stores and DIY stores.

Enzyme digesters

Enzyme digesters are chemicals, created by micro-organisms that eat away organic matter. So they're effective on organic stains – including unpleasant substances as urine, vomit, faecal matter, protein stains and the odours associated with them.

Use enzymes around the toilet and flooring to keep your bathroom smelling fresh by digesting soil, spills, bodily oils and bacteria. You'll also find enzymes in drain openers and in carpet, upholstery and laundry products. Enzymes are safe for use in septic systems and can also be used in waste disposal drains. Enzymes are temperature sensitive, so don't use them with hot water.

Disinfectants will also render them ineffective. Remember that once you open an enzyme digester, it has a short shelf life.

Enzyme digesters come as a powder that you activate with warm water, triggering a feeding frenzy on organic matter. If you've ever cleaned spilled milk from a carpet, only to have the mark return days later, you need to use an enzyme product. Most ordinary cleaners mask the odour but can't remove the organic source.

When treating a carpet stain or odour with an enzyme cleaner, first soak up as much of the stain as possible with old bath towels. (Use a wet vac if there's a lot of volume.) Apply the enzyme according to the package directions. Pour it over the stain and make sure the enzyme penetrates to the underlay. If it doesn't, you're wasting your time – the stain and smell will remain. Keep the carpet wet the entire time the enzyme is 'eating' the cause of the odour. It's a good idea to cover the area with plastic and place weights on the edges until the recommended time is up. Then rinse with 100ml of distilled white vinegar per 3 litres of water. Rinse a second time with plain water.

Enzyme digesters make a great laundry pre-soak that works away at organic stains before you run garments through the wash. Use warm water in the soak, according to the package directions (the exception being blood, which requires cold water). Be careful: enzymes will eat away at animal fibres, including silk and wool.

To purchase enzyme products, pet shops are your best bet for products such as *Simple Solutions Stain and Odour Remover*, available from *Pets at Home*. You can select proteolytic enzymes for protein stains such as meat juice, egg, blood and milk, or amylolytic enzymes for starch and carbohydrate stains. Since enzymes are costly and starches and carbohydrates generally do not leave stains, you're probably better off buying proteolytic enzymes.

Floor care products

Floor cleaners, polishes and finishes are not interchangeable. Floor cleaners, as the term implies, remove dirt. Floor polishes remove scratches because they're slightly abrasive and seal and protect the cleaned surface. Real wax isn't usually used any more on the most popular kinds of modern flooring. It has been replaced by various polymers.

What does your floor's manufacturer recommend? Each manufacturer has recommendations for cleaning and protecting its products, so try to check the manufacturer's directions and follow them. As a general rule, you should remove all dirt from the floor before you apply the appropriate protective finish. Otherwise, you'll end up with a shiny, but dirty floor.

If you don't have the cleaning instructions from your floor's manufacturer, here is a general rundown of the products you'll need. Be sure to read any product's label to make sure it's safe for the floor you're working on.

For vinyl floors, start by cleaning with a mild detergent or all-purpose cleaner such as *Flash*. After rinsing, apply a water-based floor polish and finish, such as *Johnson's Klear Floor Shine*, according to the package directions. You can find one-step clean-and-polish products, but you probably won't be as happy with the results. This same approach works for asphalt and rubber flooring. Solvent-based paste wax will also add shine to vinyl flooring (it requires buffing) but shouldn't be used on asphalt or rubber.

For wood floors try not to use any cleaners at all – just a damp mop. When that's not enough (and for laminate floors as well) choose a specialist product like *Pledge Soapy Cleaner*, that won't leave a residue.

For ceramic tile floors, a general household cleaner such as *Cif Liquid* will do a good job or use a specialised tile-cleaning product. Avoid abrasive cleaners. Grout is easier to clean when it has been treated with a silicone sealer.

Floor care products can be bought at supermarkets, DIY stores, discount retailers, hardware stores or specialist janitorial supply stores.

Furniture waxes & polishes

When you apply a wax or polish to your wood furniture, you're not beautifying the wood itself – you're improving the finish on the wood. Use either polish or wax – not both. If you put polish on wax, it will just puddle. Polishes don't offer as much protection as wax – they are designed as a quick way to add sparkle to a dull-looking finish.

Furniture waxes – whether they are paste or liquid – are made from combinations of synthetic and natural waxes. The synthetic element is paraffin, distilled from petroleum and other sources. The natural elements include beeswax and carnauba, a vegetable extract. Avoid waxes that contain toluene, a solvent with a paint-thinner smell.

The way wax works is to provide a barrier against moisture seeping into the wood of your furniture. This sealant will also help to speed up your cleaning because you'll be able to remove marks and dust more easily. Before you wax, check the manufacturer's instructions. Generally, most gloss or semi-gloss finished furniture can be waxed. If your furniture has a satin or flat finish, wax may give it a random, messy-looking sheen.

To apply wax, rub it on thinly with a clean, cotton cloth. Then let it sit for several minutes (check the label for precise timing) and buff it with another clean cloth.

When choosing a wax, bear in mind the colour of your furniture. If you have light-coloured furniture, pick a neutral tone; for mahogany, use clear or a red/brown wax for more richness; for cherry, use walnut or brown; for oak, use a chocolate brown to a yellow.

For pine furniture that doesn't have much of a finish, beeswax on its own is a good choice; after buffing, it produces a unique soft glow.

Furniture polishes often contain vegetable oil, alcohol, perfume (scents such as lemon or orange oil) and dye (to give them the colour of lemon or orange). Common mineral oil-based polishes, such as *Pledge*, are sold in bottles or aerosol cans and are easy to apply. However, some experts frown on polishes, saying they collect dust and create a dirt-and-oil mix on the furniture.

Polishes that act as revivers, such as *Guardsman Furniture Polish*, contain fine abrasive pumice in the polish formula and don't contain oil. They clean and protect the surface and are really more like a wax.

Polishes that contain silicone produce a good shine but can make refinishing the furniture more difficult in the future. Look for products that say they're silicone-free (*Guardsman*, for instance).

Waxes and polishes can be purchased wherever cleaning products are sold – at supermarkets, discount stores, hardware stores and home improvement stores.

Glass cleaners

Commercial glass cleaners contain either ammonia or alcohol. They clean dirt, smears and grease and can be used on surfaces other than glass, such as Formica and laminate – but not on Corian or marble.

The composition of a glass cleaner such as *Windolene*, is a mix of ingredients: detergents or surfactants to dissolve dirt and grime; fragrances; ammonia, an alkaline cleaner; colouring; alcohol,

to remove filmy residues and prevent streaks; and solvents to dissolve oily films.

Choose a glass cleaner that does not contain phosphorus, which has a tendency to smear glass. Citrus cleaners may not be the best choice for your home's windows either, since they often contain a solvent called limonene, which can damage wood and vinyl frames. Some glass cleaners are formulated specifically to stop them from dripping.

Homemade glass cleaners are cheap, effective and easy to put together. Here are two:
• For general cleaning, in a bucket mix 2 squirts of a mild washing-up liquid in 3 litres of warm water.
• For cleaning smeary glass, mix 50ml of distilled white vinegar with 400ml of distilled water (water that's been boiled in the kettle and allowed to cool) in a spray bottle and squirt lightly onto your windows. Then polish using your preferred method.

When you use glass cleaners to actually clean glass, do it in the morning or early evening – not during the day when the sun's rays will be heating the glass. The heat of the glass will cause whatever window cleaner you're using to dry more quickly and you're likely to end up with a problem with streaks.

As an alternative, use no cleaners at all – just microfibre cloths for perfect windows. Cloths and spray bottles can be bought from Lakeland (*www.lakelandlimited.co.uk*).

Glass cleaners can be bought in supermarkets, discount stores, hardware stores and DIY stores.

Hydrogen peroxide

Hydrogen peroxide is an oxidising agent, similar to bleach, that removes colour and cleans surfaces. Many products that promise to brighten or whiten clothes contain hydrogen peroxide. Use it with care. Peroxide is made of two parts hydrogen and two parts oxygen and it's the extra oxygen molecule that turns plain water into a potent oxidiser. The higher the percentage of hydrogen peroxide, the stronger it is.

Peroxide is a germ killer as well as a substitute for bleach. It's a potent enemy of Salmonella and *E. coli* bacteria. To kill these germs, spray 3 per cent hydrogen peroxide on a worktop or cutting board, for example, followed by a spray of white distilled vinegar. Then rinse with fresh water.

Other uses for hydrogen peroxide abound Here are a few examples:
• **For removing carpet stains**, 3 per cent hydrogen peroxide is a good choice. Pour the peroxide on the spot, wait 30 minutes and blot it up with paper towels. Rinse with 60ml of white vinegar mixed with 1 litre of water, blot, rinse again with plain water and blot once more. Test on an inconspicuous spot first.
• **Brighten your dingy laundry whites** by adding 200ml of 6 per cent peroxide to your wash.
• **To remove yellow underarm stains**, pour 3 per cent peroxide directly on the stain, let it sit for several hours and then rinse.
• **Remove red dye stains** caused by sweets and ice pops with 3 per cent peroxide poured directly on the spot. Wait 30 minutes and rinse.

You can buy 3 per cent hydrogen peroxide in supermarkets and chemists. Beauty salons carry 6 per cent peroxide.

Watch out Strong solutions of hydrogen peroxide can destroy skin tissue causing a pain that lasts for up to an hour. Wear gloves to protect your hands from splashes. Always measure water first and add the hydrogen peroxide, not the other way round.

Metal polishes

Commercial metal polishes remove tarnish (oxidation) and create a burnish or shine when you apply some elbow grease. Read the labels to find a polish suited to the specific metal you want to clean. (A general-purpose metal polish will give less satisfactory results.) Metal polishes typically do their job through a combination of mild abrasion with chemical cleaners.

Metal polishes come as liquids and creams Convenient polishing cloths that are lightly saturated with polish also are available.

How often you polish an item depends on how often the item is handled. Every time you handle a metal piece, you transfer acid from your hands to the item, which causes the metal to oxidise.

To apply polish, use an old cotton T-shirt or lint-free cotton cloth. Then use an old towel to remove any excess and a microfibre cloth to buff the polish on the metal. Be sure to remove as much of the residue of the polish as possible afterward, as the chemicals can damage metals over time. To reach nooks and crannies, use an old toothbrush. Some metal polishes contain strong chemicals, so always wear rubber gloves and work in a well-ventilated area.

Metal polishes are available from supermarkets, hardware stores and DIY stores.

Mops

Back in simpler times, mops came in two varieties – string or sponge. Now the choices include sponge, cotton string, cotton towelling, disposable (electrostatic or pre-moistened) and microfibre, and that's before you get to the latest 'kitchen mop systems', which combine a mop with floor wipes for a faster, fuss-free clean.

Mops are used to clean floors in two ways – dry-mopping or wet-mopping. Always keep it dry if you can: it's so much faster. However, to pick up ground-in and wet dirt, rather than just dust, you'll have to introduce water and/or cleaning solutions to your mop.

Cellulose sponge mops are made of open-cell foam and are good at cleaning vinyl. To use, dip the mop in a bucket of cleaner and warm water, wring out the excess moisture and mop. A sponge mop is also good for stripping and waxing a vinyl floor, but not for use on hardwood or marble flooring. The head of your sponge mop will need to be replaced occasionally – how often depends on usage.

String mops are usually 100 per cent cotton (although some contain polyester), with strings 30–45cm long. and can be used indoors or outdoors. They're good for cleaning garage floors and decking, tiled and linoleum floors and uneven surfaces of granite flooring. But string mops are not the ideal choice for hardwood or marble floors, because they can hold a lot of moisture, which can damage those surfaces. You can extend the life of the mop by machine-washing and drying the cotton head.

Towel mops use ordinary strips of fabric, secured with a holding device. Towel mops can be used wet on all floors, you can replace the mop head easily when it becomes soiled and you can wash and dry it as necessary. In addition to floor cleaning, you can use towel mops to dust cobwebs and clean ceilings.

Kitchen mop systems are a recent arrival on the market. They're available dry or with pre-moistened disposable wipes. Just place a wipe on the swivel head and start mopping. When it's dirty, replace it with a fresh one. Those made by *Flash*, *Dettol* and *Vileda* come with a spray bottle that holds cleaning fluid. You simply pull a trigger on the handle and the cleaner is sprayed on the floor in front of the mop. The *Mr Muscle* system simply uses wipes. These mops are convenient and easy to use and give great results with minimal effort, but at around 50p a time for the wipes, they significantly increase the cost of cleaning the kitchen floor.

You can buy mops from supermarkets, discount stores, hardware shops or DIY stores.

Oils

Oils used on natural wood surfaces or leather keeps them from drying out and makes them look healthy. Most oils for wood or leather are extracted naturally from animals, seeds or the peel of citrus fruits. Oils should never be used on stone, which is porous and will absorb the oil, producing dark spots in the stone. When you're thinking of using oil on wood or leather, always test it first on an inconspicuous spot. Some commonly used oils are listed below.

Citrus oil (orange, lemon and grapefruit), such as *Pledge with Orange Oil*, will help restore the finish on wood that has been neglected or has faded. Citrus oil penetrates to moisturise and condition wood. They are often combined with a chemical cleaner. Apply lightly, putting the oil on a cloth and then wiping onto the furniture or woodwork. Oil has a tendency to streak if you apply too much so be very sparing. Allow 30 minutes for the oil to dry.

Pine oil is a general cleaner and disinfectant for floors, counters and bathrooms. It comes from the turpentine family and has a distinct aroma. To use, dilute it in a spray bottle or in water according to the package directions.

Teak oil and linseed oil are good for natural wood, tabletops, wood panelling and wooden floors. Some brands have dyes in them, so they act like a stain. Linseed oil is also good for protecting outdoor furniture. Both teak oil and linseed oil can combust spontaneously, so be very careful not to leave oil-soaked rags lying around the house or in a rubbish bag inside. Hang such rags outside to dry thoroughly before you dispose of them in an outdoor rubbish bin. Or dispose of them in a sealed metal container

Neat's-foot oil, which is a light yellow, is obtained from the feet and shinbones of cattle. It's a great conditioner for leather (boots, saddles and such), keeping the leather soft.

To use neat's foot oil, apply it with a cloth, let it soak in for about 5 to 10 minutes and then buff or polish it dry, using circular motions. Cotton towels and old T-shirts are suitable for this.

You can buy citrus oil and pine oil anywhere home supplies are sold – supermarkets, hardware stores, home improvement stores and discount retailers.

Teak oil and linseed oil are available from hardware and DIY stores. **Neat's-foot oil** can be purchased at leather goods stores or shoe repair shops.

Oven cleaners

These are among the strongest – and most toxic – cleaners available for domestic use. Most contain a strong cleaning alkali, usually sodium hydroxide or potassium hydroxide. This caustic soda or lye, converts fats to soapy water-soluble compounds that will wipe away easily.

Oven cleaners come as aerosol sprays, liquids, pastes and powders and are usually thick so that they will stick on the vertical walls of an oven. They are highly toxic and can cause deep burns and blindness if they come into contact with skin or eyes. If swallowed, oven cleaners can be fatal. Don't use oven cleaners on self-cleaning ovens, which break down fats and other food with high heat instead of chemicals.

Watch out **Be careful with all oven cleaners** Wear rubber gloves and protective goggles and work in a well-ventilated area. Never spray commercial oven cleaner on a hot oven, electric elements, or oven lights – heat can make it even more caustic.

Purchase oven cleaners at supermarkets and discount retailers.

Paper towels

Professional cleaners use paper only for quick cleaning jobs, such as emergency spills. It would be expensive and wasteful to go through an entire roll of paper towels cleaning a bathroom. And since paper towels are major lint producers, they leave behind a paper trail on mirrors, on windows and any time you attempt any serious scrubbing with them. So, if you want to make one change to the way you do your cleaning, try to use fewer paper towels. You'll knock £2 a week off your supermarket spend.

For emergency or messy wipe-ups, paper towels are of course a top choice. When you have a spill, you need something within arm's reach and paper towels generally are. So keep on using them for liquid spills, pet accidents and wiping up anything (such as wet paint or cooking grease) that might ruin a rag or spoil anything in the same wash load with it.

Keep a roll in the kitchen, another in the garage (they're great for wiping oil and grease off hands) and another in the laundry room for bleach and liquid detergent spills.

Kitchen towels can be purchased at supermarkets and discount retailers. If you've got the room to store them, buy in bulk to save money. And don't get ones with decorative prints, since the inks can occasionally bleed.

Rubber gloves

When it comes to household cleaning, safety is essential. Gloves are important for protecting your hands when using harsh cleaning chemicals or working with hot water.

When selecting protective gloves, you can get ones made of either rubber or soft plastic polymers. The level of protection depends on how permeable they are, which typically depends on thickness. The thicker the glove, the more protection it provides.

- **For general household use,** standard latex dishwashing gloves are fine. (Choose a latex substitute if you are allergic to latex – many people are.)
- **For using paint strippers and solvents,** you'll need a thicker glove. The thicker the glove, however, the bulkier and clumsier it will be.

Replace gloves before they wear out and can't protect you. Signs that suggest your gloves need replacing include staining or colour change; softening, swelling or bubbling; stiffening or cracking; and leaking.

Disposable gloves are available in bulk containers, costing as little as 10p a pair. If you reuse your disposable gloves, be sure to wash them well with warm, soapy water. Let the outside dry and then reverse them, letting the inside dry. When the inside is dry, turn them right side out again and sprinkle talcum powder inside.

Purchase rubber gloves at supermarkets, discount stores, hardware stores and DIY stores.

Rubbish bags

Pay attention to thickness if you want a bag that won't split under a heavy load. Let your eyes tell you in the shop which one to buy: go for the thickest roll – but compare rolls with a similar number of bags.

The way the bags tie up is also something you should consider. Some bags have built-in drawstring ties. These bags cost a little more but make a neat, quick fastener. Other bags have plastic, notched wrap fasteners or twist ties like those that secure bread bags. These bags often come on a roll and are torn off along a perforated line. Still other bags have a handle cut out of the bag.

The cheapest bags may have no tie at all; you have to secure them by making a knot with the top edge of the bag.

If you have to tie your own rubbish bag, make simple overlapping knots, as commercial cleaners do. Pull the rubbish bag from the bin and shake the contents so they settle to the bottom. Next, take one corner with the left hand and the opposite one with the right hand, pull the corners to the centre and tie a tight square knot across the top of the bag. Then take the other two opposing corners and tie a second square knot. These right-over-left and left-over-right knots allow you to pick up the bag and carry it without spilling the contents.

Rubbish bags are readily available at supermarkets DIY stores and discount stores.

Sealants

Grime is toughest to remove when it gets a foothold in the materials used in our homes. When lodged in the fabric of a sofa cushion, the grains of wood in a deck or the pores of a ceramic tile grout, things like food spills and mildew can remain there permanently.

To prevent grime from taking up long-time residence, scientists have devised sealants – for textiles, grout, wood, brick and concrete – to block pores, making surfaces less susceptible to staining and easier to wipe clean.

Fabric sealants come in two varieties – fluorochemical sealants, such as *Scotchgard* and *Teflon* and silicone sealants.

Silicone sealants work only against water-based spills, such as juices; any spill containing oil may penetrate the sealant. Silicone sealants can even trap oily stains, making them harder to remove. Some upholstery comes pre-sealed. If the sealant wears off, reapply it or have a professional reapply it. Before reapplying a fabric sealant, be sure to clean the fabric well and remove all cleaning residue. Otherwise the sealant will not bond well.

Brick and concrete floor sealants, like fabric sealants, add a protective layer to floors, making cleaning easier. Always clean and prepare a floor surface well before applying a sealer. Reapply when signs of wear appear.

Wood sealants also protect against scratching and water damage. They come in the following varieties:
• **Penetrating sealers** seep into the grain of the wood and keep dust and dirt from doing the same.
• **Surface coating sealers** – polyurethanes, shellacs and varnishes – form a protective layer over the wood surface.

The most popular surface sealant is polyurethane, which is durable and relatively easy to use. Polyurethane sealers are either oil or water-based and they come in a variety of finishes, from completely matt to high gloss.

Grout sealants combat what has traditionally been one of the toughest things in the house to clean. This sealant, available at home and hardware stores and easily applied with a sponge paintbrush, prevents oil, dirt and mildew from staining grout lines in tiling.

You can purchase fabric sealants at supermarkets, discount stores and stores and warehouses that sell carpets and upholstered furniture, as well as through professional cleaning companies. Sealants for hard surfaces typically are available at hardware, paint and DIY stores.

Soap

The manufacture of soap has changed little over the centuries. Animal or vegetable fats are still treated with a strong alkali, such as sodium or potassium. Soap is not the same as detergent, which is a synthetic product first made in Germany in 1916 in response to a shortage of soap-making fats. But both contain 'surface-active' agents, or surfactants, which reduce the surface tension of water and dirt, in effect loosening the dirt, dispersing it in water and holding it in suspension until it can be rinsed away.

Soap is used today almost solely for personal skin and body care. For most other cleaning situations, synthetic detergents have almost completely replaced natural soaps, especially for machine-washing dishes and clothes. In hard water, soap is not as effective as detergent and may form a curd or soap scum that can ruin clothes and stain baths and sinks.

Don't use soap on tannin stains, such as those produced by coffee, fruit or jam if you can avoid it. Soap makes the stain harder to remove.

Soap is widely available in supermarkets and chemists.

Solvents

Water is the universal solvent, since it can be used to dissolve many different substances, from dirt to blood to certain paints. In cleaning terminology, however, solvent refers to liquids other than water that are used to get rid of substances that water can't dissolve. Water can't dissolve grease, for instance. Working on the principle that 'like dissolves like', you'd need a no water-based solvent, such as methylated spirits, to dissolve grease.

Common cleaning solvents include **acetone** (found in many nail polish removers), **methylated spirits**, **turpentine**, **dry-cleaning fluids** and **kerosene**.

Cleaning uses for solvents typically include removing greasy or oily substances, cleaning materials that can be harmed by water (for instance, spot-cleaning dry-clean-only fabrics) and removing stickers, wood finishes, oil-based paint and waxes.

Solvents are a last resort, to be used for the few things that water and detergent won't clean. Solvents tend to be strong, aggressive cleaners. Although they can be dangerous to breathe and harmful if they come in contact with your skin and eyes, they vary in their degree of toxicity.

Watch out **Always take safety precautions** when using solvents.
• Solvents are highly flammable. Never use them near open flames, including pilot lights and sparks.
• Always open windows to ventilate the area in which you are working.
• Wear the proper gear, including chemical-resistant gloves, long-sleeved shirts and long trousers, protective eyewear and, depending on the solvent, a ventilator.

Solvents are typically available in hardware and DIY stores and chemists.

Sponges

Household cleaning sponges, typically made of cellulose, are great at absorbing liquids and they hold lots of cleaning solution. For that reason, sponges are fast and efficient cleaning tools. But they also are a breeding ground for bacteria. The key to using sponges is to understand their limitations – and specifically to avoid cross-contamination.

Plain cellulose sponges are well suited to bathrooms, where being able to wipe moisture off walls, sinks, baths and showers is handy. But keep them in the bathroom and use separate ones for each task. Don't use the bathroom sponge in the kitchen, where germs can spread. Don't use a toilet sponge on the shelf where you store your toothbrush. Let a sponge dry between each use. Throw sponges away after a few weeks.

Abrasive kitchen sponges are designed for washing dishes. These sponges may be wrapped in a lightly abrasive mesh or backed by more heavily abrasive scrubbing pads. Use common sense when cleaning with sponge abrasives. They may scratch *Teflon*-coated pots and pans, stainless steel sinks, some worktops and other kitchen items. And kitchen sponges are just as apt to grow bacteria as those in the bathroom. Keep them as clean as possible and throw them out after a few weeks of use. Even if you don't use sponges on a regular basis, keep them around for spills.

Natural sponges – the brown, irregularly rounded ones – have been used for thousands of years for bathing and household cleaning. Although synthetic sponges, introduced in the 1940s, now have the lion's share of the market, natural sponges are still used for bathing, cleaning and a number of industrial applications ranging from printing to surgery.

A natural sponge is actually the skeleton of a sea animal. There are more than 2,000 species of sponge and in cleaning terms all are excellent.

Disinfecting your kitchen sponges regularly is important. Moist sponges are notorious for harbouring bacteria. You may think you're cleaning, but you're really slathering a layer of germs all over your sink and dishes.

Here are three simple ways to disinfect a sponge
First, rinse thoroughly to remove any food particles. Then do one of the following:
• Put them into the top rack of your dishwasher.

• Put it in a microwave oven for 30 seconds. (Be careful – it will get hot.)
• Fill the kitchen sink about one-third full of water, add 150ml of chlorine bleach and soak your sponges for ten minutes.

Sponges are widely available at supermarkets, discount stores and DIY stores – the cellulose variety, that is. For natural sponges, try at paint, hardware, home improvement and bath and beauty stores.

Spot removers

You'll see dozens of these on the cleaning aisle at the supermarket. In part, it's to do with marketing: it's easy to give a spot remover a particular stain that it tackles. In reality, it will probably clear up quite a few messes from similarly based items. Most products fall into two categories: wet and dry.

Wet spot removers, such as *Vanish*, are water soluble. These typically contain a concentrated laundry detergent and work best on food stains, such as drink spills and ketchup. But some wet spot removers also contain secondary solvents, such as alcohol and mineral spirits, to boost their stain-removal power and make them more effective on greasy stains.

Dry spot removers, such as *Spotless Dry Clean Liquid*, contain chemical solvents, including some that dry cleaners use. (Liquid is still involved. The 'dry' means water isn't used.) These are best for dry-clean-only fabrics as well as greasy or oily stains that water won't touch.

Carpet and upholstery spot removers, such as *1001 Spot Shot*, are specially designed for use on those materials. They are sometimes foamy, since low-moisture foams that can be vacuumed off are typically better for textiles with pads or cushions beneath.

Be sure to use the right spot removal product for the right job. To make sure the material you're

cleaning is colourfast, pre-test the product in an inconspicuous corner or seam. Always follow the manufacturer's directions carefully.

Spot removers are widely available at supermarkets.

Spray bottles

Spray bottles can be real time and money-savers. They allow you to mix your own cleaning solutions or buy bulk jugs of your favourite commercial cleaners and they also make applying cleaning solutions easier and more exact than simply pouring them on. Even when you're just using water – for instance, if you need to lightly wet a carpet stain – spray bottles do an excellent job.

To find good spray bottles – ones that are more durable and have a larger capacity – visit a janitorial supply store. These professional-grade squirters will have more pumping power, making your work easier.

When using spray bottles, the most important rule is to label them. Some bottles come with white rectangles on the side intended for labelling with a permanent marker. Some spray bottles also have handy check-off boxes that you can use to list the ingredients inside.

Don't pour in a bleach solution thinking you will label it later. Do it at once to avoid future confusion – and possible safety issues. And to avoid contaminating nearby surfaces, use the appropriate nozzle setting for the job you're doing. Use a tighter stream for smaller areas, such as toilet seats and a wider mist for larger areas, such as large bathroom mirrors.

If you're using a harmful cleaning chemical, such as bleach, in a spray bottle, avoid making the mist too fine. It will make the chemical much easier to inhale or get in your eyes.

Spray bottles are available at DIY stores and garden centres.

Squeegees

Professional window cleaners rely on squeegees. Anyone faced with cleaning smooth surfaces – such as windows, mirrors and tiles – should too. They are quicker and more effective at removing cleaning solutions and the dirt those solutions loosen. They don't streak. They don't leave behind lint, as paper towels do and they're not as messy as newspapers.

A 20–25cm-wide squeegee is the most suitable size for glass cleaning. Any bigger and it will be unwieldy. Any smaller and it won't cover enough surface area. (But get a small, mini squeegee for smaller, divided windowpanes.)

Buy a good-quality model, one that will work well and last. Get one with a high-quality (pliable and flexible) wiping blade – Lakeland do a selection. Cheaper squeegees have hard-rubber blades. When they get old and develop nicks, they leave a line of water behind, meaning you have to work twice as hard to get the window clean.

When using a squeegee, keep a dry towel in your other hand and wipe the squeegee on the towel after each swipe. For how to clean a window with a squeegee, read Windows, pages 388–391.

Small bathroom squeegees are available for wiping down wet shower walls, thus preventing soap scum build-up.

Squeegees can be bought at hardware, discount and DIY stores.

Steel wool

Steel wool is a speciality cleaning product and should never be used for general cleaning purposes. Even the finest steel wool is abrasive and can scratch (and ruin) many surfaces. That said, steel wool can be extremely useful for removing the most stubborn grime and for doing it without harsh chemicals.

Steel wool comes in grades that range from superfine (grade 0000) to extra coarse (grade 4). Traditionally, it has been used to remove baked-on food from pots and pans. Some brands, such as *Brillo*, have soap already embedded in the pads for convenience. But with the ubiquity of non-stick cooking surfaces, it is less important to keep these woolly balls under the kitchen sink these days. Besides damaging some surfaces, when steel wool scratches something, it creates a surface that attracts stains and rust. Use steel wool as a last resort or on surfaces that you don't mind scratching.

Steel wool is available in supermarkets.

Toilet cleaners

Commercial toilet cleaners tend to be strong and acid-based. Often they contain hydrochloric acid for eating away at stubborn stains and mineral deposits – the rings that seem cemented to the toilet bowl. Many have a thick consistency, which helps them stick to the wall of the toilet for long enough to dissolve stains and limescale.

For regular toilet cleaning, choose the method that suits you best. Liquid cleaners that you can squirt under the rim will be best in areas where limestone is a big problem. Otherwise, use tablets that can work overnight in the bowl.

Or try using a pumice stone Keeping the stone wet, rub it on the ring until it's gone. This works for old rings as well as recent ones. Pumice will not scratch white vitreous china, which is what most toilets are made of, but it will scratch glassfibre, enamel, plastic and other softer materials.

Toilet bowl cleaners are widely available at supermarkets. **Pumice stones** are available from chemists.

Vacuum cleaners

A good vacuum cleaner is a key cleaning ally for any homeowner, both for routine dust and dirt removal and for emergency situations, such as party crumbs and soil from upturned potted plants.

• **Manual pile adjustment** is important not only for better dirt retrieval when you're vacuuming carpets, but also for better carpet protection, since the 'standard' setting on many beater bars can destroy a carpet's fibres and wear down the vacuum's motor.

Choosing a vacuum cleaner is actually quite simple. Only uprights beat the carpet; cylinders simply suck up the dust. Unless there is a good reason – you find uprights too heavy to push around, or your big concern is stair cleaning – go for the upright.

In addition to uprights and cylinders, there are also wet/dry vacuum cleaners. On the whole you will be compromising on the 'dry' bit in order to be able to tackle 'wet' cleaning.

Features to consider when buying a vacuum include the following:
• **Is the vacuum bagless** or is it one where you have to change bags? Since **Dyson** pioneered the concept, the bagless vacuum has become the dominant choice – and with good reason. Cleaners start each vacuum session with no loss of suction. There are no costs for replacement bags and emptying a bagless vacuum is a simply tip-out job at the rubbish bin.
• **The power of your cleaner** Look at the wattage and, if you want plenty of power, go high.
• **The onboard tools**, such as crevice and upholstery tools, extension wands and nozzles with rotating bars. You'll use these more than you think for essential cleaning on items other than floors (curtains and upholstered furniture, for instance). Choosing a vacuum that has tools 'on board' cuts a great deal of hassle.

Filtration systems are among the best features to find their way onto vacuum cleaners in recent years. These systems improve air quality by capturing tiny particles that otherwise would be blown back into your home in the machine's exhaust. The machines with the best filters, known as **high efficiency particulate air (HEPA) filters**, are expensive and the filters themselves are expensive to replace – but for people with asthma or allergies, they are extremely beneficial.

Handheld vacuums are usually portable battery-operated machines. Ever since the introduction, more than 20 years ago, of the *DustBuster*, handheld models have been hugely popular. Most are powerful and surprisingly inexpensive. But since they have limited battery power – often less than ten minutes at a shot – they are useful only for quick jobs, such as spills and cleaning up crumb trails. A small plug-in handheld with a long flex can be very useful for stairs. If you keep your main vacuum handy, you probably don't need one.

If you have stairs to clean, most vacuums now have an exhension hose that will take an entire flight, no problem. Always keep your cleaner at the bottom and work up the stairs.

Buy vacuum cleaners from electrical appliance and department stores and online suppliers.

Index

Writer Jeff Bredenberg
Consultant, UK edition
Gill Chilton
Editor Lisa Thomas
Art Editor Julie Bennett
Photographer Michal
Kaniewski, Ad Libitum
Illustrators Sue Ninham,
Stephen Pollitt,
Cartoonist Geoff Waterhouse
for Just for Laffs
Proofreader Ron Pankhurst
Indexer Marie Lorimer
Cover digital manipulation
Ian Atkinson

Jeff Bredenberg

Jeff Bredenburg has been writing and editing home and health advice for newspapers, books and websites for more than 25 years. Among the many books he has edited or written are Clean It Fast, Clean it Right; Beat the System; Make it Last; Home Remedies from the Country Doctor; and Food Smart.

Gill Chilton

Gill Chilton is the consumer expert for Woman magazine, writing each week on household subjects with the emphasis on testing products and on sharing tips that save time, effort and money; in addition, Gill writes for, among others, Family Circle and Good Housekeeping magazines and is also the author of Reader's Digest Home Basics: The Complete Guide to Running Today's Home, and Cleaning & Stain Removal for Dummies (Wiley). Gill has 20 years experience of writing on practical issues and a totally upbeat approach: cleaning may never be our idea of a good time, says Gill, but armed with the right techniques and tools, you can't fail to be impressed at how great your home and possessions will look.

Note The information in this book has been carefully researched and all efforts have been made to ensure accuracy and safety. Neither the authors nor Reader's Digest Association Limited assumes any responsibility for any injuries suffered or damages or losses incurred as a result of following the instructions in this book. Before taking any action based on information in this book, study the information carefully and make sure you understand it fully. Test any new or unusual cleaning method before applying it broadly, or on a highly visible or valuable area or item. The mention of any product or web site in this book does not imply an endorsement. All product names and web sites mentioned are subject to change and are meant to be considered as general examples rather than specific recommendations.

Reader's Digest Books

Editorial Director Julian Browne
Art Director Nick Clark
Managing Editor Alastair Holmes
Picture Resource Manager
Martin Smith
Pre-press Account Manager
Penny Grose
Product Production Manager
Claudette Bramble
Senior Production Controller
Deborah Trott

Origination Colour Systems Ltd
Printed in China

Other images 43 Home Laundering Consultative Council; 205 Punchstock/ Bananastock; 316 Red Cover/Niall McDiarmid; 373 Red Cover/Mark Williams; 395 Red Cover/Dan Duchars

Concept code US4513/G
Book code 400-181-01
ISBN 0 276 44070 6
Oracle code 250007690H.00.24

How to Clean Just About Anything was originated and first published in 2005 as **2001 Amazing Cleaning Secrets** by the editorial team of The Reader's Digest Inc., USA.

This edition was adapted and published by The Reader's Digest Association Limited
11 Westferry Circus, Canary Wharf, London E14 4HE
www.readersdigest.co.uk
© 2006 Reader's Digest Association

We are committed both to the quality of our products and the service we provide to our customers. We value your comments so please feel free to contact us on **08705 113366** or via our web site at **www.readersdigest.co.uk**.

If you have any comments or suggestions about the content of our books you can contact us at gbeditorial@readersdigest.co.uk